— Feb. 1962

Call Her Blessed

Call
Her
Blessed

by Charles B. Broschart

Copy 2

SOCIETY OF ST. PAUL, STATEN ISLAND 14, NEW YORK

NIHIL OBSTAT:
Rev. Eugene H. Sullivan
Censor Librorum

IMPRIMATUR
✠Thomas F. McNally
Vicarius Generalis Philadelphiensis

September 30, 1961

Library of Congress Number 61-15618

*My sincere thanks to all who helped
in obtaining data on numerous shrines and sanctuaries;
to those who assisted in translations;
and to my wife Anna and daughter Margaret
for editing and typing these stories.*
C. B. B.

INTRODUCTION

The Blessed Virgin has been more celebrated, loved, venerated and invoked than any other woman who ever lived. To what other woman have been dedicated so many churches, shrines, chapels, sanctuaries and monuments? Mary, more than any other woman, has received homage from literature, oratory, poetry, painting, sculpture and music.[1] She is unquestionably the most titled personage who who ever lived.

Each title that has been bestowed on the Virgin has a particular significance—a reason—and in many cases there is a story concerning the title and its origin. The stories of these titles narrated in this book are based on: (a) historical testimony, (b) tradition, (c) legend.

"Historical testimony" requires no clarification but perhaps we should point out what the words "tradition" and "legend" usually mean.

"Tradition" is the delivery of opinions, doctrines, rites or customs from father to son or from ancestors to posterity; the transmission of any opinions or practices from forefathers to descendants by oral communication, without written memorials.[2]

"Legend" is a narrative, usually entertaining, based on tradition with some intermingling of fact, springing up naturally among a people. Or, any unauthentic narrative handed down by tradition and having a basis in fact.

Legends then are a medley of fact and fiction with the proportion of one to the other varying considerably in different legends. In any particular legend, it is impossible to determine how much is fact and how much is fiction, as the two are inextricably mingled.[3]

In view of the above the question arises as to how far Catholics may go in giving credence to legends. Thus a Catholic, writing for Catholics should draw attention to the derivation and ecclesiastical use of the term. Legends, or reading, are pieces of sacred literature ("legenda," to read, as distinct from things "credenda" or "agenda," to be believed or done), not matters of faith and therefore not of precept, but edifying narratives which the faithful may read with profit and which may be the means of arresting the attention of others to the marvels of the spiritual world.[4]

Regardless of whether the stories in this book are based on historical testimony, tradition or legend, certainly it is salutary for everyone, especially Catholics, to be familiar with them; to know the stories of the numerous titles of the Mother of God. When Our Lady appeared to the children on the mountain of La Salette in 1846, before leaving them she said: "Well, my children, you will make this news known to my people." This volume is a modest and humble effort to make the news concerning the Virgin's titles known to many who otherwise would not know of it.

1.—"The Queenship of Mary," by Most Rev. Ameleto G. Cicognani, Our Lady's Digest, May, 1956.
2.—The word "tradition" is not used here in its technical sense. In theological terminology tradition is one of the two sources of supernatural revelation —the other being Sacred Scripture. Tradition in this sense is the unwritten word of God—the body of truths revealed by God to the apostles. The apostles did not commit these truths to writing, but passed them on by word of mouth. These truths were later written down by the Fathers of the Church and have thus been preserved to the present day.
3.—There is a striking feature about legends—the fact that the same basic ideas or concepts will appear in legends of peoples whose habitats are widely separated.
4.—Legends of the Blessed Virgin by J. Collin de Plancy, P. O'Shea, New York, 1852.

CONTENTS

Titles of the Americas

OUR LADY OF HIGHEST GRACE

THIS TITLE and the shrine at Higuey in the Dominican Republic are credited as the oldest in North America. Of the several legends regarding its origin, the one best known concerns a Spanish official and his daughter, La Niña.

The family lived near Higuey in the early years of the 16th century. In the chapel on their hacienda was a small statue of Our Lady and here La Niña often prayed. One day when her father was saddling his horse to begin a cattle drive to the markets at Santo Domingo, La Niña asked that he bring her a present from the city. What she wanted was a picture of Our Lady of Highest Grace. He had never heard of such a picture or title and asked where his daughter had heard of it, and how he would recognize it if he found it.

The child replied that on the previous night, the Virgin dressed in blue and wearing a white scapular had appeared to her. As he rode off he promised that he would do his best to find the picture.

When the rancher had disposed of his cattle, he set out to buy the picture, but could find no trace of such a one. As a last resort, he called on the bishop for help. But His Excellency had not heard of the picture either; indeed he suggested that La Niña was probably making up the story about Our Lady and her appearance, and that she should be given a good talking to.

Regretfully giving up the search, the man started for home. On his way he stopped overnight at an inn in a small settlement called Dos Rios. The only other guest besides himself was an old man with a white beard, and the innkeeper invited them to have dinner with him. The old man did not accept but sat quietly on the other side of the room watching his saddle bags while the rancher and his host ate their meal.

Meanwhile the rancher spoke of his unsuccessful search for the painting of Our Lady of Highest Grace and what a disappointment it would be to his daughter when he returned home without it. "I believe there is no such picture," he said. Hearing these words the old man spoke, saying that indeed there was such a picture; in fact he happened to have one in his saddle bag. Opening the bag he took out a roll of parchment and spreading it before them, he revealed the figure of Our Lady gowned in blue wearing on her breast a white scapular.

The rancher offered to pay handsomely for the picture, but the old man refused to accept anything. He gave it freely as a present from himself to the rancher's daughter. A few minutes later it was discovered that the man, saddle bags and all, had disappeared.

The next day as the father neared his home, he found his daughter waiting for him under an orange tree which stood near the house. With a quiet confidence she asked to see the picture: there was no doubt in her mind but what he had found it. When he opened the roll of parchment, the girl, overjoyed, said that the Virgin in the painting was dressed the same as she had been in the vision.

They placed the picture in their chapel and the girl put fresh flowers before it each day. For the time her happiness seemed complete, but not long after, she died, and they buried her beneath the orange tree.

Then one day a strange thing happened: the painting was missing from the chapel! After much searching, they found it resting in a crotch of the orange tree. Unable to find out who had moved the picture, they returned it to the chapel. But the following day they found it once more resting in the orange tree. After the same mysterious transfer had taken place several times, the family realized that the Blessed Virgin evidently wished the painting to remain on that spot, so they erected a church on the site and placed the picture in it.

The church and painting of Our Lady of Highest Grace soon became well known and was the scene of many wondrous happenings. During 1575 and 1576 a Basilica was built and consecrated by Archbishop Andres de Carvajal. In 1953 the cornerstone was laid for a new and larger one. The image was crowned on August 15, 1922.

Recently a letter, dated 1649, by a prebendary of the Cathedral of Santo Domingo, was found in the archives of the National Library at Madrid, saying that in 1506 two gentlemen from Plasencia, Spain, had brought to Higuey, on the Island of Hispaniola, the picture of Our Lady of Highest Grace.

BIBLIOGRAPHY:

Historia del Culto de Maria en Iberoamerica
by R. V. Ugarte, S. J.
Editorial Huarpes, Buenos Aires, 1947.
"Mary's First Shrine in America,"
Art. by Addison Burbank,
Our Lady's Digest, June-July 1953.

OUR LADY OF APARECIDA

APARECIDA, a small town in Brazil, lies between São Paulo and Rio de Janeiro. A literal translation of "Nossa Senhora Aparecida" is "Our Lady Who appeared." [1]

One morning in 1717, three fishermen, Joao Alves, Domingos Garcia, and Felipe Pedroso poled their boat into the Parahyba River which flowed along the outskirts of their village. [2]

Their luck was bad—for hours they cast their nets but caught no fish. By late afternoon they were pretty well discouraged and they decided to quit. Turning the boat about, they headed for the shore.[3]

Then, for some reason, Alves decided to make one more try. He threw out his net and slowly pulled it in. To his great surprise there was something in it—not a fish, but something that looked like a chunk of wood. When he lifted it from the net, it turned out to be a headless statue of the Blessed Virgin.

Laying it in the bottom of the boat, he cast again. This time when he withdrew it, it again held a roundish piece of wood—the head of the statue. Putting the net aside, he picked up both pieces of wood and found they fitted together perfectly.

Now, obeying some impulse, Alves lowered his net once more. When he attempted to pull it up, he could hardly lift it for it was bulging with fish. His companions, seeing Alves' catch, threw out their nets and they too brought them in loaded with fish. A few more casts and their boat was filled up to the gunwales.

They started toward shore, silent and very much awed, for in their hearts they felt they had witnessed a miracle.

The next day they fastened the head firmly onto the body of the statue, carefully cleaned it, and one of them set it up in a place of honor in his humble cottage.

The story of the finding of the image spread throughout the village and every evening the people came to pay homage to the Blessed Virgin who had given them her image in such a strange fashion. And hearing the story of how the statue had "appeared" or "revealed itself," someone gave it the name: Our Lady Who appeared.

Within a few years a little chapel was erected in order that the image would be more readily accessible to those who wished to visit it. In 1745, a larger chapel was built. And it is said that Our Lady well repaid those who honored her, for numerous cures and even extraordinary miracles took place at her shrine.

In 1846, work began on the construction of a new church. It was completed in 1888 and the statue was transferred to it. In 1904, by order of the Holy Father, the image was solemnly crowned by the Bishop of São Paulo.

In 1909, this church was raised to a minor Basilica; in 1930 Pope Pius XI promoted it to a Basilica and officially declared Our Lady of Aparecida the Patroness of Brazil.

1.—Although the image and shrine of Our Lady at Aparecida is usually called Nossa Senhora Aparecida or Nossa Senhora da Aparecida, the full title is Nossa Senhora da Conceicao Aparecida (Our Lady of the Immaculate Conception of Aparecida).

2.—One story says the fishermen were on a routine fishing trip such as they took every day—another says the Governor of the Province was that day coming to visit their village and that the Mayor or Town Council had charged the three fishermen to catch some especially fine fish for the Governor's supper that evening.

3.—Probably the harbor of Itagcassu.

BIBLIOGRAPHY:

"Brazil's Queen"
by N. J. Muckermann, C.SS.R.,
Clipping in Marian Library, Dayton, Ohio.
"Nossa Senhora Aparecida"
by Harry Felski, S. V. D.,
Clipping in Marian Library, Dayton, Ohio.
"Statue of Our Lady Has Strange History in Brazil,"
Clipping in Marian Library, Dayton, Ohio.
"La Madonna Santuari e Feste,"
by Fr. Umberto Bonomo, C.SS.R.
Vatican City Religious Book Co., Inc., New York, 1948.

OUR LADY OF CAACUPE

CAACUPE, Paraguay, South America, nestling in the hills, has been likened to a lovely jewel case—the precious gem it guards is the Virgin of the Miracles. The Lady's full name is The Virgin of Miracles of Caacupé. She is also called the Blue Virgin.

The story begins in the village of Tobatí about the year 1600. One day a converted Indian of that town, a carver by trade, had gone into the nearby mountains and while pursuing his peaceful way was set upon by a band of Mbayaes, Indians of another tribe. He managed to escape by dashing into a thick forest where he hid behind a large tree, crouching down between two of its projecting roots. During those terrible moments, while each second he feared his enemies would find him, he prayed fervently to the Blessed Virgin promising her that if he escaped with his life he would carve her image from the wood of the very tree which was sheltering him.

His enemies were unable to discover him, and after making good his escape he lost no time in carrying out his promise. Returning soon after with axe and wedge he hacked and split from that huge trunk a piece of wood sufficient for his purpose. After drying it thoroughly he then proceeded with all the skill of his practiced hands, to carve out two statues of the Blessed Virgin. One, quite large, he donated to the little church of Tobatí; the other, very small, he kept for himself. The latter (following a series of adventures), is the image that is today venerated in Caacupé.

Legend then loses sight of the tiny statue until a later year—probably 1603—and finds it suddenly in another locale; that of a town called Arecayá. Near to Arecayá there lived a converted Indian, a venerable old fellow named Tapaicuá. On his property there was a walled up spring that always sent forth its waters in great abundance, so much so that it supplied not only his own house but most of the others in the vicinity. Then one day, so the story goes, the spring overflowed, sending out huge quantities of water, and in a few days had flooded most of the Pirayú valley. Just when it appeared that the whole region would be inundated the good Franciscans, led by the saintly Father Luis de Bolaños, besought Heaven for aid. In answer to their pleas the spring was returned to its normal flow and the waters rose no higher. Thus, according to the legend, was Lake Ypacaraí formed.

A few days later an Indian carpenter named José, of the town of Atyrá, was combing the lake shore for bits of furniture, lumber and other articles of salvage, when he spied a dark cylindrical object floating some fifty feet offshore. On closer inspection it proved to be a leather satchel containing a small, beautifully carved statue of the Virgin. It was of course the tiny statue carved from the tree trunk by the Indian of Tobatí. The statue was such a lovely piece of work that José was puzzled about what to do with it. Should he keep it or try to find the owner? He consulted Father Bolaños who told him to keep it until the rightful owner could be found. He further assured José that Divine Providence surely had a good reason for appointing him as its savior and protector.

Over the years there has been considerable conjecture as to how the little image came to be floating on the waters of the newly formed lake. Perhaps, they say, the Indian wood-carver of Tobatí had taken up his residence near Arecayá shortly before the flood, or perhaps he was on a journey through the region and was trapped, satchel and all, by the rising waters, but in any event, he never again appeared to reclaim his precious statue.

When, after several months, no one claimed the image, José considered it rightfully his and enshrined it in a place of honor in his house, he and his family regarding it ever after as their most valuable possession.

Some years later a group of Indian converts, having been transferred to Atyrá from a settlement called San Vicente de Lloys, required additional homes. As there was insufficient timber in and around Atyrá, the parish priest gave to José the job of cutting and hauling the required logs and dispatched him to Cáaguy cupé where timber was plentiful. José remained there for a year carrying out his lumbering assignment and when he returned to his home in Atyrá he found that he no longer felt contented there. He had fallen in love with the delightful climate and natural beauty of Cáaguy cupé. After careful thought he decided to go and live there so he moved his wife, his only son and all his belongings, including the beloved statue of the Virgin. After building a new home on a site about one mile southwest of what is now Caacupé he erected alongside the house a modest oratory and within it he placed the little statue. José's oratory thus became the first sanctuary of this Madonna, and as other people gradually settled in the vicinity the oratory became celebrated as a center of devotion to Our Lady.

Some years passed and José died, followed soon thereafter by his wife, whereupon José's son gave the statue to a relative who took it to his home in Tobatí. From thence forward there is a complete silence regarding the image until many years later.

Sometime around 1750 an anonymous native of Tobatí offered the long forgotten little statue to a family by the name of Aquino who lived in the settlement (now called Caacupé) on condition that they would erect a chapel worthy of housing it. For some reason the Aquino's did not accept the offer but a certain Doña Juana Curtido de Gracia heard about the matter and she donated the necessary parcel of land. On it the chapel was erected and the image enshrined therein.

In 1770 the statue was transferred to a church, newly built to replace the chapel and dedicated to the Virgen de los Milagros—the Virgin of the Miracles. And in the same year the Spanish Governor, Carlos Morphi, noting the great devotion of the people of the vicinity, established Caacupé as a Religious Center. Later, during the presidency of Don Carlos Antonio López (1840-1862), a town was built as a civil center. Caacupé, finally, was officially born. Father Juan José Jiminez was named as the town's first parish priest. And shortly thereafter, in 1883, the church of Caacupé was constructed—a fine building of brick and stone. The present Basilica was begun in 1945 and when finished will be one of the finest in the Americas.

The image of The Virgin of Miracles of Caacupé is only about twenty inches high but it is most delicately carved. The feet of the Virgin rest on a small globe, blue in color and dotted with white stars. The figure is partly shrouded in a blue mantle overlaid with flowers and stars done in gold. Numerous favors have been attributed to the intercession of Our Lady of Caacupé.

1.—Probably an Indian name—meaning "Behind the Mountains"—later contracted into the more phonetic "Caacupe."

BIBLIOGRAPHY:

    La Virgen de los Milagros de Caacupe,
        by Jose Maria Recalde,
        Editorial El Arte, S. A., Asuncion, 1954.
    Historia del Culto de Maria,
        by Ruben Vargas Ugarte, S. J.,
        Editorial Huarpes, S. A., Buenos Aires, 1947.

OUR LADY OF THE CAPE

THE HOME OF OUR LADY OF THE CAPE is at Cap de la Madeleine on the north bank of the St. Lawrence River, near Three Rivers in the Province of Quebec, Canada.

The story of this title began in 1634, when Champlain founded the settlement of Three Rivers. Jesuit missionaries who accompanied him dedicated it to the Immaculate Conception.

Later, a larger settlement grew up adjacent to Three Rivers and it was named Cap de la Madeleine in honor of St. Mary Magdalen. Then the Governor of Three Rivers built a small chapel at Cap de la Madeleine. The Jesuits took charge of the new chapel in 1651, and in it set up a shrine of the Blessed Virgin. In 1694, a confraternity of the Holy Rosary was established there.

In 1680, the Jesuits relinquished responsibility for the chapel and diocesan priests took over.

In 1714, Father Paul Vachon built a new church (which still stands) to replace the earlier chapel. He died in 1720, and thereafter for more than a century the church and parish were without a pastor.

In 1845, Father Léandre Tourigny came to the parish, and in the same year, someone presented him with a beautiful statue of the Blessed Virgin, which he enthroned on the altar of the church—the same statue that is at the shrine today.

Over the preceding years during which the parish had been without a priest, the people's faith had almost vanished, and Father Tourigny's best efforts to rekindle the spark met with little success.

In 1864, Bishop Cooke of Three Rivers sent a Father Luc Désilets to the Cape to see what he could do. For three years he labored but with no greater success than Father Tourigny. Then suddenly things changed.

On the eve of the Ascension in 1867, Father Désilets waited for several hours in the sacristy for his people to come to confession. None came. Somewhat discouraged he left the sacristy, entered the church and walked toward the altar, intending to ask Jesus in the tabernacle to help him. He heard a grunting sound and, on investigating, discovered a pig on the steps of the Lady altar. Hanging from its mouth was a rosary. Horrified at the sight, he knelt before the altar and vowed he would devote all his time and effort to re-establishing the Rosary devotion in his parish, and through it revive the faith of his people.

The next day during the sermon he showed them the chewed-up rosary, and recounted how he had found the pig chewing on it. He summed up by saying: "The people drop the Rosary and the pigs pick it up." [1]

This struck a responsive chord. The people changed and their ancient faith was renewed. The numbers coming to church soon grew so large that a bigger church was needed.

Then arose the question, where would they obtain the

stone to build the new church? The Cape—a marshy and sandy promontory—could provide no suitable stone, so it was decided that the old church should be torn down and its stone would build part of the new one. Additional stone would be taken from a quarry located on the other side of the St. Lawrence River.

Cutting the stone from the quarry at St. Angèle on the south bank of the river and dressing it to size required almost two years, but by the late fall of 1878 the work was finished. When the river froze solid the stone would be hauled across on sleighs.

Unfortunately, the winter of 1878-1879 was an unduly mild one and the river did not freeze over. March came and still no solid ice. It looked as though the building of the new church could not begin for at least another year.

Father Dèsilets was a very determined fellow, however, and decided now was the time to ask the Blessed Virgin to help them. So he besought her and implored her to produce a bridge of ice across the river. He solemnly promised that if she did and they could get the stone across that winter, he would not tear down the old church but would leave it standing. Moreover, he would dedicate it to her as a shrine of the Holy Rosary.

As always when she is fervently appealed to, the Blessed Mother acted promptly—on the evening of March 15, 1879, a terrific storm blew in, loosing the ice from the river banks and piling it in a solid bridge stretching from one bank to the other.

By the next morning the bridge was firm enough to support horses and sleighs and immediately the job of transporting the cut stone across the river was begun. Several days later, when the last load had crossed, a thaw set in. The bridge broke up and floated away as speedily as it had formed a few days before.

The new church was built alongside the old one of 1714 and consecrated in 1880. The old church now became a Lady Chapel of the new one, and the statue of Our Lady was enshrined therein.

Over the years the Blessed Virgin has bestowed numerous favors on those who honor her as Queen of the Holy Rosary, and since the place where she is honored is called Cap de la Madeleine, naturally she has come to be known in Canada as Our Lady of the Cape. The image was crowned on October 12, 1904.

1.—Our Lady's Digest.

BIBLIOGRAPHY:

Famous Shrines of Our Lady
 by H. M. Gillett, Vol. 2,
  Samuel Walker, Ltd., London 1952.
Shrines of Our Lady Around the World
 by Zsolt Aradi,
  Farrar, Straus & Young, New York, 1954.
Our Lady of the Cape
 in Our Lady's Digest.
Shrine to Mary, the Story of Our Lady of the Cape.
 by J. G. Shaw, Our Lady of the Cape Publications,
  Cap de la Madeleine, Quebec.

OUR LADY OF CHIQUINQUIRA

OUR LADY OF THE ROSARY of Chiquinquira has her shrine at Chiquinquira, Colombia, South America. She is Patroness of Colombia.

The story of this title of Our Lady originated in the middle of the sixteenth century. During that century, Spain conquered and colonized that portion of South America comprising modern Colombia and some of the surrounding territory. A few years later—probably 1540—one of the Conquistadores, D. Antonio de Santana, settled in the town of Tunja and was named overseer of two towns, Sutamarchán, a few miles from Tunja, and Chiquinquira, some thirty miles farther away.

In 1555, Antonio built himself a temporary house in Suta and near it erected a primitive chapel made of wood poles anchored in the ground and covered with straw. Then, since Antonio was especially devoted to the Blessed Virgin, he wished to place her image in the chapel. He commissioned Alonzo de Narváez, an artist of Tunja, to paint a picture of Our Lady of the Rosary.

The piece of cotton sheeting (fifty inches wide by forty-

four high), on which the picture was to be painted, was of
poor quality, and the colors used by the artist were also poor
(vari-colored earth mixed with the juice of herbs and
flowers). The artist painted the figures of Our Lady and
the Child in the middle portion of the cloth leaving blank
white spaces on either side. When Antonio saw it he decided
that it was out of balance and suggested that the artist paint
a saint on each side of the Madonna. After some discussion
it was decided to put St. Andrew the Apostle on one side
and St. Anthony of Padua (patron of D. Antonio) on the
other. The work was finally finished and Antonio framed it
with wood and put it on the altar of his little chapel, where
it might be venerated by the Spaniards as well as by the
Indians who were Christians.

A few years passed. The chapel had been poorly constructed and, when it rained, water leaked through the roof
and drenched the picture; rays of sunlight penetrating the
straw beat down on it. So the picture gradually lost most of its
original coloring and six large holes appeared in the rotting
cloth.

At that time (1565), Father John Alemán de Leguizamón
was Curé of Suta and in charge of the chapel. Noting the
dilapidated condition of the painting, he thought it unfit to
be on the altar, so he took it down and replaced it with a
crucifix that had recently come from New Spain. In the
meantime—1585—Antonio de Santana had died and his
widow, Catalina García de Irlos, had moved to Chiquinquira;
Father John sent the picture to her. She placed it in a straw
hut type of chapel which stood near her house.

In 1585 a pious woman, María Ramos, arrived in Chiquinquira. She was the sister-in-law of the dead Santana and a

native of Guadalcanal, Spain. She took up her abode with Catalina. María was very devoted to the Blessed Virgin and as soon as she was settled she looked about for a place appropriate for her devotions; thus she came upon the abandoned little chapel. She found it in a disreputable state; farm animals were using it as a shelter.

However, with the assistance of a maid-servant, she cleaned it up and fixed it up so it could again serve as a house of prayer. During the cleaning process she found a disfigured painting in a dilapidated wood frame—it was in such a deplorable condition that María could not even determine what saint it was supposed to depict.

On the chance that it might be some image of Our Lady, she and the maid repaired the frame, cleaned up the cloth as best they could and put it above the altar, securing it there with a strong string, tied with four or five knots. But María was still very sad, and when she returned to the house, Catalina asked what was troubling her? María told about finding the old picture and Catalina related the story of the painting and of the neglect which had been its lot.

Thereafter, María frequently visited the little chapel and always with tears in her eyes bemoaned the fact that her "Rose of Heaven" was in such terrible condition and in such an unworthy shack. Continually she petitioned the Blessed Virgin that she might see the blurred painting renovated— that she might experience the supreme pleasure of seeing the beloved face of the Divine Mother. Such loving words the pious woman repeated every day, and finally the Virgin heard her plea.

It was the morning of December 26th, 1586, and María had been in the chapel for two hours—this time she prayed with even greater fervor. She begged that the Mother of God would deign to show her features on that dilapidated "canvas." Then genuflecting reverently she left the chapel.

As she was leaving she met a Christian Indian woman named Isabel who carried her four-year-old son, Miguel, in her arms. Suddenly the child said to its mother: "Mother, look at the Mother of God, that is standing on the ground!" The mother looked toward the altar of the chapel and saw that the picture was indeed standing on the ground, and from it there came a strange light that lit up the whole interior of the chapel. Astonished and somewhat frightened, Isabel cried out to María, saying, "Look! Look! The Mother of God has come down from her place and is in your seat, and she appears to be burning (on fire)."

María turned and rushed back into the chapel, and great was her amazement to see the transformation that had taken place in the painting—colors which had been so drab and indistinct were now clear and vivid—it looked like a work that had just been finished. Overcome with joy she threw herself at the feet of the Madonna and thanked her for the miracle that had fulfilled her inmost desire and brought such a heavenly feast to her eyes. Gradually the brilliance which came from the picture faded, and in about an hour it was gone. Then with some fear and with great reverence they picked it up and returned it to its former place above the altar.

The news of the happening quickly spread—ecclesiastical authorities thoroughly investigated the whole affair, and, as a result, the first church was erected in 1588 on the site of the little chapel. Later, a larger church was built and in 1608 (or 1610) the image was placed in it.

In 1636, the Dominicans were given charge of the painting. In 1801 work began on a still larger edifice which was finished in 1812 and the image transferred to it—this church was consecrated in 1823. On July 9, 1919, the image was solemnly crowned at Bogotá and then returned to the shrine at Chiquinquira. On August 8, 1927, the church was raised to the rank of a minor Basilica.

BIBLIOGRAPHY:

    Resena Historica de la Virgen de Chiquinquira,
      by Fr. Andres Mesanza, O. P.
      Bogota, 1952.
    Celebres Imagenes y Santuarios de N. S. en Columbia
      by Fr. Andres Mesanza, O. P.
      Imprenta de "Veritas,"
      Chiquinquira, 1950.
    Historia de N. S. del Rosario de Chiquinquira.
      by Fr. Vincente Maria Cornejo y Fr. Andres Mesanza
      Editorial Centro, Bogota, S. A. 1942.

OUR LADY OF CHARITY, PATRONESS OF CUBA

THE SANCTUARY OF OUR LADY stands on a hilltop called "La Moboa" in the village of El Cobre, Cuba, some 650 miles from Havana. The village got its name from the nearby copper mines.

The earliest name of this village seems to have been Santiago del Prado. Later, probably around 1601, a rich vein of copper was discovered in the area. When Philip III (1578-1621) heard of the strike he ordered that mining should start at once.

This was done and the opening of the copper mines brought quite a number of workers to the village, most of whom were Negroes and Indians. Before very long the village came to be known as El Cobre.

The story of the origin of this title of Our Lady goes back to the early years of the seventeenth century. In 1628, three people of a village [1] got into their canoe and journeyed out into the Bay of Nipe to gather some salt. Two of these, Rodrigo and Juan de Hoyes, were native Indians of the country, while the third was a negro youngster eleven years old named Juan Moreno.

In a little while a storm blew up and they took shelter

in a place called Cayo Francés y Vigía, where they were
forced to lay over for three days until the storm blew out.

Early in the morning of the fourth day, the sea now being
calm, they set out for their destination. After paddling along
for some time they saw, a little way ahead of them, what
appeared to be a white figure hovering above the surface
of the water. Their curiosity aroused, they quickly paddled
closer and to their amazement they saw that the figure was
an image of the Blessed Virgin with the infant on her left arm.

And then, they noticed that the image was riding on a
little plank of wood and that on the plank, written in lumi-
nous letters, were the words: Yo soy La Virgen de la Caridad
(I am the Virgin of Charity).

They placed the image and the plank on the bottom of
the canoe and resumed their journey to the salt pits. Arriving there, they gathered three half-loads [2] of salt, placing
them in bag-like containers made of palm leaves. They then
pushed off for home.

Arriving back at their village, they took the image ashore
and carefully placed it on a *barbacoa* [3] while they went to
find a litter [4] on which to transport it to a "place" called
"Hato de Barajagua" located some forty miles inland.

In that "place" there was a Don Miguel Galan, the overseer [5] of that section of land. When he saw the image and
heard the story of its discovery, he immediately ordered a
rustic altar built for it. Then he sent a messenger, Antonio
Angola, to tell the news to Don Francisco Sánchez de Moya
who was the Administrator of Property in that territory.

Don Francisco came at once on hearing the story. He
ordered a hermitage chapel erected for the statue, and also
directed that a lamp fashioned from a copper vase should

at all times be kept burning before the image. The hermitage was built on a little plot in front of the overseer's house, and to assure that the votive lamp would always be kept burning, Don Francisco placed it in charge of a pious man named Diego de Hoyos, giving him the title of Sacristan.

Then one night as Sacristan Hoyos was refilling the lamp with oil, he was surprised to see that the image was not there—it had disappeared. He cried out in a loud voice and soon the overseer and several other persons arrived. They proceeded to search all around for the missing statue. But all in vain, for they did not find it.

However, the following morning it was back in its usual place on the altar. This same thing happened on two other nights: the statue disappeared but the next morning it was back again.

When the news of these mysterious disappearances came to the Administrator of Mines, he decided the Virgin did not want her image to remain at the hermitage, so he ordered it transferred to the church of the nearby town and commissioned Fray Francisco Bonilla to take care of the matter.

The good priest organized a procession of the people of the vicinity and with great joy they carried the image and placed it on a high altar of the parish church.

Sometime later—the stories do not say how long—the statue disappeared from the high altar, and in spite of the most diligent search could not be found. Three years passed and then one day a little girl named Apolonia was walking along the road to the mines on an errand for her parents. As she passed a certain spot, she saw the missing statue standing on top of a rock. She told her story to everyone she met, and soon the people began to say that evidently the

Virgin wanted her statue to be honored in that particular place.

To determine a site for a chapel, a meeting was held with all the distinguished people of the vicinity present, but everybody apparently had a different idea as to the location of the proposed shrine, and no agreement was reached.

Next a High Mass was offered to the Holy Spirit to ask His guidance—and the answer came immediately. That same night, the people, to their amazement, saw three columns of fire surrounding the very rock upon which Apolonia had seen the statue. The phenomenon repeated itself on the two succeeding nights. So a Temple was erected near, but not exactly on that spot.

When the new church was finished, a holiday (Fiesta) was declared and the people of the town, together with those from the surrounding countryside, carried the image to its new shrine, and there it seems to have remained for some twenty-one years.

Later—again the stories do not say how long—while Don Pedro de Lugo Albarrain was Administrator of the Mines, a vein of very rich copper was discovered directly beneath the church where the holy image was enshrined. In order that the new vein might be mined, another church, very grand and spacious, was built a short distance from the earlier church, on the precise spot where Apolonia had seen the image.

The image was moved to the new church and work on the new vein of ore began. Then a strange thing happened. When they started to mine, it was found that the ore had changed to "crestalillo" [6] a hard substance extremely difficult to mine. This phenomenon was considered to be another manifestation of the Virgin, and after the administrator investigated the matter, he ordered the mining stopped at that place and consigned the entire little hill to the Virgin.

In a few years, the new church proved too small to contain the multitudes of the faithful who came from all parts of the island to pay homage to the Virgin, so it was decided that a much larger church would have to be built.

It appears that the necessary funds for the proposed building were obtained by one Father Onofre de Fonseca [7] who solicited contributions from the faithful of Santiago de Cuba and Bayamo as well as in other places. So a sumptuous Temple was constructed to replace the earlier church. The statue was the center of devotion in the new Temple and Our Lady showered forth her graces—and many were the favors granted to those who sought her aid.

On May 10, 1916, Pope Benedict XV, at the request of the Veterans of the Cuban War of Independence, named Our Lady of Charity of El Cobre the Patroness of Cuba.

In 1925, work began on the construction of the present Sanctuary, and in 1927 the image was transferred to it. In 1932, a beautiful new main altar was completed and the statue was placed thereon, where it remains today.

The statue is a little wooden figure about eighteen inches high.

1.—This village does not appear to be the one presently known as El Cobre, but one—name seemingly unknown—situated somewhere along the shores of the Bay of Nipe. This bay is on the North coast of Cuba, almost directly across the island from Santiago.

2.—"Tres tercios"—an old Spanish term of weight, probably originally referred to half an ox-cart load, or perhaps half a donkey or burro load.

3.—This seems to have been a primitive sort of four-poster which the natives used when taking a rest.

4.—Andas—a litter carried on the shoulders of two men.

5.—Mayoral—an overseer or foreman or elder, etc.

6.—Possibly chalcopyrite—a copper-bearing pyrite—Pyrites are usually crystalline and hard.

7.—This name gives a clue as to the date when this happened. There is a miracle of the year 1702 recorded when a Father Onofre was the Cappellan (Pastor) of the church.

BIBLIOGRAPHY:

Breve Historia de Nuestra Senora de la Caridad del Cobre,
by Mons. J. A. Veyrunes y Du Bois, 1944, from Santuario
National y Parroquia de Ntra. Sra. Dela Caridad, El Cobre, Cuba.

OUR LADY OF QUITO

WHILE THE VIRGIN OF THIS STORY is frequently referred to as
Our Lady of Quito, a more accurate title is the Sorrowful
Lady of the College.

The origin of the title dates only to 1906. The scene of
the events leading to the title was the Colegio San Gabriel,
a Jesuit boarding school for boys in Quito, Ecuador.

In those days, on one wall of the school's dining hall,
there hung a picture of Our Lady of Seven Sorrows, representing the Blessed Virgin, her heart pierced with seven
swords.

On the evening of April 30, 1906, the boys had finished
supper and were getting ready to go to the study hall, when
the prefect, Father Roesch, entered and told them they could
have a few minutes more recreation. He then sat down and
chatted with the older boys, discussing the earthquake and
fire which had devastated San Francisco (April 18). The
younger boys meanwhile played or talked among themselves.

Four of the smallest boys were talking about their first
Holy Communion which they had made on the previous day.
One of them, James Chavez, happened to glance at the pic-

ture of Our Lady. To his amazement, he saw the Virgin of the picture slowly close and then open her eyes. He pointed it out to his companions and to the prefect. Then all four ran in haste to tell their teachers and the rest of the pupils what they had seen.

These lost no time in getting to the refectory and they too witnessed the strange sight, which lasted for some fifteen minutes.

The phenomenon occurred some twenty times in the days following. On one occasion, the whole student body was in the school chapel in the evening, saying the Rosary, when the Lady of the picture, which had been moved to the chapel, again repeatedly closed and opened her eyes. At the same time, the chapel bells began to ring with no hand touching them.

Word of these strange happenings soon came to the ecclesiastical authorities and the entire matter was subjected to rigid investigation.

After some six weeks of questioning the boys and their teachers, the authorities were satisfied that something miraculous had occurred, and they ordered the picture to be transferred in solemn procession from the school to the Jesuit church at Quito. There the miraculous phenomenon was repeated on several different occasions and was witnessed by thousands of people.

Soon the original title of the picture, Our Lady of Seven Sorrows, was forgotten and a new one, the Sorrowful Lady of the College, came into general use.

Later the picture was returned to the chapel of the college—and one day three boys, entering the chapel to pray, found the Virgin of the picture weeping.

The picture is still in the college chapel, although once each year it is transferred for a few days to a large church in Quito, when a novena is held in honor of Our Lady.

BIBLIOGRAPHY:

Behold thy Mother,
by the Marist Brothers of the Schools, 1931.
Fatima Findings, 1952.
"This is Your Mother,"
Don Sharkey in Ave Maria, September 26, 1953.

OUR LADY OF COPACABANA

THE SCENE OF THE ORIGIN of this title of Our Lady lies in Copacabana, a town in a little cove of Lake Titicaca, not far from the city of La Paz, in Bolivia.

Copacabana is an Inca word meaning "one who looks at the precious stone," probably coined by the Incas, because from the cove the distant snow-topped peaks of the Andes looked like sparkling jewels.

Christianity came early to the region through the labors of the missionaries, who came to the country with the Spanish conquerors.

There seem to be several stories regarding the origin of the statue and title of Our Lady of Copacabana. One says that by the latter part of the sixteenth century devotion to the Blessed Virgin had fallen off in Bolivia. The earlier fervor was no longer evident. Then around 1581, a famine struck and once again the people began to pray and intercede with the Blessed Virgin for relief. But relief was not forthcoming.

Then a simple Indian lad, Francisco Tito Yupanqui, decided that his village should be dedicated to the Blessed

Virgin, and to further this idea he would make a statue of her. He hoped that this might induce the Virgin to aid his famine-stricken country, and also, that the statue would be the means of re-establishing devotion to her in Bolivia.

Another story tells of a group of fishermen, who, somewhere around 1576, were fishing far out on Lake Titicaca when a terrific storm descended upon them. Their little craft was soon shipping water and floundering badly. Things looked quite desperate. They prayed to the Blessed Virgin to save them. She supposedly appeared to them, the raging waters calmed down, and they rode safely to the shore.

In thanksgiving they decided to build a shrine and in it place a statue of the Blessed Virgin. They gave the job of constructing the statue to Francisco Yupanqui.

Regardless of which story is the true one, it seems quite evident that sometime between 1576 and 1581, Francisco decided, for some reason, that he would make a statue of the Blessed Mother. It also seems fairly certain that Francisco had never received any instruction in carving or sculpturing, and had never previously done any such work.

Here again, the stories differ. One says he immediately set to work, and in about a year finished the statue. The other tells how for a year he worked as an apprentice with masters in several cities of Bolivia and then went to work on the statue.

Still another says that Francisco had a vision in which the Virgin appeared to him as a swarthy Indian woman, holding the Child in her left arm and a scepter in her right hand. He therefore believed that this was how she wished to be represented in his statue.

At any rate, after some months Francisco evidently made

a statue and he gave to the Lady and to the Infant the features of his own race.

Now it appears that when Francisco offered his masterpiece to the townspeople, they at first rejected it on the basis that it lacked artistic merit. Soon, however, their attitude changed and they welcomed it. In 1583 they built a chapel for the statue.

There is another ancient tale regarding the reception of the statue by the people of Copacabana, which seemingly has no evidence to substantiate it, yet, the Blessed Virgin sometimes manifests her desires in strange ways and who is to say she did or did not do so in this case?

This story holds that when Francisco first offered his statue to the people, no one wanted it, so he temporarily placed it in the house of a sympathetic Franciscan Father.

Shortly after this, a peculiar light was observed in the room containing the statue, and the light seemed to emanate from the statue. The news of this strange phenomenon spread about until the authorities of the town suggested placing the statue in the parish church of the village.

Then in 1583, when the new chapel was completed, the statue was transferred.

Regardless of the particular path the statue followed in arriving at the chapel, it is evident that soon thereafter crowds filled the chapel. Many favors were obtained and before long the statue came to be known as Our Lady of Copacabana.

Years later the present church was built and the statue transferred to it. In 1940 the church was raised to Basilica rank. Over the years the fame of Our Lady of Copacabana, Patroness of Bolivia, spread throughout South America. The image was crowned on August 1, 1925.

BIBLIOGRAPHY:

Apparitions & Shrines of Heaven's Bright Queen,
    by Wm. J. Walsh,
    T. J. Cary Co., New York, 1904.
La Reina de Bolivia y Su Santuario,
    by Fr. Arnoldo Magyar, O. F. M.,
    Centro Mariano Franciscano, La Paz, Bolivia.
"Copacabana,"
    by Frederick A. Walker, in Maryknoll Magazine.

OUR LADY OF GUADALUPE

Mexico City was founded by the Aztecs somewhere about 1325. Cortez and his Spanish followers landed at Vera Cruz in March 1519, and in November of that same year entered Mexico City, the Aztec Capital, encountering no resistance.

Later however, the Aztecs attacked Cortez and his men, and a terrific battle ensued. The Aztecs were defeated and by August 1521 the Spaniards were in full control of the city and surrounding country.

Missionaries who came with Cortez, and others who followed them, very soon converted many of the Indians to Christianity.

One of these Indians was a Juan Diego—his name originally was Cuatilatoatzin, but on his conversion he changed it to the Spanish Juan Diego, which in English would be John James. He and his wife, María Lucia, lived in an adobe house of Tolpetlac, a short distance outside Mexico City. The year was 1524.

Juan and María had no children, and little or nothing is recorded of any relatives they may have had, with the exception of an aged uncle, named Bernardino, who lived a short distance from them.

Juan and his wife were devout Catholics, hearing Mass and receiving Holy Communion regularly at a little Franciscan church, Santiago Tlaltelolco, a mile or so distant from their home.

María died in 1528 or 1529. Juan was then very lonely, and each morning he walked to the little church to hear Mass and to offer prayers for María's soul.

One morning, Saturday, December 9, 1531, as the first light of day began to break through the darkness of the night, Juan, as usual, left his home and started to walk to church. As he approached a little hill called Tepeyac, he noticed a lovely, brilliantly shining cloud resting on the top of the hill. And suddenly music of great sweetness seemed to ring out from within the cloud, and all around him. Juan Diego stopped and gazed in wonder and astonishment. He wondered if he had been carried off to heaven. The singing stopped and at that moment, a voice seemingly from the very midst of the cloud, called out his name: *Juan Diego!* The voice was kind and reassuring, so Juan hurried up the hill. Near the top, he beheld a beautiful lady standing in the middle of the shining brilliance. Rays like those of sunlight radiated from her. Her gown was rose-colored and she wore a blue-green mantle decorated with gold stars. She smiled at Juan Diego.

Again she spoke, calling him her son and telling him that she was the Blessed Virgin, Mother of the true God, and she urgently desired that a church be built there—a church in her honor, where people could come to ask her help in their troubles. She then asked Juan to act as her messenger; to go to Mexico City and tell the Bishop everything he had seen and heard and to give him her request that a church be built at that spot. Juan Diego promised to do her bidding; then the Vision disappeared, and he went on his way.

Arriving at Bishop Zumárraga's residence, three miles from Tepeyac Hill, Juan Diego was told by some of the Bishop's household that the Bishop was too busy to see him. However, he was so persistent that they finally took him to the Bishop.

Juan stammered out his story of spectacular wonders, but as might be expected, the Bishop did not believe him. He dismissed Jaun and suggested that he return sometime when the Bishop had more time to listen. Very discouraged, Juan turned back home. As he neared Tepeyac Hill, there was the same translucent and the same beautiful young lady. Somewhat fearfully Juan told her of his failure to convince the Bishop, and begged her to send a priest or a noble who might be believed. She merely smiled and told him it was fitting that he continue as her ambassador, and asked him to go again to see the Bishop and repeat her command to build a church there.

Juan promised her he would go the following morning, Sunday, directly after Mass, and he assured her that he would return to the hill to tell her how he made out with the Bishop.

His next call on the Bishop proved just as difficult as the previous one; the servants were quite determined that he should not bother His Excellency. Nevertheless Juan was so insistent that they finally gave in and ushered him into the Bishop's room. There he repeated his story of seeing the Blessed Virgin and of the church that she wanted built. The Bishop cross-examined him at length, over and over again. But he finally told Juan Diego that he would have to have some heavenly sign that the Lady was truly the Blessed Virgin before he could build a church there.

So, rather dejectedly, Juan Diego left and made his way back to Tepeyac, and once again the Lady was waiting for him. He told her how he had talked with the Bishop and that he demanded some heavenly sign to prove that Juan was telling him the truth. She replied that if that was what the Bishop wanted, she would give Juan Diego the sign. She promised that if he would return to the hill on the morrow, she would give it to him. Assuring her that he would be there to receive it, he returned to his house. She asked him to be sure not to forget.

But Juan Diego did not keep his promised appointment the next day. On reaching home he found his uncle, Juan Bernardino, very ill, groaning with pain, hot and feverish. The old man had the dreaded typhus. Juan Diego did what little he could to help him, giving him sips of herb tea but as the night faded out, the next day wore on and evening followed, the old man kept growing steadily worse. Before dawn on Tuesday his uncle insisted that he was dying and asked Juan to hurry to Tlaltelolco and get a priest for him.

Juan Diego started out on the lonely walk to the church. As he was half-way up Tepeyac, he remembered that he had failed to keep his appointment with the Blessed Virgin on Monday morning. He stopped to think, and decided to take a path on the other side of the hill, so if she were waiting for him, she would not see him; then he would not have to delay in getting the priest for his uncle.

When Juan Diego was rounding the foot of the hill on the other side, he suddenly saw the Lady coming down to meet him. He dropped to his knees in fear and embarrassment as she approached. She asked Juan what he was doing on that road. He told her of his uncle's illness and how he had spent all of the previous day nursing him—that even now his uncle was dying and he was hurrying to bring the priest. By tomorrow, he assured her, when he could safely leave his uncle, he would come back and go on her errand as he had promised.

The Blessed Virgin told him not to worry, that his uncle was not going to die, that even at that very moment he was cured and entirely well. Juan believed her implicity and said he was now ready to do as she wished, and go again to the Bishop.

She told Juan to climb to the top of Tepeyac where they had always met previously and pick the flowers he would find blooming there, put them in his tilma (cloak) and return to her.

It was December, and flowers did not bloom in those hills at that time of the year; almost nothing grew there, at any time, except a few wretched cactuses and briars. But Juan Diego did not question her word, and obediently climbed up the hill.

When he reached the top he found to his surprise a garden of magnificent roses. He plucked all that his cloak would hold, laid them carefully in it, gently gathered it up around them and hurried down the hill to where the Virgin Mary was waiting for him.

She took the roses from his tilma, rearranged them and told Juan that these roses, blooming in winter, would be the heavenly sign the Bishop had requested. He was to take them to the Bishop, and she was certain that when he saw them, he would believe Juan Diego's story. He must take great care not to open his cloak or show the roses to anyone but the bishop. He promised, and at once started for the city.

Arriving at the Bishop's house, he again had the same old trouble with the servants. They made him wait even longer, until finally his constant insistence on seeing the Bishop broke through their resistance. They noticed that he had something wrapped in his cloak, but he would not show them what it was. Finally they tried to pull it open, and did manage to get a sight of the roses. They tried three times to take some out, but could not—the roses, at their touch, seemed not to be real, but painted or embroidered on the cloak—yet they could smell their fresh fragrance and see the dew shining on the petals. They took Juan Diego to the Bishop at once.

Approaching the Bishop, Juan told him he now had brought the heavenly sign the Bishop had requested; he told the whole story and, opening the tilma, he allowed the roses to fall on the floor at the Bishop's feet.

The Bishop was astounded at the sight of the roses, but even more amazed at what he saw on the fabric of Juan's tilma—a beautiful picture of the Blessed Virgin exactly as Juan Diego had described her so often. The Bishop and all his company fell to their knees and begged Our Lady's pardon for not believing her messenger sooner.

The Bishop took the tilma from Juan and hung it over the altar in his private chapel.

He invited Juan to spend the night as his guest. The next day they visited Tepeyac and sent some of the company with Juan Diego to escort him home. There they found his uncle completely recovered and in the best of health, of course.

Juan Bernardino told him that the Blessed Virgin had visited him and made him well, and had told all about the roses and her picture on Juan's tilma. She also told him that the church or shrine that she wanted built on Tepeyac Hill, was to be known as Our Lady of Guadalupe.[1]

Juan Diego and Juan Bernardino went back to Mexico City to stay with the Bishop. The next day Juan's tilma with the miraculous picture of Our Lady was placed on display in the Cathedral of Mexico City with great ceremony.

A shrine—an adobe hermitage—was built on the plain at the foot of Tepeyac Hill, and the tilma was carried in procession and placed in the new shrine on December 26 of that same year. Time passed, and in 1622 a much larger shrine was erected, and in 1709, a still larger and richer one. Additions to this one were made at various times during the 18th century, and thus it grew into the magnificent basilica that today stands at Guadalupe—and in this basilica, in a triple frame of gold, silver and brass, over the main altar, you can see Juan's tilma and on it the miraculous picture of Our Lady of Guadalupe. Pope Pius XII in 1945 formally ratified her traditional titles of Queen of Mexico and Empress of all the Americas.

The tilma spoken of in the story is made of cactus fibre, coarsely woven, and is thin and open like sacking or burlap. It consists of two strips about seventy inches long by eighteen inches wide, held together by a cotton seam. Artists have not been able to understand the laying on of the picture's colors, because the cloth was not only unfit, but unprepared. And the picture seems to be done in four techniques: watercolor, oil, tempura and fresco. And all experts are puzzled by the fact that it has endured for over 400 years. The cactus cloth—"agate"—usually disintegrates in a few years. The image was crowned on October 12, 1895.

1.—Guadalupe in Estredamura, Spain, is also renowned for its wonder-working statue of the Blessed Virgin. There are many theories about the name Guadalupe. Since the Blessed Virgin spoke to both Juans in Nahuatl, their native language, she obviously used some Aztec word which to the Spanish sounded like Guadalupe, and almost every writer of Our Lady of Guadalupe has his pet interpretation. But as Becerro Tanco, an early Mexican authority puts it: "The reason which the Virgin had for calling Her Image that of Guadalupe, she did not give, and so it will not be known until God will be served by disclosing this mystery."

BIBLIOGRAPHY:

Famous Shrines of Our Lady,
  by H. M. Gillett, Vol. 2,
  Samuel Walker Ltd., London, 1952.
La Madonna Santuari e Feste,
  by P. Umberto Bonomo, C.SS.R.,
  Vatican City Religious Book Co., Inc., New York, 1948.
Shrines to Our Lady Around the World,
  by Zsolt Aradi,
  Farrar, Straus & Young, New York, 1954.
The Dark Virgin:
  The book of Our Lady of Guadalupe, a Documentary anthology, edited and translated by Donald Demarest and Coley Taylor, 1956; Academy Library Guild, Fresno, California.
Our Lady of Guadalupe,
  by Rev. George Lee, C. S. Sp.,
  Catholic Book Publishing Company, New York, 1947.
The Grace of Guadalupe,
  by Frances Parkinson Keyes, Julian Messner, New York, 1941.

OUR LADY OF LA LECHE

WHILE THE CENTER OF DEVOTION to the Blessed Virgin under
the title of Our Lady of La Leche is today in St. Augustine,
Florida, the beginning of that devotion dates back many
centuries.

The image of Our Lady of La Leche depicts the Virgin
as a mother nursing her child. This picturing of Our Lady
as a nursing mother began in the early years of the Christian era.

The first picture so portraying her—probably painted in
the second century—is found in the Catacombs of St. Priscilla,
in Rome.

Probably the most famous today Our Lady of La Leche
is that in St. Augustine, Florida—the first shrine dedicated
to the Blessed Virgin in the United States.

On September 8, 1565, Father Francisco López de Men-
doza Grajales, a diocesan missionary priest from Spain,
landed on the Florida sands at St. Augustine. He had come
with the Spanish fleet commanded by Don Pedro Menendez
de Aviles. Menendez had actually sighted land on August
28, the feast day of St. Augustine, so he named the colony
for that saint.

As soon as the party landed, on the Feast of the Nativity of the Blessed Virgin, they erected a crude altar and Father López offered Mass.

Soon a little settlement grew and within a year or two, Catholic priests established there the first and oldest Mission of the Catholic Church in the United States, naming it the Mission of The Holy Name of God.

During the early years of the seventeenth century, some-time between 1602 and 1620, these Spanish settlers, established, on the spot where Father López had offered the first Mass, the first shrine of the Blessed Virgin in this country. The title under which they honored her here was Nuestra Señora de La Leche y Buen Parto.[1] This first shrine must have had a statue of Our Lady, probably brought from Spain.

Over the succeeding centuries, several chapels were built on this site, but were destroyed during the English-Spanish wars and by hurricanes. The present chapel was begun in 1915. It contains a replica of the earlier statue of Our Lady.

In 1598, Madrid had a quite famous statue of Our Lady of La Leche. It fell into irreverent hands, but was rescued by a devout couple who enshrined it in their home. The wife was pregnant, and when her time was accomplished, she was in great distress and it appeared that she and her unborn child might both die. Her husband implored Our Lady to come to their aid. She heard his prayer and his wife was granted a happy delivery.

In thanksgiving, the couple spread the story of this example of our Lady's power to their friends and neighbors. Hearing of this, King Philip III (1578-1621) of Spain caused a special shrine to be erected in Madrid to Our Lady, to honor her Motherhood.

Soon the devotion to Our Lady of La Leche became

famous throughout Spain and from there, the early Spanish settlers brought it to the new world.

1.—A translation of Nuestra Senora de La Leche Y Buen Parto is Our Lady of Milk and Safe delivery.

BIBLIOGRAPHY:

Mission Nombre de Dios and Shrine of Our Lady of La Leche
Shrine of Our Lady of La Leche.
America's Most Sacred and Historic Spot,
    Leaflets, from Shrine of Our Lady of La Leche, St. Augustine, Fla.

OUR LADY OF THE MARIAN LIBRARY

THIS TITLE OF OUR LADY is comparatively new, dating only to 1951. The Marian Library is located on the campus of the University of Dayton, Dayton, Ohio.

It was founded in 1943 by Father Lawrence W. Monheim, S.M. The objective of this library as envisioned by Father Monheim was to "collect, catalogue and make available to anyone interested in the Mother of God, books, pamphlets, magazines, clippings, recordings, films, and pictures of the Blessed Virgin."

Father Monheim expressed the whole idea extremely well when he said: "The job of the Marian Library is to make Our Lady better known. We cannot love what we do not know. We cannot be devoted to a person of whom we are ignorant. And so we cannot have a devotion to Our Lady unless we know her, and we cannot practice an ideal devotion to her unless we know her very well. This is the job of the Marian Library."

Some few years after the library was launched and was a growing concern, it was felt that the library should have a special image of Our Lady. A design deemed appropriate was sketched by Father Monheim and turned over to Xavier Hochenleitner, a wood carver of Oberammergau, Germany.

The image, depicting the Virgin as a young woman seated in a chair and reading from a book resting in her lap, was received by the library in 1952.

Father Monheim himself named the image Our Lady of the Marian Library.

Other libraries in the United States which have secured copies of the original statue have called it simply, "Our Lady of the Library."

OUR LADY OF MARYKNOLL

THIS TITLE OF OUR LADY came into use around 1930. The Maryknoll Fathers have a Seminary at Maryknoll, New York. The property was given the name Maryknoll, by His Excellency James Anthony Walsh, Titular Bishop of Sien. The name was coined from "Mary" referring to Our Lady and "knoll" deriving from the fact that Bishop Walsh spent his vacations at a place called "The Knolls."

After the Seminary was built and functioning—in 1930— it received a statue of the Blessed Virgin, a gift of a convert through the intercession of His Grace, Archbishop Dowling of St. Paul.

The statue was placed in a kiosk on the Seminary grounds and it was only natural that it soon came to be called Our Lady of Maryknoll.

Over the years, the statue has figured prominently in the life of Maryknoll, and is a focal point at the departure (leaving for work in foreign fields) ceremonies.

MADONNA OF THE MOHAWKS

THIS SHRINE AT AURIESVILLE is the oldest religious shrine in New York State, and marks the point where America's first canonized martyrs shed their blood.

They were French Jesuits—Isaac Jogues, René Goupil and John Lalande—who were working with the Mohawk Indians in the early seventeenth century.

The image of Our Lady is venerated at Auriesville under three titles—Madonna of the Mohawks,[1] Our Lady of Martyrs, and Our Lady of Foy. The traditional center of Marian devotion at Auriesville has been the statue of Our Lady of Martyrs in the Old Chapel, an idealized copy of an ancient statue of Our Lady of Foy.

When Father Jogues was a Jesuit novice in France, devotion to Our Lady of Foy was very popular with the Jesuits, and they were most zealous in spreading that devotion. Indeed, wherever the Jesuit Missionaries went they invariably carried with them a little statue of Our Lady of Foy, carved from oak trees in the forest of Foy.

Father Jogues (1607-1646) came to Canada in 1636, and was assigned to the Huron Mission—his priestly work would be among the Indians.

In 1642, Father Jogues, together with René Goupil and

some Christian Hurons were captured by the Mohawks. Their captors proceeded to take them to the village of Ossernenon (near what is now Auriesville). Along the way, as they passed through other Indian villages, the prisoners were subjected to severe tortures, among which were "running the gauntlet" and being seared with hot embers.

Eventually captors and prisoners arrived at Ossernenon. There on September 29, 1642, Goupil was killed by tomahawk. Father Jogues hid Goupil's body in a near-by ravine, hoping that later he could give it proper Christian burial. However, when he returned to the spot a day or so later the body had disappeared.

Sometime during 1643, Jogues decided to escape. He was helped by the Dutch from Rensselaerswyck (now Albany), and managed to return to France, arriving there on December 25, 1643.

Father Jogues returned to Canada in 1644 or 1645. While he was away, a peace was worked out between the French and the Mohawks. When he and a surveyor named Jean Bourdon again visited the village of Ossernenon in the summer of 1646 he was apparently received in a friendly fashion by his former captors. Possibly this was due to the fact that he now came as a representative of the French Governor of Quebec rather than as a missionary.

In August of 1646, he set out again for Ossernenon, this time as a missionary and with him was John Lalande, a lay brother. Unfortunately, they arrived in the village at the very time when the Mohawks broke their peace treaty with the French. On October 18, 1646, they murdered Jogues and on the following day killed Lalande. Their heads were impaled on the village palisades as a grim warning to other Frenchmen who might seek to enter the village.

Thus ends the story of the sufferings of America's first canonized martyrs. However, other missionaries took their places—some coming even to Ossernenon—and as they went about their work of converting the Indians it may be presumed that they told them the story of Our Lady of Foy, and that they invoked her assistance in their priestly labors.

Then in 1669, it appears that the first statue of Our Lady of Foy was brought to America by the missionaries in order that it might be used to teach the Indians devotion to the Blessed Virgin. In 1675, a statue of Our Lady of Foy was taken into the Mohawk Valley by Father James de Lamberville. And in 1676, Father Bruyas, S.J., Superior of the Jesuit Mission among the Iroquois, wrote: "I attribute these conversions to the goodness of the Most Blessed Virgin, a miraculous image of whom, as Our Lady of Foy, has been sent us. We displayed this precious statue with all possible pomp on the feast of the Immaculate Conception of the Blessed Virgin, while litanies were chanted in the Iroquois tongue."

Auriesville was acquired by the Jesuits in 1884, at which time some ten acres of land were purchased by Rev. Joseph Loysance, S.J. In that year General John S. Clark, an archeologist, and Dr. John Dawson Gilmary Shea, an authority on early Indian missions, had established Auriesville as the site of the martyrdom of Jogues, Goupil and Lalande.

A small oratory was built in 1885 under the title of Our Lady of Martyrs; then in 1894, a little church, the Chapel of the Martyrs, was completed, and in 1930, the Colosseum, called the Church of Our Lady of Martyrs was built.

Devotion to the Blessed Virgin at Auriesville under the title of Our Lady of Martyrs has apparently from the beginning been intimately connected with Our Lady of Foy. Father Loysance, one of the founders of the shrine at Auriesville, stated in *Pilgrim Magazine* of January, 1886, that Auriesville as a place of pilgrimage is an American Sanctuary of Our Lady under the title of the *Faithful Virgin, Queen of Martyrs;* and that the shrine is intended as a commemoration of the historic Mission of the Martyrs and particularly as the restoration of the devotion to the Blessed Virgin Mary which existed in the Mission of the Martyrs along the Mohawk, in connection with the veneration of the statue of Notre Dame de Foy.[2]

1.—The Mohawks were the chief people of the Iroquois Confederation. They occupied the valley of the Mohawk River, and although they were first associated with the Dutch they later became firm allies of the English.

2.—QM Magazine, February 1955.

BIBLIOGRAPHY:

"Shrine of Our Lady of Martyrs," *QM Magazine,* February, 1955.
The Mohawk Martyrs,
   by Joseph MacFarlane, S. J.
   The Paulist Press, New York, N. Y.
Lives of the Catholic Heroes & Heroines of America,
   by John O'Kane Murray, James Sheehy, New York 1881.
Madonna of the Mohawks *Lily of the Mohawks,* March-April and May-June, 1954.

OUR LADY OF PROMPT SUCCOR

IT WOULD APPEAR that we are indebted to the Ursuline Nuns for this particular title of the Blessed Virgin. For the story of how it came into existence, we will have to consider four countries—the United States, France, Italy and Spain.

There is in New Orleans a Convent of the Ursulines established in 1727 by French nuns. These French Ursulines set sail on the *Gironde* from L'Orient, a port of Brittany, on February 22, 1727, and arrived at the Crescent City on August 7, 1727. In 1763, Louisiana became a Spanish possession. In the years following, it naturally came about that most of the nuns of the Ursuline Convent were Spanish. By 1800, when Louisiana reverted to France, the superior and fifteen of the nuns were Spanish, and seven were French.

Fearing that some of the excesses of the French Revolution might reach Louisiana, and they might thereby be persecuted, the sixteen Spanish sisters left New Orleans in 1803 and went to Havana.

The seven remaining French sisters carried on as best they could, but soon realized their numbers were too few. It was imperative that they secure additional nuns to help them. One of the sisters, Mother St. André Madier, remembered a cousin of hers, also an Ursuline, who had been attached to the Convent of Pont St. Esprit, in France, prior to the French Revolution. Mother St. André wrote her, telling how badly the convent in New Orleans needed sisters, and asking if she could help by sending to America some of those dispossessed by the Revolution.

Her cousin, whose religious name was Mother St. Michel (Gensoul) was no longer at the Convent of Pont St. Esprit, as she and her sisters in religion had been expelled by the Revolutionaries and scattered far and wide.

After the Revolution had spent its fury and there was some sign of religious toleration, Mother St. Michel, assisted by another Ursuline, opened a boarding school at Montpellier. Here, the letter from her cousin in New Orleans eventually reached her.

Mother St. Michel was in a quandary—she was needed in France, to help re-establish the school system, which had been completely demolished by the revolution, and yet, might not the sisters in New Orleans need her still more? What should she do? She asked the Bishop of the diocese, and he, not wanting to lose her, told her that only the Pope could advise her, and that if he counseled going to America, only he could give her authorization.

Mother St. Michel composed a letter to Pope Pius VII outlining what she wished to do, ending her letter: "Most Holy Father . . . I am ready to submit to your decision. I await your orders."

Now that she had written the letter, she began to wonder how she could get it to the Pope. He was in Rome, she in France, and he was virtually a captive of Napoleon, who had ordered that the Pope should have no communication of any kind from anyone. Even if she could find a trusted messenger, how long would it take him to go to Rome, and when he arrived, how could he reach the Pope?

Several months passed and she had found no means to dispatch her letter. In despair, she knelt before a statue of the Blessed Virgin and prayed to her: "O Most Holy Virgin! if you obtain for me a *prompt* and *favorable* answer, I promise to have you honored at New Orleans, under the title of Our Lady of Prompt Succor."

The Virgin, as always, came to her aid—shortly a trustworthy messenger appeared. Mother St. Michel's letter left Montpellier on March 19, 1809. And on April 29, she received the Holy Father's reply fully approving her request: ". . . His Holiness approves of you putting yourself at the head of your religious aspirants to serve as their guide during the long and difficult voyage to New Orleans, which you are about to undertake." The Pope having approved, the Bishop then gave his consent.

Mother St. Michel had obtained the *prompt* and *favorable* answer she had requested the Blessed Virgin to obtain for her. She immediately had a sculptor carve a statue of Our Lady of Prompt Succor and the Bishop himself blessed it. Soon thereafter, Mother and the companions she had gathered together sailed for America. They arrived in New Orleans on December 31, 1810. The statue was solemnly placed in the chapel of the Ursuline Convent. From that day on, the Blessed Virgin has been venerated under the title of "Our Lady of Prompt Succor."

On January 8, 1924, a new Votive Church of Our Lady of Prompt Succor was blessed and dedicated by Archbishop John William Shaw; and on January 6, 1928, this new shrine was solemnly consecrated. On June 13, 1928, Our Lady of Prompt Succor was confirmed as the Principal Patroness of the City of New Orleans and of the State of Louisiana.

The original statue brought over by Mother St. Michel

stands over the main altar in the new shrine. (The statue is four feet high, carved in wood, and covered with gold leaf).

As a matter of interest, the old convent of the Ursulines, erected in 1745, still stands at 1114 Chartres Street, New Orleans. It is believed to be the oldest existing building in the Mississippi Valley.

BIBLIOGRAPHY:

Apparitions and Shrines of Heaven's Bright Queen,
Wm. J. Walsh, T. J. Cary Co., New York, 1904.
Manual of the Pilgrim to the Shrine of Our Lady of Prompt Succor,
Ursuline Convent, New Orleans, La., 1943.

OUR LADY OF THE RIVERS

THIS TITLE OF OUR LADY seems to have originated in the United States in 1951, in the town of Portage des Sioux, Missouri, which was settled by the French in 1779. At this point the Sioux Indians on their journeys used to disembark and carry their canoes across the narrow neck which separated the Missouri and Mississippi Rivers, thus saving a journey of twenty-five miles by water.

The Illinois river also flows near this town, so that a great deal of damage can result from the frequent floods.

In 1951, for instance, the property and lives of hundreds of the residents of the area were in imminent danger.

As the raging flood waters of the Missouri River rose higher and higher, breaking a levee and completely cutting off Portage, Father Edward B. Schlattmann, pastor of St. Francis Church, organized a Legion of Mary. He placed his parish and the surrounding territory in the protection of the Blessed Virgin, under the title of Our Lady of the Rivers.

The flood ran its course, but no one in the community was injured, and the damage to property was small.

Soon after the waters subsided, a non-Catholic boating enthusiast became interested in the story of Our Lady of the Rivers, and as a result he became a Catholic. Shortly before his death, he requested that instead of friends sending flowers, they send a gift to be used in erecting a shrine to Our Lady of the Rivers. The idea spread among other recreational groups and commercial river men, and within a few years enough money had been accumulated to begin the construction of the shrine.

A design of the statue by Mrs. Norma McGlory of Mattoon, Ill., was chosen as the model to be used. Then a site for the statue was considered, and it was decided to place it in the Mississippi River at Portage des Sioux.

The twenty-five foot statue is mounted on a concrete pedestal, which rises twenty feet out of the water. A causeway connects the statue with the shore. Work on the project began early in 1957, and it was dedicated in that same year.

The white brilliance of the statue made of polyester reinforced with fiberglas, can be seen for miles along the Mississippi, especially at night, when it is illuminated.

BIBLIOGRAPHY:

"River Town to erect Religious Shrine in middle of Mississippi," St. Louis Globe-Democrat, Sept. 3, 1956.

Fr. Edw. B. Schlattmann, Pastor, St. Francis Church, Portage Des Sioux, Mo.

OUR LADY OF TELEVISION

THE TITLE, Our Lady of Television, was originated in 1954 by Bishop Fulton J. Sheen, National Director of the Society for the Propagation of the Faith. To the Bishop must also be credited the idea of the statue depicting the Blessed Virgin under that title. Working from the Bishop's initial concept, the statue was executed by the noted sculptor, Louis J. Feron.

Prior to this, television had been without a patroness. Bishop Sheen decided Our Lady would be a most appropriate patroness, for inasmuch as television is the projection of the *human word* to the world, so Mary was the first to give the *Divine Word* to the world.

In the statue of Our Lady of Television, a globe—representing the world—supported by the Virgin and the Child, is surmounted by a cross symbolizing the world mission of the Society for the Propagation of the Faith. The hand of the Infant and the hand of the Blessed Mother both touch the world as spiritual antennae by which all peoples are enlightened and brought to Truth and Love.

OUR LADY OF THE WORKSHOP

THIS TITLE OF OUR LADY is a very recent one, dating only from 1951. It appears to have been coined by Father Richard M. McKeon, S.J.

Father McKeon, a member of the Faculty of LeMoyne College, Syracuse, N. Y., over the years had written numerous articles on industrial relations. In these articles he invariably paid tribute to Christ the Worker and to St. Joseph as both Worker and Capitalist. It seemed but natural to Father that Mary would have displayed a keen interest in the trade of her husband and her Son. Undoubtedly, she frequently would drop into Joseph's workshop to marvel at the products which her loved ones were making. Thus, it appeared only logical to apply to her the title of Our Lady of the Workshop.

The idea of such a title came to Father McKeon in November 1951, while he was working on an article touching on the feast of Our Lady's Immaculate Conception.

BIBLIOGRAPHY:

"Our Lady of the Workshop,"
by Rev. J. McKeon, S. J., in *Our Lady's Digest,* Aug.-Sept., 1954.
Data from Richard M. McKeon, S. J., LeMoyne College, Syracuse, N. Y., 1956.

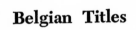

Belgian Titles

OUR LADY OF ABERDEEN
also known as
OUR LADY OF GOOD SUCCESS

THIS TITLE OF OUR LADY is very old, dating back to some indefinite time prior to the eleventh century.

In the reign of David I, (1084-1153) King of Scotland, Aberdeen, at the mouth of the River Dee, was the see of a bishop and his cathedral was the church of St. Macarius. In this church there was, and had been for some hundreds of years, a wooden statue of the Blessed Virgin, called Our Lady of Aberdeen. Who first gave it this name or when, does not seem to be known. The church and its shrine to Our Lady was a center of great devotion to the Blessed Mother and continued so until the sixteenth century.

During the early years of the sixteenth century an arched bridge was built across the Dee and Gavin Dunbar, Bishop of Aberdeen, had a small chapel erected on the first arch of the new bridge· and placed the statue therein,[1] so that all who used the bridge might pause and pray to the Virgin.

However, it was removed soon thereafter to save it from possible disrespect in such a public place, and returned to its former location in the cathedral. It remained there until the Reformation when, sometime between 1623 and 1626, it was secretly smuggled on a Spanish ship with the intention of taking it to Flanders to preserve it from destruction by the Calvinists.

Soon after sailing from Aberdeen, the ship ran into a terrific storm which blew away the masts and sails. After the storm died out, it encountered a pirate craft but succeeded in fighting it off. The ship then drifted helplessly until the wind and tide drove it into the bay and port of Dunkerque where the Governor took possession of the statue.

Shortly after this, the archduchess Isabella, daughter of Philip II of Spain, Holy Roman Emperor, visited Dunkerque and the statue was presented to her. She placed it in her palace at Brussels. Later, probably 1626, it was transferred with great ceremony from the palace chapel to the altar of a new church of the Augustinian Fathers, where it would be more readily accesible for public veneration.

Many and extraordinary were the favors and blessings bestowed on all who prayed before the statue—so numerous in fact, that before long the statue became known as Our Lady of Good Success.

It remained the center of devotion to the Blessed Virgin in Brussels until 1796, when the French Revolution spilled over into that city. The Augustinians were forced to flee from their monastery, but before leaving, they entrusted their statue to a good and pious man, John Baptist Morris, who kept it safely hidden for nine years.

In 1805, after the turmoil had ceased, the Augustinians returned and restored the statue to its former home. In 1814, it was transferred to the church of Notre-Dame de Finestère, not far distant, where it remained until 1852, when it was placed on the altar of a side chapel which had been added to the church, where it remains to this day.

1.—It was at that time called Our Lady of the Brig O'Dee.

BIBLIOGRAPHY:

Celebrated Sanctuaries of the Madonna,
    by Rev. J. Spencer Northcote, D. D.,
    Peter F. Cunningham & Son, Phila., 1875.
Famous Shrines of Our Lady
    by H. M. Gillett.
    Newman Press, Westminster, Md., 1952.

OUR LADY OF BANNEUX (Bahn-err)
also known as
OUR LADY OF THE POOR

THE SEQUENCE OF EVENTS leading to the origin of this title took place in the early part of 1933. The scene Banneux, a little village in Belgium, some ten miles east of Liège.

There, the Blessed Virgin appeared eight times to Mariette Beco, eleven years old, and eldest daughter of a very poor family of seven children. The father, Julian Beco, was a hard working laborer, who, over the years, had fallen away from the Church and was at that time practically an atheist.

About seven o'clock on the evening of Sunday, January 15, 1933, Mariette was staring through a window of the living room, watching for her ten-year-old brother to return from visiting a friend who lived nearby.

Suddenly she saw a young woman, dressed in white, standing in the garden in front of the house. She smiled sweetly and motioned for Mariette to come out to her, but the child's mother refused to let her go. Soon the lady vanished.

Three days later on the evening of Wednesday, January 18th, the lady reappeared. Mariette, accompanied by her father, went out into the garden. The father saw nothing—but he was so impressed with a 'certain power of sanctity' that he was instantly converted, and the next day he went to confession and Holy Communion.

The lady left the garden, beckoning for Mariette to follow her. She glided down the road, stopping momentarily at several places and finally came to a spot where a spring at the side of the road sent a little stream of water into a ditch along the roadway.

She told Mariette to wash her hands in the water. She also said: "This spring is reserved for me."

On Thursday, January 19th, she again appeared. Mariette asked her to tell her who she was and the lady answered: "I am the Virgin of the Poor." Then, as on her previous appearance, the lady led Mariette to the spring. Mariette asked her what she had meant when she had said that the spring was reserved for her.

The lady told her it was to cure the sick of all nations and that she had come to relieve the sick and the suffering.

The next apparition was on Friday evening, January 20th, during which Our Lady asked that a small chapel be erected and dedicated to her.

For days nothing happened and then on Saturday, February 11th—which was the seventy-fifth anniversary of the first apparition at Lourdes—she again appeared. She told Mariette that she "came to relieve suffering."

She appeared again on Wednesday, February 15th, and she confided a secret to the girl—what it was no one knows; Mariette never revealed it to anyone.

During the next apparition on Monday, February 20th, the Virgin asked Mariette to pray much and fervently.

Then came the final appearance on Thursday, March 2nd,

during which she told Mariette that she was "the Mother of the Savior, Mother of God. Pray much. Goodbye." She then vanished, to appear no more.

Then, as is usually the case when something occurs foreign to the ordinary course of events, Mariette's story was believed by some, doubted by others. She was subjected to numerous questionings by psychiatrists, doctors, and ecclesiastical authorities. Nevertheless, a few months later a small chapel enclosing the little spring was built on the spot where Our Lady had appeared.

Soon there were reports of many extraordinary cures and, in 1935, Bishop Louis Kerkhofs of Liège appointed a commission to check into every phase of the matter.

In 1942, Bishop Kerkhofs officially approved the veneration of Our Lady of Banneux—Our Lady of the Poor.

In 1949, the Belgian Bishops issued a pastoral letter declaring: "We can and must acknowledge without any reserve these facts, that is, the truthfulness of the eight apparitions of Our Lady to Mariette Beco."

In the latter part of 1955, the Bishop of Liège authorized the immediate construction of a huge new basilica at Banneux to be dedicated to Our Lady.

BIBLIOGRAPHY:

I am the Virgin of the Poor, Leaflet, Caritas Banneux-Notre-Dame.
Famous Shrines of Our Lady,
   by H. M. Gillett, Vol. 1, Newman Press, Westminster, Md., 1950.
Our Lady of Banneux, color book—Grail Publications, St. Meinrad, Ind.
Shrines to Our Lady Around the World,
   by Zsolt Aradi; Farrar, Strauss & Young, New York, 1954.
"Banneux Basilica will Mark Site Where Mary Appeared Eight Times,"
   by Rev. Henry G. Aerts, S. J. in Catholic Standard & Times, Dec., 1955.

OUR LADY OF BEAURAING (Bo-rang)
also known as
OUR LADY OF THE GOLDEN HEART

IN THE LATTER PART OF 1932 and the early days of 1933, the Blessed Virgin appeared thirty-three times to five children of Beauraing, Belgium. These five were: André Degeimbre, fourteen; Gilberte Degeimbre, nine and one-half; Fernande Voisin, fifteen and one-half; Gilberte Voisin, thirteen; and Albert Voisin, eleven.

The story begins late in the afternoon of November of 29, 1932. Albert Voisin and his sister Fernande, accompanied by their friends, Andrée and Gilberte Degeimbre, started towards a school located a short distance from their homes. They intended to meet Gilberte Voisin at the school and walk home with her.

The school, maintained by the Sisters of Christian Doctrine, was situated on a street which at that point ran under a stone railway viaduct. The railway ran on an embankment a short distance beyond the school buildings. Between the school and the railway embankment there was a fenced-in garden containing a stone grotto enshrining a statue of Our Lady of Lourdes.

Arriving at the school, the youngsters walked to the

door, rang the bell, and waited for the portress to answer. While waiting, Albert happened to glance down the street toward the viaduct, when, to his surprise, he saw a young lady, dressed in a white gown, walking on the railway tracks directly above the archway.

He cried out to his companions, "The Blessed Virgin is walking on the railway." They turned and also saw the lady as did Gilberte who at that moment stepped out from the school. Somewhat startled and perhaps a bit frightened by the strange sight, they dashed home and told their parents what they had witnessed. However, nobody believed them.

The next afternoon, November 30th, the four again set out as usual to meet Gilberte Voisin at the school, and once more all saw the lady walking on the railway embankment. She appeared to them again on the afternoon of December 1st, but on this occasion they first saw her in the garden near the grotto. In a few minutes she vanished but, a little later, reappeared near a hawthorn tree growing just inside the fence enclosing the garden. All the subsequent appearances occurred on that spot.

The apparitions continued almost daily. On several occasions the children spoke to the Lady and she answered them.

By this time, the news of these happenings had aroused the interest and curiosity of quite a number of people and many, including psychologists and doctors, were present at the apparitions, although at no time did anyone but the five children actually see the lady.

During the appearance of December 17th she requested that a chapel be built so that people might come there on pilgrimage. On December 21st, for the first time, she confirmed who she was when she told them: "I am the Immaculate Virgin."

Then on December 29th, the Virgin revealed on her breast a heart of gold, surrounded by bright rays of light. The heart of gold was visible in all the remaining apparitions.

On December 30th, she asked for more prayers. On January 2nd, she promised the children that the following evening she would speak to each individually.

On January 3rd, the time of her last appearance, a great crowd assembled in the street outside the garden and as darkness approached, she appeared. True to her promise, Our Lady addressed each child separately. To Gilberte Voisin she said: "I will convert sinners." To Andrée Degeimbre: "I am the Mother of God, the Queen of Heaven. Pray always." To Gilberte Degeimbre and Albert Voisin she merely smiled and said "Goodbye." To Fernande Voisin she said: "Do you love my Son? Do you love me?—then sacrifice yourself for me. Goodbye." Thereupon she slowly faded from view, no more to reappear.

Then, as is usually the case when something occurs contrary to the course of events, various arguments and opinions began to be heard—some firmly believing the children's story, others as strongly doubting it. This all led to a lengthy and thorough investigation of the entire matter by the Bishop of Namur, with the result that in February 1943, he officially authorized the special devotion to Our Lady of Beauraing, under that title.

In August 1946, the Bishop blessed a statue representing Our Lady of Beauraing. This statue stands in the garden, beneath the boughs of the hawthorn, on the spot where the children saw her.

On July 2, 1949, the Bishop of Namur declared that two cures—that of Maria Van Lear (Sister Prudentia of the Franciscan Sisters of the Holy Family) and of a Mrs. Acar—were miraculous and must be attributed to the intercession of Our Lady of Beauraing.

The chapel requested by Our Lady in the apparition of December 17th, was begun in 1947 and was finished and consecrated on August 21, 1954.

BIBLIOGRAPHY:

I Will Convert Sinners,
  by Don Sharkey, Booklet of Divine Word Missionary Publications, Techny, Ill.
Our Lady of Beauraing, Color Book,
  Grail Publications, St. Meinrad, Ind.
Famous Shrines of Our Lady,
  by H. M. Gillett, Newman Press, Westminster, Md., 1950.
Pro Maria Committee Leaflet, Lowell, Mass.

OUR LADY OF FOY

UNDER THIS TITLE the Madonna has her shrine in Foy, a little town in Belgium southeast of Dinant. In the early 17th century, the hamlet of Foy consisted of several houses, the homes of farmers and workmen, clustered around a large estate owned by the Baron de Celles.

On July 6, 1609, a woodman, Gilles de Wanlin, was engaged in cutting down a huge oak tree the Baron had sold to a boatbuilder from near-by Dinant. When the tree was felled, Gilles discovered that it was badly decayed inside and of no use in making planks. It could only be cut up for firewood, so he set to work sectioning it into logs. Suddenly his axe struck something which certainly was not wood—it rang as though he had hit iron. Cutting cautiously, Gilles soon located three rusty iron bars and beneath the bars, a hollow section in the tree trunk.

He removed the bars, and to his amazement discovered in the hollow a little statue of the Blessed Virgin with the Infant on her right arm. Also in the niche were a cluster of beads and several strands of hair.

The statue was about nine inches in height, made of sandstone. Some authorities believe the statue was probably made in the early years of the fifteenth century, possibly in Utrecht.

Presumably, in the niche of the oak tree at Foy, it served as a wayside shrine for workers in the neighboring fields. The three bars of iron probably formed a grill in front of the statue. As time passed, the shrine was forgotten, trees grew around the oak and over the years the tree closed the niche.

The statue was placed on the mantel in the home of a neighboring farmer but it remained there only a short time. As soon as the Baron heard the story of its strange discovery, he claimed it on the plea that since the oak in which it had been found belonged to him, so did the image.

He had a niche hollowed out in a near-by oak and placed the statue in it. After a few years, the Baron decided to build a chapel on the spot where the image had been found, and set about making plans for the structure.

However, before the work began, something else happened. In 1616, a Martin Peiltemps, father of the parish priest at the town of Sorrine, was troubled with an infirmity. Some accounts say a hernia, others a malignant tumor. He went to the spot in the forest where the image was found, prayed to Our Lady to cure him, and was restored to full health. As soon as the story of his cure spread about the countryside, pilgrims in quite considerable number came to the spot, and many were aided.

The Baron asked the Bishop of Liège for permission to build a chapel on the site of the original oak. Before giving his assent, the Bishop instituted an investigation of the entire matter, and after a thorough examination of the story of the finding of the image, and of the numerous favors credited to the intercession of the Lady of the statue, he authorized the work to proceed.

So the chapel was built and the image was enshrined on

November 21, 1619. Soon the statue and the shrine came to be called Notre-Dame de Foy—Our Lady of Foy.

In a few years, the pilgrims who came to venerate Our Lady became so numerous that it was decided to build a large church, which was finished in 1624 or 1625.

In the last years of the nineteenth century and the early years of the twentieth, the Church was rebuilt and restored to its present state. The statue of Our Lady of Foy was crowned by order of Pope Pius X in 1909.

BIBLIOGRAPHY:
Famous Shrines of Our Lady,
    by H. M. Gilbert, Vol. II, Samuel Walker Ltd., London, 1952.

English Titles

OUR LADY OF DALE

THERE ARE WRITINGS DATING BACK to the thirteenth century which record the story of Our Lady of Dale.

Very early in the twelfth century there lived in Derby, England, a very good man who was a baker. Every Saturday he distributed food and clothing to the poor of his neighborhood and offered it up to the Blessed Virgin.

One Saturday when he had completed his charitable rounds, he was exceedingly tired. He fell asleep, and in a dream the Blessed Virgin seemed to appear to him, telling him he had done well with his alms, but if he wished to be perfect he should close his bake shop and go to Depedale, (as Dale was then called) and spend the remainder of his life in prayer and solitude.

Awakening, he did as the Virgin suggested, sought out Depedale (which was really not far away from Derby), found a secluded dale near-by and dug himself a little cave in the sandstone rock. In the cave he built a small altar in honor of God and His Blessed Mother.

Some years later, after the good baker's death, a chapel was built on the site of his shrine. Then around 1150, Depedale was granted to the Austin Canons of Calke, but they found it difficult to keep the Priory going.

About 1204, a William Fitz Ralph provided them a new house in the park of his estate and promised to provision it. The new Abbey soon began to flourish.

Still later, an Abbey church was built, which soon became known as that of Our Lady of Dale.

From the middle of the twelfth century to the middle of the sixteenth century, Our Lady of Dale was greatly revered in England, and devotion to the Blessed Virgin under that title was widespread. Then sometime during the Reformation, when England left the Church, the church and shrine of Our Lady of Dale were totally destroyed.

BIBLIOGRAPHY:

Celebrated Sanctuaries of the Madonna,
by Rev. J. Spencer, Northcote, D. D., Peter F. Cunningham & Son, Phila., 1875.

OUR LADY OF EVESHAM
also known as
OUR LADY OF THE FIELDS

THERE ARE SEVERAL PLACES in the world where the Blessed Virgin has long been honored under the title of Our Lady of the Fields. Two of these are in France (Paris and Strasbourg), the other in Evesham, England.[1] Evesham probably predates the other two.

Evesham is a town in Worcestershire on the bank of the Avon River.

Our story begins in the early years of the eighth century. One day during those years—the exact date is not known—a poor uneducated swineherd (or shepherd) by the name of Eoves was looking after his pigs in a marshy little valley along the Avon River, on the outskirts of the village of Evesham.

Suddenly a beautiful lady dressed in a lovely white gown appeared to him. She did not speak, but smiled in a friendly way, and in a little while she vanished. This strange happening puzzled Eoves so he decided to go and tell the story to a good and holy man named Egwin (St. Egwin—?-720) who lived nearby-by.[2]

Egwin listened to his story. On the following day, he and several companions went with Eoves to the marshy valley.

Again the lady appeared, and this time she was reading prayers from a book which she held in her right hand.

Realizing that the Lady was the Blessed Virgin, Egwin decided the appearance indicated her desire that a church be built on that spot. So he gathered together a number of monks to drain the marshy land and convert it into a grassy park. Thereon, probably in 701, they built a church and a monastery dedicated to Our Lady.[3]

Soon great multitudes of people were coming to the shrine to pay their respects and to pray in the spot where she had prayed in the fields. Over the years [4] the shrine came to be known as that of Our Lady of Evesham and Our Lady of the Fields.

The shrine in the valley continued to be a center of devotion to the Blessed Virgin for hundreds of years. Then, during the reign of Henry VIII, probably in 1536 or 1538, it was destroyed.

In 1954, for the first time in some four hundred years, ceremonies were held in Evesham, so there is hope that this ancient shrine may be reestablished.

1.—At one time Eovesham.

2.—Third Bishop of Worcester.

3.—King Ethelred granted Egwin the land upon which to build. As to the precise date of the founding, although the monastic traditions of later generations set it in 714, recent research points to some year previous to 709. (C. E.).

4.—There seems rather good evidence that the church was rebuilt around 960, by the Lady Godiva, of Coventry Fame.

BIBLIOGRAPHY:

    Celebrated Sanctauries of the Madonna,
        by Rev. J. Spencer Northcote, D. D., Peter F. Cunnigham & Son, Phila., 1875.
    England, the Dowry of Mary,
        by H. W. R. Lillie, S. J., Catholic Truth Society, London, 1954.

OUR LADY OF WALSINGHAM

WALSINGHAM IN NORFOLK, ENGLAND, is noted for the ruins of an Augustinian Priory, traditionally dated from 1016. The shrine of Our Lady of Walsingham was at one time the most famous and honored shrine to Our Lady in all of England. To it came barefoot pilgrims from all over Europe.

The story of the origin of the title of Our Lady of Walsingham goes back many centuries.

In the middle of the eleventh century a widow of Walsingham, Lady Richeldis de Faveraches (Faverches), was favored with a vision in which the Blessed Virgin seemed to appear to her. She "showed" her the House of the Holy Family—at that time still in Nazareth; it had not yet been miraculously transported to Loreto—and asked her to build a chapel of the same dimensions in Walsingham.

Lady Richeldis immediately set about doing what the Virgin requested and soon her carpenters had the little building completed.

There were two possible sites upon which the newly constructed chapel might be set. One was close to two wells and the other, a clearing, some two hundred feet from the wells. The widow earnestly besought the Blessed Virgin to tell her which location would be better, and then retired for the night.

When she awoke the next morning, she discovered that during the night the chapel had been moved—perhaps by angels—and placed on the site away from the two wells.

Lady Richeldis then installed an altar in the chapel and on it placed a wooden statue of Our Lady and Child. The shrine soon became famous as that of Our Lady of Walsingham and pilgrims came there from all over the known world.

The earliest recorded data on the shrine of Our Lady of Walsingham seems to be that of a grant or gift by Sir Geoffrey de Faveraches (Faverches), a son of the widow Richeldis—made probably between 1165 and 1170—"To God and Our Blessed Lady—the chapel in Walsingham in honor of the Blessed Virgin together with the Church of All Saints near by. . . ."

Seemingly the care of the chapel and Church was to be given to the Canons Regular of St. Augustine and a Priory was established. There is a difference of opinion as to when this Augustinian Priory was founded, some authorities holding it was between 1146 and 1174, others that it was as early as 1016.

In 1538, the chapel, Priory, and several other buildings were plundered and leveled to the ground on order of Henry VIII and, in 1539, the statue of Our Lady of Walsingham was taken to London and burned at Chelsea.

Devotion to Our Lady of Walsingham slowly began to revive in the latter part of the nineteenth century. In 1895, an ancient chapel, called the Slipper Chapel, was completely restored by Charlotte Boyd. It had first been built about 1338, a mile or so from the site of the ancient shrine.

In 1934, a new statue was fashioned and enshrined in the

restored Slipper Chapel. In that same year, the first national pilgrimage to the restored shrine of Our Lady of Walsingham took place. The statue was crowned in 1954.

It now appears that Our Lady of Walsingham's Shrine will again be a center of devotion for all England.

The apostate Bishop Hugh Latimer (1485-1555), when he advocated the burning of the image of Our Lady of Worcester, states, "Our great Sibyl (Our Lady of Worcester) with her old sister of Walsingham and her younger sister of Ipswich, would make a jolly muster in Smithfield." If his chronology is correct, it would indicate that the title and sanctuary of Our Lady of Walsingham predates that of Our Lady of Worcester.

BIBLIOGRAPHY:

Pietas Mariana Britannica,
    by Edmund Waterton, F. S. A., St. Joseph's Catholic Library, London, 1879.
Celebrated Sanctuaries of the Madonna,
    by Rev. J. Spencer Northcote, D. D. Peter F. Cunningham and son, Philadelphia, 1875.
England, the Dowry of Mary,
    by H. W. R. Lillie, S. J. Catholic Truth Society, London, 1954.
Famous Shrines of Our Lady,
    by H. M. Gillett, Vol. I, Newman Press, Westminster, Md., 1952.
Some English Shrines of Our Blessed Lady,
    by Ellis Schreiber in Ave Maria, May 28, 1892.

OUR LADY OF THE WORKERS

THIS TITLE OF OUR LADY, a very recent one, had its origin in Leeds, England, where a special devotion started in a Jewish owned clothing factory—Burton's by name. It is the largest of its kind in the north of England. It employs many Catholic workers, most of whom are members of the Legion of Mary. One of the Legionaries conceived the idea of having a special statue of the Blessed Virgin made; accordingly a statue was designed and made by a student at the Leeds School of Art—a non-Catholic incidentally.

Then the question arose as to what title should be given to the new statue. The Legionary who had originally conceived the idea of the statue suggested Our Lady of the Factory.

However, His Excellency John C. Heenan, Bishop of Leeds, changed the title to Our Lady of the Workers, so as to include all types of workers, and also because Our Lady, although a most industrious worker, was not a factory worker.

So the statue, now appropriately titled, was blessed by the Bishop of Leeds in October 1955, and then solemnly erected in the clothing factory.

During the ceremony, the Bishop remarked: "Our Lady

was a Jewish maiden. It is fitting that her statue should be in a Jewish factory."

BIBLIOGRAPHY:

Data from Most Rev. John C. Heenan, Bishop of Leeds, Bishop's House, Old Park Road, Leeds, England, 1956.

French Titles

OUR LADY OF BOULOGNE
also known as
OUR LADY OF THE SEA

BOULOGNE, OR BOULOGNE-SUR-MER, dates back to the time of Caesar, and the shrine of Our Lady of Boulogne is one of the oldest in France.

The story of how the original statue of Our Lady came to Boulogne runs as follows: In the late afternoon or early evening of a day in the year 635, a small boat was observed moving slowly into the harbor of Boulogne. The boat had no oars, no sails, and no crew, but did have passengers—the Blessed Virgin standing upright in the middle of the boat and, on her left arm, the Child Jesus. Both were carved in wood.

Where the boat came from or who fashioned the carved statue it carried, no one knows. Some say it was the work of Angels.

The news of this strange sight spread quickly throughout the little seaport, and by the time the boat and its passengers touched the shore, quite a crowd had assembled. Reverently, the statue was removed from the boat and placed on the shoulders of several men. A procession formed, led by the local priest, and the statue was taken to the church [1] at the top of the hill.

That night the priest or some other good soul (the stories vary on this point) experienced a dream or vision during which the Blessed Virgin requested that a new church be built on the shore at the very spot where the boat had landed, and that her statue be enshrined in the new church. A new church was built and the statue, already named Our Lady of Boulogne, was placed therein, and it was a center of devotion to the Blessed Virgin for many years.

Centuries passed, then in the beginning of the twelfth century, the ancient church was rebuilt by the Countess Ida, the mother of Godfrey of Bouillon (1058-1100), one of the notable leaders of the First Crusade.

In 1544 during a war between the French and English, the English captured Boulogne. As part of their spoils, they removed the statue from the Cathedral and carried it off to England. Peace was made in 1550 and Boulogne was restored to France. In thanksgiving, King Henry II (1519-1559), ordered a silver statue made to replace the original one stolen by the English, and had it placed in the refurnished Cathedral.

The good people of Boulogne did not take kindly to the new silver statue of their Lady. They wanted their old one returned. After considerable negotiation with the English, arrangements were made to return the original image to the French. Sometime between 1550 and 1553 it was brought back to Boulogne. With much ceremony and great rejoicing it was replaced in the Cathedral.

In 1567, the Cathedral was plundered by the Huguenots who attempted to burn the statue of Our Lady. However, every time they tried to start a fire around the statue, rain fell. After repeated attempts they gave it up and instead buried it.

It was completely forgotten for some forty years. Someone then dug it up and placed it in a near-by abbey. Ten years later when the cathedral was rebuilt and restored, the statue was returned to its former home.

In 1791, during the excesses of the French Revolution, the cathedral was demolished and the statue was again desecrated; it was burned except for one hand which was saved. This was later encased in gold and a new statue was made in 1803.

About 1820 Abbé Haffreingue decided to rebuild the cathedral and again provide a suitable home for Our Lady of Boulogne. Work proceeded slowly, stopping from time to time due to lack of funds, but it was finally completed and consecrated in 1866. In a Lady Chapel of the new cathedral there was placed a new life-size image of Our Lady of Boulogne. She is shown standing in a boat as she was that day back in 635.

During World War II, the cathedral, its Lady Chapel and Our Lady's statue were badly damaged, but have since been restored.

The event which took place in 635 is each year commemorated on August 21st by a solemn procession. A silver statue of the Blessed Virgin is carried from the basilica of Notre-Dame through great crowds of sailors, miners, fishermen, and pilgrims who come from far around.

1.—This apparently was once a temple of a Roman Goddess, but was converted to a Catholic church sometime during the 4th century.

BIBLIOGRAPHY:

Apparitions and Shrines of Heaven's Bright Queen,
   by W. J. Walsh, T. J. Cary Co., 1904.
Famous Shrines of Our Lady,
   by H. M. Gillett, Vol. II, Samuel Walker, Ltd. London, 1952.
Celebrated Sanctuaries of the Madonna,
   by Rev. J. Spencer Northcote, D. D.
   Peter F. Cunningham & Son, Phila., 1875.

OUR LADY OF CHARTRES

THE FAMOUS CITY OF CHARTRES is roughly 55 miles southwest of Paris, in the valley of the Eure, and the highest point of the town is crowned by the Cathedral of Notre-Dame de Chartres, built chiefly between 1194 and 1260. In Chartres, the Blessed Virgin is honored under three titles—Notre-Dame de Chartres, Notre-Dame du Pilier (Our Lady of the Pillar), and Notre-Dame Sous-Terre (Our Lady of the Underground). All three of these titles had their origin in Chartres, at the spot today occupied by the Cathedral.

As a place of devotion and dedication to the Blessed Virgin, Chartres is undoubtedly the oldest in France and possibly the oldest in the world. The history of the shrine of Our Lady of Chartres is distinctive and different from all other shrines of Our Lady, because there was apparently at Chartres a shrine dedicated to a "very special" Virgin, almost one hundred years before the Blessed Virgin was born.

There is general agreement that on the spot where the Cathedral at present stands, the Druids raised a prophetic statue of a Virgin, almost one hundred years before Mary's birth, and they called it Virgini Pariturae.

The Druids were a fraternity of priests, religious teachers and judges who ruled over the Celtic inhabitants of ancient Gaul, Britain and Ireland. They did everything they could to uphold the national cause against the Roman conquerors and urged the people to rebel. Tiberius (Emperor from 14 A.D. to 37 A.D.) and Claudius (Emperor from 41 A.D. to 54 A.D.) deemed it necessary to officially forbid the practice of druidical rites.

There seems to be good evidence that at the time Julius Caesar was in Gaul (58-49-B.C.), the Druids had a place of worship at Chartres, and that, even then, they had an altar in a grotto on the hill now occupied by the Cathedral, and this altar was dedicated to the *"Virgin who would bring forth a son"*—traditionally also at that grotto there was a wooden statue named "Virgini Pariturae." [1]

It would be but natural to wonder where these Druids obtained the idea of a *"Virgin who would conceive."* There are several theories on this—some hold that: (a) they might have learned it from the Jews who, after the conquests of Alexander (356-323-B.C.), had scattered all over the earth; (b) they might have received it by a revelation direct from God; (c) they may have gotten it from ancient tradition running back to the early patriarchs and prophets.

Regardless of whence the idea came, it seems certain that when the Christian missionaries [2] arrived in Chartres, they found there a somewhat ancient shrine of a Virgin. Soon after the arrival of these missionaries, the grotto (shrine) of the Druids was transformed into a shrine dedicated to the real Virgin Mary.[3]

According to tradition, a wooden church was built over the Druid grotto sometime during the first century—but this is not a matter of record. There appears to be rather definite evidence that a church was built there early in the fourth century.

What happened to the fourth-century church is not known

—some say it was destroyed in 743—but apparently some time later another was built and it lasted until 858, when the Normans destroyed it. It was rebuilt, then ruined by fire in 1020. Bishop Fulbert (960-1028), decided to build a new and much larger church and this one endured until 1194, when fire ruined most of it.

Immediately it was decided to rebuild again—an edifice that would stand alone in grandeur and beauty, and this time to build with stone. Work proceeded rapidly and in 1260 the new cathedral, practically as it is today, was consecrated.

Somewhere between the first century, if we wish to rely on tradition, or the fourth century if we prefer rather definite historical evidence, and the thirteenth century the church and shrine was given the name of Our Lady of Chartres.

Now to get back to the ancient wooden statue of the early Druids—the one they named "Virgini Pariturae." All down through the centuries, through building, fires, and rebuilding of the several churches, it remained in the original Druid grotto. When the present cathedral was built the grotto became part of the crypt. Somewhere during the years the statue [4] came to be known as Notre-Dame-Sous-Terre (Our Lady Underground). Then around 1650, the grotto was walled up and, at that time, a chapel was built close by in the crypt, and the statue was transferred to it.

Over the years the statue became quite celebrated throughout Europe and was the center of many pilgrimages and great devotion to Our Lady. However in 1793, during the French Revolution, the revolutionaries removed and burned the statue and badly damaged the chapel. Years passed, and it was not until 1857 that the underground shrine was restored and a new statue carved in stone placed in it.

There is also in the Cathedral at Chartres another statue, carved in wood, known as Notre-Dame du Pilier (Our Lady of the Pillar), and also known as the Black Virgin. This statue in the upper church of the cathedral dates to the middle of the seventeenth century (some date it to the fifteenth century). In 1806 the statue was placed upon a column or pillar —hence the title Our Lady of the Pillar.

The Cathedral of Chartres also has a veil which tradition holds was one worn by the Blessed Virgin. The Veil was presented to the shrine 876 by Charles I (The Bald), King of France. Previously the veil had been given to Charlemagne (742-814) by his wife, the Empress Irene, and thereafter was for many years kept in one of the churches of Constantinople. Later it seems to have been in the cathedral at Aachen (Aix-la-Chapelle). Just how the veil came into the possession of Charles the Bald does not seem to be known, but since he was the grandson of Charlemagne, he probably received it through the regular channels of family succession.

1.—Some authorities hold that it was a custom among the Druids to erect shrines to the Virgin Mother—Virgini Pariturae.

2.—How or when Christianity first found a foothold in Gaul seems to be purely a matter of conjecture. Most likely the first missionaries came by sea, touched at Marseilles and then worked their way up the Rhone and established the religion at Lyons, which was then the metropolis and center of communications for the whole country. There is some mention that around 67, Sts. Altenus and Eodoldus were sent from Sens by Sts. Savinianus and Potentianus (or Protentianus or Polentianus) and they built a small church over the Druid grotto. Whatever may be held as to the time in which Sts. Savinianus and Potentianus lived, it would seem that the foundation of the primitive church at Chartres was laid in the days of Constantine Chlorus (beginning of the 4th century). The church of Gaul first appeared in history in connection with the persecution of Lyons under Marcus Aurelius (177). St. Pothinus, Bishop of

Lyons, disciple of St. Polycarp (69-115), was one of the first martyrs of the Church of Gaul. At that time the church of Lyons seems to have been the only church organized in Gaul.

3.—It appears highly improbable that the statue venerated by the early Christians was the same one venerated by the Druids. It is more probable that the early missionaries destroyed the ancient idol of the druids and replaced it with a new image of the real Virgin.

4.—Some hold that it dates back no farther than the 12th century.

BIBLIOGRAPHY:

Chartres,
by George Monmarche, Editions Alpine, Paris, 1950.
Shrines to Our Lady Around the World,
Zsolt Aradi: Farrar, Straus & Young, New York, 1954.
Celebrated Sanctuaries of the Madonna,
Rev. J. Spencer Northcote, D. D.
Peter F. Cunningham & Son, Phila., Pa., 1875.
Famous Shrines of Our Lady,
H. M. Gilbert, Newman Press, Westminster, Md., 1952.

OUR LADY OF FOLGOET

LE FOLGOET ON THE TIP OF FRANCE, about ten miles north-east of Brest in Brittany, has a lovely fifteenth century church of Our Lady and a Holy Well. The main pilgrimage (Grand Pardon) to the shrine is on September 8.

In the late 1300's, there lived near Lesneven (what is now Le Folgoet) a very devout old man whose name is lost to history. He was apparently a recluse, not associating much with the people of the neighborhood, but spending most of his time in the chapel of the Blessed Virgin, for whom he had exceedingly great devotion.

He seems not to have had a house or home, but for some years slept under a tree which grew above a fountain (or well) near the little church.

One cold winter evening, as the good people were leaving the chapel, they came across the old fellow lying in the snow. He was almost frozen stiff, and as they tried to lift him up, he murmured "Ave Maria" and died.

With a mass for the repose of his soul, they buried him in an unmarked grave in a field outside the village.

In the spring, as the first flowers were beginning to bloom, one of the villagers, while walking in the fields, passed the spot where the old man was buried. He noticed a beautiful white lily blooming on the mounded earth of his grave. And on the petals of the lily in letters of gold were the words, "Ave Maria".

He rushed to the village and told what he had seen. None of the villagers had planted a lily. There was no way to account for its growing on the grave nor for the golden words imprinted on it.

Soon the Bishop heard of this strange occurrence and came to Lesneven. After celebrating a high mass, the Bishop and all the people went in procession to the grave, where the lily was still blooming. They opened the grave and found that the lily's root was the old man's heart. Soon a little chapel was erected on the spot.

In 1419 a church was built over the grave. Still later, around 1808, the present church of Our Lady of Folgoet was erected over the fountain.

BIBLIOGRAPHY:

Apparitions & Shrines of Heaven's Bright Queen,
by Wm. J. Walsh, T. J. Cary Co., 1904.
La Madonna Santuari e Feste,
by Fr. Umberto Bonomo, C.SS.R.,
Vatican City Religious Book Co., Inc., New York, 1948.

OUR LADY OF FRANCE

IN LE PUY, FRANCE, there is a massive rock, probably of volcanic origin, called Rocher Corneille (Cornelian Rock). It towers almost 2500 feet above sea level.

On the very top of this huge pedestal, there is an enormous metal statue of the Blessed Virgin and Child, erected in 1860.

The figure of the Virgin, approximately fifty-five feet high, stands upon a globe; above her head is a starry crown, her feet crush a serpent. The infant sits on her right arm, his right hand raised in blessing of the entire countryside.

The statue was cast from metal obtained by melting down two hundred or more cannons donated by Napoleon III—cannons the French had captured from the Russians at Sebastopol during the Crimean War.

Here atop the majestic rock the Blessed Virgin is honored under the title, "Our Lady of France."

BIBLIOGRAPHY:

Apparitions & Shrines of Heaven's Bright Queen,
by Wm. J. Walsh, T. J. Cary Co., 1904.
Famous Shrines of Our Lady,
by H. M. Gillett, Vol. I, Newman Press, Westminster, Md., 1952.

OUR LADY OF LA SALETTE

LA SALETTE, where this title of Our Lady originated, is a village high in the French Alps, about thirty-eight miles from Grenoble.

The apparition took place on a plateau, six thousand feet or so above sea-level on a slope of Mt. Planeau, a few miles outside the village of La Salette.

The date was September 19, 1846,—the time, early afternoon of a sunny day.

Two young shepherds, Mélanie Calvat, fourteen or fifteen years old, and Maximin Giraud, eleven, were that day tending their cattle on the grassy plateau. They ate their lunch around noon and since the warm sun had made them a bit sleepy, they stretched out in the shade of a little clump of trees and promptly fell asleep.

They awoke around three and were starting to round up the cows, when suddenly, a short distance away, a dazzling whirling ball of light burst into view. After a few moments of incandescense, it slowly faded and disappeared. On the spot where it had blazed, there was now a woman weeping.

She was sitting on a boulder lying on the dried-up bed of a stream, the Sezia. She was dressed in a long white gown, had a white, jewelled scarf draped over her shoulders, and white shoes on her feet.

She sat with her elbows resting on her knees, her head bowed, her face buried in her hands—and she was weeping as though her heart would break.

This unexpected sight frightened the children and they started to run away. Mélanie cried out "O My God!" and dropped her stick. Maximin said to her, "Keep your stick now, I'll keep mine. If it does anything, I'll give it a good knock." But! the lady raised her head, stood up, and called out to them: "Come near, my children, be not afraid, I am here to tell you great news."

She told them why she was weeping—why she was so sorrowful. It was because of the sins of people everywhere—especially blasphemy, neglect of prayer, disobedience, breaking of the laws of the Church and violation of Sundays and holydays.

She also told them that if people continued to do these things, Her Son would be forced to punish them—that famine, disease, and other dire calamities would strike; but if they changed their ways and repented, abundance and many good things would be their reward. She asked them to tell all the people the things she had related to them. Then with a friendly wave of her hand she slowly vanished from sight.

The children herded their cows and hurried down to the village. Soon their story of the lady and the things she had told them spread throughout the area. But most people did not believe them; some said the children had dreamed it all; others, less kind, accused them of outright lying.

A few days later, a spring, long dry, suddenly began to flow from the very spot where the children had seen the lady. A sick woman who drank some of the water was soon cured.

The news of these happenings soon came to the attention of the Bishop of Grenoble. He questioned the children at quite some length, and after years of investigation he declared that the apparition: "'bore all the marks of truth and that the faithful have good reason to believe it.'"

In the meantime Pope Pius IX interested himself in the story and had the children write him an account of what they had seen and heard. He was greatly impressed with their tale, so much so that in 1851 he gave his permission for the erection of a new church on the place of the apparition, in honor of Our Lady of La Salette.

A Basilica was built and the statue of Our Lady (of Reconciliation) of La Salette enshrined therein was approved by the Pope; he dispatched his Legate for the canonical crowning.

The fountain of water which sprang up on the spot where the Blessed Virgin sat weeping has ever since continued to flow, and the water has been the instrument of numerous miracles.

BIBLIOGRAPHY:

Celebrated Sanctuaries of the Madonna,
  by Rev. J. Spencer Northcote, D. D.,
  Peter F. Cunningham & Son, Phila., 1875.
Famous Shrines of Our Lady,
  by H. M. Gillett, Vol. 1,
  Newman Press, Westminster, Md., 1952.
Shrines to Our Lady Around the World,
  by Zsolt Aradi,
  Farrar, Straus & Young, New York, 1954.
She Who Weeps,
  by Leon Bloy, edited by Emile la Douceur, M. S., Academy Library Guild,
  1956. (Celle Qui Pleure, 1908; Le Symbolique de l'Apparition, 1917, (France).

OUR LADY OF LAUS (Le Laus)

LE LAUS IS A LITTLE village in southeastern France, sixty miles to the southeast of Grenoble.

The story of Our Lady of Laus (pronounced Lows) and her shrine, center around a young woman named Benôite Rencurel, who was born on September 29, 1647, of humble parents in the little village of St. Etienne, not far from Le Laus.

Her father died when she was seven, and after his death her mother found life rather difficult. So when Benôite was twelve, she went to work on a neighboring farm, tending the farmer's sheep. Each day while the flock grazed she spent a few minutes praying to the Blessed Virgin at a little wayside chapel.

One day in 1664, Benôite led her little flock into a small valley near St. Etienne and there toward the end of the afternoon, a Lady and Child appeared to her, standing on top of a large rock, known locally as Les Fours. (Some say the Lady and Child were standing in a grotto hollowed of the rock).

The Lady did not speak to Benôite, but smiled in a very friendly way and after a few minutes Lady and Child vanished. However, similar apparitions continued almost daily for two months. Of course rumors of what was occurring gradually spread around the neighboring countryside.

Finally M. Grimaud, a district magistrate, questioned Benôite at length and suggested that if the lady appeared again, Benôite should ask her who she was. The girl agreed and on the very next day the Lady appeared, she asked her to please tell her who she was—was she the Mother of God? The Lady answered: "Yes, I am Mary Mother of Jesus. My Son wishes to be specially honored in this valley, but not on this spot."

With these words she vanished. Benôite did not see her again for a few days. On September 29th, while tending her flock at another pasture, at Pindreau, a very brilliant light suddenly appeared on top of some rock. In the center of the light stood the Blesed Virgin.

She told Benôite to go to Le Laus where she would find a little chapel, filled with a delicious perfume, and there she would also see her. Benôite soon found herself at the little chapel of Our Lady of Good Meeting (Notre-Dame de Bon Rencontre) and going in, she saw the Blessed Virgin over the high altar, on which stood her image. And the Virgin said to her, "On this spot I wish a church built—a privileged sanctuary, wherein many sinners will repent. Means will not be wanting, desipte the poverty of the country people around."

The news of this event soon spread; crowds came to the little chapel, which was too small to contain them. So in 1665, Msgr. Lambert, Vicar General of the Archdiocese, gave permission for a church to be built over the little chapel.

Since there was very little money available with which to hire workmen, the villagers and peasants for miles around carried the stone and built the walls—aided by the many pilgrims who came to worship and remained a while to help in the building of the church.

In 1692, during an invasion by the Duke of Savoy, the church was partly destroyed, but the statue of Our Lady of Good Meeting was not damaged. The church was soon repaired and restored.

In 1716, a new statue of the Virgin was carved and enshrined behind the main altar of the church. It is said that Benôite wished the new statue to be named Our Lady of Laus. The original of Our Lady of Good Meeting was transferred to a chapel behind the main altar. In 1885 Pope Pius IX gave official recognition to the title *Our Lady of Laus,* when he ordered the new statue to be solemnly crowned.

Benôite Rencurel died on December 28, 1718, and was buried in a vault in front of the altar in the church at Le Laus.

BIBLIOGRAPHY:

Apparitions and Shrines of Heaven's Bright Queen,
by Wm. J. Walsh, T. J. Cary Co., 1904.
Famous Shrines of Our Lady,
by H. M. Gillett, Vol. I, Newman Press, Westminster, Md., 1952.
Celebrated Sanctuaries of the Madonna,
by Rev. J. Spencer Northcote, D. D., Peter F. Cunningham & Son, Phila., 1875.

OUR LADY OF LIESSE

WHEN THE CRUSADER Foulques d'Anjou became King of Jerusalem in 1131, he set about rebuilding the fortress of Bersabee to protect the frontier of his kingdom against raids by the Saracens. He garrisoned this outpost with Knights of St. John of Jerusalem. Among these knights were three brothers whose home was in Picardy. One day during some fighting outside the fortress, all three brothers were captured and sent to Cairo, to Saladin, Sultan of Egypt and Syria.

Saladin decided he would make the three renounce Christianity and embrace Islam. He tried every strategem he could devise to bend their will, but to no avail.

As a last resort he sent his lovely young daughter to their cell to see if she could influence them. She could speak some French, having learned it from a war-prisoner slave. The three knights listened to her courteously and then they began to tell her about the Christian religion, of Jesus and the Blessed Virgin. They told the story so eloquently and so convincingly that the princess was partially won over to their way of thinking.

Then, according to the legend, two angels appeared in the cell, with a very beautiful statue of the Blessed Virgin. Seeing the statue the young girl was suddenly filled with faith; she fell on her knees in rapture before it and then and there decided to become a Christian. The knights immediately named the statue Our Lady of Liesse (a French word for joy) because of the happiness it had brought into their lives.

A few nights later the Sultan's daughter bribed the guards, released the three brothers and fled with them from the palace grounds. They carried the statue of Our Lady of Liesse with them.

Crossing the Nile in a small boat the princess had hidden in the rushes, they set out for Alexandria, thinking they would hide out there until the search for them would be abandoned. However, after walking a few hours, the princess became very tired and could proceed no further, so the knights made her lie down in the grass, promising they would take turns staying awake and on guard. But they, too, were extremely weary, and soon all three were asleep.

When they awoke, the rays of the morning sun were peeping over the tree tops. But they were bewildered—where the trees should have been palms, they were oaks. There was no Nile River, only a freshet bubbling along and, in the distance, where the pyramids should have been, there rose instead the familiar towers of an Old French castle, the brothers' ancestral home. During the night, the three brothers, the princess and the statue of the Blessed Virgin had been miraculously transported from Egypt to Picardy.

You may believe this story or not as you wish, but you *can* believe that in one way or another in 1134 the statue of the Blessed Virgin was brought to France from Egypt by three brothers, nobles of Picardy. The three brothers built a stately church and placed the statue in it. Within a short time a town named Liesse grew up around it. Later the Sultan's daughter was baptized in the cathedral at Laon.

Liesse has for centuries been a center of devotion to the Blessed Virgin. Since 1134, on Whit-Monday, there has been a pilgrimage every year to the church of Our Lady of Liesse.

Here is what the matter-of-fact history book has to say concerning Our Lady of Liesse: "Three young crusaders and a converted Egyptian princess came to France at the beginning of the twelfth century, bringing with them a statue of a Black Virgin. They built a sanctuary at Liesse which became the object of a pilgrimage very popular in the middle ages." The image was crowned on August 18, 1857.

There used to be another quite well-known monastery, called Our Lady of Liesse, at Yang Kia Ping, China, the motherhouse of the Chinese Trappists. The last Mass was celebrated there on July 8, 1947, for on that day the Reds began to plunder the Chinese monasteries. Ten of the Chinese Trappists fled to exile in Canada and the United States. They spent three years as refugees at Our Lady of the Prairies, near Winnipeg. Later they were received by the monks of Our Lady of the Holy Trinity at Huntsville, Utah, and some of them with their prior visited the Trappist monastery of Our Lady of Guadalupe, then in Picos, New Mexico. In 1955 they returned to Lantao Island, Hong Kong.

BIBLIOGRAPHY:

Legends of the Blessed Virgin,
by J. Collin de Plancy, P. O'Shea, New York, 1852.
Itineraries in France—The North,
Bulletin of Direction Generale du Tourisme, Paris, France.

OUR LADY OF MARINERS

THE STORY OF THIS TITLE OF OUR LADY goes back seven
centuries. Here is the tale as it has been handed down. Late
one afternoon, during one of the early years of the thirteenth
century, a solitary French fisherman was plying his trade
several miles at sea, off the harbor of Marseille.

Engrossed in his task of baiting and pulling in his lines, he
failed to notice the lowering dark clouds which had appeared
in the sky. Before he became aware of it, a terrific storm
burst upon him.

Soon his small boat was tossing around like the pro-
verbial cockleshell, shipping water faster than he could bail
it out. Then his rudder was lost and finally his mast snapped
off. Only quick work with his knife in cutting free the rigging
saved him from capsizing.

Everything looked pretty hopeless, and he felt sure he
could never get back to the harbor. He thought of his family
that he would never see again and cast a despairing look
at the city, and the huge rock which stood like a sentinel
or guard on the mountain which overtopped the city and
harbor.

Then dimly through the gloom he perceived the figure
of a lady, dressed in white, standing firmly on the very top

of the rock. She seemed to be extending her hand, as if she would help him to the shelter and safety of the harbor. At once it came to him that the Lady so calmly defying the wind and the rain could only be the Blessed Virgin, so he prayed to her and asked her to help him.

His boat ceased its wild tossing almost immediately, righted itself and, pushed by a friendly gust of wind, raced into the calm water of the harbor until it drove onto the shore at the very foot of the mountain.

Falling to his knees he cried out his thanks to the Blessed Virgin, then hurried home to his worried family.

The story of his rescue through the assistance of the Blessed Virgin quickly spread throughout the port. It was then remembered that other sailors, on numerous occasions during severe storms, had also seen the figure of the Lady on top of the rock. Always when she had appeared, the angry seas had calmed and their craft had ridden safely in to shelter.

Soon everyone came to believe that the rock was the spot on which the Blessed Virgin would appear whenever her help was desperately required. In thanksgiving to her, the sailors of Marseille, in 1213 or 1218, erected a chapel on the top of the rock. In it they enshrined a lovely statue of her. They named it Our Lady Help of Mariners.

Around 1544, the chapel was replaced by a large church and the statue transferred to it. Sometime during the French Revolution (1789-1799) the statue was destroyed, but during the 1830's a new statue was dedicated.

It was found that she did not confine her help to sailors only. This was proved in 1832, when a severe epidemic of cholera struck Marseille. The people of the port decided to appeal to Our Lady. They formed a procession, climbed the mountain, removed the statue from the chapel, brought it down, and solemnly carried it through the streets of the city. Almost immediately the epidemic waned and in a few days vanished. So they gave a second title to the statue—Our Lady of Help.

Some years later, as the fame of the shrine on the top of the rock spread, with more and more people coming up to pay their respects, it acquired still another name—Notre Dame de la Garde (Our Lady The Guardian).

In Marseille today, the hill of Notre Dame de la Garde is topped by a basilica, at an altitude of 550 feet, built in 1864. This commanding site has been occupied by a chapel since 1214. The interior has a multitude of sailors' votive offerings and models of ships are hung in all parts of it. A statue of the Virgin and Child dominates the city from its place on top of the western tower.

BIBLIOGRAPHY:

    Apparitions and Shrines of Heaven's Bright Queen,
      by Wm. J. Walsh,
    T. J. Cary Co., New York, 1904.
    Provence,
      Booklet of French Tourist Service, New York.

OUR LADY OF PELLEVOISIN

PELLEVOISIN IS A PEACEFUL LITTLE FRENCH VILLAGE about 175 miles southwest of Paris.

The story of Our Lady of Pellevoisin centers around Estelle Foguette, who was born in 1843, near Châlongs-sur-Marne. Shortly after her birth, the family moved to Paris.

After a normal childhood, Estelle, at eighteen, became a novice in the convent of the Augustinian Nuns in Paris. Some three years later, fearing she would not be able to perform her duties because of an injury, she reluctantly gave up the idea of becoming a nun and left the order.

Aided by the Sisters of Charity, with whom Estelle had become acquainted some years before and who were now solicitous for her, she secured employment as a maid with the Countess Arthur-de Rochefoucauld.

The Countess became very fond of Estelle and in order not to overtax her strength, gave her very light duties. Estelle eventually became the Countess' personal maid.

But after some ten or eleven years with the Rochefoucaulds, Estelle's condition became serious; she had contracted tuberculosis, not only of the lungs but also of a bone in her right arm and, in addition, a large internal tumor had developed.

By the middle of August 1875—when Estelle was thirty-two—her condition had worsened to such an extent that the doctors agreed she could not live more than a few more months. The Count and Countess, in order to make her few remaining days as pleasant as possible, moved her to their country home at Pellevoisin.

A few months later, the Count and Countess found it necessary to return to Paris, but, before leaving, they established Estelle in a small cottage on the estate, and arranged with the Sisters of Providence in the near-by convent to take good care of her.

However, in spite of the excellent care the good nuns could provide for her, she grew gradually weaker, and in February, 1876, peritonitis set in. The village doctor could do nothing for her and said she had only a few more hours to live.

On Sunday, February 13, Father Salmon, the parish priest, administered the Last Sacraments. But she did not die that night, nor on the next day, Monday.

And then it happened—sometime during the night of Monday, February 14th, or the early morning of Tuesday, February 15th, Estelle awakened from an uneasy sleep; it seemed to her that a hellish monster, in a form half human, half animal, was about to attack her. As she gasped in terror, a very lovely lady suddenly appeared in the room. She ordered the demon to depart and as he vanished, she smiled at Estelle and told her not to be afraid, and called her "her child."

She then told Estelle that she would suffer a few more days and by the following Saturday, she would either be completely cured or dead. If she were cured, she wanted Estelle to spend the rest of her life in making her known in and around Pellevoisin. Estelle promised that she would do this and with a final smile the Lady vanished.

The Lady appeared again on the nights of February 15, 16 and 17. During her visit on the 15th, she told Estelle that her Son would permit her to live, and that she would be completely cured on Saturday.

Early in the morning of Saturday, February 19th, the Lady again came to Estelle's little room, and after giving her some words of advice, disappeared. Soon thereafter the pain in Estelle's body began to ease and then vanished completely. She slept.

When Father Salmon and several of the nuns came into her room at daybreak, they found her just awakening, but to their great astonishment saw that her right arm was perfectly normal in size, all swelling gone. They called the doctor who, upon examining her, found that the tumor in her abdomen had also subsided, and that her lungs were altogether sound.

After receiving Holy Communion, Estelle arose from her bed, dressed, and was ready to take up the work she had promised the Lady she would do.

First, she and the sisters transformed Estelle's room into a shrine. Then Estelle began to wonder just how she should go about promoting the Blessed Virgin's glory—she was only a poor servant girl, virtually unknown, and she did not know how to proceed.

Months passed. If only the Lady would come to her again and tell her what she should do! Then she did come again—three times on the nights of July 1st, 2nd, and 3rd. But while she spoke to Estelle of many things, she gave her no specific instructions.

More months passed. Then on the afternoon or early evening of September 9th, while Estelle was praying in her room, the Virgin suddenly stood before her. She was clothed in a white gown, and a white veil covered her head and shoulders, extending to her feet. She was framed in an oval of vari-colored roses. Suspended from her neck and resting on her breast was a small piece of white wool on which was imprinted a red heart, encompassed by thorns and surmounted by a small cross. There was a gash or wound in the heart, and from it drops of blood and water fell.

The Blessed Virgin held up the piece of cloth so Estelle could better see it and told her: "I love this devotion. It is here that I shall be honored." Then Estelle realized that the piece of wool with the bleeding heart was a scapular of the Sacred Heart, and that her real task was to make it known and loved in Pellevoisin.

Estelle experienced five more appearances of the Blessed Virgin, on September 10th and 15th, November 1st, 5th and 11th.

When Estelle had first told Father Salmon of these visits of the Blessed Virgin, he had been quite skeptical, thinking they were mere hallucinations induced by her illness. But in the course of time he became thoroughly convinced that they were real and conveyed the whole story to the Archbishop at Bourges.

The Archbishop counselled patience and prudence, telling Father Salmon that perhaps Estelle was "day-dreaming." However, he did permit Estelle to turn her room into a little chapel, wherein the neighborhood children might come to pray. A statue of Our Lady of Lourdes was placed on the mantlepiece.

When Estelle learned that the Archbishop was not yet ready to give permission to promote the use of the scapular of the Sacred Heart, and might perhaps never give it, she was at a loss as to what to do next. If only the Blessed Virgin would come again and tell her how she should proceed.

On December 8th, Our Lady did reappear. She told Estelle that would be the last time she would see her, but that she would always be near to her. She instructed Estelle to take the copy of the scapular she had made to the Archbishop, and to tell him that the Blessed Virgin would be greatly pleased to see the scapular on every one of her children. Also, that the Archbishop was to assist Estelle in every way possible. She told Estelle that she had been chosen to spread devotion to the Sacred Heart of her Son and she could feel assured that the Blessed Virgin would bestow numerous graces on all who wore it and who worked to make it known.

Soon after the last apparition of December 8th, the Archbishop sent for Estelle and carefully examined her as to the happenings at Pellevoisin. He was apparently convinced of the truth of the apparitions for he authorized Father Salmon to have copies of the scapular made for distribution.

He also appointed a commission to check into every phase of the matter. After receiving the commission's report that the apparitions were genuine and of supernatural nature, and obtaining approval from the Pope, he established in July 1877, a confraternity to promote devotion to the Sacred Heart, through the use of the new scapular. The Confraternity was raised to an Archconfraternity in 1896. Multitudes came to Pellevoisin to pray in the chapel, and to be invested in the Sacred Heart Scapular.

Then trouble struck. Early in the nineteen hundreds, someone started a rumor that Estelle had made up the entire story of the apparitions, that she had never actually seen the Blessed Virgin. This rumor grew to such proportions that finally the chapel was ordered closed.

However, in a few years, the originator of the rumor re-tracted, the blot on Estelle's reputation was wiped out, the chapel reopened, and devotion to the Sacred Heart was re-established. Membership in the Archconfraternity is increasing year by year.

OUR LADY OF PONTMAIN

THE YEAR WAS 1871. The place, Pontmain, some thirty miles from Laval, France, at that time a little farm community of about five hundred inhabitants.

As the new year dawned, the Franco-Prussian war was six months old and the German armies had overrun most of France. Paris was besieged and the people at Laval expected the Germans to attack momentarily. Should Laval fall, Pontmain would be trampled on as the enemy dashed westward toward the Atlantic coastal ports.

Nevertheless, in Pontmain life went on pretty much as usual. Children went to school, mothers prepared meals for their families and fathers toiled at their daily tasks.

One of these was Cesar Barbadette. He, with his wife, Victoria, their two sons, Eugene, twelve years, and Joseph, ten, lived near the center of the village. A step-son, Auguste was fighting somewhere with the French armies.

Sometime between five and six o'clock on the afternoon of January 17th, Eugene and Joseph came home from school, and after warming up a bit, went to the barn with their father, to help him feed and bed down the stock. Several inches of snow blanketed the ground and it was extremely cold.

Soon after they began their chores an elderly neighbor, Jeanette Detais, came into the barn and she and Cesar began to chat about the war and the misfortunes that were rapidly crushing the country. Eugene suddenly had a strange feeling that he must step outside the barn. As he later explained, he just had an idea that he should go "look at the weather."

Stepping through the door, he found that darkness had enveloped the countryside, but the sky was clear and sparkled with innumerable stars. And yet, as he gazed at the sky something about it did not appear quite right. Then he saw what was wrong. In the sky, above Augustin Guidecoq's house, on the opposite side of the road, there was a peculiar triangular blank space, empty of stars, but with three especially bright stars making the corners of the triangle.

As he continued to look, suddenly a tall beautiful lady appeared in the center of the blank space. She wore a blue dress, sprinkled with stars, blue shoes with gold buckles. Her head and shoulders were covered with a black veil on which sat a crown with a red band around the middle.

At that instant Jeanette came out of the barn and Eugene asked her if she could see the lady standing in the sky—right there, directly above Augustin's house. But she, peering intently, told him she saw only stars.

Hearing their conversation, Cesar and Joseph came outside and Eugene, pointing to the sky, asked them what they could see. Cesar, like Jeanette, saw only stars but Joseph immediately cried out that he saw a beautiful smiling lady, and then described how she was dressed.

Their father impatiently said the two boys must have lost their good sense and told them to go back into the barn and help him finish the chores. However, in a few minutes he felt a bit sorry and told Eugene that if he wished to, he could go outside and take another look at the sky. Eugene did so and in a moment dashed back in to report that the lady was still floating there in the sky.

Now Cesar did not know what to think, and as most men when they are perplexed, he sent Eugene to the house to get his mother. After protesting that the supper would be ruined and that it was too cold to be walking around outside, she finally slipped into a heavy wrap and went to the barn with her son.

But even with Eugene and Joseph pointing to the exact spot where they could see the lady, Victoria, like Cesar and Jeanette saw only stars. However, since the two boys were not given to playing jokes and seemed so very insistent about seeing a lady, she suggested that they all go into the barn and say five Our Fathers and Hail Marys in honor of the Blessed Virgin. This they did, and coming out of the barn again the boys declared that the lady was still there.

Victoria, thinking her spectacles might help, went to the house to get them. But even with spectacles, she still could not see a lady. Losing all patience, she told the boys they were "little liars." This, from their mother, shocked and hurt them, so they turned back to the barn, finished the chores, and then went to the house for supper.

Hurrying through their meal, they asked their mother if they could go out to the barn once more and see if the lady was still visible. She gave them permission, and in no time at all the boys returned saying they had both seen her again, and that now she appeared to be about as tall as Sister Vitaline, a nun who taught them in school.

The mention of Sister Vitaline's name gave Victoria an idea. Perhaps the good sisters could straighten all this out? She sent one of the boys to the convent to ask Sister to come over for a few minutes. When Sister arrived, she also failed to see any lady but, suggesting that only children might see, went back to the convent and returned with three girls: Francoise Richer, eleven years old; Jeanne-Marie Lebosse, nine; and Augustine Mouton, a few years younger than her companions.

Arriving at the barn, Augustine could not see anything unusual, but Francoise and Jeanne-Marie immediately saw the lady and described her appearance in pretty much the same terms used by Eugene and Joseph when they had described her.

By this time, rumor that something very unusual was happening down by Barbadette's farm began to spread throughout the little village. Another nun, Sister Mary Edward, came from the convent; also Father Michael Guerin and his housekeeper Madam Friteau with her six-year-old, invalid grandson Auguste; Madam Boitin, the shoemaker's wife, carrying her two-year-old daughter Augustine. In all, some fifty to sixty were presently stamping around in the snow outside Cesar's barn, trying to keep warm and endeavoring to learn what all the commotion was about.

Father Guerin was perplexed, for while he could not see anything out of the ordinary in the sky, it seemed evident from the radiant look on the faces of the four youngsters that they were witnessing something that firmly held their attention. So he stood quietly and awaited developments.

They came almost immediately, for now the children were describing a change in the apparition. They stated that a red cross had appeared over the lady's heart and now an oval band had formed itself around her figure.

At this moment some of the onlookers began to joke and argue about what was taking place. As this hubbub seemed to disturb the four children, Father Guerin, to calm things down, asked everyone to kneel and say the Rosary. The Rosary finished, he asked one of the nuns to lead in singing the Magnificat, and then the Litany of Loreto.

The vision was again changing and the children were telling how a long white streamer had unrolled at the lady's feet and on it had appeared the words: "But pray my children."

Now additional words were forming on the streamer and they spelled them out, "God will soon hear your prayers." Then came a concluding sentence: "My son allows Himself to be moved in compassion."

By this time the crowd was deeply impressed and all were sure the four children were indeed experiencing an apparition of the Blessed Virgin. Presently the children began to speak again. The lady was no longer smiling, her expression was now one of great sadness; a crucifix, blood-red, had appeared and she was clasping it to her bosom. The crucifix was unusual in that above the customary cross-bar there was a second bar, white in color, and on it in red letters were the words, Jesus Christ.

Then, according to the children, four small lighted candles had appeared inside the oval band, surrounding the lady, two at her shoulders and two at her knees. Now the red crucifix was disappearing and two bright crosses came into view on her shoulders.

Hearing this, the crowd began singing another hymn, and as they sang, the youngsters told them that the lady was smiling once again. Then she was extending her hands as though she would embrace all of them.

A white cloud, which everyone could see, slowly began to fill in the space outlined by the three bright stars, and only the children saw it gradually erase the lady's figure, first her feet, then her body and finally her head. The apparition of "Our Lady of Pontmain" was concluded.

Father Guerin lost no time in reporting this strange event to the Bishop of Laval. He visited Pontmain shortly thereafter and, after questioning the four children at great length, was convinced they were telling the truth about what they had seen.

But, to be abosolutely sure, he appointed a special investigating committee or tribunal to check into every phase of the incident.

Their findings and conclusions were such that the Bishop, with the permission of the Holy Father, was able to declare that an apparition of the Blessed Virgin had actually occurred at Pontmain.

Several things took place in connection with the apparition at Pontmain which a skeptic would find hard to explain: First, in the sky where the four children saw the lady, there was in view of all present a triangle formed by three very brilliant stars. Yet none of the fifty or sixty persons who saw these three stars had ever noticed them prior to that particular night, and no one ever saw them afterward.

Second, consider how utterly improbable, if not absolutely impossible, it would be that four children, ranging in ages from nine to twelve years, could "make up" the words they declared they saw as they occurred on the streamer beneath the lady's feet; "But Pray, my children, God will soon hear your prayers. My Son allows Himself to be moved in compassion."

Third, it seems to be an historical fact that on the evening of the apparition the General commanding the German army outside Laval declared his soldiers would march into the city that very night. Yet within hours after the apparition he received an order forbidding him to take Laval, and telling him to withdraw his army. A few days later an armistice was signed and shortly the war was over.

There is a large twin-spired church at Pontmain, the building of which began soon after the apparition. It was consecrated in 1900 and raised to the rank of basilica in 1905. Our Lady of Pontmain is also known as "Our Lady of Hope," and as "Our Lady of Hope of Pontmain."

BIBLIOGRAPHY:

    Our Lady of Pontmain,
       Color Book, Grail Publications, St. Meinrad, Ind.
    Famous Shrines of Our Lady,
       by H. M. Gillett, Vol. I, Newman Press, Westminster, Md., 1952.

German and Austrian Titles

OUR LADY OF KEVELAER

IN KEVELAER about forty-five miles from Dusseldorf, in Germany, there is a chapel of Grace (Gnadenkapelle), a small, red brick building, pentagonal in form, topped with a domed roof. For centuries it has been a famous pilgrimage center with October the great pilgrimage month.

The story of Our Lady of Kevelaer goes back to the early years of the sixteenth century, when the village of Kevelaer was completely wiped out by fire and was not rebuilt; the site of the former town and much of the surrounding countryside became a drab wasteland.

Around 1641, there lived a peddler, a man named Buschmann (or Busmann), who owned a little store in the town of Gueldres not far from the ruins of Kevelaer.

Late one afternoon he was riding across the deserted plain, near where Kevelaer had stood, when his path brought him to a wayside cross. He halted his horse, dismounted, knelt for a moment of prayer for the souls of those who had perished in the fire, and to ask the Blessed Virgin to see him safely home.

As he was about to remount and resume his journey, he heard a voice say: "You will build a sanctuary in my honor in this place."

Startled, he looked all around but saw no one and, as on the bare plain there was no place anyone could hide, he concluded his ears were playing tricks on him. He mounted his horse and started for home.

Several weeks later he was traveling the same route and again heard the voice; and again a few days after that. Each time it repeated the same words.

By this time he was pretty well convinced that the Blessed Virgin had spoken to him, and that he would have to build a chapel for her. Yet how to do so was a real problem for he had little or no money.

He discussed it with his wife and they determined to save a little each week. In time they might accumulate enough to at least start the chapel.

Months passed and then one night his wife was awakened by a very bright light shining in the corner of their bedroom. In the center of the light there appeared a little shrine, in which was an image of the Blessed Virgin. She recognized the image as that of Our Lady Consolation of the Afflicted. This image had been for many years venerated in a shrine at Luxemburg and of which she had somewhere seen a picture.

The husband slept through all this and in the morning when she told him, he did not believe her; he assured her it must have been only a dream. But later in the day when several of his neighbors mentioned that during the previous night they had seen the windows of his bedroom all lit up, he was convinced that his wife was telling the truth.

Buschmann decided that he could delay no longer; he must now build a shrine at the spot where he had heard the voice.

But first, he and his wife searched the neighboring towns for a picture of the Virgin as she had appeared in the vision.

They finally succeeded in obtaining one from an army officer who was recuperating from a wound, in the hospital at Gueldres. The picture was a rough woodcut some five inches high by three inches wide.

He set about constructing the shrine and it seems to have been just a simple little brick column, with a niche or recess on its front face, and topped with a peaked overhanging roof. Next he attached the little picture to a board and mounted it in the recess of the brick column.

The little shrine soon became a center of devotion to the Blessed Virgin, numerous processions and pilgrimages coming to it from the surrounding territory, and numerous indeed were the favors granted there.

Some years later the present Chapel of Grace was erected over the little brick shrine, and it was consecrated in 1663 by the Bishop of Roermond.

And thus, "the humble little shrine built by a poor peddler on a deserted moor, it's sole attraction a common paper print, has, by the will of God, who chooses the weak things of the world to confound the strong, become one of the great sanctuaries of Christendom."

Kevelaer was badly damaged during World War II, but the shrine of Our Lady was unhurt and it is today a noted place of pilgrimage.

In the United States, there is an impressive shrine of Our Lady under the shortened title, Our Lady of Consolation, at Carey, Ohio.

The parish of Our Lady of Consolation was organized by the Reverend Edward Vatmann in 1868, under the title of St. Edward. Father Vatmann's successor, the Reverend Joseph P. Gloden, obtained his Bishop's permission to change the name of the church to Our Lady of Consolation, and secured from the mother shrine in Luxemburg a replica of the image of Our Lady.

Shortly after the statue arrived at Father Gloden's house in Berwick, Ohio, a procession was organized to carry the statue to the Church of Our Lady of Consolation, seven miles distant. On May 24, 1875, the statue was enthroned on a lavishly decorated portable platform, and about one thousand people marched in the procession, singing hymns and reciting prayers.

BIBLIOGRAPHY:

Apparitions and Shrines of Heaven's Bright Queen,
    by William J. Walsh,
    T. J. Cary Co., New York, 1904.
"Our Lady of Kevelaer,"
    by Ellis Schreiber in *Ave Maria*, April 11, 1896.
Famous Shrines of Our Lady,
    by H. M. Gillett, Vol. 2,
    Samuel Walker, Ltd., London, 1952.

OUR LADY OF THE LILIES

THE TITLES OF OUR LADY OF THE LILIES seems to go back to the first part of the seventeenth century (around 1620). It was given to a picture of the Blessed Virgin which hung above the altar of a little mountain chapel at Elend, Germany, in the foothills of the Brocken in the Harz Mountains.

On a cold, stormy, winter night, a teamster with a load of wine was driving slowly along the rutted mountain road. He and his team seemed to be the only living things outdoors that blustery night. The tired horses struggled and tugged at the reluctant wagon, and the snow drifted deeper and deeper. It became increasingly difficult to gain any headway at all.

Then the worst happened; with a sickening lurch, the front wheel of the wagon suddenly dropped into a deep rut, sinking up to the hubs in snow and freezing mud, and there the wagon stuck. The horses, already exhausted, strained at the traces but could not even budge it, much less pull it out. Unless they could move soon, man and beasts would perish from the bitter cold.

No human help was near. The teamster cried out to the Blessed Virgin to come to his aid. As she always answers prayers, the Virgin came to help him.

Almost immediately a whitish female form emerged from the dark woods alongside the road and glided silently toward the bogged-down wagon. She lightly touched the wagon tongue and then the horses easily pulled it out of the rut.

Instinctively realizing that the white-gowned figure who had come at his call could only be the Blessed Virgin, the teamster fell on his knees and poured out his thanks. Then he told her that he was sorry he had nothing of real value of his own that he could offer to her at her shrine in the little chapel at Elend. Hearing this, the Lady smiled and, reaching out her hand, lightly touched a naked little bush standing by the side of the road. At her touch the bush seemed to spring to life, leaves and buds appeared on it, and in a moment it was covered with lovely white lilies.

The Virgin broke off one of the lilies and with her delicate hands, shaped it into a golden chalice. She then handed it to the awe-struck teamster, gave him a parting smile and slowly vanished.

Pulling himself together, he started the team and proceeded on his way. When he arrived at the chapel at Elend, he halted the team and went to thank God and the Blessed Virgin for saving his life. As he prayed, he raised his eyes to the picture of the Virgin above the altar, and then he saw that the Lady of the painting was the Lady who had come to his aid in the forest. So he placed the golden chalice, which she had fashioned from the lily, on the altar as an offering of thanks to her.

The story of the lily-chalice quickly spread throughout Saxony and even all of Germany. Many pilgrims came to honor Our Lady of the Lilies at her mountain shrine in the chapel at Elend—the Chapel of the Lilies.

Later on, according to tradition, the lily chalice was sent

to Rome, but first an exact copy of it was molded in clay and was preserved in Elend for many years.

Since Elend is in the Communist section of Germany, it is not known whether the shrine of Our Lady of the Lilies exists now or not.

In pictures of the Madonna by the old masters, often there will be three lilies on one stem. These supposedly signified either the Holy Trinity or the Immaculate Conception, the Annunciation, or the Birth of the Savior.

In ecclesiastical architecture a pot of lilies over a doorway or window, is a symbol of the Blessed Virgin.

BIBLIOGRAPHY:

Apparitions and Shrines of Heaven's Bright Queen,
by Wm. J. Walsh,
T. J. Cary Co., New York, 1904.
La Madonna Santuari e Feste,
by P. Umberto Bonomo, C. SS. R.,
Vatican City Rel. Book Co., New York, 1948.

OUR LADY OF MARIA ZELL

THIS TITLE HAD ITS BEGINNING about 800 years ago. Today the shrine of Our Lady of Mariazell is undoubtedly the most famous shrine of Austria, and perhaps even of all central Europe.

Mariazell is near the little village of Gratz, high up in the mountains, in the province of Styria some seventy miles southwest of Vienna.

According to legend, in the year 1157, a pious Benedictine monk, Magnus, a member of the Abbey of St. Lambrecht, went out to preach the gospel to the people who worked in the salt and iron mines in the countryside.

After nightfall on the evening of December 21st, he found his journey blocked by a high rock formation. The rocky barrier was too sheer to climb over, so it seemed as though he would have to abandon his quest until daylight.

However, before giving up, he decided he would appeal to the Blessed Virgin for guidance. So, from his knapsack he took a small wooden statue—about 19 inches high—of the Virgin with the Divine Child, which he had himself carved, and placing it in the fork of a tree, he knelt and prayed for assistance.

According to the legend, almost immediately there came

a shattering rumble and the rocky barrier split from top to bottom, leaving an opening wide enough for him to pass through.

Picking up his statue, he walked through the pass. A short distance beyond he built himself a shelter and there made his home.

Several years went by and then, with the help of some neighboring people, he built a small chapel and in it placed his statue. About the year 1200 this chapel was replaced by the first church. The sanctuary soon became famous throughout the neighboring countryside. Later, Henry I of Moravia was cured of a serious sickness by praying to the Blessed Virgin and, in thanksgiving, he enlarged the church. In 1363, Louis I (the Great), King of Hungary (1326-1382) replaced the first church by a larger one. He built it in gratitude to the Blessed Virgin for his victory over the Turks and Bulgars. In 1377, Louis I built the chapel of Grace (Guadenkapelle) and donated rich vestments.

The fame of the sanctuary grew from year to year, and the little statue became known as Our Lady of Mariazell.

The church built by Louis was expanded into the present great one by Emperor Ferdinand III. The work began in 1642, and was finished in 1704. Still later it was raised to Basilica rank. The Virgin under this title is Patroness of Austria.

BIBLIOGRAPHY:

History of the National Shrine, The Mary Book, 2,
   by Rev. Bernard McKenna, D. D. & Wm. P. Kennedy, Litt. D. D.
Shrines to Our Lady Around the World,
   by Zsolt Aradi
   Farrar, Straus & Young, New York, 1954.
"Mariazell, The National Shrine of Austria,"
   by Jerome Gassner, O. S. B., The American Benedictine Review, Winter, 1957-1958.

OUR LADY OF MARIENTHAL

MARIENTHAL MONASTERY IS located on the north bank of the Rhine River in the Rhinegau about fifteen miles from Weisbaden.

According to legend, someone, in the early years of the thirteenth century, placed a wooden statue of the Blessed Virgin in the recess of a hollow tree—the statue represented the Virgin as Our Lady of Sorrows, with the wounded body of Christ from the cross held in her arms.

Soon the people of the neighborhood came to pray before the little statue framed by the niche of the tree, and reports began to circulate of cures obtained through the intercession of Our Lady.

One day a blind man came to pray before the image. He regained his sight. The story of this outstanding favor quickly spread far and wide and pilgrimages began to come to Marienthal from all parts of Germany.

Shortly thereafter, the people erected a church—probably 1225—and in it enshrined the statue. As the fame of the place grew, the grateful recipients of Mary's favors began to speak of the statue as Our Lady of Marienthal. Still later a much larger church was built and the statue was transferred to it.

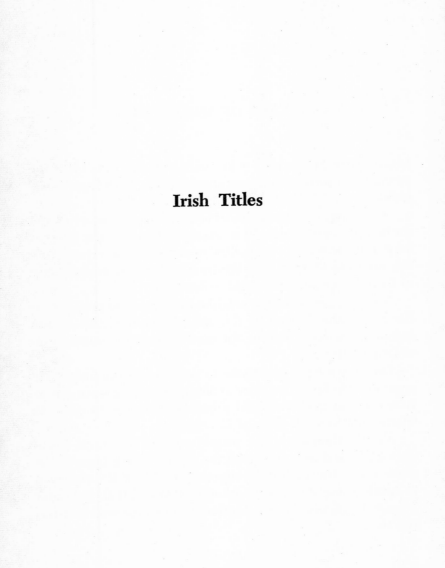

Irish Titles

OUR LADY OF DUBLIN

THE STATUE which is named Our Lady of Dublin is in the Lady Chapel of a Carmelite church on Whitefriars [1] street, in Dublin. It is almost life-size, carved in oak, which over the centuries has weathered to a dark brownish color, causing it to be also known as the Black Madonna.

The statue is very old, just how old seems to be uncertain, but most authorities think it dates at least to the fifteenth century. Some of these ascribe it to the school of Albrecht Durer (1471-1528) [2] —others think it was the work of an Irish sculptor.

Be that as it may, there seems pretty general agreement that the statue was enshrined in the Cistercian [3] Abbey of St. Mary's in Dublin, which in those days lay cross the river Liffey from a Carmelite church. [4] There it became quite a popular object of veneration and came to be known as Our Lady of Dublin.

In 1534, when the definite break of England with Rome took place, Henry VIII (1491-1547) became the supreme head of the Church of England. In 1536, the lesser monasteries were dissolved and in 1538 Henry suppressed all the remaining ones. Included among these was St. Mary's Abbey.

In 1543 or 1544 the statue of Our Lady of Dublin was

ordered burned. However, when it was only partly consumed it was rescued by some friendly person who took it to the yard of a near-by inn. There it was partially buried, face down in order to conceal it from the enemy, and the hollow-ed-out portion [5] was used as a watering trough.

There, strange as it may seem, the statue appears to have laid, half-buried, for some two hundred years. Then it reappeared in a newly built chapel, erected not far from the ruins of St. Mary's Abbey. The time must have been some few years prior to the year 1749, because a pamphlet of that year notes: "In Mary's Lane is a parochial chapel . . . . On the epistle side of the altar stands a large image of the Blessed Virgin, with Jesus in her arms, carved of wood; which statue before the dissolution belonged to St. Mary's Abbey." [6]

Around 1816, a church was built to replace the chapel, and the chapel was converted into a school—the statue remained in the school for a few years and then it appears to have been sold to a second-hand dealer.

In 1824, a priest of the Carmelites—a Father Spratt—one day saw the rather dilapidated statue standing in the dealer's shop window. He bought it and had it repaired as well as was possible.

A few years later in 1827 or 1828, the Carmelites returned to the site of their ancient thirteenth century home. There they built a new church and in it placed the refurbished statue of Our Lady of Dublin—where it remains to this day.

1.—The Carmelites in England and Ireland have been called White Friars—from the white mantle over a brown habit.

2.—If the statue is of the Durer school, it must have been by a pupil rather than Durer himself, for Durer was a painter and engraver and a designer of woodcuts rather than a sculptor.

3.—The Cistercians made their first foundation in England about 1127 and probably were in Ireland soon thereafter. Details of their activities in Ireland at this early period seem to be non-existent.

4.—The Carmelites came to England sometime between 1240 and 1247 and there made foundations at several places. It could be presumed they were in Ireland shortly thereafter. Knowledge of Carmelite activities in Ireland at this early period are meager due chiefly to the loss of many documents.

5.—Sculptors frequently hollowed out their statues to cut down the weight and to make them less subject to cracking.

6.—Quoted by Doran Hurley in "The Black Madonna of Dublin" in the April 1955 issue of The Marianist.

OUR LADY OF KNOCK

KNOCK IS A VILLAGE in County Mayo, Western Ireland.

The apparitions which contribute this title of Our Lady were unique in several respects. One, the Blessed Virgin appeared, not alone, but accompanied by two companions, St. Joseph and St. John; two, throughout the apparitions, the heavenly visitors spoke no word.

It was early evening; the date was August 21, 1879. A warm rain was falling and a brisk wind blowing.

After drying the supper dishes and tidying up the kitchen, Mary McLoughlin, housekeeper for Father Cavanagh, the parish priest, decided to run down and visit her friend, Margaret Beirne.

She walked along the village street, bucking the gusty wind, and as she passed near the church she turned her head to keep the rain from her face. To her surprise she saw standing at the rear wall of the church what looked like three life-size statues, together with a small white altar.

She wondered why Father Cavanagh had not had them placed inside the church instead of leaving them out in the rain. However, it was really no affair of hers, so she dismissed it from her mind and hurried on to the Beirne cottage. She and her friend had a half-hour's chat and a cup of tea. Then

Mary said she must be getting back to the rectory. Mary Beirne, Margaret's twenty-six year old daughter, said she would walk to the rectory with her.

As the two neared the church, they noticed a mysterious bright light seemingly coming from the wall at one end of the building. Drawing nearer, they saw three figures standing in the midst of the light.

Mary Beirne also thought they were statues that the good Father had bought for the church, but then the figures moved and both women realized they were not statues at all. As they hurried forward, it became quite evident that the lady in white, in the middle of the group, was the Blessed Virgin, the bearded figure at her right was St. Joseph, the one on her left, St. John, the Apostle. Farther to the left and a bit to the rear of St. John, there was a white altar with a lamb standing on it.

Mary Beirne ran back to her home and told her mother, brother, and sister of the strange sight. All three hurried to the church, spreading the news to their neighbors as they passed their houses.

Soon some fifteen persons were gathered by the church and all clearly saw the mysterious visitors. The apparition lasted for about two hours, while the people knelt in the rain and repeated the Rosary.

One elderly woman, Bridget Trench, walked up to the figures intending to kiss the feet of the Virgin, but to her amazement, her lips contacted only the wall of the church. However she did notice that the wall behind where the figures appeared to stand, and the ground beneath them, was entirely dry, and this, in spite of the rain which had been driving down for several hours.

Finally the figures began to fade, the bright light dimmed and soon all was darkness. The apparition was ended.

Soon people began to refer to the Virgin of the apparition as Our Lady of Knock. Cures of various infirmities and diseases began to occur through the intercession of Our Lady.

The Archbishop of Tuam set up a commission to investigate the entire matter, and after hearing the testimony of all who had witnessed the appearance, it was reported that there seemed to be no reason to doubt the story, but rather that it should be accepted.

From that day in 1879 to the present, many pilgrimages from all parts of the world have come to pay homage to Our Lady of Knock.

BIBLIOGRAPHY:

Our Lady of Knock,
Color Book, Grail Publications, St. Meinrad, Ind.
Our Lady of Knock,
Picture-story in *Our Lady's Digest*, taken from the *Treasure Chest*, Geo. A. Pflaum, Publisher, Inc., Dayton, Ohio.
Shrines to Our Lady Around the World,
by Zsolt Aradi,
Farrar, Straus & Young, New York, 1954.

OUR LADY OF TRIM

ST. PATRICK WITH SEVERAL COMPANIONS, landed in Ireland in 432, and is supposed to have founded an Abbey at Trim, dedicated to the Blessed Virgin. Specific information regarding the history of Trim seems to be lacking, but it is pretty well acknowledged that pilgrimages have been made to the shrine at Trim for some 800 years.

There are writings as far back as 1397 referring to the image of Our Lady of Trim. One of 1412 refers to Our Lady of Trim and speaks of miracles wrought at the shrine. Still another of 1444, tells of miracles wrought through her intercession. In 1472, a parliament held at Naas, granting certain privileges to the abbey and convent of Our Blessed Lady of Trim, mentioned the "image of Our Lady . . . in the church . . . ." There also exists a letter of the year 1538 which mentions Our Lady of Tryme (Trim).

So there is documentary evidence that at least as far back as the fourteenth century Our Lady of Trim was a shrine of the Blessed Virgin, and that the abbey church at Trim did have an image or statue of Our Lady.

The statue may have been destroyed with the abbey, around 1539 or 1540, but one story has it that the statue was saved and taken to the house of a family named Hammonds, where it remained until 1642. At that time, Sr. Charles Coote occupied Trim, and his son had the statue cut up for firewood.

BIBLIOGRAPHY:

Apparitions and Shrines of Heaven's Bright Queen,
  by Wm. J. Walsh,
  T. J. Cary Co., New York, 1904.
A Dictionary of Mary,
  by Donald Attwater,
  P. J. Kennedy & Sons, New York, 1956.

Italian Titles

HOLY MARY OF ABUNDANCE

THE BLESSED VIRGIN under this title is venerated at Cursi, Italy.

The story begins in the first half of the seventeenth century. At that time the Puglie region of Italy was suffering from a severe drought. For almost three years not a drop of rain had fallen. By the spring of 1641, matters were desperate. April had arrived and already the heat was as in midsummer. Thus prospects for relief and a good harvest that year appeared dim indeed.

Then the people of Cursi and the surrounding territory prayed fervently to the Blessed Virgin; they begged her to come to their aid and save them from the famine that drew ever nearer. And she heard their plea.

Soon thereafter she appeared to a shepherd named Biagio Orlando Natali. The unexpected appearance of the lovely Lady frightened him and he started to run away. But she called him back, reassured him and told him she was the Queen of Heaven and felt sorrow for the misfortune which had fallen on him and his fellow-citizens. She told Biagio to go to the pastor of the parish and to tell him in her name to assemble all the people of Cursi and come with them to this place—for here on this spot she wished a Church to be erected.

And when it was completed, she would take Cursi and the surrounding countryside under her protection. As a token of her deep regard, that very year there would be a harvest of such abundance as none had ever seen before. Finally she told Biagio that he was to change his way of life, for she had selected him to be her true follower, and that he was to serve in the new temple when it would be completed. So saying, she vanished as suddenly as she had appeared.

Biagio lost no time in telling the pastor of this strange happening. The good Father gathered together the people, and led by Biagio they all marched to the spot where the Virgin had appeared. There they fell to their knees and with one voice raised their hearts in prayers of praise and love to the Most Holy Virgin. After some little time they reassembled and started on the return march to the town. They had gone but a short distance, when a little cloud drifted into sight—then another and another, until the entire sky was overcast. Rain fell and drenched the whole crowd; but not one minded—in fact all were so happy, that they laughed and shouted and played around in the downpour. It rained for three days.

The news of this happening quickly spread and great crowds hurried to the place of the apparition to offer their thanks to the Madonna. When the time of harvest arrived, the crops in that whole area were so abundant that every barn was filled to overflowing.

Soon thereafter the grateful people erected a church in honor of Holy Mary of Abundance. And Biagio, his old life behind him, donned the garb of a hermit and vowed to spend the rest of his life in prayer and in looking after the new shrine.

Some years later this church was destroyed by fire resulting from a lightning stroke. But the people, recalling the goodness of the Virgin, immediately set to work and built the present beautiful sanctuary. On the high altar of the sanctuary there is a Greco-Byzantine fresco of the Madonna of Abundance—it depicts the Virgin with the Divine Infant. In their hands both hold sprigs of olives and ears of corn.

ST. MARY OF THE ALTAR OF HEAVEN

ST. MARY OF THE OF HEAVEN is the name of a Basilica in Rome. It dates to the sixth century, and is located on the highest point of Capitoline Hill, on the site where a Sibyl is supposed to have prophesied the birth of Christ to Emperor Augustus.

The name, "Ara Coeli" (Altar of Heaven), is based on a legend which tells how Augustus enjoyed a vision in which he saw the Virgin and Child standing on an altar of Heaven. The chapel of St. Helena in this church is supposed to be on the very spot where the prophecy was made and where subsequently Augustus erected an altar to "the First-Born of God." On the high altar of the church is the Madonna of the Altar of Heaven, an image in Byzantine style.

Here is the legend:

At a certain time during the reign of Caesar Octavianus (63 B. C.-14 A. D.) the Roman Senate, wishing to vest him with a supreme honor, resolved to proclaim him God. Augustus heard of this resolution, and while the idea did indeed please his vanity, yet for some strange reason he was not completely happy about it. So he advised the senate to withhold the proposed honor until he consulted the Sibyl of Tivoli regarding the matter.

He summoned the Sibyl to Rome and conferred with her. She requested him to give her three days before she would give him an answer, during which days she would invoke "those on high" to make known to her the proper response.

The three days passed. The Sibyl returned and presenting herself to the Emperor said, "Augustus, most powerful Sir, hearken to my words. It is not necessary that I tell you whether the deification of your person be a good or an evil thing. (Because) there is no one who should be called God unless he really is God, and you know that you are only a man even though you are truly celebrated throughout all the world for your glorious works. No, not you, but another who is truly God is about to descend upon the earth and he will assume human flesh in the womb of a Most Pure Virgin."

The instant the Sibyl finished her momentous pronouncement a brilliant light burst forth from the sky; it churned and swirled forming a halo. Within its center Augustus saw a most beautiful lady with a baby in her arms. She stood upon a splendid white altar and her figure was surrounded by little angels. And from the heavens a voice rang out: "This is the promised young girl who will give a Savior to the world, and that is the Altar of the Son of God."

Augustus, overcome by the marvelous sight, fell to his knees and with his forehead to the ground remained for a long time in silent adoration of that Mother and Child.

At length he arose, hurried to the Senate chamber, and there announced to the Senators and to all the Roman people that he must decline the title (God) they proposed to confer on him. He told them it had been revealed to him that one other, much greater than he, would ere long be born to the world and that to this one alone could that title be given.

Soon thereafter Augustus commanded that an altar be

erected on the Capitoline Hill—an altar dedicated to the
Only-begotten Son of God, called therefore, Altar of the
First-Born of God or Altar of Heaven (Ara Coeli).

That is the legend—it is inscribed on the wall of the
Chapel of St. Helena [1] in the church of Ara Coeli. The image
of the Madonna di Ara Coeli was crowned on March 29,
1636.

The Church of Santa Maria in Ara Coeli is a great gathering place for Roman children during the Christmas season.
The attraction is a life-size statue of the Christ Child, carved
of olive wood supposedly from the Mount of Olives in Jerusalem.

There is a legend concerning this image. It relates that a
Franciscan monk living in Jerusalem carved it sometime
during the fifteenth century, but was unable to finish it as
he could not obtain the proper colors to paint it. So he set it
aside in the corner of his lowly cell and that very night
Angels came and finished it for him. Later the Monk was
recalled to Rome and he carried the statue with him, but
unfortunately his ship ran into a storm and was wrecked
near the port of Leghorn. The statue was lost but floated to
the shore where it was recovered and eventually found its
way to the Church of Ara Coeli.

1.—Wife of Constantius Chlorus and mother of Constantine the Great. In
326, she visited Jerusalem and there with Bishop Macarius discovered
the Holy Sepulcher and the True Cross.

BIBLIOGRAPHY:

L'Anno di Maria,
   by I. M. Vigo, Torino, 1904.
Highlights of Rome,
   by G. Fanfani & N. Ruspantini, Tip. Ramella, Florence.

OUR LADY OF CARAVAGGIO

THIS SHRINE is located at Caravaggio, Italy. The story of this title of Our Lady begins in the first half of the fifteenth century. In those days there lived in Caravaggio a young woman, Giovannetta, daughter of Pietro Vacchi. She was a good, pious person and intended to become a nun, but her father had different ideas. To please him she married a farmer named Francesco Varoli.

The marriage was an unhappy one, for Francesco was not a nice fellow, and he made things miserable for his wife. Then on May 26, 1432, even though Giovannetta was not feeling well, Francesco sent her out to the fields to cut grass for his cattle.

After spending some time gathering a large bundle of fodder, she felt tired and sat down to rest. Perhaps she dozed a bit, for when she lifted her head the Blessed Virgin stood before her. She spoke to Giovannetta, telling her to be of good heart, that her troubles would soon be over—that her Son was displeased by the sins of the people and would punish them, but that she could obtain mercy for them if they would repent and change their ways. She also told

Giovannetta that she wished a church built in that spot in her honor—she charged her to make known her wishes to all the people and promised that if they obeyed she would bless them with many favors and miracles. So saying, she vanished. But as a memento of her appearance, she left the imprint of her feet on a stone upon which she had stood, and from beneath the stone a spring of pure water gushed forth.

Giovannetta hurried to Caravaggio and told everyone of the apparition and the things the Virgin had confided to her. But few believed her. In fact, they greeted her story with scorn and derision.

A little later some of the people chanced to bathe in the stream flowing from beneath the rock and were amazed to find their aches and pains had mysteriously vanished. Others followed and the same thing happened to them. Then they remembered Giovannetta's story of the apparition and began to believe her. The story spread far and wide and soon the people, assisted by Filberto Maria Visconti, Duke of Milan, built a shrine on the place of the vision.

As great crowds came to the shrine to offer homage to Our Lady, the Shrine was too small to contain them. So in 1575, Carlo Borromeo (later St. Charles) employed the celebrated architect, Pellegrino Pellegrini to enlarge it. Later additions and changes were made resulting in the present sanctuary.

A statue of the Virgin was placed in the enlarged sanctuary—this statue depicts Our Lady blessing Giovannetta. It supposedly occupied the very spot on which the Virgin stood during the apparition. And, from beneath her feet the little stream of water still flows.

BIBLIOGRAPHY:

La Madonna Santuari e Feste,
    by Fr. Umberto Bonomo, C.SS.R., New York, 1948.
Santuari Mariani D'Italia,
    by D. Alfonso Salvini, O. S. B. V., Rome, 1954.
L'Anno di Maria, Vol. V.,
    by I. M. Vigo, Torino, 1903.
I. Santuari d'Italia,
    April 1928, Milano.

OUR LADY OF THE CARMELS

THE BLESSED VIRGIN under the title of Our Lady of the Carmels is venerated in the Church of Santa Maria del Carmine in Naples, Italy. In Naples, however, she is more likely to be called Santa Maria della Bruna, or just La Bruna—due to the brownish color of the image's face.

The name "Del Carmine" came about in this way: the picture [1] came to Naples around the middle of the twelfth century, being carried there by some eastern monks, who migrated from Mt. Carmel in Palestine. At that time, the Carmelites began to leave their ancient home and take up new quarters in various parts of Europe.

These particular Carmelites had a little church and convent given them just outside the walls of Naples. They placed the picture of Our Lady over the high altar of their church. The church soon became quite a place of devotion for local people and before long the image came to be called the Madonna del Carmine—Our Lady of the Carmels or Carmelites.

And there, in the little church of the Carmelites, the image might have remained, attaining a measure of local fame, but for a series of events which were soon set in motion.

In 1262, Pope Urban IV invited Charles of Anjou to assume the crown of the Two Sicilies. As a result, several battles subsequently took place and in 1268, Conradin, the legitimate heir to the throne of Naples, was defeated and captured in a battle near Tagliacozzo.

His mother, Empress Elizabeth, arranged for the payment of ransom to Charles of Anjou for the release of her son, but through some mischance he was beheaded [2] in 1268, before Elizabeth arrived in Naples with the agreed-upon ransom.

Although cruel circumstance prevented Elizabeth from saving her son's life, she determined that the ransom, which she had brought with her, should nevertheless, in some way be used to commemorate Conradin. Accordingly she had his body removed to the Carmelite church and then set about rebuilding it on a scale of magnificence worthy of a royal mausoleum.

The rebuilding completed, the picture of the Madonna del Carmine, which had hung over the altar of the original church, seemed now too small for the larger edifice and it was replaced by a much larger picture of the Assumption. The small picture was placed in one of the side chapels of the church. There it remained for over two hundred years, and gradually it seems to have fallen into neglect in both the veneration and affection of the people of Naples.

Then came the year 1500—a jubilee year—and a number of pious Neapolitans decided they would go on a pilgrimage to Rome. So it was organized and the leaders thought it should be placed under the protection of the Blessed Virgin. Then someone suggested that it would be most fitting to have a picture of the Virgin, which could be carried at the head of the procession.

Next, they persuaded the Carmelite Fathers to lend them their picture of the Madonna della Bruna and, proudly placing it at the head of the column, they started the journey to Rome on April 5, 1500.

Now, it happened that, a mile or so from the church where the pilgrimage started, one Thomas Saccone lay by the roadside. Thomas had been a cripple all his life, his body deformed and his legs useless, for they would not support him.

When he saw the procession coming toward him, he was filled with a great wish to go along with it, but this he knew was impossible, for he could not even stand up, much less walk. But then he wondered—was it impossible? Could not the Blessed Mother do the impossible? Anyway he would ask her. So as the picture of the Madonna slowly passed before him, he cried out to her for help, and he vowed if cured he would join the pilgrimage. And in that instant he felt cured and, standing up, he found he could walk. Rejoicing, he joined the procession.

Naturally, the story of Thomas' cure raced ahead of the procession, and as it progressed from village to village, it was found that the townspeople had carried forth their sick and infirm and had placed them alongside the highway, so all might ask Our Lady to help them when her image passed by. It seems that many were healed.

So it went until the ninth day, when the pilgrimage arrived in Rome. There, the picture was placed in St. Peter's, where all might come to see it. The Holy Father, who had heard of the many cures that had taken place throughout the journey, came with many Cardinals and clergy to pay homage to the Madonna del Carmine.

The image was carried by the pilgrims to numerous basilicas and churches in Rome, and everywhere the people received it with great delight and manifested their sincere devotion.

When it came time to return to Naples, all the way back the procession encountered the same outpouring of people, all anxious to see the image and to pray to Our Lady.

The Carmelite Fathers together with a great multitude met the pilgrims at Aversa, a town some ten miles outside of Naples. With great rejoicing they welcomed the return of their now famous Madonna. It was restored to its original place over the high altar of their new church and henceforth great crowds came to ask the Virgin to help them in their trials and troubles.

Soon after this a most amazing thing happened. Frederick II, then King of Naples, had a really wonderful idea. He decreed that all the sick, the deaf, the blind, and the lame of his whole kingdom be brought to Naples. Then he prepared a hospital alongside the church of the Carmelites, and as the unfortnate ones arrived they were quartered therein.

When all had been collected, they were taken to the church on the appointed day. A High Mass was then celebrated and at the "Gloria in Excelsis" [3] the image was unveiled. At that same instant a ray of light appeared to descend from Heaven and shone brightly upon the face of the Madonna. Then it seemed to reflect and scatter its brilliance over the assembled multitude, and as it rested on them, all were forthwith cured.

From that day, Our Lady of the Carmels, or Santa Maria della Bruna, if you prefer, has been a very great favorite of the people of Naples, and numerous have been the favors and graces she has bestowed upon them.

1.—The picture is painted on a tablet—it is now contained in a marble tabernacle, a precious work of the sixteenth century.

2.—In the Piazza del Mercato (Market Place), Naples on October 26, 1268. Conradin of Swabia was the last descendent of the Imperial House of Hohenstaufen, a son of Conrad IV (1228-1254). His uncle, Manfred, had assumed the crown of Sicily on a rumor of Conradin's death. Pope Clement IV's dislike for the Hohenstaufens led him to offer the crown of the Two Sicilies to Charles of Anjou. Charles immediately invaded Italy and met his antagonist at Benevento where the defeat and death of Manfred in 1266, gave him possession of the kingdom. Conradin appeared in Italy at the head of an army of 10,000 and gained several victories over the French, but was finally defeated and captured in the battle of Tagliacozzo.

3.—Some say it was at the end of the Consecration.

BIBLIOGRAPHY:

Marian Shrines in Italy,
Booklet of E. N. I. T., Rome.
Celebrated Sanctuaries of the Madonna,
by Rev. J. Spencer Northcote, D. D.,
Peter F. Cunningham & Son, Phila., 1875.
La Madonna Santuari e Feste,
by Fr. Umberto Bonomo, C.SS.R.,
Vatican City Religious Book Co., Inc., New York, 1948.
Santuari Mariani D'Italia,
by D. Alfonso Salvini, O. S. B. V., Edizioni Paoline, Pia Societa S. Paolo, Rome, 1954.

OUR LADY OF THE CAVE

THE EVENT WHICH LED to the origin of this title of Our Lady took place on the outskirts of the village of San Cedsaero, eighteen miles southeast of Rome.

The setting of the story is a deep, narrow ravine a short distance outside of the village—at the bottom of the gorge there was a swiftly flowing stream. The walls of the ravine were honeycombed with numerous caves and at the time of our story, a narrow footpath ran along one wall of the ravine. The place seems to have had a bad name—many of the people were sure it was a haunt of evil spirits.

One day in 1654, a priest, Don Federico, was walking along the path on his way to the hamlet of San Pietro di Dragonea, a mission of the parish of San Cesareo. As he passed a certain cave he heard peculiar screams and groans issuing from inside it. He saw devilish figures prancing around in the semi-darkness of the grotto.

Don Frederico thought this dangerous state of affairs should be corrected. He decided to place the cave under the protection of the Blessed Virgin. So he fastened a little picture [1] of the Virgin and child to the rock just outside the entrance to the cave and the noises ceased.

The picture remained there, unharmed by time or

weather, for forty-eight years. The picture was titled Santa Maria Avvocata dei Peccatori (Holy Mary Advocate of Sinners) and thus over the years the cave's old name, Grotta degli Sportiglioni (Cave of the Bats) was forgotten and instead it came to be known as Grotta dell' Avvocatella, (Cave of the Little Advocate or Defender).

In 1702, Fra Angiolo Maria di Majuri, a member [2] of a Franciscan Monastery in La Cava, chiseled out a niche in the wall of the cave. In the niche he had the picture of the Madonna and Child done in fresco. Later, someone built an altar beneath the fresco and from then on devotional exercises were frequently held there.

On May 19, 1703, a poor farmer, Antonio Casaburi, and his six year old son were going along the path, driving their donkey which was loaded with a bag of corn. Just as they arrived before the cave of the Madonna, the donkey slipped and fell over the edge of the ravine, taking the boy with him.

Because the drop to the stream and the rocks below was over a hundred feet, the distraught father gave his son up for lost. Nevertheless, he knelt before the fresco of Our Lady and begged her to save his boy.

Then, with several others who had seen the accident, he worked his way to the bottom of the gully, where to his joy and amazement he found the donkey grazing and his son gathering up the scattered corn. Save for a few scratches and bruises, the boy was unharmed.

The news of this intervention of Our Lady quickly spread around the countryside. The people decided to erect a chapel at the site of the grotto. However, before actual building began, the Bishop of Cava decided that the whole matter should be thoroughly investigated. The grotto was closed off and all were forbidden to go there while the investigation was in progress.

After fifteen days, the Bishop was convinced of the truth of the marvelous stories in circulation about the cave, and he gave his permission to go ahead with the building of the chapel.

So the chapel was built and the first mass in it was celebrated on September 7, 1704. The dangerous little path along the canyon wall was enlarged into a road, guard rails and other improvements were made, and great multitudes came to honor the Madonna della Grotta.

1.—As to the picture, the stories vary. One says that Don Federico had it in his pocket; another, that it adorned his room in the monastery and he had to go home and get it.

2.—Again the stories differ, one says Angiolo was a monk; another that he was a lay brother.

BIBLIOGRAPHY:

Celebrated Sanctuaries of The Madonna,
by Rev. J. Spencer Northcote, D. D.,
Peter F. Cunningham & Son, Philadelphia, 1875.
La Madonna Santuari e Feste,
by P. Umberto Bonomo, C.SS.R.,
Vatican City Religious Book Co., Inc., New York, 1948.

MADONNA OF THE COLUMN

UNDER THIS TITLE, the Blessed Virgin is venerated in the Cathedral of Savona, Italy.

This ancient cathedral, known as the Cathedral of Santa Maria del Priamar, was demolished by the Genoese between 1528 and 1542—in order to obtain a site upon which to erect a castle or fortress. Thereafter the Church of St. Francis served as a Cathedral. In 1499, a pious lady named Violantina Riario Sansoni commissioned the artist Robertelli to paint an image of the Virgin and Child on a column or pillar of this church.

The image was a fresco representing the Madonna in a sitting position—a large mantle covered her head, draped over her shoulders and arms, and entwined itself across her knees. Seated upon her right knee was the Infant, holding a bird on His right hand. The child's left hand pointed to the bird while his head was turned toward his mother. Her left hand held a locked book.

This little image quickly became an object of great devotion and over the years came to be much loved by the people of Savona, who regarded it as the image of their special advocate.

In the latter years of the sixteenth century the authorities decided to erect a new Cathedral. The site chosen was exactly that occupied by the church of St. Francis. So they tore down that church, intending to use the stones in building the new one—tore down all but the column of the Virgin. And on July 19, 1589, the first stone of the foundation for the new cathedral was blessed and laid by Bishop Pier Francesco Costa.

The work proceeded rapidly and by the early part of 1601, had reached a stage where something had to be done about the old column, as it was impeding certain work. Although the ecclesiastical authorities patiently explained to their people the necessity of removing the column, the faithful were equally insistent that their beloved Madonna should not be ruined. "Tear it down," they said, "but first remove and preserve the revered little image."

Now this was easy to say, but how could it actually be done, since the column was built of bricks, faced with plaster, and the image frescoed onto the plaster. So the authorities turned to the architect, one Battista Sormano, and asked him if he could devise a means of removing the entire image intact from the column.

He soon gave his report: "I went to look it over, and examined it with my hands and with tools, and sounded it to see how firmly it was attached to the bricks of that column; I found it to be so tightly attached and incorporated that I would judge it impossible to remove it (the image) intact." And the master-mason remarked that "it would be practically impossible to remove intact that image without the miraculous help of heaven."

So a stalemate developed—if the column were left standing, it would be an ugly obstruction in the new cathedral; still the people would not permit it to be torn down. What to do? However, the Virgin had her own method of solving that knotty problem.

Came Wednesday, March 14, 1601. It was a little past noon and the workmen had gone for their mid-day meal. Father Giovanni Maria Lamberti, Curate of the Cathedral entered. He walked toward the middle of the building, picking his way over piles of rubbish and around scaffold timbers, until he came to the pillar of the Madonna. There he paused to speak to some people [1] who were guarding the treasured image from those who would destroy it.

The good Father and the self-appointed guardians were soon engaged in a lively discussion concerning the column, the image, and the dispute over its removal.

In the midst of their discussion, a strange thing happened! Suddenly the plaster containing the image of the Virgin detached itself from the bricks of the column and slowly began to slide down its face. Father Lamberti, the first to perceive what was happening, shouted, "Holy Mary, mercy, miracle!" And he and several of the others, spurred to action by his cry, leaped forward and caught the image before it hit the ground.

Carefully they lowered it to the floor and minutely examined it. It was quite thin at the top and gradually thickened toward the bottom to about a finger's width; on the front was the image, bright and completely intact and on the back, plainly visible, the outline of the bricks from which it had detached itself. [2]

They carried the precious fresco to the nearby Sistine Chapel. Then by order of the Bishop all the bells of the city rang in festivity. All the people came to honor the image and the Virgin it represented. Soon the crowds became too large for the Sistine Chapel to contain them, so Bishop Costa had the image transferred to a side chapel in the new Cathedral [3] —which chapel soon came to be known as the Chapel of the Madonna della Colonna (Madonna of the Column).

The entire marvelous happening was later subjected to the rigorous Canonical process of the episcopal curia—much testimony being taken under oath from all who had witnessed the phenomenon—experts testified to the practical impossibility of removing the painting intact from the wall of the column; all to the final conclusion that the happening was indeed miraculous.

Over the years many favors were granted through the intercession of the Madonna della Colonna—actually the fact that the image has been preserved over the centuries is itself a marvel, since it consists only of a quite thin crust of plaster. And in spite of its fragility it was undamaged during an explosion on July 7, 1648, which shattered portions of the marble in the chapel wherein it was enshrined; and it was unharmed by an earthquake on Feb. 23, 1887.

1.—They were:
Giovanni Battista De Soglio, blacksmith.
Giovanni De Micheli Fu Martino, baker.
Giovanni De Micheli di Domenico, carpenter.
Giovanni Antonio De Maestri, clothes carder.
Lorenzo da Reposseno, master-mason.
2.—The thin sheet of plaster had the curvature of the column from which it came.
3.—The new cathedral was practically completed in 1602, but was not dedicated until March 24, 1605.

BIBLIOGRAPHY:
Maria Santissima della Colonna in Savona,
by Rev. Francesco Martinengo, Savona, 1930.
Pastoral Letter of Bishop Giovanni Battista,
dated December 8, 1950, Savona.
L'Anno di Maria,
Vol. III by I. M. Vigo, Torino, 1904.

ST. MARY OF THE CROSS

THERE IS A SANCTUARY of the Madonna on the Bergamo
Road, about a mile away from the City of Crema, Italy. The
structure is circular in form, with four additions in the shape
of a cross, which gave rise to the name of Santa Maria della
Croce (Holy Mary of the Cross). The Sanctuary is located in
a place where, in years gone by, there stood a dense little
wood called "Il Novelletto."

The story begins in the late years of the fifteenth century.

In those days, a young woman named Caterina Uberti
lived with her brother in the city of Crema. When she
arrived at marriageable age, her brother induced her to wed
one Bartolomeo Petrobelli. It was an unfortnate arrangement, for while Caterina was a good and pious girl, Bartolomeo was quite the opposite, tending toward the wicked and
corrupt.

The marriage was an unhappy one for Caterina and an
uncomfortable one for Bartolomeo—his rather crude and
brutal ways shamed her, while her refined and holy life was
a silent reproach to his somewhat scandalous mode of living.
So after a year of turmoil, Bartolomeo decided to kill her.
Having made up his mind, he lost no time in carrying out his
evil design.

He suggested to Caterina that they journey to Bergamo and visit his parents. She agreed, and in the late afternoon of April 3, 1490, they mounted their horses and set forth from the city.

Now, about a mile from Crema, there was a dense little wood called "Il Novelletto," and when they arrived there, Bartolomeo left the highway and rode into the forest. Caterina was puzzled by this strange maneuver, but not knowing what else to do, followed him.

When they reached the middle of the wood, Bartolomeo dismounted from his horse and made Caterina get down from hers. Then without warning, he drew his sword, raised it and fiercely brought it down, intending to split her head with one clean cut. Instinctively, she threw up her arm to ward off the savage blow and thus saved her head, but lost her right hand—the poor severed hand hung from the stump of her arm by a strip of skin and Bortolomeo brutally tore it off and flung it to one side.

Now Bartolomeo, panicky at not having killed her with his first furious blow, began to slash about like a maniac until finally overcome she fell to the ground in a pool of blood. Thinking his fiendish work accomplished, he leaped onto his horse and fled from the scene.

But despite her numerous wounds and the quantity of blood she had lost, Caterina was not dead; however she well knew that her time was short. She was not afraid to die, but she did not wish to embark on that last journey without the consolation of the last rites—she wished with all her dying heart to have the comfort of Confession and the grace of Holy Communion.

So she prayed to the Mother of Consolation. The prayer was heard. Almost immediately a glow of light pushed back the gathering darkness, and a beautiful lady appeared approaching her.

The lady bade Caterina to be of good heart and not to fear. Reaching down she took her by the arm and helped her to her feet. At the lovely lady's touch, Caterina felt a surge of new life course through her mutilated body and more marvelous, she saw the flow of blood from her numerous wounds suddenly stop. The throbbing pain left her.

Telling Caterina to follow her, the Lady turned and started to leave the wood. Caterina however, asked if she might first look for her lost hand. The Lady told her not to worry about it, and promised it would be returned to her in due time.

Then together they moved from the little wood and soon arrived at two huts situated on the outskirts thereof. In the huts lived two families named Mongia and Sormanni. The lady told Caterina these good people would help her, and with a last reassuring smile she vanished.

Caterina knocked at the door of one the huts, and when the kind peasants saw her pitiful condition they took her in and did all they could to make her comfortable. While she partook of their poor food and drink she recounted the horrible happenings of that evening, and of the appearance of the lady. They, seeing her condition, readily agreed that heaven had intervened in her behalf, and that the lady could only have been the Blessed Mother of Mercy.

On the following morning two of the Mongia tenderly placed her on a rude stretcher and carried her back to Crema. On the way, the lady's promise about the severed hand came true—as they passed throuh the wood, one of the Mongia found it and returned it to her.

Arriving in the city, they took Caterina to the church of

St. Benedetto. The pastor, after listening to her story, heard her confession, gave her Holy Communion and anointed her—whereupon Caterina, all her last desires having been fulfilled through the power of the Virgin commended her soul to God and died.

The story of this marvelous happening quickly spread about and all phases of it were rigidly investigated—doctors who had examined Caterina, seen her grevious wounds, and knew the amount of blood she must have lost, were positive she could not have lived an hour, much less a whole night— the mysterious stoppage of the bleeding—all the evidence led to but one conclusion; heaven had interved.

But, while most believed, a few doubted, and as if to confound these doubters, the Blessed Virgin produced still another wonder.

At that time there was in Crema a young chap named Marazzo. He was eleven years old and for some three or four years had been plagued with an abscess on one of his feet, which the doctors had not been able to heal. When he heard of the great happening at the Novelletto, he begged his mother to take him to the little wood—he had a feeling that if only put his useless foot on the spot where the lady had stood, he would be cured.

So his mother, together with a group of relatives and friends, carried him to the wood and arriving at the place where she had appeared, they set him on the ground and all prayed to the Virgin. After a few minutes, the youngster gave a cry of joy and leaping to his feet found he could walk. Moreover, all trace of the abscess had disappeared.

The news of this was quickly noised about. Soon many other infirm came to that place, and many were aided. Then the people erected a small chapel on the spot and in it placed a little plaster image of Our Lady.

More favors followed, and many were the offerings made by the faithful—sufficient that in a few years it was possible. to begin the construction of a sanctuary fitting for their Madonna. It was completed in 1500.

Later a fine new statue of Our Lady was enshrined in the Sanctuary, and in 1873 it was crowned with a gold crown by order of the Vatican.

BIBLIOGRAPHY:

Santuari Mariani D'Italia,
   by D. Alfonso Salvini, O. S. B. V., Rome, 1955.
L'Anno di Maria, Vol. IV.,
   by I. M. Vigo, Torino, 1904.

OUR LADY OF DIVINE LOVE

THE STORY OF THIS BEAUTIFUL TITLE of Our Lady begins back around the year 1200. Somewhere about that time—the exact date is uncertain— a family by the name of Savelli built [1] a castle along the Via Ardeatina, [2] some seven miles outside the city of Rome. They named it Castrum Leonis (Castle of the Lion) but sometime later it was changed to Castel di Leva. A prominent feature of this castle was its tower.

Sometime during the fourteenth century, an artist— his name is lost—painted a picture of the Our Lady of Divine Love [3] on one side of the castle tower.

During the sixteenth century [4] the castle was destroyed, but the tower and its picture of the Madonna was somehow preserved. Then for many years the tower and its image appear to have been neglected and almost forgotten, except for some shepherds who grazed their flocks in the surrounding fields. These shepherds frequently came to the tower to offer prayers to the Virgin.

In 1740, something strange happened there: a pilgrim on his way to Rome wandered off the highway and became lost. In the near distance he spied the tower and started toward it, hoping he could there take his bearings and so get back to the highway. Suddenly, as he neared the tower, several savage dogs from some near-by farm leaped from the underbrush and set upon the man. He was in imminent danger of being killed. Raising his eyes to the picture on the tower, he cried out to the Virgin to save him. She heard his plea. The dogs were immediately paralyzed and fell to the ground. The pilgrim was saved.

Falling to his knees he poured out his thanks to the Madonna; then locating the highway he resumed his journey. To everyone he encountered along the way he related the story of how the Lady of the Tower had saved his life.

The news of this marvelous event quickly spread and soon great numbers came to the tower to pray. Many blessings were bestowed on those who came.

In 1744, at the earnest request of the people, a church was erected on the site of the Castel di Leva, and in 1745, the image was solemnly transferred to it. On May 13, 1883, the image was crowned by Cardinal Lorenzo Nina. In the years that followed the Sanctuary of Our Lady of Divine Love became one of the outstanding shrines of the Blessed Virgin in Italy.

During World War II the image was removed from the Sanctuary at Castel di Leva and brought to a small church inside the walls of Rome. But the church proved entirely too small to contain the multitudes who came to honor Our Lady, so the image was again moved, and this time to the large church of St. Ignatius.

When things began to look badly for the city of Rome, a special novena began on May 28, 1944, on the Feast of the Holy Ghost—a novena to ask the Blessed Virgin to bring peace, and especially to save Rome from further devastation by the enemy. During this novena great crowds came to pray at the feet of Our Lady.

On June 4, the Feast of the Holy Trinity, and the day the

novena ended, the enemy began to quit Rome and the American Army entered. Indeed, some of the American soldiers arrived at the Church of St. Ignatius and the image of Our Lady of Divine Love at the very moment the novena came to an end.

Pope Pius XII, and the grateful people of Rome, gave full credit for saving the city to Our Lady of Divine Love and she was officially given the title of the Salvation of Rome (or Savior of Rome.)

After the war, the beloved image was returned to its original Sanctuary at Castel di Leva where it is the object of numerous pilgrimages from Rome. Perhaps the greatest of these take place on Whitsunday, when a parade with carts and coaches all gayly decorated with flowers, leaves Rome for the Castle.

1.—Probably built by the Orsini, a noble family of Rome who first came into prominence toward the end of the twelfth century.
2.—The Via Ardeatina runs south from the Gate of St. Sebastian (Porta San Sebastiano), one of the South Gates of Rome.
3.—Whether the artist gave it this name or if someone applied it later seems to be uncertain—although it appears that for centuries it was known as La Madonna del Divino Amore.
4.—Some say the fifteenth century.

BIBLIOGRAPHY:

Sanctuaries of Italy,
    Booklet of E. N. I. T., Rome.
Sanctuaries of Italy for Motorists,
    Booklet of E. N. I. T., Rome.
La Madonna Santuari e Feste,
    by Fr. Umberto Bonomo, C.SS.R.,
    Vatican City Religious Book Co., Inc., New York, 1948.
Shrines of Our Lady Around the World,
    by Zsolt Aradi;
    Farrar, Straus & Young, New York, 1954.
Cause of Our Joy,
    by Rev. Edward A. Bates, C. R. in Our Lady's Digest, October, 1953.

OUR LADY OF DOLORS

THE ORIGIN OF THIS TITLE of Our Lady belongs to the Order of Servites (Servants of Mary, or Religious Servants of the Holy Virgin), founded by seven noblemen of Florence, Italy in 1233.

The prime object of the Order was to foster meditation on and thus increase devotion to Our Lady of Dolors or of the Seven Sorrows. [1]

In thirteenth-century Florence there was a society or confraternity made up of some 200 devout men; the members of this society were called "Laudesi," "Praisers of the Blessed Virgin." These men were apparently from all walks of life, some being merchants, some artisans, others nobles, but all were animated with a zeal to increase devotion to the Blessed Virgin, so that through her, Christ the Redeemer and Judge of the world would have mercy on sinful man.

The seven joined this society. Their names were: Amideus de Amedei, Manettus Antellensis, Alexis Falconieri, Bonajuncta Manetti, Bonfilius Monaldi, Sostene de Sostegni and Ugo Uguccioni.

These men assembled regularly and pursued their devotions as a group. On August 15, 1233, the Feast of the Assumption, they were gathered together in the Society's chapel where Our Lady appeared to them and told them to give up the world and live for God alone.

Losing no time in following her instructions, they sought the counsel of Ardingo, Bishop of Florence. Upon hearing their story, he advised them to give their worldly possessions to the poor and needy. This they proceeded to do, and then on September 8, 1233, the Feast of the Nativity of the Blessed Virgin, retired to the Villa of Camarzia, outside the walls of Florence.

There they spent their time in prayer, penance and fasting, offering everything to the greater honor of Our Lady. For their meager sustenance they depended upon alms obtained by humbly begging in the streets of the city. And it is told that as they passed along the streets, little children and even infants had their lips miraculously opened to utter the praise of these seven men—they were heard to exclaim "Behold the Servants of Mary." [2]

Shortly after this, the seven, desiring more opportunity for meditation on the Sorrows of the Blessed Virgin, left Camarzia and established themselves on Monte Senario, some ten miles distant from Florence. There they lived in caves with very little to eat and spent much time in prayer. And quite a number of good people sought them out and requested entrance to their little group. Noting this, Bishop Ardingo suggested they set up definite rules for their society, so that it could eventually evolve into a formal religious order. Now the Virgin manifested her wishes in a miraculous manner. On the third Sunday of Lent, 1239, a little vine which the seven had planted on Monte Senario suddenly burst into bloom, with flowers and luscious ripe grapes.

Then she appeared to them again on Good Friday, 1240, and herself outlined the plan and scope of the Order she wished established. She told them the members of the new Order were to wear a black habit to commemorate her Sorrows; they were to follow the Rule of St. Augustine; and they were to take the name "Servants of Mary."

Having obtained the approval of the Bishop, the new Order was inaugurated. As their Patroness, they chose the Blessed Virgin giving her the title, Madonna Addolorata— Our Lady of Dolors. It was natural that they should also refer to her as Our Lady of the Seven Sorrows.

The Order received Papal sanction during the Pontificate of Innocent IV (1243-1254). All seven of the founders were Canonized by Pope Leo XIII on January 15, 1888. They were buried under the high altar of the monastery chapel, on Monte Senario.

1.—The Seven Sorrows Are:
    The Prophecy of Simeon.
    The Flight into Egypt.
    Losing the Child Jesus in Jerusalem.
    Meeting her Son on the Way to Calvary.
    Standing at the Foot of the Cross.
    Jesus Being Taken Down from the Cross.
    The Burial of Jesus.
2.—It is stated that St. Philip Benizi, who later became a shining light of the Order of Servites, used this phrase when only five months old in calling his mother's attention to these holy men. Pope Innocent VIII, in 1488, in an Apostolic Letter in which he confirmed privileges given to the Order, said "the title 'Servants of Mary' was, as it were, divinely given out of the mouths of babes."

BIBLIOGRAPHY:
    The Apparitions & Shrines of Heaven's Bright Queen,

by Wm. J. Walsh,
T. J. Cary Co., New York, 1904.
La Madonna Santuari e Feste,
by Fr. Umberto Bonomo, C.SS.R.,
Vatican City Religious Book Co., Inc., New York, 1948.
Third Order of Servites,
by Gerard M. Calkins, OSM, in*QM* of Feb. 1955, quoting Pope Leo XIII's
Apostolic Letter of Jan. 22, 1888.

OUR LADY OF THE ELM TREE

THIS MADONNA is venerated at Thiene, Italy, thirty miles northwest of Padua. The title and the sanctuary had their origin back in 1530. Thiene and the nighboring countryside were hit by a severe cloudburst which ruined all the crops and destroyed many homes. A few days later the Blessed Virgin appeared to three young farm girls as they were walking along a country road. She was seen on top of a large elm tree.

Our Lady told the girls that the country had been visited by the cloudburst because the people had been neglecting their religious duties—they had practically forgotten their God; their ways were evil. God had decided to wake them up by allowing disaster to strike them. They were to return to their former practice of attending church and worshipping God. So saying, she vanished.

When the girls reached home they told everybody of the vision, but of course no one believed them. Later the Virgin appeared a second time, then a third. On this last visit, she told the girls that she was very disappointed that the people had disbelieved their story. She then asked them to go and tell the civil and ecclesiastical authorities, and to impress on them that they must take immediate steps to correct things.

So the girls might have a sign to convince the people that she had really appeared, she commanded the elm tree to be shorn of all its bark but still to retain its luxuriant foliage. And immediately the miracle took place.

The people, however, paid no attention to the girls' story, some even saying that it was no miracle at all, but only lightning which had stripped the bark from the tree.

Our Lady tried something else—in the little village of Centrale, a short distance from Thiene, there was a man named Simon. He was a hunchback, and had for years been paralyzed and practically helpless. The Virgin appeared to Simon and asked him to go and tell the people of Thiene that they must change their ways—they must repent and go back to their former way of living. Then she told Simon to get up from his bed and be about her work.

Simon found his paralysis gone and his hunchback straight. He went at once and informed all the people of what the Virgin desired. And seeing him who had always been deformed and paralyzed whole and well, the people finally listened and believed.

Forthwith they reformed and returned to their ancient Christian way of life. They built a chapel in honor of the Virgin and therein placed her image. As the people recalled the miracle of the elm tree, they began to call the image the Madonna dell 'Olmo—Our Lady of the Elm Tree.

In 1609, the building of a large church was begun—this still exists, although it has several times over the years been restored and enlarged.

BIBLIOGRAPHY:

La Madonna Santuari e Feste,
by P. Umberto Bonomo, C.SS.R.,
Vatican City Religious Book Co., Inc., New York, 1948.

OUR LADY OF THE FLOWERS

THE SANCTUARY of Our Lady of the Flowers is near the town of Bra, Italy, about twenty-five miles from Turin.

The strange events which gave origin to this title of Our Lady took place in the early part of the fourteenth century.

Rather late in the evening of December 29, 1336, a young bride, Egidia Mathis, was returning to her home on the outskirts of Bra, after paying a visit to one of her friends. The night was quite cold, and the road along which she was walking was rather lonely and desolate. She really should not have been out at all, for she was pregnant—indeed the time of her delivery was close at hand.

Suddenly from the side of the road, two ruffians leaped out and grabbed her, intending to take what little money she might have, and perhaps to assault her.

She managed to break away from them and, spurred on by fright ran to a column which stood alongside the road a short distance away, thought to be part of the ruins of an ancient Benedictine Monastery. On this column there was painted a picture of the Blessed Virgin.

Arriving at the column, Egidia fell on her knees imploring the Blessed Mother to come to her rescue. Her prayer was answered—immediately a very regal lady appeared and placing herself between the girl and the pursuing ruffians, in a commanding voice she ordered them to be gone. They turned and fled.

Then the lady turned to help the unfortunate young girl. And she was greatly in need of help, for the fright she had received had induced labor, and at that moment she was giving birth to her baby.

The lady received the new-born babe into her own hands and carefully wrapped it in the girl's scarf. Telling Egidia that she would be all right, the Lady placed the child in her arms and, with a final reassuring smile, vanished.

Her strength renewed, Egidia hurried to her home and related the strange tale to her parents. Quickly the story spread around the neighborhood. Soon a number of friends and neighbors hurried to the column, hoping that they too might see the Lady—but they were disappointed, for she was not there.

However, to their amazement, at the foot of the column, directly beneath the picture of the Virgin, they saw a cluster of lovely white flowers growing in a bramble bush—they were sweet-smelling and their perfume filled the cold night air.

They were mystified, for it was unheard of for flowers to bloom there at that time of year. Looking at the picture of the Virgin on the column, and at the flowers blooming beneath, they named her Our Lady of the Flowers.

Not long after these events, the good people of the vicinity built a small chapel on the spot. Some three centuries later the little chapel was replaced by the present sanctuary.

Since that centuries-old event, every year, even unto today, the white flowers bloom in the month of December, commemorating the appearance of the Virgin to the frightened young bride and the phenomenon of the flowers.

The phenomenon of these flowers that bloom in the cold winter month of December is generally regarded as something supernatural, or at least scientifically unexplainable. Expert and experienced botanists have examined them and given considerable thought and study to the unnatural behavior. They have no answer to the question. Why do these particular flowers bloom only in the winter rather than in the summer as would be natural? Why is it that flowers of the same species, growing elsewhere and there blooming normally during the summer, when transplanted to the soil at the foot of the column will grow, but will bloom only in December?

Perhaps the only possible answer is the one arrived at by the people on that night back in 1336, when they decided it was a miracle.

BIBLIOGRAPHY:

Marian Shrines in Italy,
   E. N. I. T., Rome.
La Madonna Santuari e Feste,
   by Father Umberto Bonomo, C.SS.R.,
   Vatican City Religious Book Co., Inc., New York, 1948.
Santuari Mariani D'Italia,
   by D. Alfonso Salvini, O. S. B. V., Edizioni Paoline, Pia Societa S. Paolo, Rome, 1954.

OUR LADY OF GOOD AIR

THE SHRINE OF OUR LADY OF BONARIA (Good Air), is at Cagliari, on the Island of Sardinia.

The origin of the shrine and of this title of Our Lady date back to the latter years of the fourteenth century.

According to tradition, on March 25, 1370, a ship enroute from Spain to Italy ran into a terrific storm at a spot some miles off the coast of Sardinia. Soon she seemed in imminent danger of sinking and the sailors, in a last desperate effort to save her, began to jettison the cargo.

When they heaved a large packing case [1] into the sea, the waves immediately died down and became calm. The ship was saved. The case floated away and, pushed by the tides, eventually landed on the shore of Sardinia at the foot of a hill called Bonaria. [2]

There the Mercy Fathers found it and took it to their church, where it was opened in the presence of a large group of people, and, to the surprise of all, they found it contained a beautiful statue of the Virgin and Child. Thus a prophecy was fulfilled—the church had been built around 1330 by Fra Carlo Catalan, while he was the ambassador to the Argonese Court. At the dedication Fra Carlo told the monks, "A Great Lady will come to live in this place. After her coming the malaria infecting the area will disappear and her image will be called the Virgin of Bonaria."

So when the statue floated in from the sea and the Fathers placed it in their church, remembering what Fra Carlo had said, they named it Our Lady of Good Air.

The statue is in colored wood, probably of Spanish workmanship. Pius X, in 1908, declared Our Lady of Bonaria the patron Saint of Sardinia.

1.—Still preserved in the Sanctuary. Another story says the ship sank in the storm and the case with the statue floated to the shore.

2.—The malaria apparently was due to a swamp which lay at the bottom of the hill upon which stood the church and monastery of the Fathers. The air around the swamp was so bad that the disease was called malaria (bad air).

BIBLIOGRAPHY:

La Madonna Santuari e Feste,
   by Fr. Umberto Bonomo, C.SS.R., New York, 1948.
Santuari Mariani D'Italia,
   by D. Alfonso Salvini, O. S. B. V., Rome, 1954.
L'Anno di Maria, Vol. IV,
   by I. M. Vigo, Torino, 1904.
I Santuari d'Italia,
   Febbraio, 1929, Milano.

OUR LADY OF THE LAMP

IN THE MIDDLE OF THE TIBER RIVER about a mile downstream from St. Peter's is the Isola Tiberina (Tiber Island). Here the Ponte Fabricio, possibly the oldest bridge in the world, built in 62 B. C., spans one arm of the river connecting the mainland to the island.

On the Island at the end of the bridge are the church, monastery and hospital of St. John Calybit which belongs to the Brothers Hospitaller. These buildings are thought to have been built before the thirteenth century. In the lower wall of the monastery, just above the water of the Tiber, there is a niche. Around the years 1290 or 1291, a picture of Our Lady was painted on the wall of this niche. The picture soon came to be known as "Mary by the River."

For some hundreds of years thereafter the eyes of the picture gazed serenely over the flowing water and Our Lady became a particular object of veneration to the boatmen who plied their craft up and down the river. Saluting her as they passed by, they would devoutly ask her blessing and thank her for favors already granted. And while the little niche in the wall was dark, still the face of the Madonna was always clearly visible, lighted by a little candle-lamp which burned in constant vigil.

In the spring of 1557 the usually calm and placid Tiber
went on a rampage—the waters rose higher and higher, covering the niche and the painting of the Madonna. Then a
strange thing happened—the little candle-lamp, entirely unaffected by the water, still burned brightly. Even through the
muddy water it could be seen—faithfully it kept vigil before
the beloved Lady. The news of this event quickly spread
throughout the city and soon the people began to call the
image, "Our Lady of the Lamp." A few years later the Brothers of St. John of God, in whose monastery wall the niche
was located, carefully removed the wall and the miraculous
painting from the niche and placed it in their chapel—where
it can be seen today. Over the years that followed the Virgin
of the Lamp became the center of great devotion and many
miracles were attributed to her—so many in fact that on
March 19, 1664, the image was crowned by the Vatican
Chapter.

Years sped along. The morning of July 9, 1796, marked
the beginning of troubled times. Soon Napoleon would force
the surrender of the papal territories and Pius VI would be
exiled. Then a curious phenomenon occurred—the eyes of
twenty-four of the pictured Madonnas in Rome were seen to
move. The picture of Our Lady of the Lamp also moved its
eyes. According to Marchetti, "the witnesses all agreed and
confirmed that this deteriorated and almost unrecognizable
picture was seen in an instant to show distinct features and
to return to its ancient beauty, as if an excellent artist had
just painted it. Especially the eyes appeared full of grace and
majesty that ravished the heart. The upper eyelids were lowered but not completely closed, and from the small opening
which remained there appeared to sparkle a living eye. The
half-closed eyelids opened several times, uncovering the

pupil of the eye. Then, sparkling with a powerful brightness, the eyes turned lovingly three or four times toward those present.

There was also noticed "the turning of the head from the left side, toward which it originally looked, bending to the opposite right side toward the high altar where the Blessed Sacrament is kept, and in which position it still remains."

The painting of Our Lady of the Lamp is today enshrined on the altar of a chapel off the main church of St. John Calybit's. A copy of the picture of Our Lady of the Lamp has been installed in Our Lady's Tower at Hammond Hall, Gloucester, Massachusetts, the Monastery of the Hospitaller Brothers of St. John of God. This reproduction was blessed by Richard Cardinal Cushing, Archbishop of Boston, on July 14, 1957.

BIBLIOGRAPHY:

Data from The Hospitaller Brothers of St. John of God, Hammond Hall, Gloucester, Mass.

OUR LADY OF POMPEII
also called
OUR LADY OF THE ROSARY

UNLIKE SO MANY OF OUR LADY'S TITLES, which go back centuries for their origin, this one is quite recent. The events which gave rise to this title took place less than one hundred years ago.

By the last half of the nineteenth century the Valley of Pompeii, near Naples, was practically deserted. Of the comparatively few people who still lived there, most had lost their ancient Catholic faith; ignorance and superstition prevailed. Only a handful of people bothered to attend the services in the little parish chapel.

In October 1872, a man named Bartolo Longo came to the valley. He was the husband of the Countess of Fusco, who had some property there, and Bartolo came to see what condition it was in. He had been reared a Catholic and was probably still one in name, although it seems he was not very devout.

On October 9th, a few days after his arrival, he was walking along a rather desolate road when suddenly a voice seemed to speak to him. It told him that if he wished to be saved, he should spread devotion to the Rosary and that the Blessed Virgin had promised that that was the way to find salvation.

Bartolo fell on his knees and replied that if the Virgin had truly so promised then he would be saved; he would not leave the valley until he had popularized the Rosary.

His early efforts to interest the people in the Rosary devotion do not seem to have been very successful, but he persisted, and in two or three years he had gathered quite a group around him for daily recitation of the prayers in the little chapel.

The Bishop visited the valley in 1875, and complimented Bartolo on the good work he had done. He suggested that a church be built there and then, turning prophet, the Bishop pointed to a field near the chapel and declared that some day a basilica would stand on that spot.

As the number of people taking part in the daily recitation of the Rosary grew, it was decided to obtain a picture of the Blessed Virgin, to help the faithful meditate as they prayed. On October 13, 1875, Bartolo went to Naples to see if he could find a suitable picture, but after searching for several days, to his great disappointment, he found that any really good picture would cost around four hundred francs, and he had nowhere near that amount to spend.

He did not want to return empty handed, however, and disappoint the good people of Pompeii, so he somewhat reluctantly accepted a secondhand painting from a Dominican friend, who had bought it in a junk shop for five lire.

The picture was too large for him to carry, so he wrapped it with paper and an old sheet and gave it to a trucker who hauled between Naples and Pompeii. The trucker, not knowing the package contained a picture of the Blessed Virgin, unceremoniously pitched it on top of a load of garbage, and in such an undignified manner the picture arrived at the Chapel in Pompeii!

The people were really pleased with the somewhat dilapidated image and enshrined it in their chapel. At various times artists were called in to retouch and restore the painting.

Several miracles took place, almost as soon as the picture was installed, through the intercession of Our Lady of Pompeii. As a result, it was decided that a church should be built in her honor to accommodate the numerous pilgrims. It was begun in 1876, completed in a few years, and later enlarged and consecrated in 1891.

In 1934, Pope Pius XI ordered a new basilica to be built. It was completed in 1939.

BIBLIOGRAPHY:

Famous Shrines of Our Lady,
    by H. M. Gilbert, Vol. 1, Newman Press, Westminster, Md., 1952.
La Madonna Santuari e Feste,
    by P. Umberto Bonomo, C.SS.R., Vatican City Religious Book Co., Inc., New York, 1948.
Santuari Mariani d' Italia,
    by D. Alfonso Salvini, O.S.B.V., Pia Soc. S. Paolo, Rome, 1954.
I. Santuari D'Italia,
    Milano, December, 1932

OUR LADY OF THE SNOWS

ACCORDING TO THE LEGEND, there lived in Rome during the reign of Pope Liberius (352-366), an extremely wealthy patrician named John. Among his possessions was a plot of ground on the Esquiline Hill—where the Basilica of Our Lady of the Snows now stands.

John and his wife had no children, in fact no heirs whatever and, being a very pious couple, decided to leave all their worldly possessions to the Blessed Virgin. They prayed to her, asking her to reveal to them the manner in which they should dispose of their wealth so as to bring the greatest honor to her name.

On the night of August 5, 350, (some say 358) John and his wife had a dream, or a vision, during which the Blessed Virgin told them she desired a church built in her honor on Esquiline Hill at the place they would find outlined with snow on the morrow. Snow in Rome, in August!

On awakening the next morning, John and his wife lost no time in acquainting the Pope of their dream and of the Blessed Virgin's request, but found he had also had a similar dream and knew just what had to be done.

They all hurried to Esquiline Hill and found a section of ground covered with snow, and it was obvious that the covered space traced the outline and floor plan of a church. They staked off the place and site outlined by the snow, whereupon it immediately melted.

Liberius ordered that work on the church should begin at once. Some hold that while Liberius started the work on the church, it was not actually finished until 432, when Pope Sixtus (432-440) dedicated it. Others hold that Liberius built the original edifice and that Sixtus merely rebuilt and enlarged it.

Because of its size and splendor, the new church was named St. Mary the Greater (Major). It was also known as St. Mary of the Snows in commemoration of the event that brought it into existence.

Then, still according to the legend, Pope Liberius began to search for an image of Our Lady for the new church. He finally settled on one in the pontifical oratory, which tradition holds had been brought to Rome by St. Helena (274-337), mother of Constantine the Great, and which is assumed to have been painted by St. Luke. [1]

The image was placed in the new church. The exact date when this was done does not seem to be certain, but it is known that Pope Symmachus used to pray before it, and as he reigned from 498 to 514 some clue is provided as to the time.

Down through the ages, as the painting became identified with and a part of the church of Our Lady of the Snows, it came to be generally called Our Lady of the Snows.

Additions were made to the original church at various times so that by the early part of the seventeenth century it appeared pretty much as it is today.

In 1613, the painting was removed from its original place behind the high altar of the church and placed in the newly built chapel of the Madonna di San Luca (Our Lady of St. Luke). This chapel also known as the Pauline Chapel, was built by Pope Paul V (1605-1621) on the north side of the original building and became part of the basilica.

Because of the numerous occasions throughout the years on which the Blessed Virgin has saved Rome from the horror of plagues, cholera, etc., the image has also come to be known as Our Lady Protectress of Rome. It was crowned in 1838.

The image—also known as "Salus Populi Romani"—is painted on a slab of wood (probably cedar) about five feet in height and approximately three feet in width. On November 1, 1954, Pope Pius XII, officially crowned the famous Madonna "Salus Populi Romani" (Salvation of the Roman People) under the title, "Queen of the Universe."

The Basilica of Our Lady of the Snows is probably the greatest church in the world dedicated to the Blessed Virgin. It is also called the Basilica of Santa Maria Maggiore (St. Mary Major).

1.—The present image dating, it is held, to the thirteenth century is probably a copy of the earlier one attributed to St. Luke.

BIBLIOGRAPHY:

Celebrated Sanctuaries of the Madonna,
    by Rev. J. Spencer Northcote, D.D., Peter Cunningham & Son, Philadelphia, 1875.
La Madonna Santuari e Feste,
    by P. Umberto Bonomo, C.SS.R., Vatican City Religious Book Co., Inc. New York, 1948.
Shrines of Our Lady Around the World,
    by Zsolt Aradi, Farrar, Straus & Young, New York, 1954.
Highlights of Rome,
    by G. Fanfani & N. Ruspantini, Ramella, Florence, 1956.

OUR LADY OF THE STONE

THE SANCTUARY OF THIS MADONNA is some seventeen hundred feet above sea level, on one of the hills in the range of Mt. Giovi twelve miles northeast of Florence.

As the stories put it, "in ancient times" a little shrine stood on the hill and it contained a tablet depicting the Blessed Virgin and Child. Since the tablet is, according to experts, a work of the Giotto School, it must have been done some time between 1300 and 1490. Giotto was himself in Florence in 1300, 1302, 1307 and 1334 and died in 1336. Many people came to pray at the shrine and among these were two young shepherdesses of the Ricovera family.

On July 2, 1490, the two girls were praying at the shrine. As their father was gravely ill, they were imploring the Virgin to restore him to health.

They heard a sound and, looking around, they saw sitting on a near-by stone a lovely lady with a child in her arms. Before they recovered from their surprise, the lady spoke to them. She told them not to be afraid and not to worry, that she was the one to whom they had been praying so fervently, and that she wished to have a church built on that spot in her honor. She asked them to go and bring their father, as she wished to speak to him.

The girls told the Lady that their father could not come because he was so sick he could not even get up out of his bed. But she assured them that he was now well again and that they should go and get him.

Obeying, the girls hurried to their home and found their father completely recovered. They returned with him to the shrine and the Lady was still sitting on the stone. She told the father of her wish that a church be built on that spot.

The man and his daughters spread the story of his recovery and of how the Virgin had appeared, but very few believed them and nothing at all was done about the church.

Then on August 15th, the Feast of Her Assumption, when a goodly number were gathered at the shrine, the Virgin appeared for a third time. She told them she was displeased at the delay and demanded that they get busy and build her church. This time they believed her and started to work.

However, since the ground around the stone on which she had appeared seemed too steep to attempt to put a building there, they started to lay the foundation at a place some few hundred feet away. But when the masons arrived for work the following morning, they found that the walls they had laid the day before were demolished and the stones strewn all around.

After this had happened several times, they decided that the Virgin did not want the church built there, but over on the spot where the stone was. So they bowed to the inevitable and with great labor levelled off the ground around the stone and there erected the church.

And since the Virgin had appeared on the stone and, moreover, insisted that the church be erected on that very spot, it was natural for the church and the image to be called Madonna del Sasso, Our Lady of the Stone.

BIBLIOGRAPHY:

La Madonna Santuari e Feste,
   by P. Umberto Bonomo, C.SS.R., Vatican City Religious Book Co., Inc., New York, 1948.
Santuari Mariani D'Italia,
   by D. Alfonso Salvini, O.S.B.V., Pia. Soc. S. Paolo, Rome, 1954.

OUR LADY OF THE TEARS

THE BLESSED VIRGIN under this title is venerated at treviglio, Italy, a town about eighteen miles east of Milan.

The origin of this title of Our Lady goes back to the early
years of the sixteenth century, when Lombardy was a theatre
of war between the French and the Germans.

In 1522, the French General Lautrec received reports
which seemed to indicate that the people of Treviglio were
showing more sympathy for the Germans than for the
French. So Lautrec came to Treviglio and told the authorities that to punish them he was going to burn their town.

The town fathers apologized to Lautrec and even offered to pay reparations if he would spare them, but to no avail.
When the townspeople heard the sad news, they gathered
together and marched to the church of the Augustinian
Monks, where there was enshrined an image of the Virgin
and Child—a fresco then known as the Madonna of St. Augustine.

The people prostrated themselves before the image and
implored the Blessed Mother to come to their aid—to induce
Lautrec to change his stern decision. And the image of the
Madonna was seen to shed copious tears. (February 28,
1522).

The news of this occurrence soon reached Lautrec and he hurried to the church. When he saw the tears falling from the eyes of the image, he paid homage to the Virgin, removed his sword and placed it on her altar. He promised the people of Treviglio that he would not harm their town.

In thanksgiving for their deliverance, the grateful people named the image, La Madonna delle Lagrime (Our Lady of Tears), and soon after decided to further honor her by erecting a beautiful church, which was completed in 1619.

BIBLIOGRAPHY:

La Madonna Santuari e Feste,
 by Fr. Umberto Bonomo, C.SS.R.,
 Vatican City Religious Book Co., Inc., New York, 1948.
Santuari Mariani D'Italia,
 by D. Alfonso Salvini, O. S. B. V., Pia Societa S. Paolo, Rome, 1954.
I. Santuari D'Italia, Milano, February, 1932.

OUR LADY OF WATER

THE MADONNA OF THIS TITLE is venerated in Rimini, on the east coast of Italy on the Adriatic.

The image depicts the Blessed Mother holding the lifeless body of her Son in her arms. It is supposed to have been done sometime during the fourteenth century by a sculptor —name unknown—of the French School. It is at present on an altar in one of the chapels of the Tempio Malatestiano. This church is dedicated to St. Francis, and the first church erected on the site was built during the thirteenth century.

Just when the image first came to the church of St. Francis seems to be uncertain. However, it was before 1563 since there are historical records that in that year St. Charles Borromeo (1538-1584) prayed before the image and also counselled the people of the vicinity to place their trust in her. According to the same records, the church of St. Francis appears at that time to have been in charge of the Conventuals, [1] and the image apparently was known as the Madonna della Pieta (Our Lady of Pity).

Sometime later, the people of Rimini discovered that their Madonna could be of special help to them in time of severe drought. And on numerous occasions when their crops were in imminent danger of being lost due to lack of rain, they prayed to her and held processions through the city streets. Each time they were rewarded by the coming of rain.

Due to her unfailing help on these occasions, Our Lady's image came to be known as the Madonna dell'Acqua (Our Lady of Water).

There is a modern occasion recorded in 1893. In that year there was a most severe and very long drought, and it looked as though all the crops would be destroyed. So, on April 24, an enormous procession was formed and it moved slowly through the streets of Rimini, imploring Our Lady to send them the much-needed rain. Their plea was answered almost too quickly; rain fell in torrents and all the people were thoroughly drenched. But the crops were saved and the harvest that year was more abundant than even the oldest inhabitant could remember.

The image of the Madonna dell'Acqua was crowned on March 8, 1814 by Pope Pius VII, when he passed through Rimini on his return to Italy after his imprisonment in France.

1.—The Conventuals are one of three separate bodies, forming with the Friars Minor and the Capuchins what is commonly called the First Order of St. Francis (C. E.).

BIBLIOGRAPHY:

La Madonna Santuari e Feste,
   by Fr. Umberto Bonomo, C.SS.R.,
   Vatican City Religious Book Co., Inc., New York, 1948.

OUR LADY OF THE WAYSIDE

THE PICTURE OF THE BLESSED VIRGIN AND CHILD, known for centuries as Our Lady of the Wayside, or Our Lady of the Way, is enshrined in the church of the Gesu, in Rome.

No one seems to know exactly how old this picture is, but some authorities place it in the early years of the fifth century. Others hold that it was painted right after the time of Constantine (274-337).

Be that as it may, it appears quite certain that for many years prior to the sixteenth century the painting graced a little wayside shrine along a highway in ancient Rome. Due to its location by the side of the road it came to be known as Our Lady of the Wayside.

Sometime during the first half of the sixteenth century, a pious Roman family, the Astalli, erected a building to shelter the picture from the elements. This was probably the church known to history as the Church of Santa Maria degli Astalli, later demolished to build the Gesu Church.

During the reign of Pope Paul III (1534-1549), the painting was acquired by the Jesuits, who transferred it to the church of St. Mark. St. Ignatius Loyola, founder of the Society of Jesus, is known to have had great devotion to the Blessed Virgin under the title, Madonna della Strada. In

1575, the Jesuits having completed the church of the Gesu as a shrine to the Blessed Virgin, the picture was moved to it and placed in a chapel especially designed for it.

At the present time Our Lady of the Highway is the Patroness of travelers. This modern version of the ancient title originated in 1937 in Little Falls, New Jersey. Father Giles Lawler, O. F. M., Pastor of Our Lady of the Angels Church, had a medal struck showing our Lady of the Highway in an attitude of prayer. The following words are on the medal: "Our Lady of the Highway, be with us on our journey; for all thy ways are beautiful and all thy paths are peace."

The Blessed Virgin is honored under the title Our Lady of the Highway in virtue of her numerous journeys: The Visitation, when she went to Ein Karim to see her cousin Elizabeth; her journey from Nazareth to Bethlehem; the trip when Jesus was presented in the temple; the flight of the Holy Family into Egypt; the return from Egypt; journeys to Jerusalem; and above all, the sorrowful journey when she accompanied her Son on the Way of the Cross.

BIBLIOGRAPHY:

Apparitions and Shrines of Heaven's Bright Queen,
  by Wm. J. Walsh, T. J. Cary Co., New York, 1904.
La Madonna Santuari e Feste,
  by P. Umberto Bonomo, C.SS.R., Vatican City Religious Book Co., Inc., New York, 1948.

Spanish Titles

OUR LADY OF COVADONGA

THE BLESSED VIRGIN is venerated under this title at Covadonga, a small village in the Cantabrian mountains of Asturia, Spain, not far from the City of Oviedo.

The story of Covadonga and it's nationally famous Virgin goes back many centuries—it can clearly be traced to the years that marked the beginning of the Spanish Reconquest; of anything prior to that time, all details seem to be lost.

In 711, the Moors crossed over from Northern Africa and landed near the site of modern Gibraltar. Moving inland they were engaged by the army of the Visigoths, led by King Rodrigo. The battle of Guadalete (July, 711, A. D.) ensued and the Visigoths were severely beaten. Rodrigo having fallen in the fighting, a kinsman, Don Pelayo, regrouped the scattered surviving Goths and slowly retreated into the hills and mountains of Asturia, finally taking shelter around a place known as Covadonga. [1]

Sometime thereafter one of Pelayo's troopers was guilty of some breach of discipline and, fleeing the wrath of his superior, hid himself among some high and craggy rocks. Pelayo, intent on punishing him, set out in pursuit. He finally spied the culprit just as he dashed into a cave on Mt. Auseba.

Pelayo was about to follow and apprehend him when a venerable hermit stepped forth from the cave and said to him: "This cave is the dwelling place of the Most Holy Mother and this man has placed himself under her protection. If you will pardon him, you too will one day find here a haven, and you will rebuild the Empire and your name will live in glory."

Pelayo undoubtedly knew that for centuries this cave had been a sanctuary of the Virgin whose image was there venerated by the hermits. So he pardoned the man and then knelt in prayer before the statue. He proclaimed the Virgin patroness of his army and of all Spain.

In 718 the Moors dispatched a powerful army under command of General Alcamah, with orders to wipe out Pelayo and his troops. When word of the approaching enemy forces reached Pelayo, he immediately retired to the cave of Covadonga and prayed to the Virgin, asking her to aid his outnumbered men.

Alcamah arrived and deployed his archers in the valley below the rocky cliffs. He ordered them to hurl their arrows against the defenders hidden among the crags above. Arrows soon filled the air, but strangely enough all fell short of Pelayo's men. Many, rebounding from the hard rocks, killed those who had shot them.

Then Pelayo's men rolled huge rocks and trunks of trees down onto the Moors. A section of the mountain broke loose, sliding down and crushing great numbers of the enemy. These mishaps disorganized the Saracens and finally they fled in utter confusion, making for the plains of Auceba. Then a terrific cloudburst broke over the mountain, causing the Deva river to overflow, and many perished in its raging waters.

This unexpected defeat of the Moors was actually the beginning of the eight-century-long Reconquest of Spain. Don Pelayo attributed the astonishing victory of his vastly outnumbered troops to the powerful aid of the Virgin of Covadonga.

Sometime around the middle of the eighth century Alfonso I (739-757) erected the first little chapel of the cave and also a Benedictine Monastery of Holy Mary. Later a collegiate church was built nearby. It was destroyed by a fire on October 17, 1777, but was later rebuilt. The present Basilica—higher on the mountain-side than the cave itself— is a work of the nineteeth century, initiated by the Bishop of Oviedo, according to plans by Aparicio. It is known as the Basilica de la Virgen de los Batallas (Virgin of the Battles).

In the cave itself, there is today the little chapel of Santa Maria and the image of Our Lady of Covadonga. The present statue was carved in 1908 by J. Samso Lengli. (Nothing is known of the fate of the image enshrined in the cave in the time of Pelayo). The image was solemnly crowned in 1918.

1.—Probably an ancient contraction of Cueva (Cave) honda (deep).

BIBLIOGRAPHY:

Ano Mariano,
by Robles, S. J., and Figares, S. J., Madrid, 1958.
Reina y Madre,
Editorial Luis Vives, S. A.,
Zaragoza, 1957.

OUR LADY OF THE FORSAKEN

THE STORY OF THIS TITLE of Our Lady begins in Valencia, Spain, during the early years of the fifteenth century. One Lorenzo Salom, who may have been a converted Jew, assembled nine friends and all vowed to "devote their time and efforts to the assistance of the sick, the poor, the aged, the orphans and the infirm, and to found a home wherein poor pilgrims and travelers, without friends or money, might find shelter."

The group of ten men organized a religious community which they named "La Confradia de los Desamparadoa"— the Confraternity of the Unprotected. Next they secured a large house, filled it with orphans, feeding and clothing them, obtaining the wherewithal by begging from door to door. Others soon joined them in their work.

The King of Spain became interested and built them a new and much larger house. At that time (1413) the community solemnly placed itself under the protection of the Blessed Virgin, and changed the name to "the Brotherhood of Innocent children and the Mother of the Forsaken."

Having placed their institution under the protection of the Virgin, they were anxious that the chapel of their new house should be graced by a statue of her. But they had no funds with which to have one made, so they reluctantly gave up the idea.

Then, early one evening in 1414, three young men knocked at their door and asked if they might stay there over night. During a chat that evening after supper, the superior happened to mention the statue the community wanted but could not afford to buy.

The young men said they were sculptors and since the superior had been so nice to them, they would be happy to repay him and at the same time honor the Blessed Virgin by carving a statue. All they needed was a block of marble, some tools, and a room in which they could work for several days undisturbed. These things were quickly provided the next day. They locked themselves in the room.

Several days passed, and strangely enough, no sounds of hammers, or chisels, or any other sounds came from the locked room. There was no answer when the monks knocked on the door.

On the fourth day, the monks, fearing something serious had happened to the three young men, kicked the door open. To everyone's amazement, in the center of the room stood a beautiful statue of the Blessed Virgin. The rough block of marble and the tools were also there, but no trace of the three young men. It was concluded that they were angels in disguise, sent by the Blessed Virgin and that they had in some miraculous way materialized the statue.

The story of the statue and of its origin soon spread throughout the city. Great crowds came to offer thanks and pay devotion to Our Lady. It was not long before the statue came to be called "Our Lady of the Forsaken" (Nuestra Señora de los Desamparados).

Seventy-five years later, in 1489, the statue was transferred to one of the chapels of the Cathedral. In 1667, it was removed from the Cathedral and transferred to a new church in the Plaza Mayor, at which time Our Lady of the Forsaken was publicly proclaimed the Patroness of the City and Kingdom of Valencia.

The image was crowned in 1923.

BIBLIOGRAPHY:

 Apparitions & Shrines of Heaven's Bright Queen,
  by Wm. J. Walsh,
  T. J. Cary Co., 1904.
 La Imagen Original de Nuestra Senora de Los Desamparados,
  Ediciones "Mater Destetorum," Valencia, 1955.

OUR LADY OF GUADALUPE (Spain)

WHILE WE OF THE AMERICAS usually think of Mexico when we consider the title of Our Lady of Guadalupe, the title actually originated in Spain two hundred years before it was used in Mexico.

The real beginning of the story of Our Lady of Guadalupe, goes back to the early years of the eighth century. At that time Spain was ruled by the Visigoths, most of whom, like the original Spanish, had been converted to the Catholic religion.

In 711, Rodrigo, leader of the Visigoths, was defeated in the battle of Jerez de la Frontera, on the banks of the Guadalete by the Saracens [1] or Moors, who quickly overran all of Spain.

Following their defeat, some of the Visigoths fled northward to the Province of Asturias, on the Bay of Biscay. With them they took a statue of the Blessed Virgin, traditionally held to be a present from Pope Gregory the Great, (590-604) to Leander, Bishop of Seville. [2]

Fearing they might be captured by the pursuing Saracens, and their beloved statue destroyed, they sealed it in an iorn box and buried it in a cave in the mountains of Estremadura. [3]

As time passed, none remained of those who had buried the statue, some being killed by the enemy and the rest dying in the natural course of time, far from home. Thus the image was completely forgotten—for six centuries.

Then the Blessed Virgin must have decided it was time for her image to be brought to light. In 1326, she appeared to a simple cowhand named Gil, and showed him where the iron box containing her image was buried. He dug at the place and unearthed the box.

Gil reported all this to the church authorities who came to open the box. In it they found the statue which had been buried centuries before by the fleeing Visigoths. The statue was in perfect condition, as were also certain papers giving details of the burial, which were enclosed with it.

The statue was turned over to the Franciscans in the near-by town of Guadalupe [4]—a shrine was built and quickly became a center of great devotion to the Blessed Virgin. Soon the image came to be known as that of Our Lady of Guadalupe and many pilgrimages were made there to honor her and to ask her help in freeing Spain from the Saracen or Moorish occupation—which came about in 1491. And today, in the chapel of the Franciscans at Guadalupe, she continues to be honored under that title, as she has been down through the centuries. The image was crowned on October 12, 1928.

1.—Saracen is the name used to designate the Mohammendans of Syria and Palestine, the Arabs generally, or the arab-berber races of North Africa who conquered Spain. By 709, the Saracens or Moors had extended their sway over Northern Africa to beyond the Strait of Gibraltar—they then crossed over to Spain (711), nearly the whole of which they subjugated. While they remained in Spain for almost seven centuries, their power for all practical purposes was broken in 1212, in the battle of the Plains of Tolosa, by the combined forces of the Kingdom of Castile and Leon.

They were finally defeated by the forces of Ferdinand of Aragon and Isabella of Castile and Leon, his wife.

2.—According to some Spanish historians, the statue of Our Lady of Guadalupe was venerated as early as the fourth century.

3.—Estramadura was an old province of Spain, lying between Portugal and New Castile. It was bounded on the north by Leon, and on the South by Andalusia. It was the home province of Cortez and many of the other Spanish Conquistadores.

4.—Guadalupe (Caceres) lies some 100 miles southwest of Madrid. The Monastery was founded in 1340 by Alphonso XI in commemoration of his victory over the Moors at Salado.

BIBLIOGRAPHY:

Historic Shrines of Spain,
by Isabel Allardyce
Franciscan Missionary Press, New York, 1912.
Spanish Shrines,
Booklet of Spanish State Tourist Dept.,
Spanish Tourist Office, New York.
Paraynfo Celeste Historia,
by Juan de Luzuriaga,
Madrid, 1690.

OUR LADY OF THE HOLY FOUNTAIN

ACCORDING TO AN OLD SPANISH LEGEND, in 1442, there lived in Cordova, a poor family named Garcia—Gonzalo, the father, his wife and a young daughter. Gonzalo was a cloth weaver and the family managed to get along fairly well until misfortunes befell them. The wife had a long illness and was a semi-invalid; the daughter became partially demented and Gonzalo, trying to do his daily job and also tend to the wants of his family, eventually broke down and he too became very ill.

Finally Gonzalo could no longer bear it and one night, in a moment of despair, he decided to end his troubles by hanging himself.

Making sure his wife and daughter were soundly sleeping, he quietly arose, found a piece of rope, fastened one end to a beam overhead, tied a slip-noose in the other and, climbing on a stool, settled the noose around his neck. Before taking the final leap, he paused and thought of his immortal soul. He prayed fervently, asking God and his Blessed Mother to forgive him for the terrible thing he was about to do.

Then to his amazement a soft light suddenly shone in a

corner of the room and in its midst a beautiful lady appeared. She smiled and asked him not to be frightened. She told him that suicide was the coward's way out, that if he would give up the idea of killing himself, she would be happy to help him.

She told him to go to a certain spot outside the city walls where he would find a fig tree. Beneath the tree there would be a spring of water. He was to drink of the water and bring some home for his wife and daughter to drink, and all three of them would be restored to health at once. Then he was to dig out the ground under the tree and a little way beneath the surface he would find a statue of her.

So saying the Lady smiled and slowly vanished. Gonzalo put away the rope and hurried forth to carry out her instructions. Locating the fig tree and the bubbling spring, he knelt and drank of the water. Immediately his sickness left him and he was well. Scooping up some of the water into an earthen jug he ran home, awakened his wife and daughter, gave each a drink, and they too were restored to health.

He quickly returned to the tree, his wife and daughter with him, and, digging down, soon discovered a statue of the Blessed Virgin.

No one knows how the image came to be buried under the fig tree, but it is supposed that it was hidden there long before to prevent its being taken by the Moors.

Naturally the story of the spring and the finding of the buried statue quickly spread throughout the countryside and everybody had to drink the water. Many were cured of their ills, both physical and mental.

In thanksgiving the people of the city erected a chapel over the spot—probably in 1454—and Gonzalo placed the little statue in it. The image soon came to be generally known as Nuestra Señora de la Fuensanta—Our Lady of the Holy Fountain. The Virgin under this title is Patroness of Cordoba.

BIBLIOGRAPHY:

Historic Shrines of Spain,
by Isabel Allardyce, Franciscan Missionary Press, New York, 1912.

OUR LADY OF RANSOM
also known as
OUR LADY OF MERCY

THESE TWO TITLES of Our Lady seem to have come into general use in Spain, during the early part of the thirteenth century.

The titles seem to be synonomous, and both apparently came into popular use as a consequence of the founding of an Order whose prime object was the recovery or rescue of Christians who were held captive by the Moors.

Three men, at about the same time, conceived the idea of establishing such an order. The three were St. Peter Nolasco (1189-1256), St. Raymond of Pennafort (1175-1275) and James I (1208-1276) King of Aragon.

It is said the Blessed Virgin appeared to these three on the same night. She instructed them to work together to form an Order whose purpose would be the ransoming or recovering of Christians who had been captured by the Turks.

On the night of the vision—probably August 1, 1218—the Blessed Virgin appeared to James and instructed him to assist in the institution of a religious society to be known as the Order of Mercy for the Redemption of Captives. A similar vision was granted to St. Raymond of Pennafort, the king's confessor, with identical instructions; St. Peter Nolasco, who was at that time in Barcelona, experienced a similar vision, but here the Virgin specified that her Divine Son desired that the Order be founded by Peter, aided by Raymond and James.

The three conferred after these visions and did as the Virgin had instructed. The new Order appears to have been formally launched on August 10, 1218, at a ceremony in the Cathedral of Barcelona—apparently the name they first selected for the organization was the Order of Our Lady of Ransom for the Redemption of Captives.

Later, probably in 1235, the movement was officially approved by Pope Gregory IX (1227-1241), but the name was changed to the Order of Our Lady of Mercy. Still later, probably in 1238, James granted to St. Peter Nolasco a large part of his royal palace, which became the first convent of the Order. There, in 1249, they built a sanctuary to Our Lady of Mercy.

The original carving of Our Lady of Mercy—still in Barcelona—was done by an artist under the personal direction of St. Peter Nolasco and King James. The present image, substituted for the original dates to the fourteenth century. It was crowned in 1888. The Virgin under this title was proclaimed Patroness of Barcelona in 1687.

BIBLIOGRAPHY:

Apparitions and Shrines of Heaven's Bright Queen,
   by Wm. J. Walsh,
   T. J. Cary Co., New York, 1904.
Our Lady of Puig,
   by George Propsero,
   in *Ave Maria,* June 6, 1892.
La Madonna Santuari e Feste,
   by Fr. Umberto Bonomo, C.SS.R.,
   Vatican City Religious Book Co., Inc., New York, 1948.
Booklet of Spanish State Tourist Dept., Madrid.

Miscellaneous Titles

OUR LADY OF AFRICA

THE STORY CONNECTED with this title of Our Lady has its beginning in the early years of the nineteenth century. The French seized Algeria after a dispute in 1827 in which the Dey struck the French consul with a fly-swatter, an incident which led to war. Algiers was captured in 1830 and the Dey and the Turks were driven out. In 1838 Bishop Dupech was appointed the first bishop of the See of Algiers. When he arrived there it was only to find that he had no church in which to officiate, nor a house in which to live. After a year or so of laboring under these handicaps, the bishop decided to return to France and attempt to collect money to build a church and a rectory.

He set about his task and while on a visit to the Religious of the Sacred Heart at Lyons told them of his problems; the Sodality of Our Lady gave him a lovely bronze statue of Our Lady of the Immaculate Conception. They told him that the dark-hued bronze Madonna seemed most appropriate for Africa and that they would pray that the Blessed Virgin would take the Mohammedans and Negroes of that continent under her loving protection. The grateful bishop thanked them for the beautiful statue and shortly thereafter, having finished his fund-raising campaign, returned to Algiers. Upon

his arrival there in 1840 he entrusted the image of Our Lady
to the Trappists who had recently come to Algiers to found a
monastery; they were to keep it until the bishop could build
his church. However, Bishop Dupech did not live to see his
project fully realized. After an administration of some ten
years he returned to France and died there soon afterwards.

Bishop Dupech was succeeded by Bishop Pavy who, in
1858, laid the cornerstone of the basilica that today overlooks
the Mediterranean. When the shrine was completed Bishop
Pavy asked the Trappists to return the statue of Our Lady
which Bishop Dupech had lent them, and which in the meantime they had enshrined over the front entrance of their
monastery. The monks, however, had come to be very fond of
the image and not one of them would help in removing it.
Eventually Bishop Pavy had to send men with a cart to
remove it and transport it to the new church. And now the
faithful, who by this time were quite numerous due to an
influx from France and Spain, came to visit the shrine. The
Blessed Virgin showered her favors upon the poor, the maim-
ed, the crippled, the blind, and especially upon sailors and
soldiers who called on her for aid—so much so that this image
gave rise to a cult of Mary under the title of Our Lady of
Africa, Comforter of the Afflicted.

Bishop Pavy died in 1866 and Lavigerie, then Bishop of
Nancy, on March 27, 1867, was appointed Archbishop of
the See of Algiers. On December 22nd of that year, he em-
barked at Marseille for his new field on a vessel which,
although one of the smallest of the line, carried some seven
hundred passengers and a large cargo of merchandise.
Accompanying the Archbishop were a number of ecclesias-
tics, the Trappist Abbot, several religious of the Sacred Heart
and of other communities. Soon after clearing port, the vessel

ran into a heavy storm. The captain attempted to turn and run for shore but the ship's rudder was damaged and the waves crashing through the hatches flooded the boiler room putting out the fires. The frightened passengers became panicky and the Archbishop attempted to calm them. He gave them general absolution and asked them to join him in a vow to Our Lady of Africa and to pray with him for her assistance.

Later, going below decks, he met the Trappist Abbot. "Oh, dear Father Abbot," he said, "We have just made a vow to Our Lady of Africa. All here will see that the Blessed Virgin will deliver us from this peril; and you, what are you doing for her?" "I also," replied the Trappist, "am recommending myself to our good Mother. I am telling Our Lady of Africa, in all simplicity, that this disaster is not to her credit, for everyone knows that you and the priests and the religious are invoking her aid, and if she allows us to perish no one will ever place confidence in her new shrine." The Archbishop smiled at this filial familiarity, but he himself had just made a vow to the Virgin in behalf of the sailors and passengers on the ship. And the ship was saved. She rode out the storm and a few days later entered the harbor of Algiers.

Archbishop Lavigerie immediately took up his duties, and under his administration the See of Algiers flourished and grew. One of the first things he did was to erect a cenotaph under the portico of the church with this inscription carved thereon: "To the memory of those who have perished in the sea, and who have been engulfed by the waves."

A few years later he obtained from Pope Pius IX the title of Basilica for the shrine of Our Lady of Africa. It was consecrated in 1872 and in 1876 the image was crowned with a golden diadem studded with precious stones—a gift of the Holy Father.

Archbishop Lavigerie also instituted a special ceremony which takes place even to this day. On Sundays, a priest vested in black cope, as for the absolution at a funeral, attended by choir boys, goes to the top of the cliff overlooking the Mediterranean. There he intones the *"Libera me, Domine,"* and while the boys hold a pall over the waters below, the priest casts holy water to the East, North, and West, meanwhile praying for the souls of all who rest in the watery tomb. Next, as burning incense perfumes the air, he asks Our Lady to watch over all who may be on the seven seas and to bring them safely to their journey's end.

Thus, over and over again, is fulfilled the vow made in 1867 by Archbishop Lavigerie and the passengers of the vessel in that far-off moment of peril—the vow that resulted in their being guided into port and safety by the protection of Our Lady of Africa.

BIBLIOGRAPHY:

    Cardinal Lavigerie, Primate of Africa,
      by Rev. J. G. Beane,
      St. Joseph's Seminary for the Colored Missions, Balto., Md., 1898.
    How the Shrine of Our Lady of Africa Originated,
      Leaflet of the White Fathers of Africa, Washington, D. C.

OUR LADY OF THE AIRWAYS

THIS TITLE OF OUR LADY appears to have originated in Malton, Ontario, Canada, some 15 miles distant from Toronto, the site of Toronto's airport. During World War II, large numbers of Canadian Air Force personnel were stationed at Malton, and a large aircraft factory was also located there.

To care for the spiritual needs of the airport, aircraft factory, and Air Force Base personnel, a church was erected at Malton and the first mass in the new church was celebrated by Father Ralph J. Egan on December 8, 1944, the Feast of the Immaculate Conception.

Inasmuch as Malton was at that time a center of aviation, it seemed most fitting to Father Egan that the new church be given some appropriate title of the Blessed Virgin.

After devoting considerable thought to the matter, he decided that Our Lady of the Airways would be a fitting title. He submitted it to the Chancery Office of the Archdiocese of Toronto, and His Eminence, James Charles Cardinal McGuigan—at that time, Archbishop McGuigan—gave his official approval.

From 1944 to 1948 the church was a Mission church—then in June 1948, Father W. Vincent Egan, P. P., became the first resident pastor. In the summer of 1949, he began to propogate devotion to the Blessed Virgin under her new title of Our Lady of the Airways.

The church itself is located some two miles north of the Malton airport. It has a picture of Our Lady of the Airways painted on the wall, near the altar on the epistle side of the church. The painting was designed by Father Vincent Egan and Scott Young, a church decorator, in 1948.

The painting depicts Our Lady standing on top of the world, her feet pinning down a serpent, her head encircled with a halo of stars—rays of light stream from her open hands and spray down upon two airplanes circling the globe—her figure is pillowed in two cloud banks. Beneath her feet is a ribbon with the words, "Super Pennas Ventorum," which phrase is taken from the Book of Daniel, Chapter 3, and is translated, "Upon the wings of the winds."

There is a lovely prayer to Our Lady of the Airways:

O Mary, Our Lady of the Airways, my Heavenly Mother, I place myself under thy protection upon this journey which I am about to undertake, and I ask that with your heavenly aid and upon the Winds this earthly journey may be brought to a safe landing.

May I also ask that upon the Wings of Prayer, and through your heavenly intercession my last journey in this life may end at the Eternal Airport of Life Everlasting with you and your Divine Son in Heaven. Amen.

There is a beautiful Chapel of Our Lady of the Airways at Logan International Airport, in East Boston, Mass. It was dedicated on January 20, 1952 by His Excellency, Archbishop Richard J. Cushing, now Cardinal. At the time of dedication, it was the world's first permanent airport chapel.

Our Lady of Loreto is known as the Patroness of Aviators.

OUR LADY OF THE AWAITING

AT SIDON IN LEBANON, there is a shrine dedicated to Our Lady of the Awaiting. It dates back to the early part of the fourth century.

Tradition tells us that once during the time when Christ was preaching, He and His Mother journeyed from Galilee north to Sidon. While Christ taught the people his mother waited for him in the shelter of a cave outside the city, in a settlement called Maghdoushe. When evening came Christ rejoined his Mother, and after spending the night in the cave they returned the next day to Galilee. The story of their sojourn was relayed from one generation to the next, in the area of Maghdoushe, until early in the fourth century St. Helena, the mother of Constantine visited Jerusalem. Here she heard the legend of the journey of Christ and the Blessed Virgin to Sidon and began to check its accuracy. She found many people in Maghdoushe who told her how it had become a tradition in the area.

Convinced of its authenticity, the Empress persuaded the Bishop of Tyre and Sidon to bless the ancient cave, consecrating it to Our Lady of the Awaiting. The Empress then sent a beautiful ikon [1] of the Virgin and Child in order that the people might have an object of devotion for the newly consecrated cave. And there for hundreds of years the picture was honored.

Early in the seventh century the Arabs swept in and conquered the entire Lebanese coast. Political difficulties soon forced the Sidonions to move their possessions across the mountains to Christian Lebanon. [2] Before leaving, they carefully covered the entrance to the cave of Our Lady of the Awaiting with stones and vines. As a result no one suspected the existence of a cave at that spot in the mountains.

During the next thousand years the legend of the cave and its image continued to be transmitted from one generation to the next, but meanwhile the details grew vague.

Then in the early seventeenth century, under the reign of Prince Fakreddin II (1572-1635), conditions made it possible for the decendants of the ancient village of Maghdoushe to return to their homeland.

After the people were settled they recalled the legend of the cave and set out to find it, but all their efforts were in vain. The intervening centuries seemed to have hidden it forever.

Then one day a strange thing happened—a goatherd on the mountain outside of the village saw a kid disappear from sight as though it had been swallowed by the mountain. Looking more closely he found that it had fallen down a crevass. He made his way into the hole, descended a few feet, then dropped into an open space. When his eyes became accustomed to the darkness he saw a shelf on the wall of the cave, and on it was a picture of the Virgin and Child.

With some difficulty, and hampered by the kid he carried, he climbed up to the surface and rushed to the village with his news. The next day the villagers returned with tools, found the entrance to the ancient cave and reopened it. With great rejoicing they carried the precious picture to the village church, placed it in the sanctuary, and then notified the Bishop of Sidon who arrived the next day to see the picture.

At this point, however, the picture could not be found in the church, but was later discovered in its original niche in the cave. They returned the ikon to the church, but by the next morning it was back again in the cave.

Thereupon the Bishop decided the Blessed Virgin wished her picture to remain in the cave. So he ordered that it should remain there. He rededicated the cave as the shrine of Our Lady of the Awaiting, [3] where the picture has remained to the present time.

1.—This picture is another one attributed by some to St. Luke The Evangelist.

2.—The Lebanese have always been Christians—even during the occupation by the Arabs they were like a "Christian Island in a Moselm Sea."

3.—In Arabic—Saiydat el Montarah.

BIBLIOGRAPHY:

"Our Lady of the Awaiting,"
  by Bruce Conde,
  Ave Maria magazine, August 11, 1956.
La Sainte Vierge au Liban,
  by Joseph Goudard, S. J.,
  Paris, 1908.

OUR LADY OF CHINA

THE BEGINNING OF THE STORY of Our Lady of China goes
back to around 1900. For some years prior to that time, the
Vincentian Fathers had a mission in a village called Tonglu
(Tong Lu), located a short distance south of Peiping.

In 1900, the Boxer rebellion hit China. In April of that
year a large force of Boxers headed for Tonglu, intending to
kill all Christians they might find there.

The several hundred Christians formed a garrison to try
to resist the enemy. Daily the Chinese priest carried the
Blessed Sacrament around among the fighting men, and all
earnestly implored the Blessed Virgin to come to their aid.

Finally, after some four months of furious attacking, the
ten thousand Boxers suddenly fled. This victory and the
retreat of the Boxers was explained by some Boxers who were
taken prisoner. They told how for days they had seen "a
woman in white over the church," and that "strange horse-
men had chased them."

In thanksgiving to Our Lady for assisting them in their
time of need, the people of Tonglu decided she should be
honored by a beautiful picture in the village church. The
local priest, Father Wu, engaged a well-known Chinese
artist to paint the picture, instructing him to clothe Our Lady

in the handsome robe of the Dowager Empress Tze-Hsi and her Son as the child Emperor standing at her side.

The painting was finished and placed in the church on March 17, 1909. When the people saw it, some of them protested because the artist had copied the robe of the Empress of China. This troubled the parish priest. He led the parish in a novena, asking the Blessed Virgin in some way to indicate whether she was pleased with the gown in which she had been painted.

There was a nine-year-old boy in Tonglu who had been sick for several years, bed-ridden and so weak he could not walk. During the novena the people prayed, saying: "Our Lady of Tonglu, if the robe in which you are shown in the picture is pleasing to you, tell us so by curing this sick boy."

By the end of the novena, the boy was up, running around with the other children and in perfect health.

In 1924, when the Bishops gathered together at the Synod of Shanghai, they dedicated all of China to the Blessed Virgin and at that time they officially changed the name of the picture from Our Lady of Tonglu to Our Lady of China.

In 1930, the Holy Father declared that May 30 should be the Feast Day of Our Lady of China.

The Church of Tonglu has since been destroyed (1942) by the Chinese Communists. However, there seems to be some evidence that the picture of Our Lady of China was saved and is now hidden somewhere in China.

OUR LADY OF CZESTOCHOWA
also known as
OUR LADY QUEEN OF POLAND

AN OLD LEGEND SAYS that St. Luke the Evangelist [1] painted a picture of the Blessed Virgin on a piece of cypress wood fashioned by St. Joseph and the Virgin herself posed for it —some hold that the piece of wood was cut from the table used for the Last Supper. Then, according to the story, St. Helena, mother of Constantine the Great (274-337), during the fourth century, probably about 326, discovered this ancient picture while in the Holy Land searching for the True Cross. She gave it to her son, Constantine, who either placed it in a chapel of his palace at Constantinople, or built a shrine for it. The records are not clear on this.

Wonderful things took place in connection with this picture. One account tells about the Saracens attacking Constantinople and at the height of the assault, when the picture was placed atop the city walls, the attackers immediately fled.

Years later Charlemagne (742-814) visited Constantinople and the painting was presented to him. However, he later gave it to Prince Leo of Ruthenia (today a part of

Czechoslovakia), as a gracious token of payment for the years Leo had faithfully served him. Then for some hundreds of years it remained in the palace at Belz in Ruthenia.

In the latter part of the fourteenth century—probably 1382—it was acquired by Duke (or Prince) Ladislau (or Ladislas) of Opal in Silesia, Poland. Ladislau invited the Paulist Fathers (monks) of Hungary to take over the guardianship of the miraculous picture. These monks had a monastery and church on the Jasna Gora, (Mount of Light or Bright Hill) so called because of its brilliant white rock composition.

The monks readily agreed, and in 1382 or 1383 the picture was turned over to them. They built a shrine and placed the painting in it. There the picture remained until 1430 when the Hussites (followers of John Huss, 1369-1415) raided and ruined the monastery and church. They broke the picture into several pieces, and cut across the face of the Virgin with a saber. In this condition the monks found it when they returned after the assault.

An attempt was made to restore the painting. Artists were able to join the pieces together without any trace of the cracks, but, try as they would, they could not eliminate the cuts on the Virgin's face. Soon the monastery and church were rebuilt and the restored picture replaced therein.

Years later the shrine was destroyed by fire, but the picture was not burned—however, the flames and smoke had darkened it and from that day it has been known as the "Black Madonna."

There are numerous recorded instances in which Our Lady of Czestochowa came to the aid of Poland in times of great need. One of them occurred during the reign of John Casimir (1648-1668), when Poland was attacked by Russia and Sweden.

By 1655 the country was practically over run. The Swedes were in possession of western Poland, including Warsaw and Krakow. In nearly all of eastern Poland the Cossacks, Tartars, and Muscovites were in control, but Czestochowa was not occupied by the enemy.

Fortunately, in 1620-24, King Sigismond II had fortified the hillock, making it a citadel capable of resisting aggression. It was as if he had foreseen the coming emergency. The hillock and the shrine were so sturdily and valiantly defended by a brave group led by Father Augustine Kordecki, that after a siege of forty days the enemy was routed and withdrew—avowing that their bullets simply bounced back at them from the monastery walls. The soldiers insisted that they clearly saw the figure of a lady in blue hovering above the monastery walls with her mantle outspread in a protective gesture.

This victory at Czestochowa was universally attributed to the help of Our Lady, and she was soon after endowed with another title. On April 1, 1656, King John Casimir, in the Cathedral of Lwow, officially pronounced her "Queen of Poland." Since then, the shrine has become a symbol of the spiritual strength of Poland, Our Lady's citadel behind the Iron Curtain.

The Order of St. Paul, the first hermit, has guarded the picture of Our Lady of Czestochowa for 600 years (since 1382), in Czestochowa, [2] Poland. The image was crowned in 1717 and again in 1925. In 1948, Poland was consecrated to the Heart of Mary.

1.—There seems to be some historical evidence that St. Luke was an artist as well as a physician. Some art experts believe that the picture was painted around 431 A. D., making it one of the oldest images of the

Blessed Virgin. The Byzantine style would indicate that it came from the Near East. Other experts date it back only to the ninth century.
2.—Czestochowa is about 135 miles southwest of Warsaw.

BIBLIOGRAPHY:

Album Pamiatkowy,
     Bul. Our Lady of Czestochowa Shrine,
     Pauline Fathers Monastery, Doylestown, Pa.
La Madonna Santuari e Feste,
     by Fr. Umberto Bonomo, C.SS.R.,
     Vatican City Religious Book Co., Inc., New York, 1948.
Shrines to Our Lady Around the World,
     by Zsolt Aradi;
     Farrar, Straus & Young, New York, 1954.

OUR LADY OF EINSIEDELN

EINSIEDELN, which means hermitage, is a town in Switzerland, some twenty-five miles southeast of Zurich. It is today, and has been for centuries, the home of one of the most famous of Catholic shrines of the Blessed Virgin. It also boasts one of Europe's most celebrated Benedictine Abbeys.

The story of Einsiedeln and its famous statue of Our Lady reaches back to the early part of the ninth century. It begins about 822, at which time a young man named Meinrad became a monk in the Benedictine Monastery at Reichenau.

After spending a few years at the monastery, Meinrad felt he should lead a more solitary life, and in the year 827 or 828, obtaining permission from the Abbot, he took himself to a spot (the Etzel Pass) on Mt. Etzel, a small mountain near Altendorf (Altdorf). However, he did not find the solitude he longed for, because too many people came to visit him. His sanctity had become well known and many wished to receive spiritual advice from him.

So, in a few years (probably 835), he moved to the denser forests on a mountainside, overlooking Lake Lucerne. There, in his rude hermit's cell, Meinrad spent the next few years. In 853 he had a small chapel built near his cell and therein placed a statue of the Blessed Virgin with the Infant resting on her arm. This statue had been given to him by the Abbess Hildegard, Superior of a convent in Zurich.

Years passed. Then on a cold winter day, January 21, 861, two men from Zurich, who thought Meinrad had some great treasure hidden in his cell, came and brutally murdered him. His body was removed to the Abbey of Reichenau, where it remained until 1039.

For some seventy-five years after Meinrad's death, his cell and little chapel seem to have been forgotten and neglected. Then Benno, a canon of Strasbourg and later Bishop of Metz, restored the chapel and cell in 906, and lived there with several companions for some years.

In 934, St. Eberhard, provost of Strasbourg and a disciple of Benno, began the construction of a church and monastery on the site of Meinrad's little cell and chapel. They were completed in 998 and Eberhard became the first Abbot of Einsiedeln.

Conrad, Bishop of Constance, came to Einsiedeln in order to consecrate the new buildings, and this led to a most strange event. On the evening before the day of consecration, shortly before midnight, a brilliant light was seen by many to appear in the church, and sounds of singing were clearly heard; then the church was seen to be filled with angels and the Savior himself was standing at the high altar, celebrating the Mass of Consecration.

On the next day, as the bishop was about to begin the consecration ceremonies, an unknown voice was heard to say: "Stop brother, the church has been consecrated by God." [1]

In 964 after much investigation and the questioning of those who had been present on the occasion of the unusual consecration, the entire episode was endorsed by Pope Leo VIII (963-965), and many indulgences were granted to all who would make a pilgrimage to the church of Our Lady of Einsiedeln.

For some years everything went along serenely at Einsiedeln. Then in 1029 a fire destroyed the church and several adjoining buildings, but Meinrad's little chapel and its image of the Blessed Virgin was untouched.

Rebuilding began at once, was completed and the church consecrated in 1039. The day of consecration was noteworthy for two happenings. Pope Benedict IX (1032-1044) on that day proclaimed Meinrad a saint and his mortal remains were transferred from the Abbey of Reichenau to the new church at Einsiedeln.

For some seven hundred years, Einsiedeln flourished and each year more and more pilgrims came to the shrine of Our Lady. True, fire struck again on several occasions, [2] each time partially damaging the church and the monastery buildings but they were quickly rebuilt and restored. And moreover, each time the statue of Our Lady was undamaged.

In 1798, during the French Revolution, the revolutionaries invaded Switzerland, seized Einsiedeln and carried away most of its treasures to France. But again the famous statue was saved; this time by the Monks who fled with it into the surrounding mountains.

In 1803, peace being restored, the statue was brought back to Einsiedeln and replaced in the Abbey. There it remained until 1817. At that time, the Lady Chapel inside the main church, which had been damaged during the revolution, was completely restored. The statue [3] was placed above the chapel altar where it remains even unto the present day.

St. Meinrad's head has been preserved and rests in the marble tabernacle of the Lady Chapel.

1.—This story is reminiscent of the miraculous consecration of the church of Our Lady of Puy in the fifth century.
2.—In 1028, 1214, 1465, 1598, and 1577.
3.—The present statue is undoubtedly not Meinrad's original image. It is thought that the present statue, known as the Black Madonna, was carved in 1466, probably in Northern Switzerland, or Southern Germany. It is a little under four feet in height. Over the years the faces of the Virgin and Child have been darkened by the smoke and fumes of votive candles.

BIBLIOGRAPHY:

Apparitions & Shrines of Heaven's Bright Queen,
    by Wm. J. Walsh.
Famous Shrines of Our Lady,
    by H. M. Gillett, Vol. 1,
    Newman Press, Westminster, Md., 1952.
Our Lady of Hermits,
    by Rev. Ludwig Raeber, O. S. B.,
    Benziger & Co. Ltd., Einsiedeln, Switzerland.
Celebrated Sanctuaries of the Madonna,
    by Rev. J. Spencer Northcote, D. D.,
    Peter F. Cunningham & Son, Phila., 1875.

OUR LADY OF THE GOLDEN FOUNTAIN

THE SCENE OF THIS STORY lies some ten miles outside Constantinople. The time is somewhere between 450 and 457. It is a sweltering hot summer afternoon. The countryside is deserted, for all living creatures have sought shelter from the blistering heat of the sun. That is, all but two.

Trudging slowly down the dusty road which leads to Constantinople is an old blind man, guided by his dog. Both are almost exhausted; they have come a long distance. Suddenly, the old man's foot catches on a rock sticking up beyond the dusty surface of the road. He staggers a moment, loses his balance and falls to the ground. The leash holding the dog breaks. Now free, he wanders off.

After lying on the ground for some time, the blind man gradually regains a little strength, struggles back to his feet and attempts to renew his journey. Lacking the guidance of the dog, he misses the road and becomes hopelessly lost and confused amid the rocks and bushes which border the highway.

Despairing of getting out of the difficulty under his own efforts, he kneels and prays to the Blessed Virgin. He asks her to help him, to send along someone who will lead him back to the road and on to the city.

Soon he hears the faint thump of footsteps and the clank of metal. The sounds grow louder and nearer, and he cries out to the approaching traveler for assistance.

The newcomer is a young soldier named Leo. He is carrying messages from his commander in the field to headquarters in Constantinople. He stops, sees the bewildered old fellow, leaves the road, helps him to his feet and leads him back to the highway.

Then he asks him where he is going. The old man tells him he is on his way to Constantinople; that he had a dream in which the Blessed Virgin had told him to go to that city and there he would see a new emperor crowned.

This statement seems a little strange to Leo, because the Emperor Marcian is apparently in excellent health, and besides, how could a blind man see anyone crowned? But, being a respectful young man, he does not argue the matter. Taking the old chap's arm, he starts off leading him down the road.

Before they have traveled a quarter of a mile the old man begins to stagger and slumps to the ground, murmuring that he can go no farther, that he is so thirsty he fears he will die if he does not soon get a drink of water.

Leo notices that a short distance off to the side of the road there is a steep little mountain, whose top is covered with trees, and he reasons that there must be water there or the trees would not be so fresh and green looking. He carries the old man to the side of the road and using his pike and a couple of sticks for supports, with a piece of his clothing erects a makeshift awning for the old fellow.

He then sets out to climb the hill. It is unbearably hot and the climb is a tough one, but eventually he reaches the top and the welcome shade of the trees. Now to find some water.

He looks around but finds only dry, caked holes. Tired and discouraged, he is about to abandon his search, but before giving up, he decides he will pray for assistance. Kneeling in the grass, he asks the Blessed Virgin to help him find water, that he may revive his aged companion.

Almost immediately he seems to hear a voice calling his name, and the voice tells him if he will go through the thicket, a few paces ahead, he will find the water he seeks.

Leo obeys without question and, pushing through the bushes, comes upon a small lake or pond of clear cold water. Then he begins to wonder if perhaps it is too late, and if the old man will still be alive by the time he can return to him with the water.

But again the voice seems to be speaking to him—it reassures him that the blind man will still be alive, and instructs him to fill his helmet with water and when the old man drinks it he will revive and regain his strength. Also, he is to take a handful of mud, place it on the blind man's eyes and his sight will be restored to him.

Then strangest of all, the voice tells him that he, Leo, will soon be crowned emperor, that he will reign for seventeen years, and after he is emperor, she wishes him to build a church on the mountainside-top at the spot marked by the little pond.

As the voice ceases, a peculiar thing happens—the appearance of the pool of water is gradually changing. The bowl of the pool turns from a sandy, muddy yellow, to a rich golden hue, and in the very middle of the golden bowl the water begins to bubble upward. To Leo it looks like a golden fountain.

Pulling himself together, Leo fills his helmet with water and with one hand full of mud, he hurries down the mountain. Reaching the old man he props him up, pours a little water between the parched lips, then some more. Soon the blind man has revived and is able to sit up. Then Leo gently rubs some of the mud on the sightless eyes and washes it off with water. Immediately the blind man can see again. After thanking God and the Blessed Virgin, they arise, resume their journey and in a few hours arrive in Constantinople.

A few years later there was an upheaval and with the assistance of Aspar, commander-in-chief of the royal guard, Leo became emperor, just as the voice on the mountain-top had foretold.

Leo reigned from 457 to 474 and was known as Leo I, or Leo the Great. He built a beautiful church on the mountain-top and, recalling the appearance of the pool on the day the Blessed Virgin had spoken to him, he named the church, Our Lady of the Golden Fountain.

Nothing remains today of this church as it was destroyed by the Turks after they conquered Constantinople in 1453.

BIBLIOGRAPHY:

    Apparitions & Shrines of Heaven's Bright Queen,
      by Wm. J. Walsh,
      T. J. Cary Co., New York, 1904.
    La Madonna Santuari e Feste,
      by P. Umberto Bonomo, C.SS.R.,
      Vatican City Religious Book Co., Inc., New York, 1948.

OUR LADY OF KIEV

AROUND 862, A BAND OF NORSEMEN [1] settled in Novgorod and organized the Slavs of that region into an independent state—the nucleus of the future Russia. Kiev, about twenty years later, became its capital. By the end of the ninth century, missionaries from Constantinople had converted many of the inhabitants to Christianity.

During the three succeeding centuries, Kiev became the intellectual and religious center of the country, and numerous convents and monasteries arose in Kiev and the surrounding territory.

One of these was staffed by the Dominicans. To it there came, in the early years of the thirteenth century, a Dominican father by the name of Hyacinth—St. Hyacinth (1185-1257), the Apostle of the North; also Apostle of Poland and Russia.

Hyacinth had a burning ambition to convert the pagans and infidels of China, Mongolia and outer Russia (the Tartars), to the Christian faith. In this dedicated task he made numerous journeys, mostly by foot, into the far countries lying beyond Kiev. Between these travels he rested and recuperated at the Dominican House in Kiev.

During one of these rest periods, (1240), word came to the monastery that the Mongols had invaded the country. They had marched across the Caucasus, swept over central and southern Russia and now Kiev itself was in imminent danger of attack by the pagan hordes.

Hyacinth, on hearing the tragic news, rushed to the near-by church to save the Blessed Sacrament from capture and desecration. He had removed the sacred host from the taber-nacle and was hurrying down the aisle when, according to the story, he heard a voice call out: "Hyacinth, are you going to leave me here at the mercy of the Tartars?"

The voice seemed to be coming from the statue of the Blessed Virgin on one of the side altars. Hyacinth stopped and turned his gaze toward the statue which was of alabaster, fairly large in size, and obviously much too weighty for one man to carry. What should he do?

Then the voice spoke again: "Take me with you Hyacinth; I will make the burden light." So, holding the Blessed Sacrament in one hand, he picked up the statue with the other and, to his surprise, found he could easily carry it. Leaving the church, he fled from the city and saved the Blessed Sacrament and the statue of Our Lady from harm.

Eighty years later, after the Mongols had been driven away, the statue was returned to Kiev. That city became a center of great devotion to the Blessed Virgin, and it was natural that people soon gave the statue the name of Our Lady of Kiev.

The statue was later taken to a Dominican Convent in Lwow in Poland. What has happened to it since the Com-munists took over Poland is unknown.

1.—Sea rovers from Norway, Sweden and Denmark—also known as Vikings.

BIBLIOGRAPHY:

"Lady of Kiev, White Russia,"
by Sister Mary Jean Dorcy, O. P.
Outline History of the Church by Centuries,
by Rev. Joseph McSorley,
B. Herder Book Co., St. Louis, Mo., 1954.

OUR LADY OF LUXEMBURG
also known as
OUR LADY CONSOLATION OF THE AFFLICTED

THE STORY OF OUR LADY of Luxemburg begins in 1607 when the Jesuits established a college in that city. Later the Bishop of Trier built a church dedicated to the Immaculate Conception; it was finished in 1621 and placed in the care of the Jesuits.

"According to a legend, in 1624, a student of the Jesuit College went for a walk along the banks of the Alzette river which ran outside the city walls. Arriving at a place called the Rocks of Crispinus, he chanced to look up at an old hollow oak tree and there in the hollow saw a statue of the Virgin and Child. Surprised, he hurried back to the college and told several students; all then returned to the tree, picked up the statue, brought it back with them and placed it on the altar of their church. However, the next morning it had disappeared. Shortly afterward it was again found in the hollow oak. It was once more carried to the church, but the next day it was gone again. Then the Jesuit Fathers decided that Our Lady wished to be honored in that particular spot, so they built a chapel on the site. [1] They enshrined the statue in it and to both chapel and statue gave the name of Our Lady Consolation of the Afflicted.

The shrine soon became quite a center of devotion to Our Lady. Numerous miracles reputedly took place there and many pilgrims visited the shrine.

Nearly two centuries passed. During the French Revolution the Duchy of Luxemburg became involved in the struggle. In 1795 the little capital was taken; all the churches were desecrated and the chapel of Our Lady was totally destroyed. The statue, however, was saved by the quick action of some faithful soul who secreted it in a vault of the Church of the Immaculate Conception.

After the Revolution was over and tranquility restored, the statue was taken from its hiding place and was again available for public veneration. The church was rebuilt and the image restored to it. As the years passed the church proved entirely too small to contain the pilgrims who came to visit it. So in 1935 work began on enlarging the original structure, incorporating it entirely as a nave of the new one. Today Our Lady resides in the enlarged cathedral shrine and while her official title is Our Lady Consolation of the Afflicted, she is popularly known as Our Lady of Luxemburg.

1.—From **The Madonna on Stamps** by Aloysius Horn.

BIBLIOGRAPHY

Famous Shrines of Our Lady,
by H. M. Gillett, Vol. 1,
Newman Press, Westminster, Md., 1952.

OUR LADY OF THE VISITATION

THIS TITLE OF OUR LADY is a very old one. There is today, in Ein Karim (Ain-Karem), a little town located a few miles west of Jerusalem, a church known as the Church of the Visitation.

While this church dates only to about 1946, it stands over the site of several much older churches, or chapels, all of which were built sometime prior to the seventeenth century.

Over the altar of the present church, there is a fresco of Our Lady of the Visitation, and there seems to be good evidence, that the churches previously built on the site have for many centuries, in one way or another, commemorated the visit of Our Lady to her cousin, St. Elizabeth.

According to local tradition, there was a chapel or church built on this same spot as early as the fourth century.

The story of the Visitation is recorded in the Gospel of St. Luke, "And Mary rising up in those days, went into the *Hill Country*, with haste in to a *City of Juda*. And she entered into the house of Zachary and saluted Elizabeth . . . and Mary abode with her about three months."

It is generally supposed that the "city of Juda in the hill

country, mentioned by Luke is what today is known as Ain-Karem.

This same Gospel also states: "and after those days Elizabeth his wife conceived and hid herself five months . . ." Here too there is a supposition that the place where Elizabeth "hid herself" was a country house which Zachary owned and which possibly was located on higher ground and thus cooler in the hot summer months than his house of usual dwelling.

According to tradition it was in this country house that the meeting of the Virgin with her cousin Elizabeth actually took place. And on the site of this house from most ancient times there came to be erected a little chapel to commemorate the event. Years later, due to the ravishes of time, the chapel fell into ruin and still later it was rebuilt. This cycle of building, falling into decay and rebuilding probably occurred several times over the centuries, culminating finally in the present Church of the Visitation built within the last few years.

It would appear logical to assume that the earlier chapels or churches erected on this spot had a statue or a painting dedicated to the meeting of Mary and Elizabeth, and that it was named Our Lady of the Visitation.

There is today in Ain-Karem, a well, called the Well of the Visitation—sometimes called the Fountain of the Virgin. These names came about from a legend or tradition that the well sprang up (probably as a spring) at the moment when Mary saluted Elizabeth—or that the well was one located not far from the site of Elizabeth's country house and that Mary drew water from it during the days in which she visited her cousin.

BIBLIOGRAPHY:

The Catholic Shrines of the Holy Land,
    by Very Rev. Paschal Kinsel & Rev. Leonard Henry
    Farrar, Straus & Young, New York, 1951.

L'Anno di Maria, Vol. 4,
    by I. M. Vigo,
    Tip. S. Giuseppe degli Artigianelli, Torino, 1904.

OUR LADY OF ZEBRZYDOWSKI

CALVARY WAS A SMALL TOWN in Poland, fifteen to twenty miles from Cracow. About six miles from Calvary, in the late seventeenth century there lived Stanislaus Paszkowski, who had in his house a statue of the Blessed Virgin. It had been in the family for several generations.

One day in May, 1671, as the family was assembled in prayer before the statue, tears of blood suddenly began to drop from its eyes.

When the story of this event spread throughout the countryside, great crowds of people came to Stanislaus' house to venerate the image.

In order to make the statue more available to the people, Stanislaus gave it to a young nobleman named Zebrzydowski, and he built a chapel for it in Calvary.

Numerous favors were granted at the shrine and pilgrims came not only from all parts of Poland, but from Hungary and more distant countries.

Pope Leo XIII (1878-1903) authorized a solemn coronation of the statue under the title "Our Lady of Zebrzydowski —Calvary."

Whether this shrine is still in existence, we have not been able to determine.

BIBLIOGRAPHY:

Apparitions and Shrines of Heaven's Bright Queen,
by Wm. J. Walsh,
T. J. Cary Co., New York, 1904.
La Madonna Santuari e Feste,
by P. Umberto Bonomo, C.SS.R.,
Vatican City Religious Book Co., Inc., New York, 1948.

OUR LADY, QUEEN OF THE UNIVERSE

WHILE IT IS entirely possible that this title may have been informally used at an earlier date, it is definite that it was formally applied in 1900.

In that year, from September 6th to the 8th, the first National Mariological Congress was held in Lyons, France. This congress expressed the desire of Catholics regarding the royalty of the Blessed Virgin in the following words: " (1) that after the consecration of the human race to the Sacred Heart — which had occurred in June, 1899 — there follow the consecration of the universe to the Most Blessed Virgin under the title of Queen of the Universe; (2) that a feast, called the feast of the Universal Royalty of Mary, be celebrated every year with its own office; (3) finally, that the Holy Father deign to add to the Litany of Loreto, the invocation: "Queen of the Universe, pray for us."

The late Pope Pius XII in a radio address to some 800,000 persons, gathered at Fátima, Portugal, on May 13, 1946, on the occasion of the crowning of the statue of Our Lady of Fátima, formally used and thus approved this title.

In the course of his address the Holy Father said: "A precious crown, indeed, expressive symbol of love and gratitude! But this immense concourse of your people, the fervor of your prayers, the thunder of your acclamation, all the sacred enthusiasm which vibrated in you unrestrainably, and, then the sacred rite which has just been accomplished in this hour of incomparable triumph of our Most Holy Mother, evokes to Our spirit another scene: When, amid other multitudes still less capable of being numbered, other acclamations still more ardent, other triumphs still more divine, in that hour forever solemn of the undying day of Eternity, the glorious Virgin entered triumphantly into the Heavenly Country. Surrounded by the blessed hierarchies, and angelic choirs, she was brought before the throne of the Most Blessed Trinity, had set upon her head a triple diadem of glory, and, seated at the right hand of the Immortal King of Ages, was presented to the heavenly court as Crowned *Queen of the Universe.*"

On November 1, 1954, Pope Pius XII officially crowned the famous Madonna "Salus Populi Romani" (Salvation of the Roman People - venerated in the Basilica of St. Mary Major, in Rome) under the title, "Queen of the Universe."

There is a huge statue of Our Lady, 32 feet high, cast of copper and bronze, weighing 6 tons, on top of Orient Heights, East Boston, U. S. A. At the close of 1954, the Marian Year, Cardinal Cushing dedicated it as "The Madonna, Queen of the Universe."

BIBLIOGRAPHY:

    Our Lady's Digest,
       May, 1956, condensed from *Fátima Findings.*
    Fátima Findings,
       November, 1954, republished from *Our Lady of Fátima,* 1949, Appendix C.
       by Archbishop Finbar Ryan, Newman Press.
    Ave Maria, August 4, 1956.
    On the Queenship of Mary
       (*Ad Caeli Reginam*), Encyclical Letter of Pope Pius XII, Oct. 11, 1954.

P9-AQK-538

SELLING OUT

SELLING OUT

How we are letting Japan buy our land, our industries, our financial institutions, and our future

DOUGLAS FRANTZ and CATHERINE COLLINS
Foreword by Congressman John D. Dingell
Chairman, U.S. House Committee on Energy and Commerce

CB
CONTEMPORARY
BOOKS
CHICAGO · NEW YORK

Library of Congress Cataloging-in-Publication Data

Frantz, Douglas.
  Selling out : how we are letting Japan buy our land, our
industries, our financial institutions, and our future / Douglas
Frantz and Catherine Collins.
      p.   cm.
  Bibliography: p.
  Includes index.
  ISBN 0-8092-4518-3 : $19.95
  1. Investments, Japanese—United States.   I. Collins, Catherine.
II. Title.
HG4910.F75   1989
332.6'7352'073—dc19   88-36662
                                                                              CIP

Published by Contemporary Books, Inc.
180 North Michigan Avenue, Chicago, Illinois 60601
Manufactured in the United States of America
International Standard Book Number: 0-8092-4518-3

Published simultaneously in Canada by Beaverbooks, Ltd.
195 Allstate Parkway, Valleywood Business Park
Markham, Ontario L3R 4T8 Canada

For our parents,
Paul and Ruth Ann Collins,
Donald and Jody Frantz

CONTENTS

FOREWORD

WOULD OUR ECONOMIC INDEPENDENCE be jeopardized if OPEC owned American oil companies? If not one American company made silicon wafers, would it hurt our national security? If foreign-owned companies financed American election campaigns, would it undermine our political sovereignty? Could we depend on foreign-owned companies to preserve and promote American jobs?

These questions were barely raised in the 1988 presidential campaign. Even more disturbing, if they had been raised, it's not clear we could have answered them. Foreign investment in the United States has tripled in the last seven years, according to the most conservative estimates. Yet we know little about its effect on our national security, economic independence, employment patterns, and political system.

Foreign investment in the United States has become too influential to remain hidden in the shadows. This provocative book sheds critical light on the subject and seems certain to turn up the heat on an issue that demands national debate. This

vii

book, and the political and economic issues it raises, deserves the attention of everyone concerned about America's ability to control its own destiny.

Fortunately, some signs indicate that the American people are beginning to recognize the significance of the issue. Senator Lloyd Bentsen, the Democratic vice-presidential candidate, struck a responsive chord during the vice-presidential debate when he voiced concern over the new influence of foreign money on American lives. In Indiana, thirty-two-year-old Evan Bayh became the state's first Democratic governor in two decades in large part by raising important questions about the long-term competitive consequences of so much government-aided investment by the Japanese.

And the House of Representatives demonstrated in the 1988 term a willingness to come to grips with the issue by approving legislation aimed at gathering data on precisely how much of the United States has been sold to foreign investors. Unfortunately, this legislation was lost in the last-minute maneuvering over the trade bill.

As this book makes clear, the subject will not go away. The question is, What should be done?

The answer, as the authors indicate early, is not to wall off the United States to investors from Japan or the United Kingdom or West Germany. Foreign investment has played a vital role in forging the economy of the United States from the inception of the nation. Foreign money built our railroads. It continues to play a significant role today.

But today that role has changed. America is addicted to foreign investment. The Japanese finance the U.S. budget deficit through their purchases of U.S. Treasury bonds. Certain industries once dominated by U.S. corporations—industries that contributed to this nation's high standard of living and made it the best place in the world to live—have already been taken over by foreign corporations. More Americans than ever work for foreign employers. This book raises important questions about whether these employers are fulfilling their roles as good corporate citizens.

But public policy has been ill-equipped to keep up with the

changes wrought by the accelerating foreign investment in the United States. The information currently collected by the government is incomplete, inaccurate, and a secret—even from the Congress—by law. It is virtually useless to the analysis and decision making of policymakers—Congress and the executive branch alike. Crucial questions raised by the growing influence of foreign corporations and governments over U.S. affairs simply cannot be answered.

We have almost no way of knowing if a hostile nation like Libya or Iran is buying one of our high-technology companies. We have almost no way of knowing whether a corrupt foreign official like Ferdinand Marcos is buying American real estate. (In fact, Marcos's American holdings were finally brought to light in the Philippines.) And we have almost no way of tracking the American investments of drug traffickers, who can launder millions through investments in the United States.

This is in sharp contrast to other countries. Japan prohibits foreign ownership of more than 50 percent in its energy companies and limits foreign ownership of high-tech firms to 25 percent. Japan, Canada, and a host of other countries require foreign ownership to be cleared in advance.

Last year, the U.S. administration and foreign interests vigorously opposed legislation requiring the most basic disclosure—a registration form the size of a postcard—of foreign investors. The truth is that America is selling its productive capacity to pay for consumption. We are now the world's largest debtor nation. Foreign investors are eager to buy not because their purchases are secret but because they are secure in the world's most stable democracy.

The problems defined so sharply in this book must be dealt with. But first we have to know the facts. Policymakers cannot operate in the dark any longer. The issue has become too inextricably linked with the nation's economic well-being to operate without the most precise data possible.

Who owns America? And who controls America's future? Once that information is in hand, Congress and the American public can begin to grapple with the complexities, consequences, and challenges of foreign investment in the United States described in the following pages.

> Congressman John D. Dingell,
> Chairman, U.S. House Committee on Energy
>   and Commerce
> Chairman, U.S. House Subcommittee on
>   Oversight and Investigations

ACKNOWLEDGMENTS

WHEN WE STARTED THIS PROJECT, the subject matter was to be foreign investment in the United States and its potential impact on the nation's economy. Over the course of our reporting, we sharpened the focus to emphasize investments by the Japanese, who emerged as the most voracious and canny of the foreigners buying up the United States. And we came to recognize that the impact of all foreign investment extends far beyond economic matters.

The conclusions in this book are our own. But they are based on the insights, opinions, and expertise of literally hundreds of other people. Some of them may object strongly to the concerns voiced in these pages, but we have tried to record the facts fairly and accurately.

These people fall into two categories, although there is overlap among them. First, we interviewed more than 200 people across the United States, from factory workers to congressmen, waitresses to leading economists. For the kindness of their time, we owe them an enormous debt.

We are indebted also to the dozens of American journalists

who have covered the emerging story of foreign investment in the United States fairly and with remarkable thoroughness. Their work added immeasurably to our own efforts and we offer all of them our sincere thanks.

We cannot single out everyone we interviewed or name all of the journalists whose work was useful in this brief space. However, we found that three publications have covered the issue of foreign investment with a distinction that bears noting.

Business Week has been excellent, particularly in its cover story on the growing political influence of the Japanese on American public policy. The *Wall Street Journal*, as always on a big business story, is a constant source of first-rate information. And the business staff of the *Los Angeles Times*, under the stewardship of our friend Martin Baron, has been exceptional. Particularly insightful from the *Times* were the articles on Fujitsu and Fairchild by William Rempel and Donna Walters and the series on working for the Japanese by James Flanigan, Michael Hiltzik, Sam Jameson, Jonathan Peterson, James Risen, Jim Schachter, Karl Schoenberger, and Nancy Yoshihara.

Two recent books provided information and inspiration, and we recommend them heartily. They are *Trading Places: How We Allowed Japan to Take the Lead*, by Clyde V. Prestowitz, Jr., and *Buying Into America*, by Martin and Susan Tolchin.

We urge readers to consult the extensive section of notes at the back of the book, where we have tried to note the many sources of information gathered by others that proved invaluable to us.

SELLING OUT

INTRODUCTION

A LITTLE MORE THAN TWO DECADES AGO, a French journalist named Jean-Jacques Servan-Schreiber wrote one of the most influential books in the history of postwar Europe. It was called *The American Challenge*, and it set forth in simple and profound terms the economic threat to Europe by the rising tide of investment from the United States.

Writing in 1967, Servan-Schreiber warned: "Fifteen years from now it is quite possible that the world's third greatest industrial power, just after the United States, will not be Europe, but *'American industry in Europe.'* "

The book was a reasoned call to action, stating its findings with clarity and emotion yet avoiding the crippling pitfalls of xenophobia and anti-Americanism. Servan-Schreiber recognized this U.S. investment for what it truly was: a symptom of the economic and political malaise of Europe, not its cause. He also realized that, unless Europe were awakened, it was witnessing "the prelude to our own historical bankruptcy."

World events changed the course of history. The giant American multinationals did not conquer Europe. One reason was

1

external: the oil crisis in the early 1970s forced the American companies to pull back. Another was internal: responding to the challenge set forth by Servan-Schreiber, Europe's industries were roused to action, and they learned to adapt the American methods and to draw on their own economic strengths.

But change did not stop there. The pendulum of history has swung so far that today it is the United States confronting a challenge from outside its borders. Today it is the United States that is on the verge of being swamped in a flood of foreign investment. Innovation and competitiveness, once thought solely the province of American industry, are now in the hands of foreign nations, most notably the Japanese.

Indeed, one need look no further than this single fact to see how radically the world has changed since Servan-Schreiber's manifesto: *The American Challenge* contains only seven brief mentions of Japan, including the observation that Japan would never be able to compete as an equal with the United States.

Today, Japan boasts the most powerful economy in the world. Its management techniques and industrial innovations are the envy of all nations. Its giant multinational firms are spreading across the globe.

And the destination of choice for these would-be conquerors is the United States. So much Japanese investment has flowed into the United States in the 1980s that the nation is in danger of seeing its economic sovereignty washed away in a tide of yen, its history pawned to a foreign power.

The parallels between the United States as it heads into the 1990s and Europe near the close of the 1960s are astonishing, and the necessity for an awakening among the economic and political leaders of the nation is just as critical.

The Japanese challenge will not be met by closing the United States to foreign investment. The wave of populist concern should stir the politicians to reasoned action but must not be allowed to sweep aside the nation's historic openness and free enterprise system. The challenge will be defeated by a concerted national policy to regain supremacy and to harness the vitality of foreign investment and ideas for the good of the United States.

And what is the challenge? It is not only financial and industrial, though there are elements of both. No. It is a challenge to a nation's intellectual creativity and ability to transform ideas into products and concepts into revolutions in the workplace. If the challenge is not met, the United States is destined to become a second-rate economic power that is always on the brink of disaster and must always look abroad for its survival.

Many Americans feel that these problems should be left to the politicians and economists. But they are wrong. The dangers have the potential to affect the job of virtually every American, and the solutions must flow from a consensus response that begins with the American public. Otherwise, the politicians will lack the guts to confront the issues and the economists and business leaders will be allowed to ignore the problems.

This book is designed to set forth the facts, raise the necessary questions, and offer some solutions, with neither malice nor antipathy toward any foreign investors. Foreign investment is changing the face of the economy in the United States and threatening the nation's economic and political sovereignty in subtle and profound ways. Unless Americans have the facts and understand the risks of the path the United States is on, there is no possibility of meeting the challenge and moving vigorously and freely into the next century.

1
LOSING SOVEREIGNTY

AT 9:30 A.M. ON MONDAY, OCTOBER 19, 1987, the bell rang on the floor of the New York Stock Exchange signaling the start of the most tumultuous day in the history of U.S. financial markets. A wave of sell orders that had built up over the weekend cascaded over the stock market, pushing its computerized trading system beyond the limits and driving the Dow-Jones Industrial Average down at an unstoppable pace.

The chaos was repeated at the futures exchanges in Chicago, where harried traders could not keep track of orders, let alone keep up with them. Back in New York, the Federal Reserve Board was forced to demand that the nation's biggest banks provide billions of dollars in credit to keep brokerage houses open. In Washington, the nation's financial regulators conducted frantic telephone conferences in a fruitless attempt to stanch the financial hemorrhage.

As news of the crashing markets spread, small investors across the country tried to call their brokers at Merrill Lynch and Prudential-Bache and countless other retail brokerages to dump shares at any price before they were wiped out. The sell orders

were so vast that phone lines were jammed and thousands of
people could not even get through.

In this era of the global economy and instantaneous communications, the panic spread, and stock markets in Tokyo, Hong
Kong, Sydney, and London quivered and prices plummeted.

By the end of what quickly became known as Black Monday,
John Phelan, chairman of the New York Stock Exchange, was
saying that the nation's markets had nearly suffered "a meltdown," appropriating the terminology of a nuclear disaster to
describe a momentous financial disaster.

The New York Stock Exchange dropped 508 points in a single
day, losing 22 percent of its total value and wiping out $1 trillion
worth of wealth. An incredible 604 million shares were traded,
three times the volume of a heavy day and double the previous
one-day record. The reverberations continued throughout the
week.

For millions of Americans, October 19, 1987, came to symbol-
ize the new vulnerability of their once-invincible nation. It was
one of those rare days in history when the shift in power from
one empire to another can be marked, precisely and indelibly.

Behind the stock market crash was a bitter lesson for the
United States, a lesson that still has not been learned by the
nation's business and government leaders. The crash demonstrated dramatically that the United States has lost control over
its own economy, that decisions made in Tokyo can affect the
standard of living and well-being of millions of Americans.

Commissions and panels were created to search for causes in
the wreckage of the crash, and they found plenty of villains
among the professional speculators and giant institutional investors who had pumped up the market like a giant balloon and
then abandoned it in a matter of hours.

But none of the reports put the official blame on the shoulders
of the Japanese investors whose actions had triggered the collapse. The nation's financial markets and the very financing of
the federal debt had become too dependent on the Japanese to
risk the repercussions of placing responsibility on the investors
they had been wooing throughout the 1980s.

The United States has become addicted to foreign investment.

As a way to finance the huge federal deficit, inflate real estate prices, grease the political system, and create new jobs. But like many addictions, this one has strong negative side effects, which could prove fatal.

No one knows how much foreign investment there is in the United States. Government attempts to monitor it are slipshod at best, and U.S. laws allow foreign investors to hide behind shell companies and wide gaps within the reporting laws. But no one disputes that foreign investment has increased dramatically in the 1980s, forcing the United States to weigh the international economic repercussions of the most basic national decisions.

No country has invested at the pace of the Japanese, who are benefiting from their own huge trade advantages and basic thriftiness. And no country has carried out its investments with the strategic mandate that motivates the Japanese. As a result, they have gained enormous leverage over certain sectors of the American economy, a fact demonstrated clearly by the stock market crash of 1987.

The most thorough and respected of the postcrash reports was produced by a commission of academics and Wall Street professionals appointed by President Ronald Reagan. The chairman of the commission was Nicholas Brady, a former U.S. senator and chairman of the Wall Street investment firm of Dillon Read & Co., who would go on to become secretary of the treasury in the summer of 1988.

Despite its thoroughness, the commission's findings were sanitized for politics, and the cause of the crash was apportioned among a variety of acceptable suspects. But six months after the crash, in a little-noticed speech to institutional investors in Washington, Brady put aside the official niceties and pinpointed the cause of the crash.

"People ask me, 'What was it that blew it off on the 19th of October? Was it the twin deficits [budget and trade]? Was it the Rostenkowski [tax] legislation? What was it?' " Brady said. "I don't think it was any of those things that really was the trigger."

"The real trigger," he said, "was that the Japanese came in for their own reasons and sold an enormous amount of U.S. government bonds, and drove the thirty-year government [bond] up through 10 percent. And when it got through 10 percent, that got a lot of people thinking, 'Gee, that's four times the return you get on equity. Here we go, inflation again.'

"That, to me, is what really started the 19th—a worry by the Japanese about U.S. currency."

Japanese concerns had heightened the week before the crash when the U.S. trade figures for August showed that imports continued to exceed exports by record amounts despite nearly three years of a declining dollar. The failure of the United States to show progress in balancing trade created a concern that the federal government might allow the dollar to slip even further.

Those fears caused the Japanese not only to stop buying but to begin selling their huge holdings in U.S. treasury bonds. The sale meant the market was flooded with bonds, and interest rates had to be increased to attract investors. An increase in interest rates can be a harbinger of inflation, which causes jitters among investors. It also can lure money from the stock market to the bond market, which in turn destabilizes the markets.

The Japanese sale and the following interest rate increase on treasury bonds caused a wave of selling that pushed the market down 108 points on Friday, October 16, and primed the pump for Monday.

The events really began a month before October 19. In September, interest rates jumped significantly because of Japanese concerns over the dollar and their reluctance to buy U.S. bonds. The lesson of the interest rate run-up was pointed out by Richard Koo, a senior economist with Japan's Nomura Securities, who smugly told *Forbes* magazine in mid-September 1987, "Think of that jump as tuition for America. Now you have learned how dependent you are on foreign capital."

By 1987, Japanese investors were exerting so much influence through their purchases of treasury bonds that they virtually determined the interest rates set by the U.S. treasury. Often before the monthly treasury bond auctions in Washington, worried U.S. officials whispered, "Where are the Japanese?"

Japanese investment in foreign securities, almost entirely in the United States, began zooming upward in 1983, doubling every year to reach a peak of $102 billion in 1986. When the dollar began to decline, they cut back their volume and as a result invested only $88 billion in 1987. Still, even the Bank of Tokyo recognized in a mid-1988 report that the level of U.S. investment by the Japanese "has become a key factor in American money and capital markets."

This dependence rolls directly downhill to determine such widespread factors as the interest rates paid on home mortgages by millions of Americans. Not only are current mortgage rates determined by the interest rate paid on federal bonds, but many of the popular adjustable-rate home mortgages are tied directly to the interest rate on the bonds.

So if the Japanese decide they need another half a percentage point in interest to buy U.S. bonds, millions of Americans wind up paying more for their homes. Such is life in a nation dependent on foreign capital.

The assertion that Japanese concerns over the dollar could trigger the crash of the New York Stock Exchange would have been unthinkable a decade before, or even five years earlier.

But by October 1987, Japanese investors were the dominant players in the U.S. bond market. They basically financed the rising federal deficit by loaning money to the U.S. government through their purchases of treasury bonds. And they were able to push it to the brink of collapse.

The crash was a graphic example of what happens when a nation loses economic sovereignty to an outside power, even a friendly one. It was a lesson in the perils of the rising levels of foreign investment in the United States, particularly the concentrated investments being made by the Japanese.

Foreign investment evolves from benign to dangerous when decisions affecting a nation's economic, political, and military destinies are made in foreign capital cities. With it comes a loss of sovereignty, putting the nation in danger of becoming a colony of its foreign owners.

It is quite possible that within a decade, the United States will find itself in the position of being a satellite of the powerful industrial machine of Japan. When that happens, the life of every American will be touched by the power of foreign investment, from conditions on the job to the cost of a home mortgage.

Already the United States is a poorer nation because of the vast amounts its citizens owe foreign investors. Real earnings of workers have fallen, and health, retirement, and vacation benefits are less generous than they once were. Although the productivity of U.S. workers has risen about 6 percent since 1977, real hourly wages have dropped 6.5 percent.

Already the growing U.S. foreign debt has made the country more vulnerable to pressure from foreign investors that influences U.S. interest rates, the value of the dollar, economic stability, political policy, and employment patterns.

"Is this the beginning of the end of the U.S. as a world economic power?" asks Senator James Exon, a Nebraska Democrat. "I'm fearful."

Cautions Senator Richard Shelby, a Democrat from Alabama: "Sooner or later, the people who own large parts of the industrial machinery of this country will influence our trade, monetary and foreign policies. If you pay the piper, you call the tune."

Foreign investors, particularly the Japanese with their penchant for U.S. government bonds, have been paying for the excesses of the United States for several years now.

The position of the United States as the world's largest debtor worsened dramatically in 1987, largely as a result of increased foreign investment to finance the federal government's deficit spending. That means a larger portion of the national income will have to be earmarked to pay the interest for years to come. A mammoth foreign debt creates a chronic drain on the vitality of the U.S. economy and strengthens the power of the foreign nations that hold U.S. debt and use their cash surpluses to acquire more and more U.S. industrial facilities and real estate.

"By the end of the Reagan administration we will owe something like $500 billion to the rest of the world," Lester C. Thurow, dean of the Sloan School of Management at Massachusetts Institute of Technology and author of *The Zero Sum Solution: Building a World Class American Economy*, said in an interview in October 1988. "We are selling America to anybody who is willing to buy. And the Japanese happen to be buying much of it."

For Thurow, the problem is not so much that the Japanese are buying up America, but that Americans are willing to sell out so cheaply.

"I've always been surprised at how cheaply we are willing to sell our technology," he said. "It is amazing that we place such a low value on it. It is partly our financial system. Technology almost never pays off in a short period of time, say five years. But the short-term outlook is something that is built into the American system. Should people care? The basic answer is that if you don't, your standard of living is going to suffer."

Since the late 1970s, American corporations have abandoned core businesses, often selling them to foreigners. They have lost their technological edge in industry after industry to foreign companies. As a result, the standard of living of most Americans has declined. Average wages have fallen, the gulf between rich and poor has widened, and foreign investors have gained unprecedented control over the nation's future.

No nation holds more leverage over the United States than Japan, which increased its U.S. investments faster than any other foreign country in the 1980s. And no nation is shaped better by its own history and nationalistic necessities than Japan to exercise control over the United States.

For unlike the United States, where corporate plans are measured by the year or the quarter, the Japanese have a centuries-old tradition of thinking twenty or thirty years ahead. This ability enables them to foresee causes and effects of economic policies and manufacturing decisions from a perspective not used by Americans. It allows them to be patient in laying the groundwork for economic domination of the United States.

Already the Japanese are making decisions that affect the lives of millions of Americans and influence the nation's political process and economic health in a way far more dramatic than the effects of any other foreign investor. More than 300,000 Americans work for Japanese bosses, and the number is expected to grow to 1 million in less than a decade. And conflicts are likely to grow, too.

Already lawsuits over sex and race discrimination are becoming more frequent as Americans discover the enormous cultural gulf that divides their nation from Japan. The U.S. Equal Employment Opportunity Commission found evidence of discrimination at the plants of all three major Japanese automakers in the United States.

"I don't think we should import those approaches which are antagonistic to civil rights or to equal employment opportunity laws in this country," says Clarence Thomas, chairman of the Equal Employment Opportunity Commission.

Even Americans who do not experience overt discrimination are finding that working in a Japanese-owned plant requires a continual effort to bridge the cultural gap that divides them from their Japanese bosses.

For thousands of assembly-line workers, the gap means working without union representation. For many executives, it means sitting through a high-level meeting without understanding a word because it is conducted in Japanese.

"We're *gaijin* [foreigners] in our own country," James Ristow said after he was fired by Toshiba's Southern California headquarters after thirteen years as a sales executive. When Ristow's division was closed, forty-one Americans lost their jobs and no Japanese were terminated.

Many labor experts feel that these conflicts will emerge as a major controversy in the coming years as more and more Americans wind up working for the Japanese, whether they are rubber workers at Firestone in Akron, Ohio, or autoworkers at Nissan in Smyrna, Tennessee, or winemakers at Chateau St. Jean in Kenwood, California.

As Japanese business interests in the United States have expanded, so has Japanese influence on the U.S. political process.

Like their American counterparts, Japanese businessmen and investors have proven adept at employing high-paid lobbyists and lawyers to carry their concerns to Congress and many state legislatures. Also like the Americans, they spend freely for these services; an estimated $100 million in 1988 alone. Unlike their American counterparts, their ultimate political allegiance lies thousands of miles from Washington, D.C.

At no time has that divergence of interests been clearer than in the spring of 1988, when Japan's hired lobbyists and lawyers created what the *Los Angeles Times* called "one of the most pervasive and sophisticated lobbying efforts in Washington in many years"—the successful muting of congressional outrage over Toshiba's illegal sale of secret submarine technology to the Soviet Union.

In March 1987, it was disclosed that Toshiba, Japan's largest semiconductor manufacturer and the world's sixth largest electronics company, had exported sophisticated milling machines and computer software to the Soviet Union illegally in 1983 and 1984 through a subsidiary, Toshiba Machine Company.

The equipment permitted the Soviets to build submarines with quieter propellers, which made the vessels and their nuclear armaments much more difficult for American listening systems to detect and raised a new threat to Western security.

The diversion of the technology violated agreements between Japan and the United States, and the Reagan administration said the transfer would cost the United States up to $100 billion to develop new abilities to track the quieter Soviet subs.

Congressional outrage was sharp. In July 1987, eight congressmen wielding sledgehammers stood on the steps of the Capitol and smashed a Toshiba radio-cassette player. One House member said the company deserved a "Benedict Arnold award."

What Toshiba got was the stiffest sanction in U.S. history, at least for a while. The Senate version of the omnibus trade bill passed that summer contained a total ban on imports from the huge Japanese manufacturing firm, which had built a $2.5 billion market in the United States. The House passed a milder, but still stinging, version that would have limited retaliation to the specific Toshiba subsidiary involved in the sale to the Soviets.

The Japanese government reacted with its own outrage, pressuring the Reagan administration to remove the sanctions in the name of preserving the alliance between the two countries and demanding the right to handle the case itself.

In February 1988, as the trade bill moved toward passage in Congress, a senior Pentagon official moved to calm the anger and pave the way for removing the sanctions by raising doubts about the extent of the damage to U.S. security from the sale of the submarine technology.

"Despite allegations of tens [of billions] or even $100 billion in damages, our Navy cannot determine the direct costs of this diversion to U.S. national security because the Soviets had quiet propellers three years before the first diversion, and we had already planned R&D to deal with this development," Richard Armitage, assistant secretary of defense, wrote to Congressman Les Aspin, the Wisconsin Democrat who heads the House Armed Services Committee.

The letter directly contradicted earlier statements by administration officials and U.S. intelligence officers. It went on to say that the Defense Department opposed the sanctions against Toshiba.

The Armitage letter was the opening salvo in Toshiba's enormous lobbying effort to gut the sanctions. The message of Toshiba's lobbyists and those from the American companies that rallied to their aid was simple and effective: if you hurt Toshiba, you hurt American workers. Nothing gets the attention of a congressman quicker than talk of losing jobs in his district.

Toshiba America employs 6,000 Americans across the country. They make television sets and microwave ovens in Tennessee, television tubes in New York, engineering controls in Oklahoma, lap-top computers in California, and copying-machine parts in South Dakota. In addition, thousands more Americans work for firms that use key components imported from Toshiba or sell Toshiba imports under their own labels.

"They came in waves, first the Washington lobbyists and then people from companies in my district," said Congressman Donald Lukens, an Ohio Republican who found out that Japanese firms were working in six of the nine counties of his congressional district.

Toshiba America hired dozens of high-level lobbyists, ranging from former Nixon administration lawyer Leonard Garment to former Democratic Congressman Michael Barnes. Mudge Rose Guthrie Alexander & Ferdon, a powerful Washington law firm where former President Richard Nixon was once a partner, received $4.2 million in fees for lobbying from Toshiba for the last half of 1987 alone.

The lobbying effort cost far more than the money paid to

Mudge Rose. Republican Senator John Heinz of Pennsylvania estimates that the actual cost of Toshiba's effort was closer to $9 million, including substantial amounts spent by lobbyists for Toshiba America, the wholly owned subsidiary of the Japanese company. But that money was not reported to the Justice Department because Toshiba America is regarded by law as a U.S. corporation, and its lobbyists are not required to register as foreign agents.

"In all the twenty-one years I have been in public office I've never seen a lobbying campaign so orchestrated at so many levels," Senator Jake Garn, the Utah Republican, told the *Washington Post*.

Garn, a strong supporter of the sanctions, said he was lobbied by Japanese government officials, representatives of Toshiba and its American subsidiary, Reagan administration officials, and U.S. distributors of Toshiba products.

The American grassroots element of the Toshiba campaign made it a watershed for Japan, according to Ronald Morse, a specialist in Japanese lobbying at the Library of Congress in Washington. "It marks a new dimension and is a warning that the Japanese are more sophisticated than they had been, and their role is much more significant," said Morse.

In the end, it paid off. In late April 1988, the final version of the trade bill was passed. It nearly obliterated the punishment for Toshiba. The bill banned imports from Toshiba Machine for three years, which could cost the company up to $300 million over the period. But the parent company was allowed to save almost all of its $2.5 billion-a-year U.S. business, because only U.S. government agencies were prohibited from buying its products for the three-year period. In addition, even that ban was lifted for products that only Toshiba supplies.

As for the Japanese handling the punishment themselves, a Japanese court gave suspended sentences to two executives of the Toshiba subsidiary, and the company was fined $15,700.

The argument that proved most effective in influencing Congress turned out to be the potential effect on American workers. But the real issue was sovereignty, or the United States' lack of it, because it had become abundantly clear that the Japanese could wage a very successful lobbying campaign in the halls of Congress and the back offices of the executive branch.

The Toshiba lobbying demonstrated convincingly that the United States is wide open to economic blackmail as a result of Japan's heavy investment in the United States and the reliance of U.S. industry on Japan for key goods. Confronted by what a high-ranking Defense Department official had labeled publicly the "single worst case of technology transfer that has ever occurred," the U.S. Congress could not react independently in punishing a Japanese company.

In early 1988, an unnamed Reagan administration representative admitted to the *Washington Post* that he was concerned that the rising Japanese investment in the United States risked a shift of policy decisions from Washington to Tokyo. "Then we will become merely the day-to-day managers," he said. "We don't want the situation to degenerate into 'their minds and our muscle.' "

That is clearly the direction in which the situation is headed, as the Japanese take the lead in high-technology and other capital-intensive industries, shift the low-end work to their U.S. factories in order to escape protectionism, and create the mechanisms to protect their growing investments in the United States.

Despite the concerns of the unnamed Reagan official and such stark evidence as the market crash and the Toshiba lobbying campaign, America's leaders have failed to recognize the Japanese challenge or the degree to which the nation's sovereignty has been lost already.

As a result, they have failed to create the proper policies to respond to what can be called justifiably an economic war with Japan, which already has destroyed some American industries and threatens the ability of the nation to rebound from its staggering trade deficit and deteriorating standard of living.

For the millions of Americans who believe they are unaffected by the selling out of the United States to the Japanese, consider the impact of the $23.5 billion in interest payments on U.S. treasury bonds paid to foreigners in 1987 alone. Most of these debtholders are Japanese.

Budget experts said the amount crowded out spending on

domestic programs and represented three times the amount requested for all federal housing programs, 50 percent more than the federal education budget, and more than the total requested to operate the national parks, airline safety, trade promotion, cancer research, and the Environmental Protection Agency combined.

As our debt deepens, the nation can expect to be paying more than twice that amount in interest payments to foreign investors in the year 2000. The implications for every person in the United States are frightening.

2
A NATION FOR SALE

FOREIGN INVESTMENT KEEPS THREATENING to become a central economic, social, and political issue in the United States.

Richard Gephardt, the Missouri congressman, tried unsuccessfully to win the Democratic presidential nomination in 1988 by campaigning on a single issue: that the country had lost control of its economic destiny to foreigners.

Governor Michael Dukakis of Massachusetts, the man who won the Democratic nomination, and his running mate, Senator Lloyd Bentsen of Texas, raised the issue briefly in the final month of the presidential campaign. Indeed, it was Bentsen who first brought the issue to the surface in his televised debate with the Republican vice presidential candidate, Senator Dan Quayle.

Bentsen voiced concern over the levels of foreign investment in the United States, but Quayle countered with the familiar Reagan administration panacea that foreign investors had created jobs and were welcome in any number. The exchange did not grab headlines and the subject faded within days.

But it is not likely to go away forever. Paul Krugman, an influential economist at the Massachusetts Institute of Technology, puts the matter this way: "The political issue of the 1990s is going to be the foreign invasion of the U.S."

The question is, can we wait that long? The answer is no.

Unless the American public and its leaders confront the issue of foreign investment in reasoned yet urgent tones today, tomorrow will be too late. Already the United States has become what *Time* magazine called "a huge shopping mart in which foreigners are energetically filling up their carts."

The most recent figures from the U.S. Commerce Department showed that foreigners owned $1.536 trillion of U.S. government and corporate securities, factories, and land in 1987, an increase of 15 percent over 1986. While the figure represents only about 10 percent of all U.S. assets, at the current spending rate foreigners would own the entire country within fifty years.

More significantly, the Commerce Department figures showed that the value of U.S. assets owned by foreigners exceeded U.S. assets overseas by $368.23 billion in 1987, a jump of $100 billion in a single year. That widening gap marked a further deterioration in the U.S. position as the world's largest debtor nation.

The Commerce Department figures, which many experts believe seriously underreport foreign investment, are still accurate enough to demonstrate the trend among foreign nations.

The 1987 data showed that the British remained the biggest direct foreign investor in the United States, meaning they owned the greatest amount of tangible items, such as factories and real estate. The Netherlands was second, partly as a result of investment that flows through the secrecy haven of the Netherlands Antilles that could actually belong to anyone in the world.

Japan replaced Canada in third place in direct investments at the end of 1987, according to Commerce Department statistics. The Japanese increased their direct investment in the United States in 1987 by 24 percent. But when direct investments are combined with their vast holdings in government and corporate securities, called portfolio investments, the Japanese become the most influential foreign investors in the United States.

Since rising from the devastation of World War II, the Japanese have demonstrated a grim determination to undergo any sacrifice in order to obtain economic supremacy at home and abroad.

Japan is a tiny, resource-poor nation of islands, about the size of Montana and jammed with half the population of the United States. Only 20 percent of its land is habitable and, once farmland is subtracted, the amount available for development drops to 5 percent.

Harvard Business School professor Thomas K. McCraw aptly says: "Simply, there is no escape from the logic of Japan's physical setting: a very large population in a small and mostly barren land mass. Thus, whatever other national goals it might conceive for itself—a strong voice in world politics, wide recognition for its artists, honors for its athletes—Japan cannot, even for a moment, forget about its need to export."

Further, because Japan lacks the rich soil of the American breadbasket and the oil fields of the Arab nations, its exports must be manufactured goods in exchange for the raw materials it simply doesn't have. Thus, the Japanese are compelled by the simple need for survival to conquer the world's markets with their export-driven economy. The largest of those markets is the United States. And what could be a better way to conquer an economy than to buy it?

And they have bought huge chunks of the United States' choicest real estate and invested in its most influential and vital industries.

Investors from the Land of the Rising Sun have gobbled up huge portions of the most desirable land in Hawaii. They own three-fourths of the beachfront hotels in Honolulu, and in 1987 they bought four out of every ten condominiums that went on the market along world-famous Waikiki Beach. They are buying office buildings and golf courses. And the biggest development project in the history of the islands—the $3 billion Ko Olina resort—is a joint venture between a local businessman and the deep-pocketed Japanese construction giant, Kumagai Gumi.

There is a joke on the islands: Two captured Japanese officers are surveying the wreckage of Pearl Harbor. One Japanese officer says to the other, "Next time, we'll just buy Hawaii."

Downtown Los Angeles is 70 percent owned by foreigners, and half of those foreign-owned towers belong to the Japanese. The imprint of the Japanese on the city's skyline will be felt most

strongly when Mitsui Fudosan completes a fifty-two-story structure of polished Brazilian and Swedish granite on the most
prestigious location in the Los Angeles business district, the
corner of Wilshire and Figueroa. Japanese investors own the
buildings that house Bank of America's headquarters in Los
Angeles as well as the West Coast headquarters for New York's
Citicorp and Chase Manhattan banks.

Far more importantly, the Japanese own five of the ten largest
banks in California, which has the richest state economy in the
United States, with an output that makes it the eighth largest
economy in the world. By 1988, an estimated 100,000 Californi-
ans worked at nearly 1,000 U.S. subsidiaries of Japanese companies.

And as they have done in Hawaii, the aggressive Japanese
investors are moving out of downtown offices into residential
developments and resort property across Southern California.

A $1 billion resort is under construction by Japanese interests
near Palm Springs. The famed La Costa Country Club near San
Diego, built many years ago with tainted Teamsters money, was
bought in 1988 for $250 million by Sports Shinko, a Japanese
resort operator. Sports Shinko, which bought Greenlefe Resort
and Conference Center near Orlando Florida in 1987, plans to
create a worldwide chain of resorts specializing in golf and
tennis.

In Los Angeles, the Japanese ruffled the feathers of local
power brokers and social mavens by purchasing the Riviera
Country Club, once the playground of film stars such as Douglas
Fairbanks and Mary Pickford and the scene of Errol Flynn's
arrest for stealing the badge from an off-duty policeman at a
lavish dinner.

The low-key furor caused Hisao Kobayashi, at the time the
head of the California subsidiary of the world's largest bank,
Dai-Ichi Kangyo Bank, to telephone a prominent Japanese-
American businessman whose name had been mentioned in a
newspaper story about the deal.

"My friend, were you truly involved with the Riviera purchase?" asked Kobayashi. After being assured by the businessman that he was not involved, Kobayashi said with relief: "I am

glad. You know, there are some things that we just should not be buying."

Public reaction to the Riviera purchase grew so strong that the anonymous Japanese buyers were forced to scale back their plans to buying a 49 percent interest in the club with an option to buy the remainder in a year, after tempers cool.

"If they perceive the Riviera sale to cause a major Japan-bashing situation, I think they will probably not proceed with the acquisition," warned William Keogh, a Los Angeles real estate agent, in the summer of 1988.

In September 1988, the purchaser came out of the closet. It was Marukin Shoji Company, a Japanese real estate and construction firm, which was making its first major purchase outside of Japan. Despite the clamor, Noboru Watanabe, chairman of the company's American subsidiary, signed a formal purchase agreement for 49 percent of the historic country club.

The Japanese hate nothing so much as public embarrassment or spectacle, and some established Japanese businessmen have been chagrined by the ostentatious and pervasive purchases made by their countrymen. They fear the potential of a backlash that would curtail their acquisitions.

Hawaii and California, with their view toward the Pacific Ocean and their cultural diversity, are the favorite investment havens for the Japanese; estimates of Japanese holdings in those two states range as high as $7.2 billion in Hawaii and $7 billion in California.

But rather than the stopping point, those two states are only the beginning of the Japanese investment invasion. Across the United States, they own skyscrapers in any city worthy of having a tall building. Of the fifteen largest purchases of existing office buildings by foreigners in the United States since 1986, all have been by the Japanese. They have included the $640 million acquisition of Arco Plaza in Los Angeles by Shuwa Investments and the $610 million Exxon Building in New York City by Mitsui Fudosan. Both were the highest prices ever paid for buildings in the respective cities.

In Chicago alone, the Japanese have bought or built thirteen major downtown buildings in recent years. Nissei Realty paid

$141 million for the forty-one-story Prudential Plaza in 1986 and announced plans to finance a sixty-four-story tower next door. Dai-Ichi Kangyo Bank, the world's largest bank, paid about half that amount for an office building at 101 Wacker Drive. Another giant Japanese bank, Sumitomo Trust, paid $50 million for the Xerox Center in the heart of downtown Chicago, and a joint venture between a Japanese life insurance company and a Japanese bank expects to complete the $360 million AT&T Corporate Center in downtown Chicago in 1989.

Late in the summer of 1988, Kato Kagatsu, a Japanese corn-syrup firm, struck a deal to acquire the 2,000-room Chicago Hyatt Hotel, one of the world's largest, for $260 million.

"American real estate is cheap, especially to Japanese firms and families," said Robert Aliber, professor of international economics and finance at the Graduate School of Business at the University of Chicago. "The Japanese came into Chicago tepidly at first, and now are moving more aggressively."

In New York, Japanese interests have acquired at least a dozen major office buildings and hotels in Manhattan. The 1987 acquisitions alone included a $670 million interest in two of Citicorp's Manhattan office buildings by Dai-Ichi Mutual Life Insurance Company; 666 Fifth Avenue, $500 million, Sumitomo Realty and Development; 919 Third Avenue, $325 million, Nomura Securities; and the Essex House hotel on Central Park South by Nikko Hotels, which also developed a giant riverfront hotel in Chicago.

In Washington, the list is almost as long and includes such transactions as Nissei Realty's purchase of the American Medical Association building at 1101 Vermont Avenue NW for $36 million; Mitsubishi Bank's development of a $200 million office complex called Washington Square on Connecticut Avenue NW; and the $87 million acquisition of Judiciary Center at 555 Fourth Street NW by the investment firm of Kondo Bosekei.

Shuwa Investment's $80 million purchase of the U.S. News and World Report complex in Washington in 1987 amounted to $480 per square foot, the highest per-square-foot price ever paid for a building in the nation's capital.

At the end of September 1988, the Japanese made their largest single acquisition of American real estate—the worldwide Inter-Continental Hotel group for $2.27 billion in cash.

While the hotels were owned by Grand Metropolitan PLC, a British brewing and hotel concern, the company had its headquarters in Montvale, New Jersey, and was registered as an American firm.

The buyer was the Seibu Saison Group, which is run by Seiji Tsutsumi, an international businessman, poet, novelist, and half-brother of Yoshiaki Tsutsumi, identified by *Forbes* as the world's richest man. The move marked Seibu Saison's first move into the international arena after creating an empire of grocery stores, restaurants, and resorts in Japan.

It was a big move. In one transaction, the Japanese acquired ownership of seventeen major hotels around the world, including the Mark Hopkins in San Francisco, part of the historic Willard in Washington, and the May Fair in London. In addition, the company became the operator of eighty-one other hotels on several continents.

In addition to the purchases of top-flight properties at top dollar, the Japanese are branching out to second-tier cities—such as Boston and Portland—and more varied projects, from shopping centers to resorts, joint ventures, and full-scale development projects. The huge construction firm of Kumagai Gumi is a partner in a $225 million, sixty-two-story office building in Seattle called Gateway Tower in addition to a huge mixed-use development called Worldwide Plaza on the site of the old Madison Square Garden in midtown Manhattan. Mitsui Real Estate Sales USA, an arm of one of Japan's giant trading conglomerates, is a general partner in a 400,000-square-foot office project in Stamford, Connecticut, called Stamford Harbor Park. A group of Japanese banks is a limited partner in the shoreline project.

The Stamford deal, along with such massive projects as Ko Olina in Hawaii and the $1 billion development near Palm Springs, represent the broadening interests of the Japanese in not just buying existing buildings but in reaping the larger profits available by developing projects. This expansion is a natural next step in Japan's investment in U.S. real estate and the result of the growing sophistication of the Japanese as they learn the ropes of commercial property in the United States.

Precise figures are difficult to come by, as noted earlier. Federal agencies do not record all foreign purchases of U.S. real estate, and when they do they often don't include value. In addition, many sizable deals often are arranged through limited partnerships or other mechanisms that conceal ownership.

A report by the Los Angeles–based accounting firm Kenneth Leventhal & Co. said Japanese invested in real estate ventures worth $13 billion in 1987 alone, bringing their total U.S. real estate holdings to $26 billion. The study predicted that Japan's real estate investment in the United States could rise by another $19 billion in 1988.

While real estate is often the most visible Japanese investment, it is not the one that raises the most concern for the nation's sovereignty. The real estate will remain here, regardless of what the Japanese do or where they go.

The truly dangerous penetration of the American economy comes from Japanese investments in financial services companies and manufacturing plants. It is these acquisitions that represent the opportunity to wield power and influence.

Japanese financial firms have purchased big stakes in some of Wall Street's most respected investment houses, most notably Goldman, Sachs & Co., Salomon Brothers, and PaineWebber. Japan is now home to all ten of the world's biggest banks, and every major U.S. city has branches of these dominant financial institutions. No U.S. bank ranks among the world's twenty-five largest.

The long-preferred form of investment by the Japanese is the "green fields" investment: starting from scratch, building a factory, and training hand-picked workers. Across the country, Japanese manufacturers have set up factories to manufacture everything from noodles to automobiles.

Often these factories are wooed by competing state governments, each offering special giveaway programs composed of tax breaks, free job training, and other economic incentives, in order to secure the jobs created by the new Japanese plants. In addition to burdening local communities with years of providing additional services with severely reduced tax bases, these enticements create a disadvantage for American firms that must compete with the Japanese.

With the closing of Pennsylvania's Volkswagen plant, all seven foreign automakers in the United States are Japanese. Studies show that each job created at a Japanese-owned auto plant in the United States costs two workers their jobs at American-owned plants. By 1991, the Japanese will have captured 50 percent of the U.S. auto market, the world's largest.

When the stock market crash triggered by Japanese investors in October 1987 sent the value of many American companies plummeting, the Japanese took advantage of the bargains by acquiring more U.S. companies. Their biggest transaction was the purchase of Firestone Tire & Rubber Co. for $2.6 billion by Japan's Bridgestone.

But there have been dozens of little-noticed, smaller acquisitions that provide the Japanese with investments in key industries, such as the $242 million purchase of California's largest and oldest cement maker, CalMat, by Japan's Onoda Cement Company in 1988. As part of the deal, Onoda received an option to buy California Portland Cement Co. in two years, which will make Onoda the state's biggest cement manufacturer and give it the opportunity to determine price and supply for a basic building commodity in the nation's richest state.

More than half of the nation's cement industry already is owned by foreigners, chiefly the Japanese and the Australians. Likewise, foreigners have gained control of the nation's chemical industry.

In 1988, Japan's Dai Nippon Ink & Chemicals paid $540 million for Reichhold Chemicals, making it the fifth of the ten largest U.S. chemical companies to come under foreign control.

Clearly the Japanese are not the only foreigners filling up their shopping carts in the United States. Great Britain, the Netherlands, Canada, West Germany, Switzerland, France, Kuwait, Saudi Arabia, Australia, and Sweden have traditionally made forays into the U.S. economy, taking advantage of America's addiction to foreign capital and its openness to foreign investment. They have taken over factories, advertising agencies, farms, mines, dairies, publishing companies, and casinos.

Some of the most common names on American grocery shelves—and sometimes, the shelves themselves—are actually owned by foreigners. Alka-Seltzer is owned by West Germans,

who also have a controlling interest in the A&P Grocery chain.
West Germany's Bertelsmann communications firm paid $500
million for Doubleday & Company. Stouffer, Beach-Nut, Carnation, and Beringer Vineyards—which was founded by one of the
half-dozen original Napa Valley families—are owned by Nestle,
the Swiss conglomerate. The French own big stakes in Mack
Trucks and American Motors. Timex is owned by Norwegians.
Santa Fe International, a leading energy company, is owned by
Kuwaiti investors.

Saudi Arabia spent $1.2 billion in June 1988 to buy half of
three Texaco refineries, 1,450 gas stations owned by Texaco, and
a distribution network of more than 10,000 independently owned
Texaco-brand stations in twenty-three states in the southern and
eastern United States.

In the biggest acquisition yet by a British firm in the United
States, British Petroleum Co. paid $7.4 billion for the 45 percent
of Standard Oil Co. it did not already own in 1987. The purchase
was only one of several huge acquisitions that helped the British
remain the biggest foreign investors in the United States in 1987.

A year later, British-owned Batus agreed to pay $5.2 billion to
acquire the Los Angeles–based Farmers Insurance Group, the
biggest acquisition in California history and a deal that caused a
ripple of concern among industry regulators in several states
where Farmers does business.

The drive by the British to repurchase their former colony was
strong in 1987 and 1988. Within days of each other in 1987, for
example, two deals allowed Britain to replace the United States
as the world's premier owner and operator of quality hotels.
Allegis Corporation sold Hilton International to the British-
owned Ladbroke Group, and Bass PLL took over the international network of Holiday Inns from US Holiday Corp.

At the same time, Hanson Trust, one of Britain's top ten
companies, consumed the New Jersey–based Kidde, Inc., including its assets of Jacuzzi whirlpools and Farberware kitchenware.
Hiram Walker of Canada, a subsidiary of the British conglomerate Allied-Lyons, also owns one of California's largest wineries,
Clos du Bois. The British also own Smith & Wesson handguns,

Ball Park Franks, and a part of Washington's famed Watergate complex.

Canadians have vast investments in U.S. newspaper, magazine, and book publishing and cable television. Just two Canadian corporations, Thomson Newspapers and International Thomson Organisation, own 100-plus newspapers and forty publishing subsidiaries. Seagram, the Canadian brewer, acquired Tropicana Products from Beatrice Companies. And in a hotly contested battle with R. H. Macy over Federated Department Stores in 1988, Canadian developer Robert Campeau paid $6.6 billion for a retailing and real estate empire that included sixteen branches of Bloomingdale's and 549 other stores. A Canadian company already owned Brooks Brothers clothiers.

The determination of these foreign bargain hunters was demonstrated by Michael Dornemann, a director of West German publishing giant Bertelsmann AG. He flew to the United States more than fifty times between 1984 and 1986 while deciding how to invest $1 billion in his company's shopping spree. He visited more than twenty American firms before selecting two targets, RCA records and Doubleday publishing.

Although Dornemann thought the possibility of acquiring both companies was extremely unlikely, he wooed publisher Nelson Doubleday and John Welch, the chairman of RCA parent General Electric, diligently. Finally, having acquired neither by September 1986, he arranged separate meetings with each company on the same day and he gave the impression that his company could afford to buy just one. "Either you sell to us, or we'll go to the others," each company was warned. By the end of the day, Dornemann had a double victory: both companies for a total price of $805 million.

Still, it is the Japanese who have poured the most money into the United States in recent years, spurring soaring real estate values and turning Main Street Midwest into a virtual subsidiary of the Japanese auto industry.

The flood of foreign investment has created jobs for American workers and helped to finance the staggering national debt. Americans drive higher-quality cars, even if they are not foreign built, thanks to competition from the Japanese. Consumer electronic goods are cheaper and better because of the Japanese. The very openness of the U.S. economic system is an essential ingredient in keeping the capitalistic engine operating smoothly and efficiently.

Yet those benefits must be countered by a realistic assessment of the full impact of foreign investment and the unprecedented challenges it poses. The nation must not be blind to the dangers in the dramatic level of foreign penetration of the U.S. economy demonstrated by the Toshiba lobbying campaign and the stock market crash.

Political and economic leaders must not be so afraid of offending the foreign moneymen that they refuse to ask the serious and troubling questions that arise from the selling of America.

Even if foreign investors, whether they are Japanese or British, can never gain control over the giant U.S. economy, they can secure strangleholds on specific sectors.

The warnings must be recognized, and questions must be answered, before the United States unwittingly sells too much control of its destiny to the highest bidders, who are more and more often the Japanese.

Too often the debate over Japanese investment has been stifled because those who seek more realistic trading policies are scorned as alarmists and accused of Japan bashing. Charges of racism too easily form a shield that protects the unfair trade policies of the Japanese while deflecting Americans from a serious discussion of the most pressing national problem of the next decade.

Facts are not colored by nationalism or ethnic background, and the facts are that Japanese investment here is different from that of other nations.

For one thing, it is growing much faster. The amount invested in the United States by the Japanese nearly tripled from 1980 to 1985, and the pace of investment has been faster than that of any other foreign nation since 1984. Figures compiled by the U.S. Commerce Department for 1986, while incomplete, illustrate the trend.

In 1986, Japanese private and government direct investments

here outstripped those of any other nation. Of the 1,051 reported transactions, 351 originated in Japan. The total Japanese investment amounted to $9.3 billion on 170 of those deals, and the government failed to list amounts for the remainder. Great Britain was second with 178 transactions and 83 identified values totaling $8.1 billion. Canada was third with 114 transactions and 57 identified values totaling $6.8 billion.

At the end of 1987, the Japanese were third in total investments in the United States behind the British and the Dutch. Once the final figures are in for 1988, many experts predict that the Japanese will have surpassed the Dutch to rival the British as the leading foreign owners of the United States.

Second, the strategy is different from that of other foreign investors. The Japanese are not interested in simple return on their capital or in the type of passive, safe haven Arabs sought for their oil dollars in the 1970s.

The Japanese are determined to buy access to a country where growing sentiment for trade protectionism threatens to shut them out. In addition, the Japanese also exhibit a definite tendency to target either a geographic area—Hawaii, for instance—or a specific segment of the economy—the auto manufacturing and related parts industries, for example.

While the strength of the yen made it less expensive for Japanese companies to invest abroad and triggered much of the surge in the late 1980s, the Japanese also diversified, buying more foreign corporations and investing in research and development projects abroad.

Japanese investments are no longer relegated to securities and government bonds and traditional real estate. They have switched to direct seizures of power by purchasing control of companies. That fact becomes important when coupled with the growth rate of Japanese investment here.

A 1988 survey by Japan's Economic Planning Agency documented the expansionist drive. After years of shunning takeovers, one out of every three big Japanese companies planned to expand into foreign markets during the year by purchasing existing companies. The market of preference: the United States.

More than any other nation, Japan is buying the United States with America's own dollars. The huge trade surplus racked up in Japan is being used to buy control of the world's richest consumer market.

There is another difference, and it may be the most critical. Decades of European investments in the United States have been the result of a free flow of trade; with some exceptions and more restrictions than Americans apply, European nations tend to be open to foreign investments.

But the Japanese are taking advantage of the U.S. commitment to free trade while maintaining the industrialized world's most stringent restrictions on foreign access to its markets. For instance, while Japan's giant construction firms built more than $3 billion worth of projects in the United States in 1987 alone, U.S. firms have been virtually shut out of the construction market in Japan.

There is no wrongdoing in expanding into the global marketplace. Americans themselves argued the concept's benefits in the 1960s and 1970s, and it would be hypocritical to reverse field now that the investments are flowing in the other direction.

But throughout those decades, the United States maintained an open door to foreign investors while the Japanese have marked their nation with a "No Trespassing" sign. It is that critical difference that makes the Japanese stance wrong. And that difference should not be ignored by those who wave the flag of free trade and a global economy to silence debate over foreign investment in the United States.

The proper response to this inequity may not be to create obstacles to Japanese investment in the United States. But reciprocity, with the attendant threat of tariffs, quotas, and other sanctions, must be on the bargaining table.

It is essential to recognize that foreign investment in the United States, particularly the strategic purchases by the Japanese, threatens to rob the nation of the ability to control its economic and political destiny. Decisions affecting the jobs of millions of Americans and the health of the economy will be made in Tokyo, not Washington.

The dilemma may have been best stated by Clyde V. Prestowitz, Jr., former counsel on Japan affairs at the U.S. Commerce

Department and author of the excellent 1988 book *Trading Places: How We Allowed Japan to Take the Lead*. At a breakfast with *Los Angeles Times* reporters in Los Angeles in May 1988, Prestowitz was asked about the impact of Japanese investment on U.S. competitiveness, and he said: "Let's remember that British investment in India turned it into a colony."

3
A FAILING POWER

FOREIGN INVESTMENT HAS PLAYED a crucial role in the economic development of the United States. From the country's earliest days, its borders have been open to investors from abroad, and its commerce and industry have benefited from that openness.

In 1791, Secretary of the Treasury Alexander Hamilton recognized the value of foreign investment when he said, "Rather than treating the foreign investor as a rival, we should consider him a valuable helper, for he increases our productivity and the efficiency of our businesses."

By the early nineteenth century, the British owned one-quarter of the entire U.S. debt, and nearly one-third of the South's cotton plantations were mortgaged to London investors. British bankers backed President Thomas Jefferson's purchase of Louisiana, and European money poured in to dig canals and construct the railways that penetrated the western frontier. Following an 1843 report by the House of Representatives that said that almost half of the nation's debt was in foreign hands, some alarmed state legislatures passed laws restricting further borrowing by state governments.

But the U.S. position as a debtor nation ended in 1914 with the onset of World War I in Europe. Between the opening of the war and the entry of the United States in 1917, more than $2 billion worth of U.S. securities was returned to the country from European investors who exchanged them for loans to help finance the war. At the same time, the United States itself was loaning huge sums to the Allied powers of Europe to help finance the war. When the battles ended, the United States advanced $9.6 billion to European governments to help rebuild the continent.

The war left Europe so depleted financially that the United States continued to be a source of capital for years to come, and American industry began a rapid international expansion.

By the 1920s, huge American business concerns such as Ford, General Motors, Standard Oil, and General Electric forged secure niches for themselves in the European economy, setting up plants or buying companies there.

Through the years, the Great Depression, and another world war, United States industry continued to expand abroad, particularly in Europe. For instance, in 1963, American firms in France controlled 40 percent of the petroleum market, 65 percent of the production of film and photographic paper, 65 percent of telecommunications equipment, and 45 percent of synthetic rubber.

Far more important to the future of Europe, U.S. corporations controlled the burgeoning electronics and computer industries that would form the foundation for the new industrial revolution. American corporations in Europe controlled 15 percent of the production of telecommunications equipment (radio, TV, and recording devices), 50 percent of the production of semiconductors, 80 percent of computers, and 95 percent of the then-new market for integrated circuits.

So complete was the transformation of the United States from debtor to creditor that Europe raised its voice in protest, spawning Jean-Jacques Servan-Schreiber's influential book, *The American Challenge*, and creating a movement to shake off U.S. economic dominance. Interestingly, the book was written and the alarm sounded when American industrial investment in Europe was less than 10 percent of the total capitalization, a figure roughly in line with the amount of foreign investment in the United States today.

"By extrapolating the present trends, it seems clear that we Europeans cannot hope to participate fully in that world of the future," wrote Servan-Schreiber. "This does not mean we will be poor; probably we will grow even richer. But we will be overtaken and dominated, for the first time in our history, by a more advanced civilization."

History intervened before the United States could overtake Europe. The reasons are many. Chief among them was the oil crisis of the early 1970s, for which the many warnings had been ignored in Detroit and throughout the American economy. American multinationals were forced to contract even more rapidly than they had expanded years earlier. But credit for the turnaround must be given also to the determined response of European industry.

Roused to action by the warnings from Servan-Schreiber and political and business figures, European managers adopted the strengths and strategies of their American counterparts and retooled their industries to become more competitive. The governments of Europe, once colonial powers themselves and well aware of the relationship between economics and politics, played a significant role in assisting in the rebound.

Since those days when American industry sat as a colossus astride the world, the nation's position has declined dramatically. In 1950, the United States dominated the world markets for goods and services, accounting for 20 percent of total world exports and more than half of the exports of many manufactured products.

By the 1980s, although the United States remained the world's largest exporter, its share of the world export market had shrunk to less than 15 percent, and a decade of trade deficits had drained its share of international trade reserves from 32 percent in 1950 to about 6 percent. The United States lost market share to international competitors in every major industrial category, and the country was trading in the red with every major trade bloc in the world.

David B. Yoffie, a Harvard Business School professor, finds

that some of America's trade decline was inevitable and even desirable. "The industrial nations of Europe and Japan would inevitably regain some of the world market share lost to the United States after they recovered from the effects of the Second World War," said Yoffie.

But others see a peril in the sharpness and rapidity of the decline. Felix Rohatyn, the Wall Street investment banker and social critic, says the United States has suffered "an astonishing turnaround." In twenty-five years, the American century turned into the American crisis.

Certainly as the end of the 1980s approached, the world's economic tables had been turned. Only twice in the seventeen years between 1971 and 1988 had the U.S. trade balance run in the black, and both of those years, 1973 and 1975, were during a recession. At the start of the downward spiral in 1971, the United States had an overall trade deficit of $2.2 billion; by 1987, the deficit had increased to $160 billion. The United States was running a deficit—importing more than it was exporting—with virtually every industrialized trading partner.

But it was to Japan that the United States was most in debt. The last year that the United States was ahead in trade with Japan was 1964. By 1987, the United States had a $57 billion trade deficit with Japan.

Even as the weaker dollar began to improve the U.S. balance of trade overall in 1988, the deficit with Japan was too imbedded to respond. A 70 percent decline in the value of the dollar, which should have spurred the Japanese to import cheap American goods and cause Americans to stop buying the more expensive Japanese products, did not work.

American industry was no more effective in cracking the nearly closed Japanese markets than American consumers were in weaning themselves from Japanese products. For example, instead of using the lower dollar to pry the Japanese out of their secure position in the U.S. auto market, Detroit's Big Three automakers lost an additional 5 percent of the market share between 1982 and 1988.

The pivotal year in the American decline was 1985. For the first time since 1914, the United States became a debtor nation.

Just three years earlier, in 1982, the United States was the world's largest creditor nation. But the figures released in 1985 by the U.S. Commerce Department showed that, for the first time since before World War I, the amount of U.S. assets owned by foreigners exceeded the amount of foreign assets held by U.S. investors. And the difference was not small: foreigners owned $111.9 billion more in U.S. assets than U.S. investors held in foreign assets.

The deterioration continued. By 1986 the figure more than doubled. Foreigners held $1.331 trillion in assets in the United States, while U.S. investors owned $1.068 trillion in assets overseas, for a difference of $263.65 billion. In 1987, the difference jumped another $100 billion.

In simple terms, that means the United States, like Mexico, Brazil, and a host of other lesser developed countries, took in more foreign capital than it invested abroad.

The United States has become what Rohatyn called "a classic model for a failing economic power: increasing levels of foreign debt, a constantly depreciating currency, and a continuing negative trade balance almost regardless of currency levels."

This huge international debt means that the standard of living in the United States will decline as the country is forced to make interest payments to foreigners.

By 1988, the federal government was already paying $24 billion in interest to foreigners, more than it spends on schools. And interest rates were higher because the United States had to lure foreign investors to finance its profligate spending.

"We are much like a wealthy family that annually sells acreage so that it can sustain a lifestyle unwarranted by its current output," Warren Buffett, the legendary investor from Omaha, Nebraska, told *Fortune* magazine in May 1988. "Until the plantation is gone, it's all pleasure and no pain. In the end, however, the family will have exchanged the life of an owner for the life of a tenant farmer."

Or, as Congressman John Bryant, a Texas Democrat, put it: "America has been selling off its family jewels to pay for a night on the town."

During the U.S. decline, Japan emerged as the world's most

powerful economic force. In industry after industry, from automobiles to machine tools to electronics, the Japanese knocked
the Americans out of first place in the world. In late 1985, when
the United States surpassed Brazil and Mexico and became the
world's biggest debtor nation, Japan emerged as the world's
largest creditor. Japan's governmental and private holdings
abroad surpassed those of Britain and other industrialized nations.

Richard Rosecrance of Cornell University predicted in 1988
that "If things continue as they are now, it won't be much beyond
2010 before Japan becomes a leading power in world politics."

Statistics tell the story. In 1950, Japan had only 1 percent of the
world's exports, and it was a follower in world trade. Not blessed
with an abundance of natural resources, Japan imports mineral
fuels, crude oil, industrial raw materials, and foodstuffs and
grinds them through the machinery of its high-powered economy to export high-tech scientific, electronic, and transportation
equipment. Japan's leading exports are autos, communications
equipment, audiovisual equipment, office equipment, scientific
and optical instruments equipment, and ships.

As the end of the 1980s approached, Japan had done far more
than simply catch up; its share of world trade had grown tenfold,
and it had built a trade surplus of $100 billion.

Much of that surplus was in dollars, for Japan's success came at
the expense of the United States. Import-hungry American
consumers have been spending billions of dollars on Japanese
cars and video equipment while the nation's manufacturers were
buying sophisticated components from Japan. The Japanese
then use the surplus dollars to step up their direct investments in
the United States.

"Basically, the VCRs and the Toyotas are coming back,"
explains David G. Shulman, director of real estate research at
Salomon Brothers in New York.

America's fading dominance began to cause fear of this rising
tide of foreign investment, which in turn fueled calls for controlling foreign purchases and setting up quotas to protect American industries from the threat of foreign competition, particularly the Japanese.

The Japanese were predictably concerned about the threat of

protectionism and bashing of their interests in the United States. They responded by stepping up a relatively new trade pattern: setting up plants in the United States. Much of the increase in Japanese investment in the United States has come in the form of new factories or acquisition of existing U.S. plants.

It's like an insurance policy: Japanese industries evade restrictions on imports by manufacturing goods in the United States through subsidiaries, and thereby also avoid being damaged by the falling dollar. There is also the added benefit of using their U.S. operations to increase their share of the nation's market without boosting the U.S. trade deficit. Such concerns were on the minds of Toshiba executives when the Japanese electronics giant decided to expand in the United States.

"We first started talking about moving our personal computer production to the United States three years ago," Daniel M. Crane, vice president for marketing at Toshiba America in Irvine, California, said in late 1987. "We wanted to insulate ourselves from currency fluctuation; we wanted to be an insider."

The increasing presence of Japanese goods in the United States has been referred to as "judo economics," a policy that deflects protectionist pressure because of Japan's huge strength in U.S. markets. Often when the United States tries to retaliate against Japanese companies for violating international trade rules, the U.S. actions must be softened because its domestic economy is hurt, too, as demonstrated in the Toshiba incident.

This is all part of a long-term plan being followed by Japanese corporations driven by the necessity of exporting. The initial phase called for grabbing a big share of the U.S. markets, frequently by reducing prices sharply and sometimes settling for a loss on exports. Establishing a capability in the United States to assemble components made in Japan and thus evade protectionism is the second phase. And the third will be shifting full manufacturing to the United States, including setting up an array of Japanese suppliers to ring its big manufacturing plants.

Japanese investment in the United States was so extensive that by 1988 a majority of Americans had come to believe that a country's economic power, rather than its military might, decides its influence in the world.

Fears over the erosion of U.S. power, a central theme of Paul

Kennedy's bestselling 1988 book *The Rise and Fall of the Great Powers*, deepened as Americans watched familiar landmarks and trademarks passing into foreign hands.

The Algonquin Hotel, the celebrated haunt of such literary luminaries of the past as Dorothy Parker, Edna Ferber, Alexander Woollcott, and Robert Benchley, was sold in 1987 to the Brazilian subsidiary of a Tokyo corporation. Another New York City landmark, the Tiffany Building, went to the Japanese. So did two Hawaiian homes, for two of the largest price tags ever attached to single-family dwellings—$40 million for the Kaiser Estate in eastern Oahu and $21 million for Casa Blanca del Mar, which was owned by seafood magnate Richard Fowler. Japan's Seibu Railway purchased one of Hawaii's best-known resorts, the Westin Mauna Kea, in 1987 for $310 million, or a record $1 million per room.

Japanese investors purchased three Las Vegas casinos, including the world-famous Dunes Hotel and Country Club. A consortium of three cash-rich Japanese companies, calling itself CST Communications, signed a three-picture deal with MGM/UA Communications, investing $5 million in Whoopi Goldberg's *Fatal Beauty*, Michael J. Fox's *Bright Lights, Big City*, and *Last Rites* with Tom Berenger.

How unsettling do Americans find this foreign shopping spree? One 1988 survey asked this question: "Ten years from now, who do you think will pose the greater threat to our national security then—our military adversaries or our economic competitors?" Nearly 60 percent of the respondents feared the economic competitors more; only 34 percent were more worried about military enemies.

Another survey uncovered a sharp division in U.S. opinion. Elite leaders fear foreign investment far less than the general populace does, a situation similar to the conflicting opinions created by U.S. reliance on European investors before the turn of the century.

Not surprisingly, a 1988 survey conducted by Smick-Medley and Associates, a bipartisan public policy advisory firm in Washington, D.C., found that Americans 50 and older are far less tolerant of foreign investment than the younger generation. But across all age groups, the biggest fear was that foreign investment causes the United States to have less control over its economic destiny and less world influence.

Yet an elite group of 100 leaders in government, business, and the media were much less concerned about the threatened loss of control than were the 1,003 members of the general public consulted in the survey.

For instance, both groups held strong views on the costs and benefits of foreign investment, and the views were fundamentally opposed to each other.

While 80 percent of the general population believed that "foreign investors can cause a financial crisis by withdrawing their money from U.S. banks," only 55 percent of the elite agreed. When asked whether foreign investors might pull their money out at any time, 77 percent of the general-population respondents felt they might, but only 39 percent of the elite held that view.

The general population clearly fears losing control to foreign investors. And, while most Americans in both groups want foreign investments to continue, 89 percent of the general population favored a law to require foreign investors to register with the U.S. government, and 78 percent supported a law limiting the extent of foreign investment in U.S. business and real estate. Among the elite, only 48 percent favored registering foreign investors, and a tiny 13 percent supported restrictions.

The American public is restless and suspicious as billions of dollars in foreign investments change the face of American industry and the shape of the country's skylines. When those fears collide with the acquiescent attitude of the nation's opinion makers, the stage is set for a contentious and bitter conflict.

That is precisely what resulted when a young Democratic congressman from Texas named John Bryant tried to pass a bill requiring foreign investors simply to sign up as they come through the open door of the United States.

4
WHO OWNS AMERICA?

JOHN BRYANT FIRST BECAME INTERESTED in foreign investment while serving as a state legislator in Texas in the 1970s. The issue surfaced when Arab investors were believed to be behind the purchases of large parcels of agricultural land in the state.

When Bryant tried to trace the source of the purchases, he found that most owners were hiding behind a screen of dummy corporations registered in the Netherlands Antilles, a Caribbean haven for investors and other moneymen seeking anonymity. The U.S. Agriculture Department listed 270,000 acres of Texas agricultural land owned by residents of the Netherlands Antilles—one acre per man, woman, and child on the tiny island. Bryant was dubious.

More significantly, Bryant was amazed at the ease with which a foreign investor could conceal his identity under U.S. law. He discovered what anyone who makes the seemingly simple inquiry "Who bought what and for how much?" discovers: there is no single U.S. agency tracking such information, collating it, or analyzing it. Although private organizations and individuals have tried to study foreign investment, their efforts are stymied from the start because of the lack of complete information.

The point was made with clarity in 1986 at hearings held in Washington by a House subcommittee.

Edward Ray, chairman of the economics department at Ohio State University, told the congressmen that the lack of data on foreign investment in the United States makes it "virtually impossible to do serious quality research" on the subject.

Ray arrived at that opinion following more than a decade of studying foreign investment. In 1977 the U.S. Commerce Department commissioned him to review several policy issues concerning foreign investment. Ray wrote a report on his findings and then left the Commerce Department at the end of the summer, assuming his suggestions would be reviewed and taken to heart.

Four years later, a graduate student who wanted to study Japanese investment in U.S. financial institutions came to Ray at Ohio State. Ray referred her to the Department of Commerce, which agreed to mail her the available information. When the envelope arrived, it contained only a copy of Ray's report.

In 1986, nine years after writing that report, Ray told Congress he was still unable to get the necessary information to do worthwhile research in the area.

The inability to do an academic study of foreign investment may seem to be of little national concern. But the same absence of hard data on foreign investment means that U.S. political leaders are unable to make sound decisions on a myriad of issues related to foreign investment. They simply lack the facts to reach a reasonable conclusion.

"We cannot assess where in our economy foreign interests are buying control, which parts of our economy are susceptible to foreign influence, or which U.S. economic policies are responsible," said Bryant. "Because of the lack of adequate reporting requirements, we cannot determine whether new foreign owners of U.S. assets are legitimate businesses, hostile nations like Libya, Iran, or the Soviet Union, corrupt Third World dictators, or organized drug traffickers laundering their ill-gotten gains."

A hodgepodge of different laws is supposed to monitor foreign investment in the United States and provide those facts. The laws

have confidence-inspiring titles, such as the International Invest-
ment Survey Act of 1976, the Domestic and Foreign Investment
Improved Disclosure Act of 1977, and the Foreign Agriculture
Investment Disclosure Act of 1978.

In addition, the list of sixteen different federal agencies
charged with tracking foreign investment is an alphabet soup of
government, including BEA, OTIA, OFIUS, USDA, SEC, DOE,
and IRS.

The two federal entities primarily responsible for monitoring
direct investment are the BEA, the Bureau of Economic Analysis,
and the OFIUS, the Office of Foreign Investment in the United
States. Both are in the Commerce Department.

OFIUS produces an annual list of transactions, arranged by
industry and country of origin. Some listings include price or
value of the investment. But the information is culled from
public sources, such as newspaper clippings, and a disclaimer
opens each report: "While every effort was made to verify the
information obtained from public sources, the U.S. Department
of Commerce is not responsible for any inaccuracies or gaps in
information presented in this report."

As early as 1980, a report by the House Committee on Government Operations said that the only function of this "obviously
unreliable" publication was "public relations."

The unreliability was backed up by a study done by Bryant's
office once he got to Congress. The examination found that the
Commerce Department's tracking mechanisms left at least $150
billion in foreign investment unaccounted for between 1982 and
1987.

The BEA, on the other hand, collects information on foreign
investments of 10 percent or more in U.S. businesses with assets
of more than $1 million, except banks. It reports aggregate data
about the investors' countries of origin and the types of industry
in which the investments were made. From that information it is
possible to identify certain trends. But the reports do not identify
either the investor or the U.S. business in which money has been
invested.

In fact, scattered liberally throughout the BEA's charts are
little capital Ds in parentheses, which signify that in those cases

even the aggregate data has been "suppressed" because it might reveal information that either the foreign investors or the American sellers want kept secret. And in the case of foreign individuals investing through intermediaries, the BEA does not require them to disclose identities at all.

Even Congress has been denied access to the raw data from which the BEA reports are compiled.

After Bryant was elected to Congress in 1982 from a district that included downtown Dallas and some affluent suburban neighborhoods, he was determined to create a more thorough mechanism for monitoring foreign investment.

Bryant's was not the first effort to pry open the lid on foreign investments. The Foreign Investment Reorganization Act of 1983 grew out of the 1980 congressional report that found serious inadequacies and redundancies in the data collected by sixteen federal agencies under existing laws. But there was little interest in the issue, and the measure died.

So it was no surprise that a reporter from his hometown paper and a wire-service correspondent were the only people who attended the 1985 press conference at which Bryant unveiled his Foreign Investment Disclosure and Reciprocity Act.

"It was like striking out in a baseball game. You know you'll come up to bat again," Bryant said philosophically in his Washington office three years later as he recalled the party to which almost nobody came.

Certainly there had been stories that year in which the issue of foreign investment played a major role. Press accounts had disclosed a secret attempt by the Soviet Union to acquire banks in California's Silicon Valley, which would have given the Soviets access to the inner secrets of high-tech borrowers. Documents seized from former Philippine president Ferdinand Marcos disclosed the existence of vast, previously secret U.S. real estate holdings purchased with funds siphoned from American foreign aid. And President Reagan ordered a freeze on Libya's U.S. assets to counter Muhummar Qadaffi's terrorist threat.

Reagan's plan to freeze Libya's assets highlighted the joke of U.S. monitoring policies when it came to foreign investments. As Bryant pointed out to the president in a letter, it was a great plan except for one thing—no one would be able to find the assets under current U.S. laws.

Bryant's initial legislation was more than a simple "signing in at the door." The measure would have required foreign investors to register each new investment publicly with the Department of Commerce, disclosing their true identities, nationality, the purchase price of the investment, and their source of financing.

These requirements amounted to no more than what publicly held American corporations must divulge in annual reports to the U.S. Securities and Exchange Commission or whenever they make a new acquisition. And the requirements were still far less than what most other nations demanded of Americans when they invested abroad. But the proposal would generate outrage from foreign investors and their supporters.

A more significant element of the proposed legislation was the reciprocity section. It would have prohibited investment in American assets by foreigners unless Americans were permitted to invest in the investor's home country on the same terms.

Testifying at a committee hearing on his proposal on May 8, 1986, Bryant said, "As ownership of our economic assets is transferred overseas, so is the power to make decisions affecting the independence and prosperity of Americans. Foreign access to sensitive high technology and research capabilities narrows our strategic and competitive edge. Foreign influence in vital energy and defense industries may endanger our national security; our oil industry is particularly vulnerable at this time. And our economy is becoming so dependent on foreign capital that many respected economists warn that its sudden withdrawal could send us into an economic tailspin."

The Reagan administration, which had financed the deficit with big help from foreign investors, was steadfastly opposed to the legislation. Officials from various government agencies countered that Bryant's amendment was, at best, redundant and that current efforts to monitor investment were adequate. They objected to the reciprocity section on the grounds that enforcement would create a bureaucratic morass and place American businesses abroad at risk of reprisals.

In an apparent coup, Bryant had arranged for supportive

testimony from Richard Perle, assistant secretary of defense for international security and a leading voice for the administration on arms matters. However, on the morning of the day his testimony was scheduled, Perle's secretary telephoned to say that he had a conflicting appearance in the Senate and would be unable to appear.

George Slover, Bryant's legislative counsel at the time, later explained what had happened: "We knew from things he had said publicly in the past that Perle was very concerned about foreign investment and how little we know about it. There was no official explanation, but what we heard later was that his testimony was not approved by the Office of Management and Budget. It wasn't approved because it didn't toe the party line."

Opposition to the proposal centered on the reciprocity section, so in January 1987, Bryant submitted a new version to the House that was titled the Foreign Ownership Disclosure Act. The reciprocity section had been dropped, and Bryant was able to line up thirty-one cosponsors.

In March, the measure was attached as an amendment to the omnibus trade legislation then under consideration in the Energy and Commerce Committee. The bill was adopted by the narrow margin of 21 to 20, after fierce opposition from every Republican on the committee.

There was a further modification of the disclosure section: it would apply only to the big players, foreign investors with a "significant interest" of more than 5 percent in any U.S. business or real estate property with assets of more than $5 million or annual sales of more than $10 million, and those with a controlling interest of 25 percent or more in a U.S. business enterprise with assets or annual sales of more than $20 million. The information required would be simpler: identity, nationality, address, date interest was acquired, percentage of investment and purchase price, name and location of U.S. property, and terms and conditions of acquiring interest.

The amendment included severe penalties for noncompliance and stipulated that the information would be public, indexed by name, nationality, and industry of the foreign investor and by name, state, and industry of the U.S. property.

Until its passage as part of the trade bill by the Energy and Commerce Committee, Bryant said, his amendment had benefited from Congressman Richard Gephardt's more controversial proposal for trade reciprocity, which distracted the administration from the Bryant measure.

But once the bill passed the committee and headed toward the floor of the House, the amendment met with vigorous lobbying from a variety of sources with links to or dependencies on foreign investment. Among those fighting the measure were First Boston, the New York investment bank owned in part by a Swiss bank, Credit Suisse; Shell Oil, a wholly owned subsidiary of Royal Dutch Shell; and the White House.

J. D. Williams, a high-powered Washington attorney representing First Boston, called on Bryant to express his concerns about the amendment. He used the good-old-boy routine, cautioning Bryant in a friendly fashion, "I've been around a lot longer than you, son. If we have to, we can stop you. Too bad, son."

In Washington, there is no better measure of a proposal's significance than the amount of money its opponents are willing to spend to defeat it. And the Bryant proposal caused plenty of spending, though there is no way to determine precisely how much. But the list of corporations, domestic and foreign, lined up in opposition to the proposal reads like a *Who's Who* of business in the United States: the American subsidiaries of the Big Three Japanese automakers, Honda, Toyota, and Nissan; British-owned Standard Oil; Swiss multinational Nestle; American Express, the biggest U.S. financial services company; Fujitsu; and even the U.S. Chamber of Commerce.

Slover fielded more than 100 telephone calls himself from representatives of foreign investors and governments in a six-week period. Most of the callers were lawyers who refused to say which foreign investors or corporations they represented.

"The word on the street was that more money was spent on defeating the Bryant amendment than on both sides combined on any other provision to the trade bill," said Slover. "But it was all very quiet. The foreign lobby did not want to arouse any public sentiment. It would be virtually impossible to stir up any grass-roots support for keeping foreign investment secret."

Ultimately, the concerns of Shell Oil and First Boston and other big foreign investors were satisfied by a round of modifications. But the Reagan administration kicked its lobbying efforts into high gear and called up heavy hitters such as Paul Volcker, then chairman of the Federal Reserve, and Treasury Secretary James Baker to lead the charge.

"As soon as the amendment hit the full committee, Baker started working the Congress hard," Bryant said. "For someone who usually just calls on chairmen of the various committees, Baker walked the halls of Congress, calling on members, like a common lobbyist."

Eventually a modified version of Bryant's amendment arrived on the House floor, and Norman Lent, the ranking Republican member of the Energy and Commerce Committee, turned up the heat.

While proposing his own watered-down amendment to the Bryant proposal, Lent said, "The Bryant provision, while well-meaning, is a highly controversial, burdensome, confusing, and inflexible provision that Paul Volcker and others have said could cause a severe outflow of capital and produce a severe, negative impact on our economy and on the present and future jobs of millions of U.S. workers. My amendment seeks to guard against this by incorporating reasonable authority for the Secretary of Commerce to exempt certain investments if their reporting or disclosure would be harmful to beneficial foreign investment."

The Lent amendment offered the secretary of commerce blanket authority to exempt entire classes of foreign investors from all reporting requirements. It would have allowed foreign investors to use economic clout in order to extort exemptions to the reporting requirements. In other words, Lent sought to punch a hole in the Bryant amendment so big that any investor could stroll right through.

Lent's amendment was defeated by a vote of 230 to 190, which meant Bryant's amendment remained in the trade bill passed by the House. Bryant began looking for a Senate sponsor. Several senators expressed interest, but then backed off in the face of political pressure. Finally Senator Tom Harkin, a Democrat from Iowa, took the ball.

Lobbying intensified in the Senate, where representatives of blue-chip foreign and American multinationals joined in opposition with some of Washington's most powerful law firms—on the payroll of foreign corporations and governments—trade organizations, foreign ambassadors, and, of course, the White House.

One lobbyist representing a large multinational corporation called Senator Harkin's office and threatened, "How would you like it if we pulled everyone right out of Iowa?" An amused member of Harkin's staff said the threat was not taken seriously, and Harkin didn't waver.

Gary J. Campkin, director of international affairs for the Confederation of British Industry, sent a dragooning letter to the Metrocrest Chamber of Commerce, located in a district neighboring Bryant's outside Dallas. Leaving all subtlety aside, Campkin wrote that if the Bryant amendment were to become law, "its effect would be to impact negatively on British operations in the United States and also to deter new and future investment proposals. This in turn would mean less job opportunities and economic benefits in the U.S. In addition, it opens the door to retaliatory and mirror actions by other countries which could affect British and American investments."

Foreign ambassadors threatened that such legislation would send their investors and their money elsewhere. The White House claimed it would undermine the president's efforts to break through other countries' trade barriers.

Surprisingly, there was also opposition from many American business groups, such as the U.S. Chamber of Commerce and the National Association of Manufacturers. Adopting one of the administration's lines, they said they were worried that foreign governments would retaliate by imposing harsher reporting requirements on U.S. firms in their countries.

Harkin, speaking on the Senate floor, addressed that brand of reasoning as well as the concerns over chasing away foreign investment: "There are those who say that this bill will discour-

age foreign investments. I take issue with that. Business people bring their money here because it is a good place to invest and because they can make money in this country. Who is concerned with anonymity? Drug traffickers, the PLO, other foreign investors who do not want us to know how much they are acquiring of certain sensitive businesses in this country?"

Harkin argued that no legitimate business would be afraid to disclose the information required by the Bryant amendment. He pointed out that the disclosure was neither more nor less than required of publicly owned U.S. companies.

He concluded by crystallizing the danger posed by the laissez-faire attitude toward foreign investment: "The short-term advantages of foreign investment should not prevent us from considering the potential long-term effects on our economy and our national security. Over time, as ownership of our assets is transferred overseas, so is the authority to make important business and economic decisions affecting the prosperity and independence of our nation."

The threats by foreign companies to abandon the United States and the fears that investments would be withdrawn, however, carried the day. The opposition won a clear victory, sending the proposal down to defeat by a vote of 83 to 11.

Despite the lopsided vote, several senators wanted to keep the measure alive, and they found a way.

When similar laws are passed by the Senate and the House, a conference committee composed of members of both bodies is convened to iron out the differences. The trade bills passed in both assemblies contained such differences, and a giant conference committee of 200 senators and congressmen got together to work out a compromise measure.

From February through April 1988, the conferees hashed out their disputes, and one of the most hotly contested issues was Bryant's provision on foreign disclosure.

House Democratic leaders wanted the provision included in the bill, with Speaker James Wright telling reporters, "I think Americans should be allowed to know who is investing in this country. I don't see any justification for secrecy."

Some Senate leaders, however, joined the administration in

arguing that such requirements might deter additional foreign investments, which they said were needed to stimulate jobs and keep the economy from dipping into a recession.

Congressman John Dingell, the influential Michigan Democrat and chairman of the Energy and Commerce Committee, offered a compromise that called for a congressional study of the issue. As part of the study, Congress would have had access, on a confidential basis, to data collected by the federal government on foreign investment.

Congressional committees obtain highly classified national security information on just such a basis regularly from the Central Intelligence Agency and the Defense Department. But the White House opposed a similar plan for information on foreign investors.

In the end, as with everything in Washington, politics drove the decision.

President Reagan had vowed to veto the trade bill if it contained certain elements, including a version of the Bryant amendment. Democratic leaders in Congress wanted to put heat on the Republican administration in an election year by putting just such "veto bait" in the bill. But the leadership decided to narrow the focus to a single issue, requiring companies to provide workers with at least sixty days notice of a plant closing.

"It was felt that this would play better politically than the foreign disclosure issue," said a congressional staff member who was involved in the negotiations. "Jobs were a better nail to hang it on than foreign investment."

Some weakened regulations covering foreign investments were included in the bill, with the administration's okay, to head off broader regulation. One was a provision granting the president power to block a foreign investment that would impair national security. Another was the three-year ban on U.S. government purchases of Toshiba products as punishment for the illegal sale of submarine technology to the Russians. The ban does not apply to products for which Toshiba is the sole source or to U.S. products using Toshiba components. And the U.S. trade representative was given broader authority to take retaliatory steps against unfair trade practices by a foreign country.

Even those provisions, part of a bill that the president had vowed to veto because of the plant-closing provision, elicited a response of mock outrage from Japanese government officials.

"It seems the measures taken are not only aimed at the trade problem but are also based on racial discrimination against the Japanese," Hajime Tamura, Japan's minister of international trade and industry, complained to American reporters.

Reagan did veto the bill, but later in 1988 the Congress sent him essentially the same legislation without the plant-closing provision, and the president signed the new trade bill. Again, however, the Japanese raised their familiar protest, claiming that the legislation failed to recognize concrete steps taken by their government to respond to criticism from the United States and other trading partners.

The legislation decried by the Japanese actually wound up being less than a sweeping overhaul of the nation's trade laws. There were no big tariff increases, new quotas on imports, or new trade barriers. It also contained no new curbs on general foreign investment.

While the final version did retain authority for the president to block a merger or acquisition that endangers national security, the president was restricted to taking action only if no other laws, such as antitrust laws, could stop the deal, and the president could prove that the foreign party was likely to take action that would harm national security.

Yet the Japanese complained loudly, using the familiar tactic of appealing to the American sense of fairness while obscuring the fact the foreign investors and corporations find it almost impossible to penetrate Japan's closed economy. But such official protests are only one of the means used by Japan to protect its growing interests in the United States.

5
CAPITOL CLOUT

THE DEFEAT OF THE BRYANT AMENDMENT and the eviscera-
tion of the Toshiba sanctions only hint at the power of the
network of paid influence peddlers who work on behalf of the
Japanese in Washington and in state capitols across the country.

In 1988, 152 Japanese companies and government agencies
hired 113 firms to represent them in Washington. The next most-
represented country was Canada, with 61 organizations representing its interests, followed by the British, with 44.

Indeed, as Japanese investments in the United States have
increased, so has Japan's determination to protect those interests
by trying to shape U.S. policy through paid lobbyists, campaign
contributions by American subsidiaries, public-relations and
advertising campaigns, and even charitable contributions.

Overall, Japan's government, foundations, and corporations
spent at least $310 million on a range of activities from lobbying
to sponsoring public television programs aimed at influencing
U.S. opinion, according to an estimate by *Business Week* magazine.

"They are interested in creating an environment in which they can make money," Bernard Karsh, director of the Center for East Asian Studies at the University of Illinois, told *Business Week*. "I see this as a major effort to come in and stay, to legitimate their presence."

It should come as no surprise that the Japanese and other citizens of foreign nations want to safeguard their interests by shaping U.S. policy and influencing debate on issues critical to their well-being. Quite surprising, however, is the cooperation provided to them by dozens and dozens of former high-ranking U.S. government officials who are willing to serve as hired guns for these foreign nations.

The list reads like a *Who's Who* from the White House to the Department of Commerce to Congress. Senior statesman Elliot Richardson, who has held three cabinet posts and more than a dozen other high-level government positions, represents foreign interests, including an umbrella organization known as the Association of Foreign Investors in U.S. Real Estate.

James H. Lake, a key adviser to George Bush's presidential campaign, has been one of the most effective lobbyists for Japanese and European interests because of his close ties to the U.S. trade representative's office. During a six-month period in 1987, he met or spoke with U.S. trade representative Clayton Yeutter or his assistants twelve times on behalf of Mitsubishi Electric Corp., just one of his firm's Japanese clients. Mitsubishi paid the firm $129,000 during the period.

Richard Allen resigned as national security adviser to former President Ronald Reagan after disclosures that he had accepted funds from Japanese interests. During a Justice Department investigation that determined he did not engage in any illegal activity, Allen acknowledged that during his time as national security adviser, he met with Japanese auto firms while the United States was negotiating import quotas for Japanese automakers. Immediately after leaving government, Allen opened a firm that represented Japanese interests.

George Bush's former chief of staff, retired Admiral Daniel Murphy, works for a powerful public relations firm, Hill & Knowlton, as head of its international division. Some of Japan's largest companies are clients of the firm, including Hitachi and the Electronic Industries Association of Japan.

Peter G. Peterson, chairman of the Blackstone Group, a Wall Street firm with major Japanese clients, is a former commerce secretary and also former chairman of the Council on Foreign Relations and the Institute for International Economics. While not a registered lobbyist for the Japanese, Peterson has emerged frequently as a defender of Japanese interests.

William Eberle, a former U.S. trade representative, and Robert Strauss, a one-time special trade envoy with the title of trade representative and one of Washington's most effective lobbyists, represent or advise foreign interests, including those of Japan. So does Roderick Hills, former chairman of the Securities and Exchange Commission. Former Defense Secretary Clark Clifford represents foreign interests, and so does William Colby, the former director of the Central Intelligence Agency.

Former Democratic Congressmen Michael Barnes of Maryland and Jim Jones of Oklahoma were among the army of lobbyists mobilized by Toshiba to weaken congressional sanctions against the company in 1988.

When Toyota wanted federal approval for a questionable special trade zone in Kentucky so it could receive imported auto parts from Japan duty-free for use at its new auto plant there, it enlisted the aid of Republican Party Chairman Frank J. Fahrenkopf, Jr., to set up a meeting between Toyota representatives and Commerce Secretary Malcolm Baldrige. The trade zone was approved.

When Eric Garfinkel was deputy assistant director of commerce and trade in the Reagan administration, he was a key player in the debate over whether to offer the U.S. machine tool industry the option of imposing sanctions on the Japanese in order to protect the American industry. When he left the White House in 1983, he went to work at a law firm where he represented the Tool Builders Association of Japan.

Walter Lenahan, a deputy assistant secretary in the Commerce Department, was the leader of the U.S. negotiating team for discussion of the extension of an international agreement gov-

erning trade in textiles and apparel, two U.S. industries that had
suffered enormously as a result of imports.

Lenahan was given proprietary information by U.S. companies and various American trade associations representing the
two industries. He knew what the top priorities of the companies
would be, and he was well aware of the concessions the U.S.
negotiators were prepared to make in order to get the agreement
renewed or at least extended.

Just days before the team's departure for the talks in Geneva,
Lenahan quit the Commerce Department and went to work for
the International Business and Economic Research Corporation,
a Washington lobbying firm that represented Japan, Hong
Kong, South Korea, and the Philippines, the very nations on the
opposite side of the table from the United States. He even attended the meeting in Geneva, saying that he was not attempting
to influence U.S. policy, but merely advising Hong Kong.

When a bill was introduced in the Senate in 1985 that threatened to increase U.S. tariffs on Japanese telecommunications
equipment, Stanton Anderson, a Washington lawyer and one-
time Nixon White House aide with strong ties to the Reagan
administration, helped organize the opposition.

One Washington reporter who covers trade issues said of
Anderson: "He's a very effective lobbyist. Stan Anderson knows
within hours what happened at any high-level White House
meeting dealing with Japan."

At the time of the threatened tariffs, Anderson's law firm
represented the Communications Industries Association of Japan, and he was chairman of Global USA, a lobbying firm with
a client list that included two Japanese high-technology companies, Kyocera and Fanuc, and a Japanese airline, All Nippon
Airways.

The Senate was unable to muster support for a bill with any
teeth. Later Robert Angel, former chief of the Japan Economic
Institute, a Washington research organization funded by the
Japanese government, told Eduardo Lachica of the *Wall Street
Journal*: "Japan hasn't lost a battle since Nixon acted against
Japanese textiles. It can buy its way out of any trouble." Angel
quit the institute in a dispute over what he viewed as undue

influence over its affairs by Japan's Ministry of Foreign Affairs.

A study by the General Accounting Office, the chief investigative arm of Congress, raised the image that virtually any sort of expertise acquired while working for the U.S. government is for sale in Washington to foreign interests.

The GAO identified seventy-six federal officials who went to work on behalf of foreign interests in Washington after leaving office between 1980 and 1985. Among them were eighteen senior White House officials, twenty-two other high-ranking officials from the executive branch, six senators, nine members of the House, four military officers with the rank of general, and seventeen senior congressional staffers.

However, persons who engage in "private and nonpolitical activities" on behalf of a foreign country are not required to register. And lawyers who represent a foreign government before a court or a government agency are exempt from registering. This exemption covers the dozens upon dozens of lawyers who work against implementation of trade laws on behalf of Japan and other foreign countries.

Because of these and other loopholes in the law on registration of foreign agents, the GAO concluded that its data was incomplete and that the "actual number is likely to be greater."

And the numbers have grown dramatically since that admitted underestimate. For instance, in 1986 alone, fifteen members of the U.S. trade representative's office, the key trade negotiating arm of the U.S. government, left government and signed on as agents for foreign powers. Most of them went to work for the Japanese.

As is the case with everything else surrounding foreign investment and involvement in U.S. society, determining the precise amount that Japanese companies and the Japanese government pay for their representation in the United States is impossible.

Anyone who lobbies public officials for a foreign interest is required by law to register with the Department of Justice in Washington and disclose what he does and how much he is paid. However, the Justice Department division that monitors the 8,000 people registered as foreign agents has a tiny staff, and the best it can hope for is voluntary compliance. Congressional testimony placed the actual number of people working as lobbyists for foreign governments in Washington at 20,000.

Further, Japanese-owned companies in the United States are not required to have their lobbyists register as foreign agents. Therefore, Japan has an enormously powerful built-in force of influential advocates for its policies and positions.

Despite the handicaps of determining precise figures, congressional testimony and experts in Washington estimate that the amount spent by Japanese interests to influence U.S. policy reached about $100 million in 1988. The figure is greater than the combined budgets of the five most influential American business organizations in Washington—the U.S. Chamber of Commerce, the National Association of Manufacturers, the Business Roundtable, the Committee for Economic Development, and the American Business Conference.

The former government officials sell their prestige and supply the access that comes with government service and party politics in a town such as Washington, where relationships and favors are the currency of choice among power brokers. And they take with them vital inside knowledge when they switch sides.

Representative Marcy Kaptur, an Ohio Democrat who has worked hard for stricter laws governing foreign lobbying by former high-ranking government officials, told a congressional hearing in 1987 about the experience of one of her constituents.

"A few years ago, one businessman from my district, engaged in auto parts manufacture and export, participated in a U.S. Department of Commerce trade mission abroad," Kaptur testified. "During that trip, he shared proprietary information about his business with U.S. officials in charge of the mission.

"When I met with him last year, he explained to me in dismay that after he returned to Washington to follow up on matters related to the mission, he discovered that the same people he had previously dealt with in the U.S. government were now working on behalf of the very foreign interests that compete with his company. He is convinced that the last place he can trust to represent American interests is the U.S. Department of Commerce."

Although Kaptur did not identify the "foreign interests" in her congressional testimony, she acknowledged later that the country was Japan.

Access and expertise are what a foreign nation or corporation buys when it hires a lobbyist in Washington or a state capitol— access to the decision makers, an opportunity to get its side of the story put out with the most possible influence and impact, and expertise gained while in the pay of the U.S. citizens and sometimes turned over at their expense to competing foreign interests.

The foreign lobby in Washington is truly "an American original," said attorney Deborah M. Levy in a 1987 issue of the journal *Foreign Policy*. There is no similar mechanism of American-paid lobbyists working in Tokyo or Osaka or London or Seoul.

That is a point that was made forcefully by Pat Choate, director of policy analysis for the U.S. technology and defense firm TRW. In 1987, he told a congressional panel: "In another nation, this wholesale employment of former senior government officials as influence peddlers for foreign interests would be unthinkable, even a national scandal. Certainly, it smudges the federal government's already limited credibility and casts doubt on the integrity of U.S. trade negotiations and the administration of trade programs."

Nothing illustrates Choate's point better than the case of Robert E. Watkins, who was a leader of the U.S. delegation in U.S.-Japan trade talks in 1987 as a senior official at the U.S. Commerce Department. He didn't even bother to wait until he left government to try to sign up with the Japanese.

In 1986 and 1987, the U.S. trade team was concentrating on negotiating an agreement to stop Japan from flooding the United States with auto parts and to allow some U.S. manufacturers to sell in Japan. Bruce Smart, the undersecretary for international trade at the Commerce Department, headed the team. But he had no experience, so the specifics of the agreement were left to Watkins, who was deputy assistant secretary for automotive affairs and consumer goods.

The year-long talks ended in August 1987 with little progress. The only agreement was a weak provision to monitor the purchases of auto parts in certain product categories between the two nations. None of the guarantees of U.S. access to Japanese markets was secured, or even in sight.

Less than two months later, on September 23, when Watkins was still at the Commerce Department, he wrote letters and sent copies of his résumé to the Japanese car manufacturers and dozens of Japanese auto parts companies, asking them to hire him as a lobbyist. Watkins said he was "uniquely qualified to establish and lead an automotive association committed to market principles." He also said he should be hired to help protect the Japanese against "xenophobic and protectionist political action."

Disclosure of the letter in October by the Associated Press prompted Congresswoman Kaptur, whose district includes many auto parts manufacturers, to take to the floor of the House of Representatives and denounce Watkins.

"I am absolutely outraged at the despicable behavior of one of this nation's leading trade negotiators who sold America down the river to line his own pocketbook," said Kaptur.

A few hours later, Watkins resigned. A Commerce Department spokesman said Watkins quit because "he couldn't be effective in his job as deputy assistant secretary."

The Commerce Department's top ethics official later testified before Congress that Watkins had spoken to one of her assistants in June about his plans to seek a job outside of government and was advised that he would be allowed to remain in the trade negotiations until a company agreed to hire him. However, the ethics official said that Watkins had not mentioned his idea for creating an association for foreign companies.

The head of the federal Office of Government Ethics later said that Watkins's action "went well beyond any permissible course of conduct," but a GAO report to Congress said Watkins had not violated any laws.

Watkins may be an extreme case. But the easy availability of former government officials ensures an effective and sophisticated lobby for foreign corporations and nations.

Consider the $200,000 propaganda campaign orchestrated to smooth the way for Japanese Prime Minister Yasuhiro Nakasone's first visit to the United States in early 1985 by the high-powered Washington lobbying firm of Gray & Co.

The firm's head was Robert K. Gray, a lobbyist whose highly visible friendship with President Reagan had earned him a reputation as "the king of clout," according to the *Los Angeles Times*.

Gray had come to Washington in 1953 to serve in the Eisenhower White House, and he had stayed on as presidents came and went, winding up as cochairman of Ronald Reagan's inauguration.

Most appropriately, his offices were on two floors of a converted electric-generating plant called "The Powerhouse" in a fashionable area of Georgetown. Although he was a Republican, Gray was savvy enough to know that long-term survival in Washington meant rolling with the sentiments of the voters, so his payroll included Gary Hymel, a top aide to Thomas P. "Tip" O'Neill when the Massachusetts Democrat was Speaker of the House, and Frank Mankiewicz, former press secretary to Senator Robert F. Kennedy and to George McGovern's 1972 presidential campaign.

In 1982, Gray organized a $100,000 lobbying campaign to push relief for foreign bankers and precious-metals dealers through Congress. He and his aides visited seven House members and three senators, talked to dozens of top congressional staff members, and sent bottles of wine at Christmas to staff aides of liberal Democratic senators.

Both houses of Congress passed a bill giving $3.3 million to the dealers and bankers for silver they had ordered but could not buy on a day in 1967 when the Treasury Department stopped selling silver from its stockpiles. It was a victory after fifteen years for the dealers and bankers.

But it was short-lived. Reagan vetoed the measure, saying that the United States could not afford such private-relief legislation.

The mere fact that Gray had almost single-handedly pushed such private legislation through Congress was one likely reason that the Japanese government turned to him in late 1984. Gray's job was to soften up the U.S. public and its opinion makers in preparation for a Nakasone-Reagan meeting in Los Angeles on January 2, 1985. The Japanese viewed the visit as critical to heading off rising pressure from Congress for legislative action to force the Japanese to open their markets to U.S. companies and help ease the soaring trade deficit.

Documents outlining what Gray & Co. did for the Japanese government are contained in the foreign agents' files at the Justice Department in Washington. The documents form a blueprint for the modern propaganda campaign, describing all the ways that sophisticated propagandists can manipulate public opinion through news outlets.

In a letter to an official at the Japanese embassy in Washington, Robert Gray outlined the campaign and promised, "It will raise the general level of awareness of the visit, reinforce the importance of the U.S.-Japan bilateral relationship, and give Americans a greater understanding of and appreciation for the Prime Minister."

Gray said he would send a five-person film production team to Japan to prepare segments to feed free to American television and radio stations in advance of the visit that would cast Japan and Nakasone in the best possible light. The broadcast end of the campaign would include interviews with Nakasone and Mike Mansfield, the U.S. ambassador to Japan, conducted by Meryl Comer, the host of a syndicated business program.

Using a "real" journalist would provide the segments with the sheen of authenticity and objectivity necessary to get them aired as news on television and radio stations around the United States.

To augment the packaged news, Gray said his staff would work with the Japanese embassy to identify experts on U.S.-Japan relations and place them on television and radio programs prior to the visit. While the documents did not specify the philosophical leanings of the experts who would be picked, there is a huge pool of academics and think-tank occupants in Washington whose bills are paid in full or in part by the Japanese and who always have a friendly opinion ready to offer.

Gray also proposed a blitz of American newspaper and magazine columnists and editorial writers to "produce positive editorials and opinion pieces." Magazine writers were targeted to produce glossy profiles of Nakasone in advance of the trip. In case that was not enough, Gray & Co. would prepare its own pieces for the op-ed pages of the nation's newspapers.

Nowhere, of course, would the carefully orchestrated news segments, expert guests, editorials, and opinion pieces be identified as having been financed by the Japanese government.

In 1986, Gray's firm was acquired by Hill and Knowlton, one of the world's biggest public relations firms and also a frequent employee of foreign interests, including a roster of Japan's largest manufacturers and trade associations.

Some of Washington's most powerful law firms have been built on a foundation of lobbying government officials on behalf of special-interest groups and companies. Few of them make a distinction on the nationality of the client, preferring only to make sure they are paying in dollars. And the dollars can be enormous.

For the last six months of 1987, for instance, the Washington office of the law firm of Akin, Gump, Strauss, Hauer & Feld was paid $741,934 by five foreign companies or governments. The bulk of the money, $486,659, came from Fujitsu, the giant Japanese electronics manufacturer, which had been fighting to acquire one of America's premier semiconductor firms in the Silicon Valley of California.

Among the services provided by the law firm for Fujitsu were visits by its lawyers to several key Reagan administration officials with responsibility for trade and foreign investment in the United States. The officials ranged from Alan Holmer, the general counsel to the U.S. trade representative, to Douglas McMinn, assistant secretary of state.

The firm also sent letters to an unspecified number of government officials—letters which it acknowledged in its Justice Department filings constituted "political propaganda."

Akin Gump, as the firm is known, is not just another law firm. It has a reputation for awesome access to the politicians and high-ranking government administrators who determine U.S. policy on virtually any key issue.

One reason for its power is the founder of its Washington office, Robert Strauss. He served in several high positions in the administration of President Jimmy Carter and the Democratic Party, and he was also Carter's special trade envoy.

But the personal charm and effectiveness of Strauss are well augmented by campaign contributions to friendly elected officials.

For years, the firm's contributions to political candidates have been at or near the top among U.S. law firms. Members of the firm themselves gave at least $121,000 to political candidates during 1981–1982. For six months in 1987, a nonelection year for Congress, the firm contributed more than $45,000 to congressmen.

Political giving by lawyers in Washington has only two purposes: insuring access to politicians on behalf of the firm's clients, and rewarding congressmen who have proven friendly in the past.

"This money holds out no pretense of constituency," says Fred Wertheimer, president of Common Cause, the self-styled citizens' group. "This is straight access buying, an extension of the hired gun principle."

Even Strauss does not object strongly to that assessment. He told the *Wall Street Journal*'s John Fialka that part of his firm helps lawmakers who are "philosophically akin to our client base."

Federal campaign law prohibits foreign interests from donating to U.S. political candidates. But the law does not stop the lawyers and lobbyists hired by these interests from making campaign contributions in their own names, although the net effect is precisely the same.

Foreign interests have also found another way around the federal campaign restrictions.

U.S. subsidiaries of foreign firms are treated the same as domestic corporations under federal election law. Like American-owned corporations, they may not make contributions to political candidates directly out of company coffers. But they may establish political action committees, or PACs, that are run by corporate personnel and solicit contributions from company employees.

The result is that U.S. election laws do not permit resident aliens to vote, but they and all foreign-owned subsidiaries are free to make campaign contributions that can exert far greater influence on U.S. policy.

More than 100 foreign companies have legally created their own PACs. Those PACs channel more than $1 million a year into congressional elections alone.

The Japanese have also sought to advocate their message by offering free trips to Japan and honoraria to American academics, journalists, and others. Take the Foreign Press Center of Japan, which is "an independent nonprofit foundation financed by the government of Japan, the Japan Newspaper Publishers and Editors Association and the Japan Federation of Economic Organizations for the express purpose of assisting foreign correspondents in Japan," according to its filing at the U.S. Department of Justice.

Another source of Japanese influence over American policy is the growing number of Japanese corporations and government ministries supporting the work of scholars and think-tank-type institutes that play an extraordinary role in shaping the ideas of official Washington.

In an article in June 1988 in the *Washington Post*, TRW's Pat Choate illustrated the point by citing the example of the Institute for International Economics, the think tank with the greatest influence over policy thinking on trade issues in Washington. The institute was created and originally financed with money from West Germany. In recent years, Japan has emerged as a chief source of its funds.

The institute is a strong opponent of government intervention in trade relations between nations. Its scholarly studies downplay the value of retaliatory actions to redress trade inequities and minimize the role played by Japanese protectionism in creating the U.S. trade deficit with Japan.

Choate cited a 1981 study by the institute in which its scholars estimated that the Japanese barred only $2 billion worth of U.S. exports from their shores. Clyde Prestowitz, an author and a former Commerce Department expert on Japan, said that amount could be accounted for by Japanese restrictions on the sale of U.S. tobacco products alone. In fact, Commerce Depart-

ment analysts calculated that Japan had barred $20 billion worth
of U.S. products in 1982.

By 1985, the institute had increased its estimates, but only
slightly. It said that Japanese protectionism contributed $5 bil-
lion to $8 billion to the trade imbalance between the two coun-
tries. Japanese trade negotiators used the figure as proof that
their trade barriers were minimal, and the Reagan administration adopted the estimate in opposing tough retaliatory provisions in the 1988 trade bill.

Yet other scholars believe Japanese protectionism probably
keeps $50 billion worth of U.S. goods from getting into Japan,
an amount roughly equal to the size of the American trade deficit
with Japan in 1988.

6
THE SHADOW LOBBY

IN MANY WAYS, THE JAPANESE LOBBY in Washington has become so pervasive that this foreign nation is emerging as a full-fledged member of the decision-making process on any issue that affects Japan. The heavy spending by the Japanese in a multitude of public-opinion fields has given them the capacity, through their hired agents and people with less overt links, to shape U.S. policy debates on key matters.

Few legislative issues have been as critical to relations between Japan and the United States in the last two decades as the giant trade bill that was put together by Congress over a three-year period running from 1985 until its final passage in the summer of 1988.

This was a piece of legislation with the potential to provide an impetus for U.S. manufacturing to reposition itself for better international competition, and to level the international playing field in ways that would help restore the nation's trade balance.

And it is a piece of legislation in which key advice in its early stages was provided to Congress by three former high-ranking U.S. government officials with financial ties to Japan. As is often the case in Washington lobbying, there is nothing illegal about what went on here. But it is another striking example of the depth to which Japanese interests have been insinuated into the political process of the United States.

The three former government officials were Robert Strauss, the Washington lawyer and former special U.S. trade representative whose list of lobbying clients in 1986 included Fujitsu; William Eberle, also a former U.S. trade representative, whose lobbying firm, Manchester Associates, represented Nissan Motors in 1986; and Fred Bergsten, a former U.S. Treasury Department official, whose Washington think tank was created with money from the Germans and was receiving substantial chunks of money from a U.S. foundation financed by the Japanese in 1986.

Here is what happened.

The House Ways and Means Committee, arguably the most powerful panel in Congress, began formulating the outline of a trade bill in 1985. By early 1986, the congressmen were trying to come up with the central theories that would be contained in the legislation.

Normally, the process at this point is devoted to congressional hearings at which expert witnesses and people potentially affected by the legislation appear to give testimony. This is also the point at which the lobbyists begin to- exert their substantial muscle.

Representative Dan Rostenkowski, the Chicago Democrat who is chairman of the committee, decided to do things differently this time. In February 1986, he announced that the committee would attend a retreat in Florida during which members would devote their time solely to trade issues. Lobbyists would be barred, and the committee members would become students in the hands of experts from academic institutions and trade-policy think tanks.

"We will meet to learn, not legislate," said Rostenkowski in a February 21 press release, "and I hope that our extended discussions will allow time for the type of comprehensive examination of issues that simply isn't possible during hearings. Trade is our priority for this year."

In the name of fairness, the committee staff selected the liberal-leaning Brookings Institution and the conservative-styled American Enterprise Institute to organize the seminar. Financing assistance came from the Ford Foundation and the Luce Foundation.

Rostenkowski's press release contained a schedule for the three-day retreat, which would be held March 14–16 at Destin, Florida, a quiet resort town perched on a narrow strip of land between Choctawhatchee Bay and the Gulf of Mexico.

What Rostenkowski's press release failed to contain, and what committee staffers later refused to release, was the list of experts who would be providing the committee members with their in-depth look at the complex issue of international trade. A congressman concerned about Japanese influence on the American political process later provided a list of the faculty.

Robert Strauss was listed as one of two keynote speakers. He was identified only as a former U.S. trade representative, with no mention of his lobbying work on behalf of Fujitsu and other foreign clients. The other was the current U.S. trade representative, Clayton Yeutter.

Among the thirteen experts chosen as faculty members were William Eberle, identified as being from Manchester Associates, and Fred Bergsten, identified as being from the Institute for International Economics.

Joseph Pechman, an official at Brookings who helped organize the retreat, said the names of virtually all the experts who would form the faculty came from the Ways and Means staff. "The names were presented to AEI and Brookings by the committee staff," he said. "Our degree of maneuverability was very limited."

Nonetheless, Pechman defended the selection of all three men, saying he was certain that the congressmen were aware of the work that Strauss and Eberle had done on behalf of the Japanese. When asked about the money that Bergsten's institute receives from a Japanese-financed foundation, Pechman indignantly defended his former Brookings colleague as a respected expert on international trade.

Questions exist, however, about whether the majority of the congressmen attending the retreat were aware of the connections between the former U.S. officials and Japanese interests. The confidential outline of the program contained no reference to any such ties.

More importantly, two congressmen who attended the session, Donald Pease of Ohio and Robert Matsui of California, said they had no recollection of any disclosure that any of the three experts were linked in any fashion to Japan or any other foreign interests.

No one is suggesting that these former government officials should be stopped from expressing their views. Most people would not stop them from working for a foreign government once they leave office. There is no law to prohibit such a step. Nothing, that is, so long as their connections are disclosed.

The issue is not influence peddling itself, but influence peddling concealed behind the facade of governmental credentials and objectivity.

The solution is called "transparency." It means simply that people engaged in lobbying and related activities disclose the interests they represent. The idea is that you can more accurately judge someone's opinions and the facts they are providing if you are aware of whom they represent, who is paying their bills.

Ronald L. Danielian, president of the International Economic Policy Association, a Washington research organization financed by American companies doing business overseas, pointed out the problem in a 1986 paper decrying the influence of foreign interests on trade policy.

"It is essential that our policymakers have an accurate, objective understanding of the [trade] situation," wrote Danielian. "Unfortunately, this objectivity is tainted by a deluge of policy advice from foreign interests and governments."

One way to combat the problem, he said in an interview, is to require witnesses before Congress or experts providing information to congressmen to make a detailed, written disclosure of who is paying them and how much they are being paid.

This is stronger than the Foreign Agents Registration Act because it would require the disclosure at the point of influence spreading. With the weak FARA provisions, the lists of lobbyists are tucked away in a small office across the street from the J. Edgar Hoover FBI Building in Washington.

But in a town like Washington, where it's often difficult to tell who represents whom, transparency is a controversial subject that has met stern resistance outside government and within government. It would upset the intricate network of old boys that flourishes in Washington.

So what we end up with is a retreat to discuss the all-important trade bill, at which three former government officials are viewed as impartial trade experts by congressmen; a session from which lobbyists had been specifically barred, except for some lobbyists in other clothing.

This is yet another graphic illustration of the unprecedented success that the Japanese have had in enlisting the aid and influence of the most important American figures in the international trade arena.

The most important service provided by these former government officials is not knocking on the doors of congressmen on specific issues or lobbying their former colleagues in the U.S. trade representative's office or the Treasury Department. It is this more subtle and sophisticated manner in which they set the tone and terms of U.S. debate on such important policy matters as the first comprehensive trade bill in more than two decades.

These are the wise men of trade, and when they talk, harried congressmen and former subordinates listen. And what they hear is not a Japanese lobbyist or an expert from a think tank financed partly by foreign interests. They hear the architects of American trade policy for the last two decades defining the terms for the coming decade.

This phenomenon was described as long ago as 1984 in an article in *The New Republic* by writer David Osborne. He urged an examination of the droves of U.S. trade experts crossing over to work for the Japanese.

U.S. government agencies, he wrote, "have become virtual training camps for our Japanese competitors, whose roster of lawyers, lobbyists and consultants reads like an all-star team of former U.S. trade specialists."

None of these all-stars is more prominent than Fred Bergsten, an assistant treasury secretary in charge of international trade in the Carter administration, former Brookings senior fellow, and author of more than a dozen books on trade and related issues.

In 1981, after Jimmy Carter was replaced in the White House by Ronald Reagan, Bergsten founded an organization called the Institute for International Economics in Washington. It was a think tank that became the premier research center on international trade issues, and through it Bergsten became the most prominent expert in the city on international trade.

Anointing his position, between January 1984 and June 1988 Bergsten was quoted as an expert source a whopping eighty-three times in news articles and columns by Hobart Rowen, chief economics writer for the *Washington Post*. In that town, there is no stronger validation for a nongovernment official than regular appearances in the capital's most influential newspaper.

Through this period, Bergsten's institute received a substantial portion of its funding through foreign entities and governments. The institute was started with $4 million from the German Marshall Fund of the United States, a foundation financed by the West German government.

The West German money was augmented for the first time in 1984 by a $100,000 grant from an organization called the United States Japan Foundation, which was created in New York with a $48 million grant from a group financed by a Japanese billionaire power broker. The Japanese grant was increased to $200,000 in 1985 and has been given in that amount annually since then. In addition, the institute has received money from various Japanese corporations and foundations over the years.

During his years at the institute, Bergsten has been an outspoken advocate of free trade. He has repeatedly downplayed the role of Japanese import barriers in creating the deficit with the United States, and he has argued against steps to impose sanctions on the Japanese.

Reports issued by Bergsten and the institute are fodder for the Japanese during negotiations with the Americans to open up Japan's markets. The papers allow the Japanese to point out that one of the most influential experts on trade in the United States says not to worry about Japan's trade barriers. And government officials who oppose strong steps against the Japanese frequently find succor in papers from the Institute for International Economics.

"The reports of the institute were used extensively to support the view that there are no trade barriers with Japan," recalled Clyde Prestowitz from his years as counsel to the secretary of commerce for Japanese affairs. "The argument was that any barriers to exporting U.S. goods to Japan were only minor, and it really was not worth spending much effort trying to negotiate opening the Japanese market. The State Department and the Council of Economic Advisers, they used Fred's work to bolster their positions."

The name of the game at Washington think tanks is influencing policy, and the most canny organizations have learned the fine art of timing their releases to have the most impact. This generally means releasing a study or a paper on the eve of an important debate or vote on the issue. No one practices this fine art better than Bergsten.

For instance, congressional pressure to punish the Japanese with trade sanctions was strong in the summer of 1985 as the U.S. trade balance with Japan worsened. Complaints of American industry were heard that Japan's barriers stopped U.S. exports there and contributed to a trade deficit that, in 1985, would top $50 billion for the first time in history.

In response, negotiators from the U.S. trade representative's office, the Commerce Department, and other federal agencies were engaged in tough talks with the Japanese on opening Japan's markets to U.S. goods in order to relieve the deficit pressure.

On July 11, 1985, at a trade seminar for government and industry officials, Bergsten released the latest study prepared by the Institute for International Economics. The conclusion was that Japan's barriers had been exaggerated.

The study claimed that even if Japan dropped "all overt and tangible" barriers to trade, its surplus with the United States would be reduced by only $5 billion to $6 billion. Further, the study contended that U.S. barriers on Japanese imports kept out nearly an equal amount of Japanese goods.

"Although both sets of estimates must be considered quite rough, they suggest that approximate reciprocity already exists," wrote Bergsten and a senior fellow at his institute, William Cline.

In an unusual display of emotion and bluntness, a senior official from the U.S. trade representative's office stood up at the seminar as Bergsten was talking and challenged the findings.

Gaza Feketekuty, senior assistant trade representative, called Bergsten's study "a whitewash for the Japanese system," and told Bergsten directly, "I fear your paper could reduce the incentive for the Japanese to make reforms and get rid of protectionism."

Bergsten responded that the report was not a whitewash and pointed to a section recommending that the Japanese take the lead in rolling back restraints because of the anger the barriers were kindling in Washington.

But the text of the report was devoted substantially to eliminating any blame for the Japanese and subtly shifting it to the United States. The report said that Japanese imports of U.S. manufactured goods had risen considerably in recent years. And it said a more important solution than wasting time on trade barriers was persuading the United States government to reduce its budget deficit.

Without question, deficit spending by the United States government has contributed enormously to its trade imbalance. And blame can also be parceled out to American consumers who are wedded to imports and to American industries which are wedded to outdated manufacturing plants and poor-quality products.

But a huge portion of the blame must also go to the Japanese, who have closed their markets to U.S. goods at the same time that they have taken advantage of the openness of American markets and manipulated the U.S. political process to ensure that their advantage remains intact.

The subtle technique of pointing the accusing finger solely at the United States has been adopted by Japanese business and government officials. It has also become a popular notion, and a more insidious one, with a variety of U.S.-based organizations having financial links to Japan.

Bergsten did not respond to repeated telephone calls by the authors of this book for comment on his relationship with foreign funding sources. But he did reply to indications in a 1988 *Business Week* article that his institute was influenced by Japanese money.

"Innuendos that Japanese funding could influence the agenda, research findings, or policy recommendations of the Institute for International Economics are so ludicrous that it is necessary to set the record straight," Bergsten wrote *Business Week*. "The institute receives no financing from any government, in Japan or elsewhere. We have never experienced the slightest hint of pressure from any of our funders and would immediately reject both the pressure and the money if that were ever to occur. Institute studies have been extremely critical of Japanese policies in both the macroeconomic and trade areas. Any fair evaluation of our work would surely reject any notion that the institute is soft on Japan."

Despite the disclaimer, Bergsten's institute has long-standing and substantial financial ties to an organization in New York with its roots deep in Japan. In addition, the chairman of the board of that organization is former trade representative William Eberle.

The organization is the United States Japan Foundation. The foundation was created with a $48 million grant from the Japanese Shipbuilding Industry Foundation in March 1981, at a time when trade problems had strained the relationship between the United States and Japan. Its expressed purpose was to strengthen cooperation and understanding between the two countries by financing studies, public television programs, and exchange programs involving lawmakers, politicians, and scholars.

The board of directors was made up of prominent former U.S. and Japanese government officials and academics. The year after its creation, former presidents Jimmy Carter and Gerald Ford joined as honorary advisers along with former Japanese prime ministers Takeo Fukada and Nobusuke Kishi.

Its first chairman, former U.S. diplomat Angier Biddle Duke,

said at the outset that the foundation would not become a lobbying organization. Rather, he promised, it would try to foster new
understandings among the leaders of the two nations.

Yet the next year, when it issued its first full annual report, the
foundation set forth some interesting criteria for determining
which projects it would finance.

"We will consider a project's capacity to achieve broader impact regionally as well as nationally," the report said. "We will
also examine the capacity of a project to influence public opinion."

The foundation's own words sound suspiciously like those of a
lobbying organization. And an examination of the background
of the man behind its creation raises more questions about the
United States Japan Foundation.

The foundation was the latest goodwill gesture of Ryoichi
Sasakawa, an aging Japanese billionaire who has spent millions
of dollars trying to buy himself a Nobel Peace Prize and, in the
view of many, to erase the sins of his checkered past.

Sasakawa's donations of $50 million to the United Nations, $12
million to Mother Theresa, millions of dollars to American
colleges, and even $1.5 million to the Jimmy Carter Presidential
Library have earned him respectability and a reputation as
possibly the world's most generous philanthropist—at least in the
United States.

Sasakawa, the son of a poor sake brewer, claims that when he
was a small child, Buddhist priests told his parents that he had
been sent from heaven to purify the world. And Sasakawa maintains that fulfilling that prophecy has been his life's mission.

Yet buying respectability, let alone a savior's purity, has not
been so easy in his native Japan. At home, Sasakawa is viewed as
a *kuromaku*, a man behind the curtain, a right-wing power
broker. At home, they know he earns his vast fortune at the helm
of a motorboat-racing concession that is the only form of legalized gambling in Japan in private hands.

And as with gambling everywhere, it's the poor, who can least
afford it, who are the source of Sasakawa's money and the
influence it buys him. They bet about $10 billion last year on

races held at twenty-four motorboat courses across Japan operated by Sasakawa.

As a condition of maintaining his monopoly on legalized
gambling in Japan, Sasakawa was required to donate 3.3 percent
of the betting take each year to a charity. So he established the
Japan Shipbuilding Industry Foundation and has bankrolled it
since shortly after World War II.

Questions about Sasakawa's fitness to finance U.S. public-
opinion makers can be traced back to the 1930s, when he formed
a national right-wing party and mobilized his own private army
and twenty-two-plane air force. The 15,000 soldiers wore black
shirts, and Sasakawa spoke openly of his desire to form an
alliance with the fascists in Italy and Germany.

Indeed, in the early 1930s he flew to Rome and was photo-
graphed with Mussolini. He told a *Business Week* reporter in
1986 that Hitler had wanted him to extend his visit in Rome
until the German leader could arrive and meet him, but he had
to return to Tokyo.

Before the war, his fascist party joined other Japanese politicians in agitating for war against the United States. In 1945, after
Japan's surrender, Sasakawa was among eighty Japanese rounded
up and sent to Sugamo prison in Tokyo with the label "Class A"
war criminals.

Sasakawa has maintained that he was imprisoned because he
had been a prominent prewar politician and had helped train
the Japanese air force. The U.S. intelligence forces at the time
had a different view, saying in a report that "Sasakawa is potentially dangerous to Japan's political future" and that he "chafes
for continued power."

But the fervor for punishing the Japanese waned, and after
three years Sasakawa was released from prison without formal
charges ever having been placed against him.

He quickly reestablished right-wing connections that continue
today and, with the help of politicians he met while in prison, he
obtained the right to manage the motorboat races.

The huge profits generated by the boat betting provide a
source of funds that Sasakawa has used to spread his influence

across the globe, and one of his most successful creations has been the United States Japan Foundation.

The list of good works financed by the foundation reads like a *Who's Who* among the organizations that influence American public opinion. In 1986, for instance, Bergsten's think tank received $200,000 in continued support of its studies on trade issues; the United Nations Association of the United States of America got $150,000 to establish a group to examine Soviet policies from Japanese and American viewpoints; and WNET-TV, the public television station in New York, received $200,000 to develop programming on Japan for broadcast over American stations.

About $700,000 was given to eight American universities and educational institutes to support programs aimed at teaching students about Japan and creating textbooks on Japanese-American relations.

Another large chunk of money, again about $700,000, went to a variety of organizations that sent American educators, business and political leaders, scholars, and journalists to Japan on expense-paid visits. The National Conference of State Legislatures got $98,622 to send state legislators to Japan; the year before, a group of congressmen had gone to Japan on a trip financed by the foundation.

The biggest grant awarded by the foundation, $250,000, went to the Japan Society of New York for its United States–Japan Leadership Program. The program sends promising American leaders to Japan on visits ranging in length from three to five months. The visitors, whose expenses are paid, range from leading journalists and think-tank scholars to elected officials and labor leaders.

Bruce Stokes, who covers trade for the prestigious Washington publication *National Journal*, spent three months in Japan on the program in 1987. Among the other participants that year were Susan Spencer, a CBS-TV network reporter; a reporter from the *Boston Globe*; and a judge from Philadelphia.

The participants are chosen from nominations submitted by anonymous selectors. Stokes, who had written articles critical of Japanese influence peddling in the United States and extensive articles on the role of the newly industrialized countries of Asia in world trade, said he was called out of the blue one day and invited to go to Japan.

"They are trying to influence the future leaders of America," said Stokes. "As long as it's transparent, I don't think there's anything wrong with it. In fact, I'm outraged that American foundations aren't doing the same thing.

"The Japanese were smart enough not to impose any restrictions on us. I got to interview everyone I wanted to see. I think I even could have seen the prime minister if I'd asked to. They seemed to indicate that that was possible, but only for a short visit."

Stokes said he is still no fan of Japan, but he has a deeper understanding of its culture and problems, and he has written more frequently about Japanese trade as a result of his visit.

"They got their money's worth out of me," he said. "My magazine couldn't afford to send me to Japan and I'm forever and a day a better reporter because I went."

Not all of the participants have the professional skepticism that allowed Stokes to remain aloof from the sense of obligation engendered by a gesture of this type. He said that some of the people on his trip, and others he has met since who participated in the program, became "gaga" over Japan.

"In the long term, the Japanese can't lose with a program like this," he said.

7
CLOSED DOORS

RECIPROCITY IS THE CONCEPT that best exemplifies the unfairness behind Japan's invasion of the United States. It also is a concept as important as quality and hard work in understanding why Japan has emerged as a world economic power since the end of World War II.

Reciprocity is the notion that the trade door should swing open both ways. Philip Trezise of the Brookings Institution, a Washington think tank, said it simply: "Reciprocity need only mean balanced opportunities to trade. That indeed is a sensible objective."

Along with being a sensible objective, reciprocity is the standard by which many believe trade relations should be measured. When that measure is applied to the Japanese, the world's emerging industrial power fares poorly. A congressional study in 1987 found Japan "among the nations with the most stringent investment restrictions."

A confidential report prepared by the U.S. trade representative's office was even blunter. The language is not shielded in the usual diplomatic tones because nowhere in the forty-page report is its source indicated. The author, a high-ranking official within the trade office, was therefore free to speak his mind in what was expected to be an internal assessment of U.S. access to the Japanese markets.

Although the report was prepared in mid-1985, it has not previously been quoted from, and, more importantly, its arguments are as true today as when they were composed.

"The issue of access to the Japanese market is one of deep concern to the United States," said the report. "Layers of regulatory control, together with the ability of many industrial associations to exercise considerable control over activity in their sectors, makes the Japanese market one of the most difficult to penetrate. This assessment of the Japanese market is held not only by American businessmen, but by businessmen from around the world. It is reflected in the low levels of manufactured imports in the Japanese market."

What this means is that the Japanese can sell their autos and stereos and computers in the United States. And U.S. companies are restricted or prohibited from selling the same products, or the ones at which they excel, in Japan.

What this means, too, is that Japanese corporations can build new plants and acquire anything from office buildings to factories without U.S. governmental restrictions in the United States. Yet whole industries are off limits to U.S. buyers in Japan.

The degree to which Japan's markets are closed is demonstrated by the trend there to limit imports while its exports have soared. Clearly there are other international economic factors at work. Among them are the monstrous deficit spending of the American government, which has required huge sums of foreign capital, and the unbridled appetite of American consumers for imports.

But the impact of Japan's protectionism cannot be ignored in assessing the trade numbers.

Between 1980 and 1985, Japan's exports rose 35 percent and its imports fell 8 percent. The decline in imports came during a period when the Japanese standard of living was improving dramatically. And it came during a period when developments in the United States were going in the opposite direction. U.S. exports declined 3 percent while imports rose 41 percent.

The numbers on the U.S.-Japan trade deficit show how Japan has benefited from open American markets and closed domestic ones.

Between 1982 and 1987, the U.S. trade deficit with Japan increased more than 200 percent, rising from $17 billion to $56.9 billion. U.S. imports of Japanese goods more than doubled, going from $37.7 billion to $84.6 billion. Exports of U.S. goods to Japan, however, rose only about one-third, from $20.7 billion to $27.7 billion.

Many factors played a role in the trade imbalance, but one of them again was Japanese protectionism. American exporters face enormous difficulties in cracking Japan's closed markets, as shown by the years of effort to ship beef there without smothering restrictions.

Japan's Livestock Import Promotion Council is an example of a misnomer if ever there was one.

The semigovernmental body was created not to promote imports of beef to Japan, but to restrict them. As one example of the industry associations mentioned in the confidential U.S. trade representative's report, the council controls all distribution of beef and sets prices, often three times higher than the actual import price. The tactic depresses demand among Japanese consumers and allows the economically weak but politically powerful Japanese agriculture sector to survive.

In addition, the council restricts U.S. beef imports to a specific quota. The quota specifies not only how much can come in, but what cuts—lots of cheap chuck and ground meat, very little sirloin. For instance, in 1987 the quota for all U.S. beef imports was 214,000 tons. Of that amount, only 52 tons could be sirloin.

The only meat that American firms can export to Japan in unlimited quantities is offal, the collection of scrap meats that the Japanese then turn into a product called "formed steak." As a result, the imported U.S. beef most widely available to Japanese consumers is of the poorest quality.

"Japanese are always complaining that imported beef tastes

bad," said Philip Seng, the top official in Tokyo for the U.S. Meat Export Federation. "But we're not allowed to sell our best products here."

The Japanese government has authorized 3,600 shops to sell imported beef, but most of the stores only sell it three hours a day because they cannot get enough to maintain a full supply.

In response to U.S. pressure and the threat of trade sanctions, Prime Minister Yasuhiro Nakasone lifted many barriers on imports during his five years in office. But he refused even to discuss removing the quota on beef.

U.S. trade negotiators made removing the restrictions on beef one of their priorities in later negotiations. They also threatened to impose financial penalties against Japan under the General Agreement on Tariffs and Trade. The potential for expensive and highly embarrassing financial penalties, which most experts were certain would be imposed on Japan for unfair restrictions of beef imports, served as a big stick to bring about change.

The breakthrough came in 1988. The government of Nakasone's successor, Prime Minister Noboru Takeshita, approved annual increases of 60,000 tons a year in U.S. beef imports to Japan until the quotas are lifted entirely in 1991.

Under the 1988 agreement, however, the Japanese tariff on beef would be allowed to increase from 25 percent up to 70 percent by 1991 before dropping to 50 percent by 1994.

More significantly, the Japanese agreed to allow U.S. exporters to bypass the import council, which will be phased out over a period of several years. That was a victory that pleased U.S. beef producers at least as much as phasing out the quotas and promised to more than offset the increased tariffs.

Americans produce beef so much more inexpensively than Japan's cattlemen that American products would be cheaper in Japan even with the tariffs and shipping costs, so long as the import council did not impose its protective pricing structure.

Not all Americans involved in the beef-import negotiations were certain the Japanese would stick to the bargain. Often in the past, the Japanese have agreed to concessions and then spent years delaying the new rules. Some were concerned that before the abolition of beef quotas in 1991, Japan might find a reason to back out of its promise.

Part of the reason for fears that Japan might welsh on the deal is the deep-seated national belief of the Japanese that they are truly unique in all the world, even when it comes to the type of beef they can eat.

According to a myth that is almost universally accepted in Japan, the Japanese have intestines thirty feet longer than those of other races, which makes it difficult for them to digest imported beef. The notion was so entrenched that Shunpei Kumon, a noted economics professor at the University of Tokyo, confessed in a newspaper column in 1988 that he had only learned that Japanese intestines were no different from anyone else's as a result of the beef dispute.

The fact that such an outrageous argument won acceptance underscores the degree to which the Japanese view themselves as unique. Such a view offers many justifications for erecting barriers to protect national industries while expecting foreigners to provide the Japanese with free access to their countries.

U.S. construction firms have been barred from bidding on major projects because of Japanese claims that their soil is unique, and foreign-made skis were barred for years because the Japanese snow was supposedly unique.

While it is of less significance, the treatment of outsiders at Japanese golf courses is another telling indicator of how closed their society remains.

Golf is a tremendous passion for the Japanese, who pay as much as $2 million for a club membership. Along with the social status conveyed through the game and membership in the right clubs, such as Kasumigaseki in Tokyo, Japanese tend to conduct a lot of business on the golf course.

While foreigners are allowed to play as guests, they cannot join most Japanese golf clubs as members, particularly the prestigious, old-line clubs. The contrast to the United States is sharp—not only are Japanese allowed to join virtually any U.S. golf club, they have bought a considerable number of them, particularly in Southern California and Hawaii.

On a more substantive side, the Japanese have been far less willing to make compromises that would open their critical industries to competition from Americans or other nations. In such fields as steel, autos, computers, and semiconductors, the Japanese government's protectionism has been instrumental in the creation of world-class industries.

U.S. government policies have been indifferent or even damaging to U.S. corporations. Their Japanese competitors benefit from a strategic industrial plan directed by the Japanese government that has left Japan's domestic markets almost impossible to penetrate. The result is that the Japanese manufacturers have the financial and strategic backing of their government along with a guaranteed market that forms a base for their exports to the United States and elsewhere.

This is a central difference in the policies of the two nations. American businessmen are left by their government to stand alone, and few would want it any differently. Japanese businessmen take a communal view, or a team approach, that makes the government and the private sector partners in planned economic conquest.

The economic advantages for Japan are enormous and must be part of the equation when calculating how the Japanese surpassed the United States.

One of the clearest illustrations of how the Japanese system was set up to take advantage of American openness and its own closed nature is the television wars. The price that the American television pioneers paid for doing even a limited amount of business in Japan was sharing their technology. They had no idea what that price would ultimately cost them.

Immediately following World War II, American television manufacturers such as Motorola, RCA, and Zenith enjoyed a tremendous, perhaps insurmountable, technological and cost advantage over the rest of the world. It seemed certain that America would dominate the world's television industry forever.

The Japanese market, however, was closed to the U.S. producers. Japan's government wanted to give the fledgling Japanese electronics industry time to get off the ground. Despite the lower price of U.S. televisions, they were unavailable to Japanese consumers. Along with keeping out the U.S. rivals, this practice meant that the Japanese firms had a captive market for their inferior, more expensive products.

It was a perfect example of the Japanese reverence for the producer and the relegation of the consumer to a distant second—a telling contrast to the United States.

Television and the larger arena of electronics were viewed in Tokyo as a strategic industry. The government placed a far higher value on developing a domestic television industry than on serving consumers with the best products.

In order to gain access to Japan, RCA and General Electric were required to license the technology for television to Japanese companies in the early 1950s. The decision was encouraged by the U.S. government as an example of the American commitment to help rebuild its former enemy.

The transfer of the technology provided the U.S. companies with some short-term profits from the licensing agreements. But the leap the transaction gave to the Japanese was priceless.

By the 1960s, the Japanese were inundating the U.S. with their black-and-white televisions. The Japanese sets were cheaper for several reasons. Labor costs were far lower in Japan, and the Japanese corporations had not had to invest the money in research and development that Americans had spent, because they had been allowed to license the technology.

More significantly, the Japanese were dumping their television sets on U.S. customers. That is, they were selling them at below-cost prices in order to gain a foothold in the U.S. market. The tactic was successful, in part because the Japanese manufacturers could sell their sets at a higher price at home, where they had no fear of foreign competition.

U.S. manufacturers responded to this wave of inexpensive imports by moving a substantial portion of their assembly offshore to compete with the low wages being paid by the Japanese. The result was lost jobs for American workers, and the loss of years of technological advantage for the industry.

But U.S. technology provided another chance for dominance

through the development of color television. In 1966, Motorola unveiled a prototype for the world's first color television, developed completely without government assistance.

The Japanese government responded with an all-out drive to create color TV technology in Japan. Just as had happened with black-and-white televisions, the Japanese government closed domestic markets to the American color sets. The Japanese program to develop color televisions also benefited from an earlier U.S. action: in 1962, RCA had licensed its color technology to Japan.

So, while Motorola had the first prototype and RCA had the early technology, it was Japan's Hitachi that advanced the technology: they marketed the first commercial solid-state color television in 1969.

Understanding the degree of cooperation employed by the Japanese in overcoming the U.S. lead in the television industry requires an understanding of how closely development and export activities were coordinated in Japan. An interesting look behind the scenes is contained in a 1983 book, *The Japanese Conspiracy*, by Marvin J. Wolf.

In the book, Wolf explains that for two decades, beginning in the 1950s and lasting until their dominance was complete, the Japanese television makers met in secret groups to control price, development, and distribution. The collusion was so well organized that each level of managers from the various Japanese companies met in separate groups to discuss strategy for marketing and pricing.

The Tenth Day Group, composed of middle management, met on the tenth of each month at the Palace Hotel in Tokyo, according to documents at the Japanese Fair Trade Commission. Recommendations were passed up to the Palace Group, which was composed of senior executives who met at the same hotel. The most important matters were handled by the company leaders who met as the Okura Group at the prestigious Okura Hotel in Tokyo.

The chairman of the Okura Group was Konosuke Matsushita, who is known in Japan as the "god of management" for the manner in which he nurtured the company bearing his name into the world's largest consumer electronics firm. The Osaka-based company includes 600 firms. Among them are Panasonic and Motorola's television production unit, Quasar, which Matsushita bought in 1974.

By the mid-1970s, Japan had replaced the United States as home to the world's leading manufacturers of television. A decade later, the only major American company still producing televisions was Zenith, and most of its assembly took place abroad.

Along with conquering the television industry, the Japanese had paved the way for a lucrative monopoly in videocassette recorders and positioned themselves to set the pace for new developments in the video industry.

U.S. technology and its free enterprise system turned out to be no match for the government-directed collusion of the Japanese electronics industry and the country's closed markets.

Along with protecting its markets from imports, Japan carefully screens and restricts any direct investment by foreign interests.

Japan employs an elaborate investment-approval process, with the Ministry of Finance, the Foreign Exchange Ministry, and other ministries having jurisdiction to review each investment and take comments from potential Japanese competitors. The ministries can demand alterations in any proposed investment or deny it outright.

Japanese law permits only joint ventures and prohibits foreign ownership of more than 50 percent of its energy companies or more than 25 percent of what the government deems "technologically innovative" companies.

To be approved, an investment must not "harm the national security, disturb the public order, or hamper public safety." In addition, the proposed deal must not "adversely or seriously affect" Japanese companies in the same or a similar type of business and must not "adversely affect the smooth operation of the national economy."

Further, a Japanese cabinet decision said that foreign investment in agriculture, forestry, fisheries, mining, petroleum, leather, and leather products "shall, at least for the time being, be dealt with, as in the past, with prudence." The policy has been widely interpreted as closing those areas to foreign investment.

As a 1987 congressional report pointed out, almost any investment of substance would probably violate at least one of these vaguely worded protectionist policies and provide the means for a ministry or a powerful industry to block the deal.

"There is broad latitude on the part of the Japanese government to discourage the investment and, for the most part wholly owned investments by foreigners are restricted to only those cases where Japan absolutely needs the investment for one reason or another," said Ronald L. Danielian, a former U.S. Commerce Department economist who heads the International Economic Policy Association, a nonprofit research organization in Washington funded by American industry.

In testimony before Congress in May 1986, Danielian explained how the U.S. auto companies had tried in vain to invest in Japan in the 1960s. The companies then began to try to buy minority interests in Japanese auto companies, again without success. In fact, U.S. auto companies were not allowed to invest in Japan until the Japanese had developed a full-fledged auto industry that supplied a growing number of cars to the world, including the United States. And that permission came only after pressure was exerted by the U.S. government.

"If U.S. companies had been free to invest in Japan back in the 1960s, our automobile trade picture would look much different today in terms of the enormous drain on the U.S. international accounts," Danielian said. "At a minimum, a portion of the income earned from imports of Japanese cars would have accrued to the United States and the U.S. automobile companies."

Automobiles and televisions are two of the most important consumer businesses in the world. They also represent areas where American technological advancements have often provided substantial side benefits for the nation's defense.

They are also two industries where the United States has watched its technological edge erode and disappear. They are only part of the list of businesses in which the Japanese have gained the upper hand through a national policy that protects domestic markets and targets the development of strategic industries.

The Japanese government often disputes that its markets are being opened slowly to foreign businesses, and its leaders frequently point out that government regulations are not as restrictive as American businessmen charge.

Yet the U.S. trade representative's unpublished report described a series of levels at which foreign investment in Japan is blocked, so that cracking the market there begins to sound as difficult as finding one's way through a maze.

"Systemic Japanese governmental measures include formal measures, such as tariffs and quotas," said the report. "While some of these explicit restrictions have been reduced over the years, tariffs and quotas continue to severely restrict imports on certain products of interest to Japan's trading partners. High tariffs effectively limit imports of wood, paper, some fisheries, aluminum and various petrochemicals, for example. Import quotas continue to restrict imports of fisheries, leather and leather goods, and an extensive list of agricultural products. Such formal governmental measures limit trade opportunities for both developed and developing countries, even though foreign supplies are frequently cheaper and of higher quality due to lower material and/or energy costs or natural endowment."

The report said the Japanese government also intervenes directly in the market to ensure that Japanese suppliers have a dominant position. New foreign-made goods are often prevented from entering Japan's market until domestic producers have developed competitive technology.

One example cited in the report involved an American company that had been the sole supplier of a certain type of aluminum sheeting for use on an aircraft. During the period when the Japanese could not produce the material, there was no import tariff on it. On April 1, 1985, after two Japanese firms began producing the material, the Japanese government imposed an 11.5 percent tariff on the American aluminum sheeting.

Just as the Japanese are not the only foreign investors in the United States, the disadvantages for U.S. investors abroad do not stop with Japan. Most other nations with substantial holdings in the United States maintain protectionist policies in varying degrees.

Canada, the biggest trading partner of the United States, grew concerned over the potential for U.S. dominance of its industrial and cultural entities and created the Foreign Investment Review Agency.

The agency was to screen all foreign investments to ensure that they offered "significant benefits" to Canada. The agency conducted its reviews in secret and offered no explanation for rejections. Among the considerations, however, were whether Canadian employment and exports were increased; whether sufficient Canadian raw material was used; whether the impact on competition within the country was favorable; and whether productivity and technology were advanced.

The agency, known as FIRA, wound up as an example used by those who argue against the concept of reciprocity, however. By rejecting about 15 percent of the proposed foreign investments, FIRA was a target for blame when Canada's unemployment rate rose to double digits, and it was abolished in the spring of 1985.

But the new legislation, the Investment Canada Act, retains many of FIRA's former exclusionary provisions. For instance, direct acquisition of any Canadian business with sales of $5 million or indirect control of one with sales exceeding $50 million is subject to review and possible rejection. And special review provisions are included covering some cultural and financial institutions.

Foreign-owned banks are limited to a main office and one branch. The potential for foreign banks to expand in Canada is limited further by requirements in the Bank Act of 1980, which stipulate that the total assets of all foreign banks are limited to 8 percent of the total domestic assets of Canadian-owned banks.

In South Korea, more than a third of the private industries are restricted or off limits to foreign investors, including dairy, communications, rental real estate, agriculture, publishing, and cigarettes. A 1983 law gave the Korean government authority to approve only foreign investments that are deemed to serve Korea's national interest. Yet Sun Myung Moon, a Korean imprisoned in the United States for income tax evasion, and his Unification Church own and publish the *Washington Times* and a small daily newspaper in New York City through New World Communications.

In 1981, the Kuwaiti government bought 100 percent of Santa Fe International, a $4 billion U.S. petroleum giant. But the converse could not happen in that Mideast nation. In Kuwait, the energy industry belongs exclusively to the government and other key sectors, ranging from banking and property ownership to participation in the local stock market. All foreign investment in Kuwait must be through a joint venture in which a Kuwaiti partner holds at least a 51 percent interest.

Australia requires government approval any time a foreign national wants to invest in media, mining, or civil aviation. Applications can be rejected if the government determines the investment is harmful to the national interest or if there are Australian investors available to invest at "reasonable terms and conditions."

Yet Australian Rupert Murdoch was able to amass a media empire in the United States that included the *Chicago Sun-Times*, the *New York Post*, and *New York* magazine free of any U.S. government review or intervention. Only when Murdoch branched out to acquire television stations was he required to take out U.S. citizenship; the broadcast industry is virtually the only place where the U.S. restricts ownership to its citizens.

When Nestle, the Swiss conglomerate that is the world's largest food company, sought to buy Britain's Rowntree candy company in May 1988, the move touched off a furor of political opposition. The critics argued that Swiss companies are protected from hostile takeover bids in Switzerland, while they are free to launch assaults on companies in Britain and elsewhere.

Indeed, Nestle expanded from its Vevey headquarters through an aggressive acquisition policy that swept up companies all around the world, including such American brands as Carnation, Stouffer restaurants and hotels, Beech-Nut baby foods, Hills Bros. coffee, and Beringer wines, while safely protected from foreign takeover by Swiss policy.

"There is no specific law against the takeover of, say, a Swiss bank by foreigners, but in actuality you cannot really do it," said a New York expert on international banking. "The same holds true for Britain, where the Bank of England will not permit any foreign ownership of English banks. They do it by regulatory controls. There is no law.

"Japan is the worst, of course. There is no law. Again, it is done through the regulators."

And it is also done in a variety of industries in Japan in a more subtle way than through the government. These investment barriers may ultimately prove far more effective than the government-imposed set.

Clyde Prestowitz, an author and former Commerce Department official, found out about these subtle barriers when he ran his own trading company and medical-equipment company in Japan.

It is a mistake, he told Martin and Susan Tolchin for their 1988 book *Buying into America,* to look at the potential for success in Japan only from the standpoint of whether you can set up a business there. Prospective foreign businessmen must examine the distribution system and their ability to hire workers.

"In order to sell, you need salesmen, warehouses, office space, distributors, trucks, secretaries, etc.," said Prestowitz. "The warehouses are very hard to get. They are controlled by big trading companies. There is cross-shareholding. The presidents of twenty or so companies meet and coordinate. They could decide not to give warehouse space to a competitor.

"In Japan there is lifetime employment till the age of 55. The pensions are not very good, and they are not vested, so Japanese workers can't transfer them if they change jobs. There is also a great deal of pressure from the company. When I tried to hire away workers, the company called their wives and parents. The pressure was very intense. I remember one man crying in my office. They make them feel as if they are betraying the company. It's hard to get good skilled Japanese employees.

"Then you need distributors. Business in Japan is done on the basis of personal relationships: ties between supplier and buyer.

Many distributors are retirees . . . and depend on these jobs; it is really a social welfare system. These personal relationships are conducted among Japanese companies. Nippondenso sells to Toyota but not to Nissan. How can American companies get a crack?"

The U.S. trade representative's report made the same point, explaining that the Japanese distribution system is another "informal means by which imports are kept under strict control. . . . Entry into the system is virtually closed to foreign suppliers."

Alongside these formal and informal obstacles, the report said, the Japanese erect "an endless source of barriers and delays in processing documentation and gaining approval to compete. In one case, a patent application for optical fiber filed in Japan by a foreign firm was pending for ten years, during which time a similar domestic product became available."

This tight control of its markets also means that Japan can decide to open the system a crack to allow in certain elements that may prove valuable in the long run, such as allowing the aluminum producer to provide material to the aerospace industry in Japan cheaply until two domestic suppliers were up and running.

The Japanese government has been enormously successful at luring selected foreign financial institutions to the Tokyo markets and extracting new skills and technology from them. Yet the government has been careful to keep them restricted enough so that there is no possibility of taking away big chunks of business from domestic Japanese institutions.

There has been no similar restriction in the United States. Efforts by congressmen to enforce reciprocity through legislation have been largely unsuccessful, partly out of fears that specific measures could trigger a trade war that would chase the golden goose from American shores at a time when the nation still needs heavy doses of foreign investment.

One exception was a provision contained in the 1988 trade bill that bars foreign companies from serving as primary dealers in U.S. securities unless their governments allowed U.S. firms to compete on equal footing with their companies within a year.

The primary dealers deal directly with the Federal Reserve Bank of New York when it buys and sells government securities, and some large institutional investors will do business only with these elite dealers.

The measure was aimed at Japan, and it was strongly opposed by the Reagan administration. It could force the three big Japanese securities firms out of the lucrative business as primary U.S. securities dealers unless Japan offered U.S. companies the same opportunities within a year.

Japan is an incubator in which strategic industries are identified and fledgling corporations nurtured to dominate them. It all takes place under the protective guardianship of government-imposed restrictions on foreign competition and a social system constructed to exclude foreign interests.

The result is a system that provides enormous competitive advantages to Japanese corporations, advantages that the Japanese are constantly using to expand their domination by investing more money in advanced technology and improved manufacturing processes.

An economic forecast by the Bank of Japan, the nation's central bank, predicts close to a 20 percent increase in capital spending by Japanese manufacturers in the fiscal year ending in March 1989. This should increase worries among U.S. industry because the primary capital spenders in Japan are the big export industries, such as the producers of microchips, chemicals, precision machinery, and a variety of technologies related to information processing at home and in the office.

The investment will make Japan's most formidable industries even stronger at home, creating new difficulties for Americans trying to break into Japanese markets. The expenditures will also provide more cash for new investments in the United States, where the Japanese expect to expand both manufacturing capacity and market share in the coming years.

By 1992, the Japan Machinery Exporters Association estimates that 30 percent of Japanese-owned auto manufacturing will take place outside Japan, compared with 11.5 percent now; 25 percent of computer manufacturing compared with 5.7 percent; 27 percent of machine tools versus 5.2 percent; and 37 percent of home electronics, such as VCRs, compared with 25 percent.

The competitive advantages for the Japanese come at the expense of U.S. industry, and the advantages and the increase in spending come at a time when the Americans can least afford to operate at a disadvantage.

8
UNDERSTANDING
THE COMPETITION

AT A MEETING OF THE U.S.-Japan Businessman's Conference in Honolulu in February 1986, the chairman of Ford Motor Company spoke the lament that characterized American industry in the 1980s.

"I wish someone would tell me that manufacturing is not un-American," said Ford boss Donald Petersen.

Yukuo Takenaka, a Japanese-American who advises many of Tokyo's leading industrialists in addition to hundreds of the Japanese companies setting up shop in the United States, used nearly the same language in early 1988 as he sat in his office in downtown Los Angeles.

"Americans seem to have given up on manufacturing," said Takenaka, head of the Japan section at Peat Marwick Main, the world's largest accounting firm. "Americans somehow think that manufacturing is second-class work. No one in this country is concerned about manufacturing anymore. It is no longer a desired job to work in a factory. It has become almost un-American."

Where does the blame lie? A substantial measure of it belongs to the decade-long orgy of merger mania that swept the nation in the 1980s. It is no coincidence that the economic decline of the United States occurred at precisely the same time that the investment bankers and corporate raiders began their destructive transformation of corporate America.

Instead of increasing spending to modernize plants and boost budgets for research and development to retain America's competitive position, the nation's manufacturers allowed Wall Street to push them into a self-destructive game of corporate checkers that drained capital and energy and creativity.

A side effect: until the early 1970s, only about 12 percent of the Harvard Business School graduating class each year went to Wall Street; by the 1980s, fully one-third of each class was going there. Wall Street became the magnet for the nation's brightest young business school graduates, the people who once would have gone to work at General Motors or Lockheed. The money was being made in moving paper, not in creating products. If manufacturing did not look un-American to the nation's brightest young MBAs, it certainly looked unappetizing.

Another consequence of the merger mania is that U.S. managers have been forced to focus on short-term profits at the expense of long-term development plans. Operations that do not drive the bottom line, such as the development of new products, are jettisoned. If it is cheaper to buy sophisticated components abroad and simply assemble them in U.S. plants, what does it matter that a company sacrifices technical innovation and devalues inventive and engineering skills?

By contrast, the biggest companies in Japan are often owned partly by their lenders, so they are able to borrow at lower interest rates and focus more on long-term outlooks than American business does. Richard Drobnick, director of the International Business Education and Research program at the University of Southern California in Los Angeles, said, "In Japan, you can invest more, ask for lower prices, develop market share, because you don't need to pay it back so quickly. That's no fault of any American company. That's the fault of American economic policy."

But the warning signs of a nation at risk were visible well before merger mania was under way.

The nation seemed to take the wrong fork in the road in the 1970s. The Vietnam War damaged the national psyche, the oil embargo threatened U.S. economic independence for the first time in more than a century, and unemployment and inflation both rose throughout most of the decade.

The manufacturing sector, weakened by malaise, came under attack from foreign producers. Market after market fell to cheap goods produced abroad—cars from Japan, shoes from Italy, apparel from Hong Kong and Taiwan.

American industry was disheartened, and its leaders stopped minding the shop. They stopped paying attention to quality and no longer were willing to invest the energy and capital that had paved the way for the post–World War I ascension of American capitalism.

While America went into decline and began living off foreign capital and developing an addiction to imported goods, Japan was reaping the fruits of an industrial development that had begun in the ashes of World War II.

Japan's principal aim in World War II had been to gain control of land that would provide the natural resources vital to its economic prosperity. After its defeat, Japan's leaders recognized that they would have to find another way to build the economic sovereignty of their nation. The alternative was evident: the nation's economic power would have to be built on a foundation of manufacturing and exports. The resources would have to be bought, rather than seized, and the value added through a new industrial base.

In order to develop that base, Japan would keep its markets closed to protect its fledgling industries, and its people would sacrifice through hard work and by paying more for domestically produced goods than they would have paid for American imports. The driving force was the strategic development of a national industrial base, not the desires of consumers for inexpensive goods—a sharp contrast to the laissez-faire policies of the United States.

Here another factor surfaces that played a role in what has become known as "the Japanese miracle." That factor is the homogeneous nature of the Japanese society. The historic sense of community and national purpose, which had been reinforced

by the stinging defeat in the war, is not only unrivaled in a
nation as diverse and young as the United States. It is barely
understood.

Perhaps no two cultures are as different as those of the United
States and Japan. Americans pride themselves on individual
initiative and outstanding personal accomplishments. The Japanese operate within a framework of team play in which the
individual's needs are always secondary to the goal of the whole.

Japanese society extols hard work, loyalty to the company, and
a desire to resolve conflicts through cooperation, consensus, and
a strong dose of deference to authority. The necessity of building
an economy based on manufactured goods became part of the
textbooks from elementary schools on up. It was preached by
government officials and business leaders and implemented with
the help of the nation's most powerful government agency, the
Ministry of International Trade and Industry, or MITI.

The national awareness of the urgency of this task, coupled
with the unique ability of Japan's leaders to harness their people
to the job, spawned perhaps the most-focused, best-educated
society in the world, producing the scientists and engineers
demanded by its national goal. The result was an enormous
juggernaut that would propel Japan to the top.

But few Westerners were aware of what was occurring in
Japan. Throughout the late 1940s and 1950s, Americans were
secure in their economic and military power. The nation was
unconcerned and even paternalistic toward the Japanese. After
all, it was U.S. goodwill that had played a central role in the
restoration of Germany and Japan, rebuilding shattered cities
and industries and sharing American technology and theories.

When it came to international rivalry, American attention was
focused on the Soviet Union and China. There was neither time
nor inclination to be concerned about the economic power of the
vanquished Japanese.

Indeed, American spending in the Korean War played a major
role in helping develop Japan's export-based society. Orders from
the U.S. Defense Department for trucks helped resuscitate a
floundering Toyota. Similar buying by the U.S. military also
assisted other Japanese industries. So while the United States was

investing greater and greater amounts of its money in military spending, the Japanese were free to devote all of their resources to industrial development—a development that benefited directly from the U.S. military spending.

As they had been a century earlier, the Japanese also were extraordinarily good at adapting Western ideas and improving upon them. It was an ability that the German economist Kurt Singer recognized soon after the war, following a period of working for the Japanese.

"They invent few things, receive passionately, and excel in the art of adapting, adjusting, fitting," he said. "What they have chosen to undertake is often reduced in scale or scope but within these limits is carried to perfection."

Singer could not have imagined how the scale would grow, but he certainly captured a key factor in the Japanese miracle.

From Henry Ford the Japanese already had learned the principles of mass production and the importance of reducing costs to develop mass consumerism. From another American, Frederick Winslow Taylor, the Japanese learned "scientific industrial management." With a stopwatch and his famous time-and-motion studies, management philosopher Taylor reduced each assembly-line worker's function to a set number of precisely timed actions. In fact, by 1911 a translation of Taylor's book *The Secret of Saving Lost Motion* had sold more than 1.5 million copies in Japan.

But it was not until after World War II that the Japanese learned the technique that would become their hallmark: quality control. This time the inventor was American Edward Deming.

Deming's methods for monitoring and improving the quality of work were used by U.S. industries during the war, but they were discarded in its wake. The Japanese, however, adopted Deming's premise, and today Japanese industry acknowledges its debt to him with the Deming Award, the most sought-after honor in Japan's business world.

Not until 1980, after a Japanese company began using Deming's methods in its American affiliate, was he really rediscovered in his native country.

This mix of factors, ranging from the personal sacrifice and homogeneity of its population to the adoption of U.S. manufacturing and management methods, produced an enormous economic success for the tiny nation. Between 1950 and 1973, the gross national product of Japan grew at the astounding rate of 10.5 percent a year, far faster than that of any other industrialized nation.

The list of industries that the Japanese came to dominate grew longer each year—cameras, televisions, stereos, home appliances, musical instruments, motorcycles, watches and clocks, machine tools.

Japan was producing half the new ships in the world by the 1960s, and its steel industry rivaled that of the United States by the 1970s. Its share of world auto production increased from almost nothing in 1960 to nearly 25 percent by the early 1980s.

At the same time, the Japanese were surpassing the rest of the world in certain products that will be the basis for the next industrial revolution—computers, telecommunications, robotics, and biotechnology. For instance, by 1984 the Japanese had mastered the use of robots in manufacturing plants and accounted for two out of every three industrial robots.

A large part of this development was financed by the massive individual savings encouraged by the Japanese government. Since World War II, Japan has developed the world's highest savings rate, climbing to 18.3 percent in 1981 before dropping to 14 percent in 1987 as Japanese consumers began exercising their new financial muscle, with government encouragement. During the same period, the U.S. savings rate declined steadily and stood at 5.2 percent in 1987.

The huge personal savings deposited in banks provided cheap capital to Japan's expanding industrial sector and helped fuel its worldwide expansion. In contrast, the low rate in the United States meant that government and industry had to finance expansion by selling ever-increasing amounts of debt on the open market and paying three to five times as much in interest as their Japanese rivals.

By the end of the 1980s, the benefits of these sacrifices and the concerted industrial development policy were being bestowed on the Japanese people.

Millions of Japanese were unemployed and hungry at the end of World War II. In 1988, the average annual household income was $40,000, well above the U.S. average. The Japanese middle class was earning large salaries, with office workers at large firms making as much as $50,000 a year and management executives taking home $100,000.

The new wealth is reflected in Japan's capital. Tokyo, with 11 million residents, is resplendent with innovative architecture and chic boutiques, and its streets are jammed with Mercedes-Benzes and Porsches.

The value of real estate in Tokyo skyrocketed faster than the Japanese economic miracle. A barber sold his shop and its tiny piece of land in Tokyo in 1988 for $7.5 million. According to rumor, a *soba* (noodle) shop owner sold his 450-square-foot patch of land in Tokyo's financial district for $14 million. The government reported that the choicest piece of commercial real estate in central Tokyo sold for the equivalent of $6.7 million per acre in 1987.

Not surprisingly, prices of residential real estate spiraled, too. During 1987, residential real estate in Tokyo appreciated 69 percent, almost doubling the previous record of 39 percent in 1973. Any condominium within a few miles of the center of the city commands a price tag of at least $1 million. Young professional couples find that they must spend $600,000 for a two-bedroom apartment an hour and a half from Tokyo.

The land prices put home ownership out of reach for many Japanese. In 1986, the average Tokyo resident paid nine times his or her annual income in order to buy a home. In New York, the average was three times income. One solution has been a return to "three-generation housing," in which children are once again living with parents, and the creation of "two-generation mortgages," in which parents and their children agree to finance jointly the purchase of a house.

The land values also created new wealth. Between 1980 and 1987, the number of Japanese who owned land worth $2 million or more tripled to 333,500 in a country of only 120 million people. When Japan surpassed the United States in 1987 as the country with the most billionaires, the basis of most of the wealth was not the export industries, but land.

The world's richest man is probably Yoshiaki Tsutsumi, whose vast properties throughout Japan and stock holdings were worth an estimated $21 billion, excluding all debt. The lead company in his empire is Seibu Group, which his father had used to buy land from broke Japanese aristocrats before, during, and after World War II. Seibu has also become active in the U.S. real estate market in recent years.

The most active Japanese investor in U.S. real estate has been Shigeru Kobayashi, who founded Shuwa Company in 1957 and built an empire of residential and commercial buildings in Tokyo worth an estimated $6 billion. From that base, Kobayashi has expanded dramatically into the U.S. real estate market, acquiring prestigious buildings such as Arco Plaza in Los Angeles and ABC's New York headquarters. Along the way he also has acquired a reputation as an egocentric and aggressive investor.

Japan's new billionaires stand out in a nation that has pulled together to overcome the devastation of World War II. In fact, the communal effort has played a central role in allowing the government to shape Japanese industrial policy and keep out forces that play a significant role in the United States, such as organized labor.

An attempt by Japanese labor unions to organize independently, in the fashion of U.S. labor unions, failed after a bitter struggle in the early 1950s. One by one, the more radical, American-style unions were defeated by company-sponsored alternate unions in industries across the country that survive today.

David Halberstam wrote about the close of the 1953 Nissan strike in his book *The Reckoning*: "From now on, each company would have its own union, which would be totally loyal to its parent company and dependent upon the marketplace success of the company for its own success. Management had won . . . it had defined labor on its own terms, incorporated labor into the company itself, and ended any possibility of labor as an adversarial force within. Years later, when Japan finally challenged Western industries, it was clear that one of the most critical factors in its success was the creation of the second unions and the elimination of the radical ones."

The bonds that hold Japanese society together are thousands of years old, and, when it comes to developing and carrying out the strategic goals set by the nation's leaders, they can be invaluable.

For example, despite the fact that rice farmers make up only 12 percent of Japan's population today, compared to 50 percent following the war, the Japanese can't even bring themselves to alter significantly their government's land-use policies that allow the country's grossly inefficient and heavily subsidized rice farmers to continue working much as they always have through the centuries. Japan's rice costs between six and ten times as much as rice produced in other countries. Because rice farms take up a full one-quarter of the country's habitable land, many argue that land for housing is costly because the government continues to support the price of rice.

In trying to explain the Japanese attachment to the land, despite the resulting distortions to the country's economy, James Fallows wrote in *The Atlantic*, "When they think of rice, even today's urbanized Japanese think of their devoted uncle or grandmother stooped over in the fields. When they go back to the home village they want to see the same familiar paddies, green, well tended, bearing the new year's crop."

Rice farming is just one example of how Japanese society, from labor relations to rural-urban relations, tends to run smoothly in part because the network of personal and traditional relationships provides a sense of loyalty and continuity missing from the American free enterprise system.

One of Japan's acknowledged masters at using a network of personal relationships to unite business, science, and government in a fashion that is virtually unknown in the United States is Shoji Tanaka.

A professor of applied physics in his sixties, Tanaka has served as the leading scientific adviser to the nation's electronics giants and to his government for many years. In many ways, Tanaka is a microcosm of postwar Japan.

He studied physics at Purdue University in West Lafayette, Indiana, in the late 1950s and early 1960s and then returned to Japan to use his newfound knowledge. His research findings have been transformed into commercial products that help advance Japan's drive for technological superiority.

In the mid-1970s, he helped lead the Japanese assault on the semiconductor industry, and the result is that Japan leads the world in producing those vital little ceramic chips that tell computers what to do.

Later in that same decade, Tanaka spearheaded research and development in a new technology that brought together electronics and optics. The result was the same as in chips: Japan now leads the world in the field of fiber optics.

In 1988, he was named the head of a consortium of Japan's forty-four biggest industrial giants brought together to conduct research on superconductors. Two IBM scientists had discovered new potential for superconducting materials, and the goal of the Japanese group was to beat the Americans to the market with commercial products based on the discovery.

Superconductors are materials that conduct electricity with little or no loss of energy. Previously the materials had to be kept at extremely low temperatures to work, which limited their usefulness, particularly in the development of new products for mass marketing. But the IBM scientists, and others, discovered superconductors that could operate at higher temperatures.

Many scientists believe the discovery opened the way for revolutionary applications that will lead to computers that operate faster, power lines that do not lose electricity, and trains that float.

A consortium of Japan's shipbuilders is designing a high-speed ship that will use superconducting motors to turn its propellers. If successful, the vessel would carry freight at up to sixty miles an hour and cut the two-week overseas trip from Tokyo to Los Angeles down to four days.

Other Japanese shipbuilders are working on efforts to create ships that are propelled by superconducting magnets, rather than by propellers. A study by the U.S. Naval Research Laboratory in Washington said such technology could "lead to revolutionary advances in marine propulsion," including the creation of superquiet submarines.

While the Japanese were working together on a unified effort to move from the lab to the marketplace, American companies proved reluctant to spend the necessary money on research. Further, the research under way in the United States was being conducted competitively by companies and universities, without an overall national aim.

The U.S. Office of Technology Assessment, a research arm of Congress, issued a report in the middle of 1988 that indicated the Japanese were already poised to beat the United States to the market with commercial applications of superconductor technology. If that occurs, it will be a classic example of Japan's ability to get a free ride on basic research done at the expense of U.S. companies and then develop the first commercial products.

While Americans took a wait-and-see attitude about superconductors, the report said, the giant Japanese companies grabbed the lead in several areas. "Japanese R&D managers see HTS [high-temperature superconductors] as a truly revolutionary technology, one that promises radical change in their business," said a draft copy of the report, which was later toned down. "The skepticism common in the United States is nowhere to be found."

The report also criticized American industry for expecting the military to develop the first applications of the technology and hoping to follow that with commercial spin-offs.

The office recommended that a new federal agency be created to assist in coordinating research and financing the resolution of technical problems that have slowed down the U.S. effort. The office recommended a budget for the agency of $100 million to $500 million.

The same sense of national purpose and marshaling of resources that motivates the Japanese research into superconductors characterizes Japan's approach to virtually every sector of its industrial society.

The ability to coordinate investments and policy was exempli-

fied at a meeting in the fall of 1986 which was first described in a
Japanese newspaper and later translated in a report issued by the
Foreign Broadcast Information Service in February 1987.

Those attending the meeting in Japan included Hiroshi Ku-
rosawa of the Industrial Bank of Japan; Akio Morita of Sony;
Masataku Okuma, the president of Nissan Motors; and Takushin
Yamamoto, the president of Fujitsu.

The session was convened to discuss how the various companies would expand their markets in the United States, and how
they could do so without further alarming the American public
and risking the backlash of protectionism.

Morita summarized the view of the United States held by those
attending the extraordinary session. He described a conversation
with a U.S. banker who had told him that there should be no
concern in the United States over the transfer of U.S. manufacturing plants overseas. Morita said the persistence of that attitude would mean that the United States would soon deteriorate
into a nonindustrial nation.

Yamamoto underscored the point, saying, "U.S. companies
have not been able to beat Japan up to now because they don't
understand Japanese competition."

Indeed, few American business leaders have been able to understand the concerted nature of the competition they face from
Japan. One reason is that the type of coordinated effort embodied in the 1986 meeting of Japanese industrialists is completely
antithetical to the U.S. mind-set. The very idea that the chief
executives of IBM, General Motors, and Citicorp would sit down
for a similar session is unthinkable.

And few Americans recognized the significance of a new
Japanese investment pattern that emerged in the middle to late
1980s as Japan switched from passive purchases of stocks and
bonds to direct purchases of U.S. companies and the creation of
new plants on American soil.

The Japanese found that their skills could be exported to the
United States, where they could manufacture goods without fear
of protectionist tariffs or the volatility of international curren-
cies.

While there have been setbacks for specific Japanese companies in the United States, the majority have been enormously successful, and their success has encouraged more Japanese firms to set up U.S. operations.

The Japanese are very averse to risk taking. No one wants to make a mistake and suffer public embarrassment. They have a saying that exemplifies this group mentality, and it translates roughly into this parable: If everyone is stopped at a red light and one person crosses against it, that person is in great danger. However, if everyone crosses at the same time, no one is in danger.

Having seen the success of other Japanese companies in the United States was a leading factor in drawing hundreds more to American shores as the 1980s progressed. And one of the key traits shared by most of these companies has been the ability to bring Japanese management practices to U.S. manufacturing plants.

9
SELLOUT AT FIRESTONE

No EXAMPLE OF JAPANESE INVESTMENT in the United States better illustrates the ability of the Japanese to export management techniques and to take advantage of the weakened U.S. manufacturing sector and the short-term outlook of American executives than Bridgestone's acquisition of Firestone Tire and Rubber in 1988.

Bridgestone started small in its move to the United States, taking over a Firestone plant in La Vergne, Tennessee, in 1983. Firestone's work force in La Vergne had been demoralized by job cuts, and the equipment at the plant was outdated and inefficient. The plant was producing only 600 tires a day under Firestone and seemed destined to be closed entirely.

Bridgestone bought the operation, added work shifts, updated the equipment, instituted new quality-control measures, and retrained the labor force. Within months, La Vergne was producing 3,000 tires a day.

By 1983, Japanese firms were just beginning to demonstrate that they could transport their management skills to the United States. Within a few years, a Columbia University business professor named Martin K. Starr would do a study of Japanese-owned companies in the United States that confirmed their success. Overall, Starr found, Japanese companies were able to get new products on-line twice as fast as U.S. companies. While U.S. manufacturers discard or rework 4 percent of their products, superior Japanese quality control means that less than 1 percent of their products are defective.

But good management was not enough for Bridgestone. The company needed to add tire-production capabilities, to serve the growing production of automobiles transferred to the United States by Japan's automakers and grab a share of the U.S. auto-maker market. So Bridgestone, following the examples of the automakers and the electronics industry, sought a far larger U.S. presence.

Its opportunity came in early 1988, and the story of how Bridgestone bought all of Firestone reflects both the decline of American manufacturing and the rise of Japanese industry on American soil.

Firestone had been having difficulty producing tires profitably for many years. The scandal surrounding its faulty Firestone 500 tires had set the company back, and its inattention to quality and outdated plants had also taken a toll.

By 1988, the company had de-emphasized its tire business in favor of a more diversified product line and a retail orientation. The company marketed building products, roofing, and synthetic rubber. It even experimented with a car-rental business. Between 1979 and 1988, its work force declined by half to 55,000 from 110,000.

In many ways, the transformation of Firestone tracked the path of U.S. manufacturing from production of goods to a new reliance on service-related business. Companies unwilling or unable to make the technological advances necessary to compete turned tail and ran to a softer arena where innovation and engineering skills were unnecessary.

As early as 1986, Firestone had engaged in discussions with Pirelli, Italy's leading tire maker, over the possible sale of some of Firestone's manufacturing operation. But in late 1987, Bridgestone entered the competition by offering to buy 75 percent of

Firestone's tire business for $1.25 billion. Firestone would retain a quarter of the business in a joint venture with Bridgestone.

As the largest tire company in Japan, Bridgestone supplied 50 percent of the tires to that nation's burgeoning auto industry. The company was founded in 1932, and its American-sounding name is an inversion of the English translation of the founder's name, Ishibashi, meaning stone bridge.

The company was a household name in Japan, but in order to be a global power and to supply tires to the growing Japanese auto industry in the United States, Bridgestone needed to establish a U.S. operation far larger than the La Vergne, Tennessee, plant.

Firestone offered the opportunity. It was the third largest U.S. tire company behind Goodyear and Uniroyal-Goodrich, and it supplied 40 percent of the tires used by Ford and 21 percent of those used by General Motors. It had five tire-manufacturing plants in the United States, a network of 3,500 independent dealers to market the products, and a substantial production capability in Europe.

The joint venture with Firestone, an increasingly common technique used by the Japanese to gain an economic foothold in the United States, offered Bridgestone the immediate capacity to become a global player in the tire industry. Bridgestone's giant leap in size would also fit with the overall Japanese strategy of creating a top-rank supplier as part of its emergence as a world automotive power. For its part, Firestone would get an infusion of cash that would help its expansion into other areas.

But Pirelli would not be put off, and the Italian firm formed an alliance with France's Michelin to counter with a $1.9 billion bid for all of Firestone. Pirelli and Michelin were also eager to become larger global players, particularly with the creation of a wide-open market in Europe scheduled for 1992. Companies not big enough to compete would be swallowed up.

Yet when the showdown came, the two European companies were no match for the cash-rich Japanese.

On February 16, 1988, Bridgestone offered to buy the entire Firestone company for $2.6 billion in cash, the largest Japanese acquisition in the United States to date. The company founded in

1900 in West Virginia by Harvey S. Firestone, the pioneer of mass production of tires, the company that once vied to be the world's largest tire maker, officially became Japanese-owned on April 25, 1988, when shareholders overwhelmingly approved the transaction.

"It isn't that Firestone is in trouble and needs to be taken over," Donald DeScenza, an industry analyst with Nomura Securities in New York, said a few days after the deal was announced. "It's that Firestone's management regards the interest expressed by Bridgestone as an opportunity to enhance its value to stockholders. It's a management that has no loyalties to tires."

Firestone's devotion to tires had begun to wane in the 1970s, when America's driving habits were disrupted by the Arab oil embargo and longer-lasting radial tires began to grab a greater share of the market. Rather than adapting to the changes, Firestone was hobbled by them, and it began closing factories and losing market share.

The weekend before Firestone's stockholders approved the sellout, General Motors said it would end its purchases of Firestone tires. The company maintained that it was trying to reduce its number of suppliers, but auto-industry analysts suspected the decision was based on the new ownership of Firestone. GM had said in the past that it wanted to do business with domestic suppliers.

The GM setback did not appear to faze the Japanese, and why should it? For $2.6 billion, equivalent to about half that amount in yen, Bridgestone had accomplished something that otherwise would have taken years and cost many hundreds of millions more: it had leapfrogged to the number three spot among American tire makers. In one day, the Bridgestone purchase of Firestone increased the Japanese presence in the American tire industry to a combined 16 percent.

For John J. Nevin, the chairman of Firestone, the sale marked a 180-degree turnaround in attitude about competition with the Japanese, a switch no doubt made easier by the fact that he profited substantially from the increased value in his Firestone shares.

In the 1970s, Nevin was the president and chairman of Zenith

Electronics, and he was a leader in the pitched battle to stop the Japanese from dominating the color television industry. He led the fight in Washington, arguing that the failure to enforce U.S. trade laws and the weaknesses in the laws themselves were allowing the Japanese to sell their products below cost in the United States, the practice known as dumping, in an attempt to gain control of the market.

But in explaining the sale of Firestone a decade later, after the Japanese had indeed conquered the color television market, Nevin failed to recognize any inconsistency in providing the Japanese with a base of operations in the U.S. tire industry.

"At Zenith it was the perception of unfair trade practices, not a fight with the Japanese," claimed Nevin. "Without arguing that dumping was a problem, it clearly has not been a problem in the tire or auto markets of the United States. I would assert that I never attacked Japan or the Japanese, but U.S. trade policy that tolerated dumping."

He offered a similarly disingenuous explanation for the sale of Firestone to a company management group, contending that Bridgestone would increase career opportunities for them.

"If we hadn't taken that action, the jobs that are left wouldn't exist," Nevin said. "We are living in a world of geometric change."

Few have changed more in that world than John Nevin, and nothing better illustrates the new U.S. order, with its drive for short-term gains and disregard for the nation's long-term economic health, than the sellout at Firestone.

The Japanese also are challenging another of America's mainstream industries—construction equipment manufacturing, which is dominated throughout the world by Caterpillar Inc. of Peoria, Illinois.

On August 31, 1988, a joint venture was announced between Japan's Komatsu, Ltd., the world's second largest manufacturer of construction equipment, and Dresser Industries, a large Dallas-based maker of equipment for the energy, construction, and mining industries.

The new joint venture, called Komatsu Dresser, started with 5,000 employees from existing plants of both companies and will produce construction equipment such as earth-moving machinery, front-end loaders, cranes, and road graders. The production will occur chiefly at Dresser's factories in the United States and Canada, which will be upgraded through the introduction of Komatsu's advanced technology, which relies heavily on robotics.

"The new joint venture will have about 20 percent of the market share compared with Caterpillar's 40 to 45 percent," said Herbert M. Ryan, director of investor relations for Dresser. "We should be able to take on anybody. No company is invincible."

Ryan explained that Komatsu spends $250 million a year on research and development, far more than Dresser. As a result, he said, the joint venture will benefit from the production know-how of the Japanese. In exchange, Komatsu will gain access to the 200 dealers in Dresser's distribution network in the United States, Canada, and South America. Like Bridgestone before the Firestone acquisition, Komatsu had had great difficulty penetrating the American market because of the lack of a distribution network.

It will not be the first time Caterpillar has encountered head-to-head competition from Komatsu on American soil, with help from American citizens.

In March 1985, Komatsu announced that it would open an assembly operation on the fifty-five-acre site of an abandoned factory in Chattanooga, Tennessee. It had chosen Chattanooga following a long courtship in which the city and state promised tax-free loans, property-tax deferral, employee training programs, special education programs for the Japanese, federal grants, and a promise to create a foreign trade zone that would reduce the tariff on components brought in from Japan.

Komatsu acknowledged to local officials that it was seeking safety from the possibility of rising protectionism in the United States. And, while the company also admitted that it would start with only 250 jobs, it vowed that more would follow.

Yet the incentives for Komatsu came at a time when Caterpillar had just lost close to $1 billion and laid off nearly half of its 120,000 workers. In an attempt to compete with lower-cost foreign producers, Caterpillar had shut down a plant in Mentor,

Ohio, that once employed 2,700 and moved the production to South Korea.

There is little doubt that Caterpillar will survive, but the company has been forced to move more production jobs out of the country. And smaller firms have gone out of business or, as occurred with Dresser's construction equipment division, been forced to merge with a cash-rich Japanese partner.

What was the payoff for the people of Tennessee? By the summer of 1988, the Komatsu plant in Chattanooga employed just 180 people. The majority of the executives at Komatsu America were Japanese nationals.

Despite the shortsighted behavior of executives such as John Nevin and local officials such as those in Tennessee, America remains the world's technological giant. According to a survey of 282 business executives in the United States, Japan, and six other Pacific nations conducted in late 1987 for the *Los Angeles Times* by the consulting firm of Booz, Allen & Hamilton, American companies continue to rank as the dominant powers in most of the critical spheres of technological innovation, ranging from artificial intelligence to superconductivity.

But that dominance is eroding, and serious questions can be raised about the findings that the United States leads in superconductors. The United States has lost world leadership to Japan in many important fields, such as robotics and microelectronics. Perhaps most significantly for the long run, the survey found that American companies seem to lack a strong will to develop improved technology and exploit innovations.

"Fixated on quick research payoffs, blind to the ability of technology to open new markets, inattentive to the contributions scientists and engineers can make to corporate success, many American managers—especially in the big companies that were the survey's focus—have lost touch with innovative power that drove their firms to technological leadership," said the *Times* in a February 21, 1988, report on the findings.

A similar conclusion was reached in a study released in 1988 by the Congressional Budget Office, which found that inflation-adjusted spending for research and development by private U.S. corporations has risen at a rate of 3 percent a year since 1984.

That is about half the rate of increase in the preceding ten years.

"Despite the greater competition from foreign firms, the portion of gross national product devoted to research and development is lower now than it was twenty years ago," said the study.

Much of the blame for this change can be assessed to the preoccupation of American executives and managers with short-term payoffs and the heavy levels of debt assumed by many of the nation's leading manufacturers as a result of mergers or fending off unwanted corporate suitors. R&D expenditures, unfortunately, tend to have long-term payoffs and American managers seem to have an aversion to long-term planning.

This pervasive attitude among U.S. industries caused the nation to lose its technological advantage to the Japanese in many spheres and opened the door to the rise of Japan at the expense of the United States. And once that door was flung wide, the Japanese demonstrated ingenuity, brilliance, and determination in taking advantage of the opportunity. In contrast to their American rivals, the Japanese have demonstrated convincingly that developing new technology is a top business priority, ranking second only to increased profitability.

It is this recognition of the long-term, essential benefits of technological innovation and giving projects many years to become profitable that positions the Japanese for even greater conquests than they have made in the last two decades. Rather than an emerging power, Japan has become a dominant force that must be reckoned with on all fronts.

Nowhere has Japan gone further than in the auto industry, and no company better illustrates that than Honda.

10
TROJAN HORSE

THE U.S. ECONOMY IS UNDER SIEGE, and the battlefronts are many—from the New York Stock Exchange to Hawaii's hotel industry. To the victor will go rich spoils—possibly entire sections of the U.S. economy, such as the auto industry. As in a military war and its resulting loss of political sovereignty, economic sovereignty will be tough to rebuild.

When viewed in the terminology of war, the competition can be divided clearly into various fronts; corporations assume the role of battalions; and the victories can be counted for what they really are—steps toward conquest.

One of the single most important fronts today is the auto industry, where the siege by Japanese companies has stripped away jobs and profits from U.S. automakers and threatens to overrun what for years has been the United States' premier manufacturing field.

In recent years, the Japanese have infiltrated U.S. lines, avoiding quotas and tariffs and gaining leverage to fight protective measures by moving an ever-increasing portion of their manufacturing process to the United States.

Today, 3,000 years after the residents of Troy pulled a wooden horse inside their walled city and opened the door for their defeat, the Trojan horse has four wheels, a shiny paint job, and power brakes.

Japan's automakers are the ultimate Trojan horse, and American cities and states are eagerly wheeling them inside. The states and towns swing open the gates and offer tax holidays, public works improvements, worker retraining centers, and special schools for the children of Japanese executives.

Like the residents of ancient Troy after the long siege, state development agencies and local chambers of commerce hungry for revenue and jobs are blinded to the long-term implications of replacing the American auto industry with a Japanese one.

"In the 1980s Japanese automakers have invested more than $5 billion in U.S.-based assembly facilities," said a March 1988 report by the General Accounting Office, the chief investigative arm of Congress. "Seven Japanese-affiliated auto manufacturers and more than 100 Japanese-affiliated auto parts suppliers are operating or constructing facilities in the United States."

The report went on to reflect a deepening worry: "The growth of foreign direct investment has led to concerns over the future of the U.S. auto manufacturing and parts supplier industries. Critics suggest that it is causing job losses, reducing the market share for U.S. companies, and contributing to industry overcapacity."

More than one in five new cars purchased by Americans is Japanese-made, and some industry analysts predict the total will reach almost half by early in the next decade. Thousands of those Japanese cars actually will be manufactured at plants in the United States, but there is little solace in that phenomenon for the U.S. auto industry or the thousands of men and women who work in the industry and its related supply businesses.

The Japanese-affiliated automakers in the United States, called transplants, use fewer workers and more foreign content than U.S. automakers, and the result that many expect is a dramatic decrease in employment in the auto industry in the United States.

As America's love affair with Toyotas and Hondas and Nissans blossomed between 1978 and the end of 1986, more than 400,000 jobs were eliminated in the U.S. auto industry and related businesses. A 1987 study by the United Auto Workers predicted that another 540,000 of the 1.8 million jobs remaining in the auto and parts industries will disappear by 1990 because of the effect of the Japanese transplant automakers and parts suppliers.

David Cole, director of the Office for the Study of Automotive Transportation at the University of Michigan in Ann Arbor, put it another way during an interview: "Japan is creating an economic success where Pearl Harbor failed."

Cole recognizes the advantages in the Japanese plants on U.S. soil—after all, the Trojan horse came wrapped as a prize. But Cole also is gravely concerned over the long-term implications.

"Clearly, if Japanese vehicles are going to be sold in the United States, it is better on a net basis if they are assembled here," he said. "But any new plant will be more efficient than an old plant, so it isn't a zero-sum game in terms of employment. The customers are the big winners. They are getting better cars at better values. But the dislocations from a social standpoint are enormous. Competition is great, but in terms of the kind of things happening today in the auto industry, competition can also get a little out of control.

"There is almost a total absence of strategic understanding in our society about what this might lead to. Long-term thinking among our politicians is the next election. The Japanese, however, are long-term thinkers. They have specific goals in mind. They look at all the implications of a decision. We don't. We live for today, sometimes tomorrow, but never next year. The long-range strategic implications of major foreign investment and competition for control of assets in the United States have got to be dealt with.

"In a sense, the Japanese are feeding Congress's insatiable desire to spend money. It's almost like Japanese Kobi beef. They take their precious cows, feed them beer, massage them, force feed them. I'm sure the cow is as happy as possible. He probably feels great as he walks up the steps of the slaughterhouse. Are we doing the same thing?"

To carry Cole's analogy a bit further, one could say that state governments across the United States have been building the steps that lead to the slaughterhouse. In what *Newsweek* called the "War Between the States," almost no concession is too great as states fight with each other to land the latest Japanese manufacturing plant.

Battling five other states for a big Japanese auto parts plant, Tennessee officials granted demand after demand from the Japanese businessmen. They agreed to build new sewer lines and improve highways to serve the plant. They provided tax benefits and cheaper utility rates than U.S. firms were paying, and they tossed in Saturday English classes. These were similar to the giveaways used to lure Komatsu to Chattanooga.

As *Newsweek*'s Bill Powell told the story, only when the Japanese envoys demanded driving lessons did the Tennessee officials stop to consider whether the demands went too far. After huddling for an hour, the Tennessee officials agreed to provide free driving lessons for the plant's Japanese employees, and the deal was inked.

The bill is not in on what it will cost Tennessee to get the jobs associated with the auto parts plant. But Kentucky officials have acknowledged that it will eventually cost the state $350 million or more for the new Toyota plant in Georgetown. The bill included $55 million in worker training grants along with millions more in tax abatements, improvements, and related costs.

The Japanese businessmen have learned how to take advantage of the American competition, causing New York lawyer Ko-Yung Tung, who negotiates many of the deals on behalf of the Japanese, to remark: "Their expectations of what the states will do for them have increased dramatically. It's financial terms, but also symbolic things. They expect, for example, that the governor will show up at the airport to meet them. If he doesn't take them to lunch, they tend to think the state must not be serious."

Ohio was one of the states competing with Kentucky for the big Toyota plant, and Ohio Governor Richard Celeste described a day-long meeting with Toyota officials at which representatives of several state agencies had discussed various possible locations for the plant and other benefits offered by the Buckeye State.

"At the end of the conversations I came into the meeting and kind of reiterated our offer," recalled Celeste. "The man leading the Toyota team said to me, 'I am curious why you haven't said what every other governor has said—just tell us what you need and we'll do it.'

"I responded that I can't make that offer responsibly. What I've presented is what I think is a responsible offer. Any more might hurt my state."

Celeste said he was later told that the Toyota officials had a great deal of respect for his position and probably would have said the same thing in that position, but that the Japanese company would probably choose another state for its plant. Kentucky was that state.

Celeste supports foreign investment as a source of jobs and competition for American industry. Ohio was not only the first state to land a Japanese auto plant, it will be the first state to land two plants. Honda announced plans in 1988 to build a second plant in Marysville, Ohio. Although Ohio has been one of the most aggressive states in pursuit of foreign investment, Celeste is also aware that there are perils in the competition between states for foreign investment.

"States have to have a very clear idea of the boundaries when we are bidding for investment," he said. "Our real source of long-term strength is the companies already doing business in our state. We should not offer someone from outside our state a deal we aren't ready to offer folks already doing business in Ohio."

Ohio's original incentive package amounted to roughly $10 million, and included widening of the road, digging wells and building a pump house, building a sewer line, and reactivating a railroad spur. Marysville's fifteen-year real estate tax abatement was more than made up for with increased personal property taxes generated by the new plant. Incentives for the second auto plant will cost the state a total of $19 million.

"Our rule of thumb," said Jim Duerk, the former development director who helped negotiate the original deal under former Governor James Rhodes, "was that we would only provide incentives based on projections that we would get our money back within the first five to seven years. With Honda we got it back in two and a half years. In terms of jobs and tax returns, for the money we put in, it may turn out to be the best industrial development project in the history of Ohio."

But sometimes the concessions granted to Japanese automakers can prove more expensive than the benefits of the plants they build and jobs they create. A fascinating example of this occurred in Flat Rock, Michigan, which went to enormous lengths to win a new Mazda plant in 1984 and will likely be paying for it well into the next century.

Many key aspects of the Mazda–Flat Rock story were contained in a paper presented in the spring of 1988 at an automotive conference at the University of Michigan. The paper was prepared by three members of the sociology department at Michigan State University—Richard Child Hill, Michael Indergaard, and Kuniko Fujita.

Flat Rock is a rural town of about 7,000 some twenty-five miles south of Detroit, the capital of the American auto industry. There is a strange irony in this small town being the site of one of the most heavily subsidized foreign assembly plants ever built in the United States.

Until the early 1970s, it was mainly a bedroom community. But Ford changed all that with the opening of its Michigan Casting Center in Flat Rock in the early 1970s. The plant employed more than 5,000 workers at its peak, producing V-8 engine blocks. By 1981, the plant accounted for 64 percent of the town's tax revenue.

Ford closed the plant in 1982, leaving Flat Rock with an enormous hole in its revenue base and sending property values plummeting. The city laid off one-quarter of its work force, and the schools cut teaching positions and extracurricular activities.

As a result, Flat Rock was desperate for a new source of revenue and jumped at the opportunity to land the Mazda plant after state officials learned in early 1984 that Michigan was among a handful of states being considered by Japan's number three automaker.

The state's governor, James J. Blanchard, visited Japan and received a list of needs from Mazda. State officials said Mazda's representatives were extremely knowledgeable about what they wanted, and the demands exceeded the expectations of Michigan's officials.

Nonetheless, the state officials enlisted the aid of regional and local officials in the Flat Rock area, determined to meet the demands and win the plant. In addition to providing necessary jobs and tax revenue for Flat Rock, the potential of the plant fit well into Michigan's efforts to restructure its auto industry in an image that would carry the state into the twenty-first century.

Even after the site was chosen, state officials said that Mazda maintained constant pressure on Michigan officials to deliver the promised assistance. In the end, Mazda got about $120 million in government incentives and subsidies to locate in Flat Rock. Among the items on the list was an $80 million tax break from the city of Flat Rock and a $19 million grant from the state for training workers. The state even provided half a million dollars to cover the cost of miscellaneous fees and permits.

In addition to the outright grants, an army of state and local officials and businesses was mobilized to make the Japanese feel at home and smooth the way for their investment in a plant to compete with U.S. automakers. There were golf outings and receptions and luncheons and dinners. The welcome wagon was even extended to the Japanese parts suppliers who were planning to follow Mazda to Flat Rock.

State officials estimated that the Mazda plant would generate, directly and indirectly, 15,000 to 20,000 new jobs. Blanchard boasted that the move enhanced Michigan's ability to attract more Japanese investment.

Flat Rock's $80 million contribution of total freedom from taxes for twelve years was the largest item in the package, and city officials thought they had traded the tax break for a guarantee that Mazda would hire 400 of the city's unemployed residents. Several other nearby cities thought they had received commitments from Mazda to hire 100 of their residents.

Flat Rock's mayor at the time, Ted Anders, crowed that the Mazda plant would be a "pot of gold" for the city and the surrounding communities. But it turned out to be fool's gold.

By 1988, Flat Rock officials estimated that only thirty-two city residents had been hired in the first wave at the Mazda plant. You could say that each job cost Flat Rock $2.5 million in tax abatement. Instead of being local people, the bulk of the first 2,000 workers hired at the plant came from outside the immediate area.

Flat Rock was left with a burden on city services and the need to spend money for mammoth infrastructure improvements, while the Mazda plant pays no local taxes for a dozen years. City officials have been forced to go, hat in hand, to state officials in Lansing and plead for enough assistance to make ends meet on their local budget.

At one point, Flat Rock officials asked Mazda for $350,000 to offset an increase in city services related to the construction of the auto plant. The Japanese executives balked, and the state ended up coughing up the money.

Ted Anders was defeated when he ran for reelection not long after Mazda came to town. The new mayor, Richard Jones, eliminated the Japanese flags that had been flying at City Hall. Two years later, in 1987, Anders sought a rematch and was trounced even more soundly by Jones. Local politicians cited the city's anger with all he had given up to attract Mazda as the reason behind both defeats.

Despite the Flat Rock experience, Michigan officials remain boosters of the plant, and they are actively seeking additional Japanese investment. And every time they try to lure a plant, they find themselves competing with representatives of the other twenty-nine states that maintain active offices aimed at attracting Japanese investment to their cities and towns.

"As long as there are people who want to work and can't find jobs, you really can't be on the sidelines," said Indiana Governor Robert Orr, who helped his state beat out a dozen others and land a new Subaru-Isuzu light truck and auto plant in 1988.

However, there are at least stirrings that some Americans are uncomfortable with the enticements being provided to Japanese manufacturers.

In November of 1988, 32-year-old Evan Bayh became the first Democrat in twenty years to be elected governor of Indiana. In upsetting Orr's handpicked candidate, Lt. Gov. John Mutz, Bayh relied heavily on dramatic television commercials that blasted the Republicans for giving $55 million in taxpayer money to the Japanese for the Subaru-Isuzu plant.

The commercials also drove home another point that appealed to Indiana voters: a Japanese construction firm was being used to build the new plant, rather than a local contractor.

In light of the lavish efforts by state governments to attract Japanese investments, particularly auto and related businesses, it is worth examining the attitude of the Japanese toward U.S. investment in their own auto industry.

"Industrial rationalization" is the "backbone of the Japanese economy," wrote Clyde Prestowitz, Jr., in his book *Trading Places: How We Allowed Japan to Take the Lead.* According to Prestowitz, the industrialization theory was introduced in the late 1920s and "asserts that since absolutely free competition tends to result in economic crises, a comprehensive industrial plan with some governmental control is needed to replace excessive competition with cooperation among firms."

The Automobile Manufacturing Law, written in the 1930s, is an example of such government control. The law attempted to force all of Japan's manufacturers into three large entities by requiring government licensing to do business. Then the government put up half the capital for those firms lucky enough to obtain licenses and eliminated taxes and import duties for five years. Toyota and Nissan were licensed. Ford and General Motors, which until then had had a large share of the Japanese market, were not. Eventually their Japanese operations went out of business. By sheltering its auto industry in its early days, the Japanese government nurtured it into the world power it is today.

In that way, Japan built a protective wall around its auto industry, as it has done with so many other sectors of its economy. After World War II, imports were restricted to taxis, and the result was that less than 1,000 foreign cars were imported every year until 1959.

In 1960, Volkswagen could have delivered and sold its Beetle in

Japan at roughly half the price of Nissan's equivalent product, according to a study by Booz, Allen & Hamilton, the U.S. consulting firm.

At the same time, the Japanese refused to allow American automakers to invest in their auto industry through joint ventures or to set up manufacturing plants of their own in Japan. The refusal was flat, outright.

By keeping foreign products and American auto firms out, the Japanese were able to build a strong auto industry designed to export to the world. The restrictions on imports were eased slightly in 1960 and liberalized in the early 1970s, which allowed a gradual increase in the number of imported vehicles.

By that time, however, Japan had established itself as a major world exporter of autos, and could defend itself against the foreign automakers and go on to conquer the most lucrative car market in the world, the United States.

While the Japanese have not yet conquered the U.S. auto market, figures on auto sales in the 1980s illustrate the penetration of the Japanese and the decline of the domestic Big Three automakers. And these changes occurred despite a 40 percent rise in the sticker price of the Japanese cars as a result of the appreciation of the yen, which began in September 1985. American sticker prices went up 11 percent during the same period.

In 1982, the Big Three accounted for 70.8 percent of all new cars sold in the United States and the Japanese accounted for 22.3 percent. The remainder of the market went to the Western Europeans.

In 1988, the Big Three's share of the pie had dropped to 65.6 percent and the Japanese portion was down to 18.3 percent. The Western Europeans, meanwhile, had fallen to 4.5 percent, and sales to Third World countries, which were virtually nonexistent in 1982, accounted for 5.6 percent.

At first glance, the Japanese appear to have lost ground. But they really picked up more than 2 percent when transplants are accounted for. Transplants, Japanese cars produced in the United States, accounted for 6.3 percent of the new car market in 1988. That brought the Japanese share in 1988 to 24.6 percent.

What's more, the share of the market held by transplants is

expected to boom in the coming years as huge new Japanese-owned plants now under construction are brought on line. At the same time, Japanese auto executives are scouting for new locations all across the country.

By 1991, the Japanese expect to be producing 1.77 million cars in the United States just from plants that are now operating or under construction. When 330,000 cars and utility vehicles being produced in Canada by the Japanese for export to the United States are added in, the total nearly equals the 2.3 million-unit limit in place under the voluntary quota adopted by the Japanese in 1981.

A major ingredient in the success of the Japanese automakers in the United States has been their reputation for quality. American automakers have tried to capitalize on the Japanese image through joint production with their Japanese rivals. The danger, however, is that the Americans will end up assembling the vehicles while the Japanese control the design and engineering functions. This enables the Japanese to continue to expand their abilities in those areas, which provide long-term payoffs, while American technology is in danger of deteriorating further.

For example, Toyota manages New United Motor Manufacturing Company, its joint venture with General Motors in California; Mitsubishi manages its Illinois coproduction project with Chrysler; and Mazda owns and manages the Flat Rock, Michigan, plant where it builds cars for Ford and itself.

In late 1988, Ford announced a project that appeared to be an advancement from the American perspective. Ford will own and operate a plant to build minivans for sale in the United States by Nissan and Ford itself. But even this project leaves the high-value work with the Japanese—Nissan will handle all of the engineering and design for the minivans. For its part, Ford gets to spend $1 billion updating a plant in northeastern Ohio, where it will assemble the vehicles.

Some industry analysts believe the Big Three can thwart the Japanese move into the United States as domestic quality standards improve and the dollar weakens against the yen, making the Japanese cars cost even more. The American carmakers showed some progress in 1988 in regaining lost market share, but the Japanese are not expected to back down from their attempt to conquer the biggest auto market in the world.

And there is little incentive for them to back down when state and local governments across the United States continue to roll out the welcome mat and line it with tax abatements, infrastructure improvements, and other concessions that provide a built-in advantage over American automakers.

"The domestics have retrieved some lost share this year, but they shouldn't underestimate the capacity of the Japanese to come out fighting to cope with the yen," Chris Cedergren, an automotive analyst with J. D. Power & Associates, a market research firm, said in mid-1988. "The Japanese will do whatever they have to do to increase their share in this country. They are still developing a strategy that would have all of their transplant units become incremental sales, on top of selling all of the imports they are allowed to sell under the quotas."

Nowhere has that strategy been implemented more effectively than at Honda, which by 1988 was the best-selling foreign car manufacturer in the United States and had its sights set on replacing Chrysler as the number three seller overall.

11
THE HONDA STORY

DON'T RECITE THOSE STATISTICS about lost jobs at American carmakers or describe David Cole's opinions to the people of Marysville, Ohio. A decade ago, Honda established the beachhead for the invasion of Japanese automakers and their affiliated suppliers in Marysville.

No one there sees Honda as a Trojan horse. And the reasons why they don't, make Honda's story worth examining in considerable detail.

Since breaking ground in 1979 for a $35 million motorcycle plant in tiny Marysville, thirty miles northwest of Columbus, Honda has added a full-blown auto factory, hired 6,000 employees, and single-handedly resuscitated the ailing local economy. In 1987, Honda turned out 360,000 cars at its Marysville facilities, including 540 shiny new Accord coupes that were exported with great hoopla back to Japan. Plans for an auto engine–manufacturing facility and a second auto plant nearby will increase Honda's employment to an estimated 8,650 and its total investment in Ohio to $1.7 billion by 1991.

By going first and succeeding, the most maverick of all Japanese automakers paved the way for its rivals to avoid import quotas and potential tariffs and take advantage of the declining value of the dollar. By the end of 1988, U.S. car and truck facilities were also being operated by Toyota, Nissan, Mazda, Mitsubishi, Subaru-Isuzu, and New United Motors Manufacturing, a joint venture between General Motors and Toyota.

By 1990, these companies are expected to be operating thirteen plants in the United States with the capacity to assemble up to 2.5 million Japanese-designed vehicles for the U.S. market.

The catalyst for all of them was Honda, today the manufacturer of the best-selling foreign car in the United States. Honda sold 738,000 cars in the United States in 1987 and plans to challenge Chrysler's number three ranking by selling 1 million cars in 1990, with more than half of them being manufactured in Marysville.

At first glance, the relationship between Honda and Marysville looks like a successful chapter in the story of the global economy.

Honda, the international automaker, brings jobs, technology, and money to Marysville, a bedrock American town in the heart of the Rust Belt. *Business Week* hailed the "Americanization of Honda" in a cover story in April 1988.

Along with the rest of the Midwest in the late 1970s and early 1980s, Marysville was foundering. Its second biggest employer, aerospace and defense giant Rockwell International, packed up and moved away, leaving behind 400 ex-employees. Westreco, a coffee and cocoa processing plant, shut down and laid off 200 more people. O. M. Scott & Sons, the lawn-care products firm whose commercials of Marysville residents watching grass grow helped put the town on the map, cut back another 200 jobs. Several home builders went out of business. The only movie theater in town shut its doors, and the Chrysler dealership went under. Unemployment rose to 18 percent. And lots of people had nothing to do but watch the grass grow.

Then came Honda.

It started small, with ground-breaking in 1979 for its plant to manufacture motorcycles for sale in the United States and export around the world. In 1981, however, the Japanese automakers and government agreed to voluntary quotas on the number of cars they could send to the United States. The quotas came in order to avoid harsher penalties threatened by the U.S. government, which was under enormous pressure from its domestic auto industry.

The voluntary restrictions were designed to give the American auto industry some breathing room so it could develop new products and adopt new technologies to compete with the Japanese. The restrictions were also viewed as a way to encourage the Japanese to build new production facilities in the United States.

Honda was the first to respond to the encouragement, opening the doors on the first Japanese auto plant in the United States the following year at its Marysville site. Its fast response allowed Honda to turn the restrictions into a terrific boost to Honda's U.S. production operation. While the other big Japanese carmakers were limited in the number of imports they could ship to the United States, Honda was free to augment its imports with as many cars as it could turn out at the Marysville plant.

And Honda could still send the profits home.

Since the early 1980s, Honda has employed steadily larger numbers of workers in Marysville. By mid-1988, the employment figure topped 6,000. By 1990, when the second auto plant and a car-engine plant are on line, employment is expected to reach 8,650.

David Baker, the director of the Ohio Department of Development, doesn't have a bad word to say about Honda.

"Honda is a major employer," he said. "They aren't the largest by a long shot. GM employs 65,000 and Ford over 40,000 in their several factories in the state. But Honda's 6,000 is not to be laughed at. Honda represents a revitalization of an industry that had been declining in this state. The numbers have been going down at GM and Ford and will continue going down. But Honda represents the part of the auto industry that is fresh and contemporary."

Baker sees no connection between the declines at GM and Ford and the surge by Honda: "Employment was going down at GM while we were importing foreign cars. If GM workers are being displaced, Honda is hiring them. I don't care where a company's headquarters is. So what if it's in Tokyo? The vast majority of the positive impact ends up being local, where the company buys all its raw materials and parts, and where it does its hiring."

In fact, Honda rarely hires workers who have spent time in U.S. auto plants. Its Marysville operation is strictly nonunion, and the company does not want to bring workers with a history of union involvement into the workplace. Two attempts by the United Auto Workers to organize at Marysville were unsuccessful, and the union has not tried again.

Honda also prefers a work force that is more receptive to its Japanese-style production techniques, which means the company does not want workers who have spent years working at a Ford plant or on a GM assembly line.

The ideal Honda worker is new to the industry, and preferably very thankful for the job.

Jim Andrews was one of Honda's local hires. When he returned to Marysville in 1983 after serving in the Army, Andrews went to work as a carpenter with his father. The first year, he earned only $15,000, and there was not enough work to support both men.

In 1985, Andrews got a job in the welding department at Honda's motorcycle plant, which first established Honda's ability to serve a worldwide market from Marysville with its top-of-the-line Gold Wing motorcycle. The motorcycle, which sells for up to $10,000, is exported to fifteen countries, including Japan.

"What we're making here is a Japanese product, made by Americans. There aren't too many $30,000-a-year jobs in a rural area like Marysville," he said. That salary has paid for his wife Pam's tuition to nursing school and enabled them to buy a house.

The housing market in Marysville has come alive since Honda arrived. Keith Castle, a local builder, was putting up fifty new rental units and seventy-five single-family homes in 1988 alone to satisfy demand generated by the Honda facility. He had never built more than twenty-five houses in a single year before.

"My company wouldn't be in business today if it weren't for Honda," said Castle. "My father started it thirty years ago. I bought it from him ten years ago. I wouldn't have lasted five years. My brother is a mortgage banker in Tampa, Florida, and I'd be down there with him right now if it weren't for Honda."

Martha Moore, a real estate agent, sold eighteen houses in 1987, 85 percent of which she said were to Honda employees.

Marysville Mayor Tom Kruse says only about a quarter of the Honda employees now live in the country surrounding the plants because of a housing shortage. "It's my belief that we could build 1,000 houses here in the next six or seven years and sell them before they are built," he said.

Kruse also has benefited personally from Honda's arrival. He runs a company that provides janitorial service for businesses. His biggest client is Honda.

Many new businesses have moved to town. Jack Gilberg, whose grandfather started a family business in 1926 in New Bremen, Ohio, about an hour's drive away, decided on Marysville for his first expansion. "We're banking on Marysville growing up with Honda," Gilberg said.

There have been other expansions. The number of banks went from five to eight. The Dairy Queen went out of business before the boom, but Marysville now boasts McDonald's, Burger King, Pizza Hut, and Kentucky Fried Chicken restaurants. Plans are on the drawing board for a new shopping center, and a town council that once worried over the source of the next tax dollar is busy approving plans for housing developments and new businesses that will rebuild the local tax base.

Who can blame the residents of Marysville for welcoming Honda? Who could blame the residents of Troy?

The source of all this manna looks like a very large, low-rise high school campus sitting along U.S. Highway 33 just outside Marysville. The complex is no-nonsense, siege-style architecture—cinderblock walls, few windows, no unnecessary details; a few plantings ease the building's relationship to the rich Ohio earth.

The austerity continues inside. Absent are paneled offices, a corporate dining room, and executive bathrooms. Assembly-line workers and executives alike compete for parking spots on a first-come, first-served basis.

Through a nondescript door off the reception area and down a short, narrow hallway lies the executive office: a large open room, filled with standard shark-gray metal desks of equal size,

where everyone wears the same white uniform with his or her
first name stitched above the left front pocket.

Honda calls its employees "associates," from president to
receptionist, and they all share the open office space. The only
way to know who is in charge is to ask, because it is impossible
to discern corporate rank by the usual visual clues. No legions of
secretaries protect the inner sanctum of the president. No one is
allowed food or drink at his desk because assembly-line workers
are not allowed either at their work on the line.

Shoichiro Irimajiri, associate and president, sits at a neat desk
at one end of the large room. A motorcycle helmet rests on the
bookshelf nearby. There is a constant ebb and flow of young
engineers around his desk.

Next to Irimajiri sits the jovial Toshi Amino, the executive
vice president and, at fifty-two, the oldest member of the admin-
istrative staff. Irimajiri is forty-seven, and the other vice presidents, Shin Ohkubo, Scott Whitlock, Allen Kinzer, Susan Insley,
and Toyoji Yashiki, are all between forty and forty-seven years
old.

When asked to characterize Honda, the University of Michigan's David Cole said: "It's a new company compared to most
auto manufacturers. If you compare the Japanese companies,
Nissan is the sophisticated citified type of company. Toyota is
more rural, the Samurai warrior type of company. But Honda is
a daring bunch of motorcycle mechanics with dirty fingernails.
It is an extraordinarily good company with a very explicit set of
goals and unwavering commitment to technology. It is a very
solid company, which happens to be kind of untraditional."

Honda's emphasis on the United States is rooted in its history.

In the early 1960s, Japan's powerful Ministry of Trade and
Industry tried to keep its usual tight rein on the auto industry by
discouraging Soichiro Honda from expanding beyond motorcycles and providing new competition for the existing auto companies, such as the established Toyota and Nissan.

The ministry's opposition and the older companies' lock on
the Japanese market meant that the new company was forced to
develop its main growth overseas. Honda was determined that he
would succeed despite the odds against him.

A Harvard University study once called Soichiro Honda "an inventive genius with a legendary ego." Honda grew up in Komyo, 160 miles southwest of Tokyo, where he spent his time tinkering in his father's blacksmith shop.

According to his biographer, Sol Sanders, Honda remembers being sent to school wearing his mother's blue sash in honor of the emperor's birthday, an ornament that resulted in the worst possible fate for a young schoolboy in Japan. He stood out among the uniformly dressed students.

Although his classmates laughed and reduced him to tears, Honda learned the value of nonconformity for an artist or an inventor. The incident also sparked his lifelong penchant for red and pink suits.

Honda's later exploits became widely known in Japan, where he gained a reputation for his capricious temperament and his occasional bouts of philandering.

Among the stories circulated in the Japanese press about Honda were that he tossed a geisha out a second-story window, climbed inside a septic tank to retrieve a visiting supplier's false teeth and subsequently placed the teeth in his mouth, and stripped naked before his engineers to assemble a motorcycle engine.

Someone who was less independent would have bowed to the government's pressure and been satisfied to prosper as one of the world's leading motorcycle manufacturers. But Honda's refusal to buckle under led to the formation of an automaking company in which sharp design and near-perfect quality created a worldwide market, particularly in the United States.

The tiny motorcycle company that started with twenty-four employees in 1948 eventually became the largest firm launched in postwar Japan, thanks largely to Americans.

War-ravaged Japan was in desperate need of transportation, and Honda was one of 248 competitors who sought to fill that void. Like many of them, Honda purchased 500 tiny war-surplus engines and adapted them to bicycles. The clip-on engines were two-stroke, single-cylinder designs.

Honda's first breakthrough came in 1949, when he developed a lightweight, fifty-cubic-centimeter, three-horsepower motorcycle with a sturdy stamped-metal frame. Its initial success was short-lived, because competitors soon introduced more powerful four-stroke engine designs.

In need of capital, Honda joined forces with businessman Takeo Fujisawa. In 1951, the new partners unveiled a four-stroke engine with double the horsepower of the competition's engines and rode it to first place among Japanese motorcycle manufacturers. And from that position, Honda was able to pursue his life's passion—racing.

Prior to World War II, when Honda had run his own car-repair shop in Komyo, he modified and raced cars. In 1936, he crashed at the finish of the All-Japan Speed Rally after setting a new Japanese average speed record of seventy-five miles per hour.

In 1954, six years after launching his new company, Honda found a commercial use for his avocation. He announced that his motorcycle would beat the world's best motorcycles at the annual Tourist Trophy Race on the Isle of Man in Great Britain.

At the time, established European makes such as Triumph of Britain and BMW of Germany dominated the race, and everyone dismissed the upstart from Japan. Shifting most of his firm's resources into the racing effort, Honda was able to design a new combustion chamber that doubled horsepower and cut weight by half. In 1959, Honda's boast became reality when one of his cycles won the Isle of Man Manufacturer's Prize. Two years later, Hondas swept all five first positions.

Since then, "the racing spirit" has taught Honda's engineers many lessons.

"The racing platform—whether motorcycles, all-terrain vehicle, or Formula One racing car—is a moving test laboratory," Irimajiri told a gathering of business executives at the Harvard Business School in 1985. From that test laboratory, the company learned to face challenges, from the Isle of Man races to the restructuring of the American motorcycle market a few years later.

It was racing and a new commercial model—the Super Cub—that gave Honda the opportunity to plunge into the international marketplace in the late 1950s. Before then, most motorcycles were sold in Japan to men as an alternative to public transportation. Women had resisted using the cumbersome, hard-to-handle machines.

Honda's Super Cub was an inexpensive motorcycle that could be managed with just one hand. The company was overwhelmed immediately with orders for the Super Cub. By the end of 1959, Honda had leapfrogged into first place among Japanese motorcycle manufacturers, and the Cub made up more than half of its 285,000 sales.

Honda's partner Fujisawa believed that the world's consumer economy began in the United States. Thus in 1959, American Honda Motor Co. was born in Los Angeles with a small office and capital of $250,000.

Growth was slow, partly because Americans still thought of the Japanese as producers of inferior products. The company's meager reputation was almost destroyed by early reports of clutch failure on its motorcycles. It was only when Honda brought the Super Cub to the United States in the early 1960s that sales began to climb.

But even as sales rose, Honda and Fujisawa discovered that the American motorcycle market was stagnant. They blamed the stagnation on the unsavory image of motorcycles derived straight out of Marlon Brando's movie *The Wild One*.

They decided to blow open the U.S. market in what was the first example of the smart marketing that later would become a hallmark, not only of Honda but of virtually all the big Japanese manufacturers.

In early 1963, an undergraduate advertising major at UCLA submitted an ad campaign for Honda to his professor as an assignment. Its theme was "You meet the nicest people on a Honda." Encouraged by his instructor, the student passed the paper on to a friend at Grey Advertising, which had been soliciting the Honda account. Grey purchased the idea and then sold a campaign based on it to Honda.

Honda created a whole new image for motorcycles through an advertising campaign that became an industry classic. Housewives, doctors, businessmen, and teachers were portrayed gadding about on Hondas. Within a year, Honda dominated the U.S. motorcycle market, and one out of every two motorcycles sold in the United States was a Honda.

The company was having a more difficult time in Japan with its fledgling auto unit. In the face of government disapproval and the threat of legislation banning it from the auto industry, Honda rushed to introduce its first model, the S360 sports car, in Japan in 1962. As he had with motorcycles, Honda sought his validation on the racetrack. By its second year of competition in the international Formula One events, Honda won the Mexican Grand Prix.

Since then, Honda has surged past five other Japanese rivals—Daihatsu, Fuji Heavy Industries, Mazda, Mitsubishi, and Suzuki—to become the country's number three auto manufacturer, trailing only the industry giants Toyota and Nissan.

Honda began exporting cars to the United States in 1970. Again the company heard yet another starting gun, in the form of the U.S. Clean Air Act.

"Unless you are at the starting line when the gun sounds, you cannot participate in the race," Irimajiri said. "Even in the business world, there are often starting guns. The Clean Air Act was one such starting gun."

The clean air legislation, designed to control the rising pollution caused by auto emissions, required catalytic converters for almost every car manufactured or sold in the United States. The devices were expensive and slowed down a car's performance, particularly in their early days.

Honda had introduced the Honda CVCC in the United States in 1971, the same year the legislation went into effect. Within another year, an eight-man team of Honda engineers in Japan had developed a special CVCC engine that did not require a catalytic converter—a totally new approach to pollution control that gave the company a technological lead in the automotive marketplace that it never lost.

When Honda announced its intention in 1977 to build a motorcycle factory from scratch in the midst of Ohio's rolling countryside, the company was pursuing its philosophic cornerstone, as described in its literature: "By establishing manufacturing facilities in the markets where the demand for Honda products exists, we can become part of the communities in which our customers live. We can give back to these communities, states and nations something in return for the support Honda products have enjoyed."

In that sense, Honda is similar to the American multinationals that spread across the globe in the 1950s and 1960s, creating production facilities in locations where there was demand or where they felt they could create it.

When production began at the motorcycle plant in September 1979, Honda employed just sixty-four people in Ohio. Although in its first twelve months the plant produced 24,000 motocross and street-bike models, employment rose to just ninety-eight.

In 1981, as other businesses in Marysville began to falter and lay off workers, Honda's payroll hit 356. So while Honda did not bring many new jobs to the community, as Jack Scott of the Marysville Chamber of Commerce said, it "helped out with the balancing act for a while."

Within a few years, however, Honda was more than just helping out. With the opening of its auto plant and expansion of its motorcycle operation, Honda's total investment in Marysville rose to $720 million in 1986, and 3,053 people were employed.

Honda has also given its domestic rivals a lesson in how to prosper in the world's largest automobile market. More than any other Japanese company, Honda relies on the individual initiative demonstrated by its founder in developing new products and breaking down the distinctions between engineering, styling, and marketing.

In late 1987 and again in early 1988, more than twenty members of Honda's American sales force drove a secret prototype all night along California roads and then spent the next day telling designers and engineers where the bugs were located.

The same total involvement is evident in the manufacturing end of the business at Honda. The Marysville workers, all nonunion, form ad hoc groups to search for the most efficient production methods, and those who come up with innovations win free trips to Japan and free cars.

Another decidedly Japanese technique is called "just-in-time," a sometimes harried form of inventory control designed to keep costs down and suppliers on their toes.

Again, racing shaped the way the company operates, like a pit crew that relies on quick response. Unlike American auto manufacturers, Honda does not keep expensive inventories. The floor-to-ceiling stacks of car seats or large bins of stereo speakers that line the Marysville auto plant are actually just enough to keep the assembly line moving for just a couple of hours.

"Just-in-time" means that Honda's parts suppliers are responsible for delivering parts as they are needed, not before and certainly not afterward. Shipments of everything manufactured outside the plant, from steel to car seats and wheel rims, arrive constantly throughout the day at Honda's loading dock.

John Geese, vice president and plant manager for Bellemar Inc., a Japanese-owned seat manufacturer, located just a half-mile away from the Honda plant, explained the concept: "Actually, Toyota developed the practice, called 'Kaban' or card system. What they found was that when inventory went down, productivity went up, quality got better and they had more floor space and less money tied up in a nonproductive product. In other words, when that seat going down the assembly line is going to be placed into a car in three hours, you make sure that it's done right."

In addition to reducing overhead, the concept provides a built-in advantage to Japanese suppliers for the auto industry. These parts manufacturers have grown up within the "just-in-time" school of management, and their experience with it is one of the reasons that Honda and other Japanese automakers cite repeatedly when justifying their reliance on parts companies from Japan.

When Honda began working with a dozen or so Midwestern steel firms to assess which companies could make steel to its specifications, a consideration process that can take up to three years, one leading company was dropped from the list of prospects when its first test steel arrived a few hours late.

"A late shipment may cause the assembly line to stop," said Honda's Irimajiri. "On our assembly line we measure downtime in seconds. When you have more than a thousand associates working together to build a car, it is the attention to the seconds, not just the minutes, that determines your production efficiency."

Geese remembers ruefully the time that Bellemar stopped the Honda assembly line for fifty-two seconds.

Bellemar's Pennsylvania-based foam supplier had a fire. The shipment left late, and Bellemar ran out of foam and could make no more seats. Honda had only a two-hour supply of seats remaining.

While a truckload of foam was en route from Pennsylvania, Bellemar chartered a twin-engine plane to fly a small amount from the Pennsylvania plant to an airport near Marysville. At the airport, Bellemar had a truck waiting to rush the small shipment to its plant, where it would be turned into seats and in turn zipped over to Honda to keep the line going until the full truckload arrived.

But the minutes were so precious that Bellemar also chartered a radio station's traffic helicopter out of Columbus to fly a few minutes' worth of foam directly to the factory from the airport, before the small truck could make the same trip. Geese himself rushed out to Bellemar's baseball field, where the stuffed helicopter landed, and helped to drag in the bulky foam.

The frenzied, expensive effort meant that the Honda line was out of seats for less than a minute. Despite the fact that company officials admired the supplier's determination, they arranged three follow-up meetings in order to analyze the system and avoid future problems.

Today, Bellemar's trucks make up to forty half-mile deliveries a day to the Honda plant. And when the seconds are running out, Honda's loading dock uses a special red-light system to give Bellemar's trucks clearance over the dozens of other trucks always lined up, making deliveries at the plant.

Such techniques have proven economical. While it originally cost Honda $500 more to build a car in the United States than in Japan, the costs were about equal by early 1988.

Along the way, Honda's share of the American market has grown dramatically. In 1980, Honda sold 375,388 cars in the United States, third among foreign cars behind Toyota at 582,195

and Nissan at 516,890. Just seven years later, Honda had surpassed both its rivals and sold 738,306 cars compared with
630,052 for Toyota and 576,663 for Nissan. Part of the credit for
the success belonged to the Marysville production facility.

Concerns over quality of the U.S.-produced Hondas, however,
were still evident. A 1988 survey by J. D. Power & Associates, an
automotive marketing consultant, found that a random sample
of Honda Accords from Marysville was slightly more prone to
rattles and other minor problems than were their counterparts
built in Japan. Power found that there were 162 mechanical
defects per 100 Marysville Accords compared with 93 in the
imported models, which still made up about one-third of the
Hondas sold in the United States that year.

For those who want to tell the difference, Hondas made in
Marysville have serial numbers that start with 1HG while those
manufactured in Japan start with JMH.

Honda made automotive history again in March 1988 when it
became the first Japanese carmaker to ship autos built at its
United States plant back to its home country.

On a chilly Monday in Portland, Oregon, 540 Honda Accord
coupes from Marysville were loaded aboard a cargo ship bound
for Japan. The luxury coupes sported leather seats, aluminum-
alloy wheels, and a prominent eagle medallion that said "Made
in the USA." The car was designed by Honda's American staff at
its sales and distribution headquarters in Southern California.

The first car, a gray Accord, was driven onto the SS *Green Bay*
by Tetsuo Chino, president of Honda's American sales operation,
and Senator Bob Packwood, an Oregon Republican, as hundreds
of reporters and cameramen watched and American flags
flapped in the blustery wind.

Chino told the reporters gathered on the dock, "It has always
been our goal to develop the capabilities to export our American-made products to the world."

Packwood called the shipment an example of how American-
made goods could compete in the world market without protectionist trade laws, adding: "America is a force. This is a day that
we prove once again that we can do anything given the proper
management and proper international teamwork."

But it was little more than a token shipment, as Chino virtually admitted when he said the export goal of 4,000 cars in 1988 would make Honda the leading U.S. exporter of cars to Japan. The cars, however, were a big hit with the Japanese, and Honda said later in the year that it would send a total of 6,000 of the American-made Accords to Japan.

Yet as that first small shipload of Honda Accords crossed the Pacific, thousands of Toyotas and Nissans and Mitsubishis were on their way toward the Port of Los Angeles and other destinations in the United States.

Honda set another record that March, settling the largest race- and sex-discrimination case ever brought against a foreign employer by the U.S. Equal Employment Opportunity Commission. The requirement that Honda hire more blacks and promote more women hinted at the profound cultural differences between Japan and the United States and at the potential for a major labor conflict as more and more Americans go to work for the Japanese.

Foreign employers, particularly the provincial Japanese, have demonstrated little readiness for dealing with the roles of women and minorities in the American workplace. In industry after industry, Japanese employers have faced complaints and lawsuits from women and minorities who felt they were treated unfairly.

The Japanese, including Honda, have come to the United States with little background in dealing with women and minorities and unions. They are steadfastly antiunion and have to be forced to adopt affirmative action programs and other projects to provide fair opportunities.

The case that Honda settled with the EEOC was the largest to date among the several investigations of employment practices at Japanese-owned companies under way at the federal agency.

About the time the *Green Bay* set forth for Japan and the EEOC announced its settlement with Honda, George Chamberlin stood inside the once-shuttered Chrysler showroom on U.S. Highway 33 a few miles from the Honda plant outside Marysville. He was surrounded by new Chryslers, and he credited Honda with providing the economic punch in town that allowed him in 1982 to reopen the dealership that had closed just years earlier.

"Honda has had a tremendous impact on the Marysville economy," said Chamberlin, his hands stuffed in the pockets of his three-piece suit, one of the few suits seen in the rural town, where most men don blue jeans and baseball caps to go to work. "I'm selling a lot of the new Dodge minivans to the Honda workers, the Japanese especially. And I sell their Honda trade-ins to a wholesaler in Columbus."

Chamberlin, who had not heard of the UAW study showing that every job in a Japanese-owned car plant in the United States costs two jobs at a domestically owned auto company, thought for a while and then started talking again: "You can't tell me that companies like Honda aren't a detriment to the bigger picture, the national economy. Somewhere along the line, they are taking away from Ford and General Motors. Foreigners have captured 31 percent of our auto market. That's the reason General Motors is closing plants."

Unfortunately, Chamberlin's skepticism over the long-term costs of inviting the Japanese into the U.S. economy is shared by few local, state, or federal government officials. In much the same way that the federal government's deficits have been spending the next generation's tax dollars, officials are happy to accept the short-term gains embodied in the plants of Honda, Nissan, Toyota, Hitachi, and dozens of other major Japanese manufacturers.

The first wave of foot soldiers is already clamoring down the sides of the Trojan horse. They are the Japanese auto parts suppliers who have followed the big car companies to the United States and begun chipping away at yet another American industry.

12
CATTAILS AND SUN VISORS

LAS VEGAS. THE PERFECT SETTING for a $7 billion showdown.

But the grim-faced men huddled around the tables in early March 1988 in the gambling capital of the United States were not card sharks or craps experts. They were leaders of the American auto parts industry and executives from eleven Japanese car companies. And the battle was over the survival of the U.S. auto parts industry.

The U.S. auto market had sustained two waves of a Japanese invasion and was in the midst of a third that spring. The first wave was the flood of imports that grew throughout the 1970s. The second was the ground-breaking for the transplant factories that began in the 1980s.

The third wave was the arrival of the Japanese auto parts manufacturers. In 1984, there were approximately 50 Japanese parts manufacturers in the United States; by 1990, the number will have soared to 300.

The American auto parts industry has been squeezed so hard that some of its leaders worry about its future. And why not, since it is a future that is increasingly dependent upon the Japanese?

History shows little reason for optimism when coming up against the Japanese and their drive to conquer the world's auto industry. The Japanese auto industry had surpassed the United States as the world's leading exporter by 1988, but Japan remained virtually closed to the American parts suppliers, as it had to American carmakers.

Further, American carmakers have been importing increasing amounts of foreign-made parts from Taiwan, Korea, and Japan in an attempt to keep prices down. Industry analysts said that by 1990 the domestic content of U.S cars will drop to 75 percent. That means that one in four American cars will be an "invisible import."

"Demand for U.S. manufactured automotive products is stagnant at best," William F. Busker, president of an automotive parts division of the Goetze Corp. of America, had told a House committee in 1987.

Julian C. Morris, president of the Automotive Parts and Accessories Association, was far blunter that same year when he told the U.S. International Trade Commission: "The very survival of our industry hinges on American success in cracking the Japanese original equipment and replacement markets."

Now, in the spring of 1988, as the Japanese transplants gained a bigger share of the U.S. market, the American companies were finding themselves shut out once again.

The Japanese were importing the most sophisticated parts from home; they shipped $7 billion worth of parts to the United States in 1987, including engines, transmissions, and electronics. And they were buying millions of dollars more worth of parts from the Japanese suppliers who had followed them to the United States.

For two days in Las Vegas, the American executives, represented by the Motor and Equipment Manufacturers Association, tried to convince the Japanese executives to put more American-made parts under the hoods of the Japanese cars they were producing in the United States.

"The Japanese are buying more U.S. auto parts now that they are setting up factories here, but they are not purchasing nearly enough U.S. parts," said William A. Raftery, president of the auto parts association. "The problem is that the Japanese have been encouraging Japanese suppliers to follow them to the U.S. and open plants here. That doesn't provide new jobs, and it takes away U.S. jobs."

Raftery said the Japanese were buying "a few hundred million dollars" in auto parts from U.S. manufacturers while bringing $7 billion a year in parts to the United States from Japan and buying increasing amounts from the Japanese producers here.

After two days of meetings, Raftery and some of the other Americans thought there had been some progress. But there were no agreements. The Japanese, as had happened countless other times in trade negotiations, succeeded in delaying any commitment that would slow their domination of another major industry.

Three months after the Las Vegas meeting, a major Japanese auto parts manufacturer announced in Tokyo that it would set up a new plant in Shelbyville, Indiana, to manufacture and sell auto parts to domestic and Japanese carmakers in the United States.

The company plans to begin production by the end of 1989 and will be called PK USA. It is owned by Press Kogyo, a major Japanese auto parts maker, and Mitsui & Co., the huge Japanese trading firm.

If that seemed an expression of bad faith to the U.S. negotiators at Las Vegas, there was ample precedent for their concerns. Eight years earlier, in 1980, the Japanese had bowed to pressure from the U.S. government and agreed informally to raise their imports of U.S. auto parts to $300 million a year. By 1988, they had reached a grudging $261 million.

The failure of the Japanese to make significant increases in the amount of imported auto parts mirrored their reluctance to increase imports across the board. In 1960, imports of manufactured goods accounted for 1.5 percent of Japan's gross national product. In 1986, they were 1.6 percent, despite years of trade talks and repeated promises to liberalize their markets. And despite the deepening penetration of foreign markets by the Japanese.

The failure to reach any new accord on auto parts in Las Vegas underlined the frustrations vented a few months earlier in a speech at a seminar on selling to the Japanese sponsored by various state governments for the auto parts industry.

"If you want to supply parts to Japanese firms, forget about going to Japan," said Michael Flynn of the Industrial Technology Institute, an American think tank. "Your only chance is the transplants, and you only have a chance if you are supplying something that must be done locally because of weight and bulk. And you only have a chance if you can do it better than a Japanese supplier."

The difficulty in proving to the Japanese that you can do it better, let alone simply doing it better, has been demonstrated many times.

Elliot Lehman is cochairman of Fel-Pro Incorporated in Skokie, Illinois, a family-run firm that has sold gaskets to U.S. auto manufacturers for seventy years.

"Selling to the Japanese or the transplants is of vital importance to the future of this firm," he said. "But until recently, it's been nothing but a con game. For example, two years ago I sent some gaskets to a Japanese manufacturer. But before they even got there, he called to tell me that they had failed the test. We keep trying, though.

"For two years I've been saying we are 'cautiously optimistic' about our chances because for two years their people have been saying they're 'interested.' We've spent fortunes in producing test products. Yet we have no commitments. No orders."

Without sales to the Japanese, either in Japan or the United States, Lehman fears being boxed out of the market and seeing his business starved into oblivion.

Long-standing protectionist measures in Japan, such as favorable tax rates and deferred taxes for costs of developing new export markets, have created almost impenetrable barriers to U.S. companies interested in selling there.

And those attempting to sell to Japanese transplants operating in the United States have run into barriers of a different ilk.

While all societies maintain distinctions between themselves and outsiders, few are as exclusionary as the Japanese. They firmly believe in their inherent superiority to foreigners, and it is a belief that extends into the business world. For a foreign business to break into a Japanese market requires not only superior quality but overcoming traditional biases that are deeply imbedded in the business life in Japan.

The focus of the Japanese is not on the welfare of the individual, but on that of the group. Thus, Japanese businessmen build relationships over years, and Japanese corporations develop relationships over decades, that are designed to foster harmony and prosperity for the group. Often this harmony results in common membership on corporate boards and friendly treatment at related banks.

This translates in a very practical way: when a Japanese company has been supplying Toyota with ball bearings for several decades, Toyota will not displace the supplier with a new one even if the new one's bearings are cheaper and better. These types of relationships are augmented by the fact that many types of companies may fall under the same corporate umbrella, which provides yet another layer of protection from outsiders.

"The unnatural growth in productivity and price competitiveness of the Japanese auto parts industry is not simply a function of optimal management practices and production techniques," explained Julian Morris of the parts and accessories association.

"The Japanese vehicle manufacturers have a long-established family relationship with most of their parts suppliers consisting of interlocking directorships and equity position, under the aegis of the Central Bank's traditional practice of selective access to credit. This has resulted in a highly nationalistic, inbred, protected, and virtually impenetrable vehicle manufacturer-supplier environment in that country."

George Galster was vice president of international sales for Champion Spark Plug Co. when he saw the Japanese making huge inroads into the U.S. auto market in the 1970s. In response, he began trying to construct some sort of relationship with Japanese automakers because he recognized that the Japanese were the wave of the future in the global auto industry.

After five years of correspondence, Galster traveled to Japan in 1978. "It was just a matter of introducing oneself and one's company, which is not done on the first, second or even the seventh trip," he explained. "It's just one of those things about Japanese manufacturing companies.

"The Japanese are always interested in the corporate image, the background of the company, who the owners are, how corporate management treats employees, what the attitude is toward employee longevity, quality control. The Japanese look at the representative of the company first and ask themselves, 'Is he a worthy individual?' Then they look at the company. And then they will consider the product.

"Eventually one submits test samples. Those are followed up by individual visits and exchanges of technical information. The Japanese like to offer suggestions. They don't like to call it advice. Often they will request a visit to a supplier plant. In reviewing operations they might offer suggestions for reducing costs and improving quality."

Galster provided his Japanese hosts with a lot of technical data about the company and its research abilities and invited them to tour Champion's research and development facilities.

"The Japanese are inclined to use their own products, not foreign products. So we had to convince them that we had the technology that would benefit them," he said.

After another two years of "developing new technology and passing a rigmarole of engineering tests" Champion finally landed an order from Honda—for ninety-four spark plugs.

Then the company had to deal with just-in-time. Champion built a warehouse near Yokohama to receive the initial shipment and a satellite warehouse next to the motorcycle plant.

As a result of the years of courtship, Champion earned a small part in the original equipment market in Japan. But that market was mostly for small engines—outdoor equipment and motor-cycles.

Although Champion has supplied original spark plugs to many American car lines and virtually all the high-performance European cars, such as Mercedes, by 1988 the company still had only minority accounts with Japanese manufacturers, and only for vehicles to be exported, not for domestic vehicles.

At one point during negotiations, Galster offered to provide spark plugs free to Japanese auto manufacturers for a set amount of time. He was turned down.

Congresswoman Marcy Kaptur, an Ohio Democrat, first learned of the difficulties when she was preparing for a 1985 congressional trade mission to Japan. Kaptur visited all the companies in her district that had tried and failed to do business in Japan, including Champion. She took several packages of spark plugs with her and presented them to the various heads of Japanese industry, whom she met on her travels.

"I made them part of my pitch," she said. "I told them, 'When you start buying these, I'll believe in your efforts to solve the trade imbalance.'"

Today, representatives of Champion will not talk about the company's relationship with Japanese clients. Galster talks unofficially because he has since retired. Kaptur says the company, like many auto-parts manufacturers, is "afraid of endangering future contracts."

Some U.S. companies have been successful in dealing with the Japanese transplants. But it has not been easy for them either.

Before Honda moved into Marysville, Ohio, William Taylor of Capitol Plastics in Bowling Green, Ohio, read a small news item in the *Wall Street Journal* saying that the company was considering opening a motorcycle manufacturing plant in the United States.

"Rumor had it that Honda was considering coming to Ohio," he said. "It made sense to us that if they made motorcycles here, it might lead to the manufacture of autos here. We were always looking for new customers. Well, we figured we were an auto parts supplier and in Ohio and that we might have a chance. So we wrote Honda a letter. And then another, and another, and another. We were determined to get a response."

Finally he and his entourage received an invitation to Honda's California office. When Honda set up a temporary office in Columbus, Ohio, several months later, Taylor had a second appointment. Then a Honda representative visited Taylor's Bowling Green facility and discussed what he felt were the small company's strong and weak points. Taylor made the suggested changes. Honda provided sample parts. Taylor replicated the test parts and submitted them along with his proposals.

The whole process, which ended up taking three years, cost Capitol Plastics about $200,000. Taylor said, "We just decided, well, if the Japanese manufacturers are going to be in the United States and become potential customers, then we'd do whatever it takes to do business with them. But we got visitor after visitor from Honda. It seemed to take forever to get a commitment from them. We did wonder, 'Holy jeez, is it worth it? Will we ever get an order?' "

In 1980, after three years of negotiation and testing with Capitol, Honda rolled the first motorcycle off its assembly line in Marysville, Ohio. And Taylor submitted his first invoice—for $216 worth of plastic parts.

However, the process did turn out to be well worth it for Taylor and his small company. Capitol Plastics has increased its business 500 percent in the last five years, and one-third of that business is with Honda. In addition, the relationship with Honda has provided an entree for other Japanese manufacturers.

Another area where Americans stand a chance is the low-end, labor-intensive jobs that the Japanese do not consider important enough to warrant a whole factory in the United States.

Kevin Kern was a seed tester for O. M. Scott & Sons, the lawn-care products firm in Marysville, until Honda moved to town. He had never done any auto-industry work, but a friend of a friend who worked for Honda got Kern an invitation to bid on the preassembly of stereo speaker components for Honda's cars.

Unlike other parts suppliers and assemblers, Kern received his first work for Honda on twenty-four hours notice. He gathered several long tables and half a dozen people willing to work for $4.25 an hour in the back of the seed-testing laboratory. Then Honda people arrived with "how-to-assemble" charts and plenty of Super Glue.

"What a mess," Kern said, recalling those harried first days. But it was a chance not offered to far larger companies, and Kern is still in business, with a bare-bones factory behind the McDonald's on the edge of town, where twenty-five people work full-time for about minimum wage.

Taylor's success may have been made a little easier to attain because plastics are often cheaper in the United States, and Kern's business is low-tech, minimum-wage work.

Congresswoman Kaptur said: "I call it the cattail and sun visor crowd. They give us the fluff. They don't buy the drive-trains, the high-value end of production where engineering is important, from domestic companies. They tend to buy the incidental parts to the basic skeleton from American firms."

Others call it a "screwdriver society." They worry that U.S. workers are becoming skilled at little more than assembling components manufactured elsewhere. Carried to its logical extension, that trend would have the already anemic research and development arms of American corporations withering away as they increase their reliance on foreign-made parts.

What little progress the American parts firms had in selling to the Japanese in 1987 and 1988 was a matter of simple economics. Each surge in the yen made it more expensive for the Japanese to ship parts to their American transplants, and the weight of those rising expenses meant they had to abandon traditional relationships in some cases and buy American. It also stepped up the exodus of Japanese parts firms to the United States, of course, so that future currency imbalances will not jeopardize the relationships.

Honda, Toyota, and Nissan claim that they have 60 percent domestic content in the vehicles they manufacture in their U.S. plants and that they aim to take it higher in the upcoming years. But time after time, the domestic-content numbers issued by the transplant manufacturers are disputed by their American counterparts and auto-industry analysts.

"It is difficult to believe the domestic content numbers," said Raftery of the Motor and Equipment Manufacturers Association. "How much is made up of parts? How much is made up of labor? We've had difficulty coming up with the same numbers in looking at the cars ourselves."

When considering parts alone, domestic content is actually closer to 25 percent, most American experts agree. And that angers them.

Others, such as an executive for a truck parts manufacturer in Ohio, demonstrated a chillingly fatalistic attitude: "Who cares? If you aren't competitive you should be out of the industry. I think the Japanese are deliberately trying to create a surplus capacity, in order to drive the market share of the old-line companies down. But if the old line can't compete, the hell with them."

But the simple fact is that mere competitiveness is not the only barrier. The Japanese have used a wide array of advantages, often including a well-deserved reputation for quality, to create a playing field that is tilted dramatically in their direction.

The net result for the U.S. auto and auto-parts industries will be further declines in market share, additional job losses, and increasing reliance on foreign parts manufacturers.

James Mateyka is a vice president and auto-industry specialist at the consulting firm of Booz, Allen & Hamilton. He foresees the 1990s as a time of intense competition in the U.S. auto industry, with the domestic Big Three fighting a pitched battle with the Japanese imports and transplants.

"Clearly the domestic builders will assemble less vehicles," said Mateyka, as the transplants grab more and more U.S. market share. "The question really becomes one of how effectively the Big Three can drop capacity and drive down their break-even points."

The battle in the manufacturing end of the industry will be replicated within the auto-parts industry, although the U.S. auto-parts suppliers are at an even greater disadvantage as the Big Three turn to cheaper foreign parts for more and more of their original content.

So, unless the auto-parts industry can break into the Japanese market in a major way, its future is in grave doubt.

This question then emerges: is the auto industry simply a blueprint for what will happen in other vital industries?

William Busker from Goetze Corp. warned a congressional committee in 1987: "Here is what lies ahead for other major American industries: Japanese bankers will finance the new plants and Japanese construction contractors will build them; Japanese machines will equip them; and Japanese steel will be used to build and equip the factories. Japanese investment, like trade, means keeping the money in the family."

13
GIVING AWAY
THE FUTURE

IN EARLY JUNE 1988, U.S. and Japanese defense officials approved the basic outline of an agreement to develop jointly a new jet fighter for the Japanese air force, the FS-X, at a cost to the Japanese of $7 billion to $9 billion.

The accord marked the conclusion of more than two years of sometimes acrimonious talks between officials from the two governments and their respective aerospace industries. The Americans felt they had achieved a substantial victory: the design of the plane would be based on the F-16 produced by General Dynamics, and U.S. firms would receive 35 percent of the development and production work on the project.

It may turn out that they won the battle and lost the war.

The United States faces a crisis in the aerospace industry. It is a crisis that threatens the long-term survival of some of its largest and most important corporations, such as Lockheed, General Dynamics, and McDonnell Douglas. National security is also at risk.

Foreign competition is eroding the U.S. lead in civilian and military aircraft technology. High-quality foreign products, shrinking budgets in foreign countries for defense purchases, and transfers of U.S. aerospace technology abroad have threatened the nation's dominance in the field.

If that dominance is lost, the effect will reverberate beyond the monthly trade-deficit figures. Aerospace, in addition to providing one of the few pluses on the U.S. balance of payments ledger, is absolutely critical to national security. Advances in technology that lead to the development of new air-defense weapons require a decade or more to get into the field. If the nation allows its lead in this arena to wither away, the chances of recovery will be slim.

For several decades, the United States has been the leader in the civilian air transportation industry. Indeed, the industry has been the last bastion of a trade surplus for the United States. The value of U.S. aerospace exports rose from $1.7 billion in 1960 to $25 billion in 1987. During the same period, however, imports have surged more than 100-fold, from $61 million in 1960 to $7.7 billion in 1987.

Unlike in the auto industry, the threat to U.S. aerospace supremacy does not come chiefly from imports or direct investment in the U.S. industry. Formal barriers such as tariffs and quotas are not even the primary obstacles to retaining a healthy trade surplus.

The danger lies in the loss of the U.S. advantage in aerospace technology through other means, and there are deep concerns within the industry and sectors of the federal government that economic and political factors could combine to weaken the U.S. position.

On the military side of the picture, the nation's position as the technology leader has declined already. The United States has been slow to move into many promising new fields, such as hypersonic aircraft and planes that take off almost vertically. Further, as the world market for commercial aircraft shrinks in the 1990s, there will be increased inroads into the American market share from other nations and rising pressure on the U.S. companies to share their technology in exchange for access to foreign markets.

There are, then, parallels to the auto industry in the 1960s and early 1970s. Even though the threat assumes a different form, the potential for the same type of disaster awaits a nation that does not wake up to the crisis.

At high levels within the Department of Defense in Washington, discussions in the middle of 1988 were focused on the viability of the nation's aerospace industry. As the defense procurement scandal widened, it cast a taint over an industry already reeling from the stock market crash in October 1987 and trying to prepare for the defense-spending cutbacks expected with a new administration.

Some defense officials viewed the threat of foreign competition as a danger potentially more harmful than reduced U.S. defense spending or the effects of the stock market crash.

"The aerospace industry pushes the frontiers of technology and is essential to our defense posture," said a high-ranking official with the Defense Department's Defense Advanced Research Projects Agency. "There are serious concerns at the highest levels of the Defense Department over the health of the aerospace industry and its vulnerability to foreign takeovers and manipulation."

The Defense Advanced Research Projects Agency, known as DARPA, finances the ultrasophisticated weapons research done by U.S. defense contractors. It is the real cutting-edge stuff, and the high-ranking official worried that American companies may soon run out of money to continue the research he and many others consider vital to the nation's defense.

"Government R&D money is being cut back considerably this year, and it will get worse under the new administration, whether it is Democratic or Republican," said the defense official in June 1988. "The companies themselves have already been asked to share more of the cost burden in researching and developing new weapons systems and, with the financial shape they are in, you just can't expect them to put up much more cash in the coming years."

The unpleasant alternative, said the official, is encouraging more joint development projects with foreign nations, which are always eager to put up development money for a shot at access to the advanced technology at U.S. defense and aerospace companies.

The joint projects also have appeal to U.S. companies, since the costs of developing a new engine or a new aircraft can often exceed a company's entire net worth. A joint project with a foreign firm can also be the only means of gaining access to the foreign nation's domestic markets. Thus, sharing the R&D burden, and the financial risk it entails, through collaboration is one of the trade-offs many feel is required in today's aerospace world.

Under consideration in mid-1988, according to the DARPA executive, was a project to develop a new fighter plane with the British for sale in Europe. Preliminary talks included the possibility of equipping the new plane with the ultrasecret "stealth" technology developed at a cost of hundreds of millions of dollars by the U.S. government and Northrop.

He said the British had come up with $350 million as their first installment in a joint development project. The lure of the money was making it hard for the American companies and defense officials to resist the deal, despite their aversion to giving up the radar-eluding secrets of the Stealth Bomber, which had been one of the most closely guarded defense projects in U.S. history.

Aerospace industry organizations, such as the influential Aerospace Industries Association of America, confront a difficult dilemma with the joint ventures. The association's member companies often need the foreign partnerships to compete in the international marketplace. Yet they are well aware of the dangers in transferring technology to foreign competitors and allowing foreign acquisition of U.S. defense companies. It is similar to the dilemma faced by Department of Defense officials.

"DOD is real concerned about Japan and other countries getting involved with major aerospace firms," said Virginia Lopez, director of research at the Aerospace Industries Association in Washington. "The interlocking of firms and the penetration of our defense industry through cooperative agreements are going to have an impact on the shape of our industry that will be greater than direct investment."

From the standpoint of foreign companies and governments, one appeal of joint ventures is the difficulty foreign firms have in acquiring controlling interests in American corporations that do defense work. It is one of the few areas where the federal government applies restrictions to foreign investment. While such an acquisition is not prohibited, compliance with the regulations can make such an acquisition extremely difficult.

Another drawback to outright purchase of a defense firm, of course, is the potential for creating a public backlash in the United States. Japan's Fujitsu discovered that when it attempted to acquire Fairchild Semiconductor, which made computer chips with critical defense applications. Fujitsu backed away from the purchase, as described in a later chapter, but eventually formed a joint venture with the American firm that ultimately acquired Fairchild.

These partnerships also appeal to American businesses, and this is an attractiveness that will increase as the crisis in the aerospace industry deepens.

"Joint ventures make sense in many ways," said Lopez. "The federal budget crunch is only going to get worse. We need foreign partners for access to some international markets. And I don't see how we can afford to undertake some of these big projects without cooperation. There are pluses and minuses, and it is a very tricky deal to come up with the best policies."

The chief minus of joint ventures is that they trade long-range competitive advantages for short-term profits. They represent yet another example of the dangerous shortsightedness of American industry and the lack of a long-term strategy by the American government.

In a joint venture, a foreign company learns about American technology and manufacturing processes. Once it learns the process, it becomes an independent competitor and can use its new knowledge to increase its market penetration both in the United States and in the other countries where the United States is trying to sell products.

In the case of the FS-X fighter, Japan might be able to build its own fighter-plane components, but compiling those components into a sophisticated, supersonic aircraft requires years and years of technical training that the Japanese aerospace industry lacks. A joint venture offers the opportunity to transfer that training from the United States to Japan in one quick stroke.

Time after time, from televisions to machine tools, the Japanese have demonstrated that their implicit strategy in joint ventures is to obtain the technology and skills so that they can develop their own competing industries and eventually obtain control of another segment of the manufacturing world.

The most perceptive thinking on the perils of these business partnerships with the Japanese is contained in a 1986 article in the *Harvard Business Review* by Eric D. Mankin, a doctoral candidate in economics at Harvard at the time, and Robert B. Reich, a political economist at Harvard's Kennedy School of Government, who was author and director of policy planning at the Federal Trade Commission during the Carter administration.

The article is called "Joint ventures with Japan give away our future," and the findings are as blunt as its title.

"On the surface, the arrangements seem fair and well balanced, indicative of an evolving international economic equilibrium," write Reich and Mankin. "A closer examination, however, shows these deals for what they really are—part of a continuing, implicit Japanese strategy to keep the higher paying, higher value-added jobs in Japan and to gain the project engineering and production process skills that underlie competitive success."

The authors contrast the lack of U.S. strategy, writing: "In exchange for a few lower-skilled, lower-paying jobs and easy access to our competitors' high-quality, low-cost products, we are apparently prepared to sacrifice our competitiveness in a host of industries—autos, machine tools, consumer electronics, and semiconductors today, and others in the future."

In the auto industry, for instance, the domestic Big Three automakers have all struck joint-venture deals with big Japanese competitors. Each of the deals has assembly taking place in the United States, which allows the Japanese to avoid import quotas and provides the appearance of creating U.S. jobs. But in each case, the Japanese automakers have retained the responsibilities for plant design and engineering, and they supply the most expensive components.

Reich and Mankin point out the troubles contained in that

pattern. By handling the complex, research-oriented tasks, the Japanese have robbed their U.S. partners of the incentive to give skilled workers the opportunity to design new products and manufacturing processes. Instead, they must turn increasingly to the Japanese for the very components that add the most value to the car and require the best-paying jobs.

The logical consequence of the relationship is that U.S. workers will fall behind their Japanese counterparts, and U.S. manufacturing will increase its reliance on the Japanese for innovations in design and processes. The danger of this is particularly grave in the field of high technology, where new products and faster, more efficient production methods render even the most recent developments obsolete very quickly.

"The problem snowballs," warn Reich and Mankin. "Once a company's workers fall behind in the development of a rapidly changing technology, the company finds it harder and harder to regain competitiveness without turning to a more experienced partner for technology and production know-how."

As one example, they cite the closing of Westinghouse's color-television tube factory in upstate New York a decade ago because it could no longer compete with the Japanese imports. The same plant later reopened as a joint venture with Toshiba, only Toshiba supplied the technology that Westinghouse no longer had the ability to produce after a ten-year hiatus.

The stakes in these joint ventures become more important than the issue of the country to which the profits flow. The stakes are the efficiency, productivity, and skill levels of a nation's work force. As Americans fall farther behind in the high-tech race with Japan, the skill levels of its workers are destined to fall, too.

The nation moves toward becoming a screwdriver society, in which the technological innovations come from Japan and the products are simply screwed together at assembly plants in the United States. As Reich, Mankin, and others have pointed out, degrees of this problem are evident in many industries, from consumer electronics to automobiles.

The joint development of the new FS-X fighter for Japan's air force represents one more example of Japan's strategic determination to take away the U.S. lead in another critical industry. And this time, it is an industry vital to the nation's security. Yet once again it is being done with the shortsighted encouragement of American government and business leaders.

The Japanese began planning the development of their own supersonic jet fighter in the mid-1980s. Japan's aerospace companies said publicly that they wanted to build the plane entirely on their own, a strategy that evoked easily anticipated anger in the U.S. Congress.

Senator John Danforth, a Missouri Democrat and a strong critic of U.S. trade policy, led the opposition. He accused Japan of closing its market to superior and less expensive American products, such as the General Dynamics F-16 and the F-15J developed by McDonnell Douglas.

He argued that it would be far more cost-effective for the Japanese to take advantage of America's advanced technology and long development history in the aerospace industry. Danforth and other members of Congress also criticized the Japanese plan because of its potential impact on the U.S. trade deficit with Japan.

At the very least, some legislators and U.S. aerospace-industry officials suggested, the Japanese should agree to a joint development project with U.S. firms. This suggestion played into the hands of the Japanese government.

There are substantial questions about the ability of the Japanese aerospace industry to develop a completely new jet fighter on its own. Japan produces excellent avionics and other components for aircraft, but most aerospace industry experts believed from the start that the Japanese would have to rely heavily on U.S. designs to integrate the components into a sophisticated fighter.

So the opposition from Congress provided the perfect opportunity for the Japanese to appear to be compromising in the name of trade relations and actually achieve access to the technology and designs required for the development of the aircraft.

When Japanese negotiators sat down with officials from the U.S. Department of Defense and Department of Commerce in the fall of 1987 for talks on a joint project, the Japanese agreed to what they termed a codevelopment plan.

The new Japanese plane would be called a modified F-16, and the Japanese would pay General Dynamics a royalty of about one-half million dollars per aircraft.

In exchange, the Japanese wanted General Dynamics to provide a full staff of engineers at the Japanese construction site and supply all the drawings and technical data on the F-16, one of the most sophisticated and cost-efficient fighters in the world.

The main components of the plane would be Japanese. The avionics, the fuselage, the weapons, and the bulk of the engines would be Japanese.

What the deal offered the Japanese was permanent access to advanced technical data at a fraction of what it would cost to research and develop the plans itself. Yet the Japanese still would be producing an almost completely Japanese airplane, which would spur tremendous growth for its aerospace industry.

U.S. officials balked at the proposal, viewing it as a clumsy attempt to buy off American anger and buy up American technology.

Several months of talks ensued, and during that time Frank Carlucci replaced Caspar Weinberger as secretary of defense. Weinberger had been a strong proponent of the "buy American" argument. Carlucci, who had been President Reagan's national security chief before taking over the Defense Department, toed the administration line that friendly relations with Japan were paramount to long-range economic concerns.

So the negotiators returned to the table. Final approval of the agreement came in early June 1988 after Carlucci and Japanese Defense Minister Tsutomu Kawara engaged in discussions over how the work would be split.

The joint venture provided that the construction would take place in Japan and the components would be developed by the Japanese. The basic design would be taken from the F-16 drawings and technical plans, and U.S. firms would receive about 35 percent as subcontractors to the Japanese aerospace firms under a final accord signed in November 1988.

In addition, it was agreed that Japanese technologies developed for the FS-X would be eligible for transfer to U.S. companies, but the U.S. firms would have to pay licensing fees for them.

The agreement also set up a joint engineering committee, to exchange technical information, that will include participation by the U.S. Air Force and Japan's air force, known as the Air Self-Defense Force.

The Japanese plan to build 130 of the new fighters, with completion of the first scheduled for 1993 and delivery of the first production aircraft planned for the fall of 1997. Carlucci promised that the U.S. teams, including the Air Force engineers, will participate in the program from the initial development through the completion of flight testing in 1996.

By then, the fast-moving Japanese will probably no longer have any need for U.S. assistance anyway. And in the meantime, one of the key Defense Department negotiators on the FS-X deal, James Auer, has left the government and gone to Vanderbilt University, where he is setting up a center to study Japan. At the same time he was negotiating on the FS-X and other key issues on behalf of the United States, he was soliciting money from Japanese companies for his center.

14
TECHNO HAWKS

THE SHERATON CARLTON IS ONE of Washington's grand old hotels. Its location at 16th and K streets, a few blocks from the White House, makes it a perfect spot for the regular breakfasts hosted by Godfrey Sperling of the *Christian Science Monitor*. Sperling invites high-ranking government officials to answer questions from reporters representing most of the important news organizations covering the officials' particular bailiwicks.

Many Washington correspondents feel the breakfasts are more get-acquainted sessions than forums for generating real news. And they grouse about the early 8 A.M. starting time and the cholesterol-laden meals. But few can afford to miss a Sperling breakfast when the subject concerns their beat. Every once in a while, genuine news breaks.

The breakfast on a frosty morning in March 1987 had the earmarks of a yawner. Secretary of Commerce Malcolm Baldrige was well liked by reporters and respected as someone who had brought a measure of clout to a second-tier agency. But he was generally viewed as a man who kept his cards close to the vest. The Nebraska native, who had made a fortune in business and still roped steers in rodeos, once observed that "Cowboys don't talk unless they've got something to say."

The reporters who attended that particular morning, however, were rewarded. Baldrige had something to say.

A few months earlier, at the end of October 1986, Japanese electronics giant Fujitsu had announced a deal to acquire 80 percent of Fairchild Semiconductor, a pioneer of American high-technology and mainstay of Northern California's Silicon Valley, for $209 million. The proposal touched off a debate that divided the highest levels of the Reagan administration into two distinct camps.

In one camp were Baldrige, U.S. trade representative Clayton Yeutter, and Assistant Secretary of Defense Richard Perle, who saw the deal as a threat to the long-term economic health of the United States and to the technological leadership vital to sustaining its military independence.

Some members of the alliance earned the name "techno hawks" because of their abiding fear that the Fujitsu-Fairchild deal was part of a Japanese master plan to take over the U.S. information industry in much the same fashion that the Japanese had come to dominate consumer electronics. The "hawks" thought that allowing the Japanese to control a company vital to American defense and economic interests would leave the nation vulnerable in the event of war, strengthen the Japanese role as competitors, and increase the potential for espionage, either military or industrial.

Aligned against them were key aides from the Treasury and State departments, who feared that rejecting the Japanese investors would have an adverse impact on the nation's financial and diplomatic affairs. This second group also had allies within the Defense Department and on the influential National Security Council.

The Treasury-State side argued that the federal government should stay out of the transaction because of the nation's need for foreign investors, particularly the Japanese, who were underwriting the staggering federal budget deficit of the Reagan years. They also contended that political interference in a commercial transaction would set back Washington's efforts to persuade the Japanese and other nations to remove trade barriers.

Supporters of the deal on the National Security Council and within the Defense Department felt there was an opportunity to improve the U.S. defense-technology capabilities by bringing aboard some of Fujitsu's advanced technology. They had sought assurances from the Japanese company that it would share technology and other resources as part of the transaction.

The first phase of the debate had been carried out behind closed doors under the auspices of a little-known interagency group called the Committee on Foreign Investment in the United States, or CFIUS. The organization is chaired by the Treasury Department and includes officials from various agencies of the executive branch of government, including commerce, defense, and state.

As the only agency within the federal government set up to review foreign investment, it is supposed to screen major, politically sensitive investments. Since being established more than a decade ago, CFIUS has never opposed a single foreign acquisition. Indeed, were CFIUS to oppose an investment, there is little it could do to block the transaction unless the deal involved a defense-industry corporation. CFIUS is widely regarded as nothing more than a paper tiger. The Fujitsu-Fairchild deal was the only foreign investment the panel considered in all of 1986, a year in which the Japanese, British, and others were buying more of America than at any time in history.

On the rare occasions that the interagency panel cannot resolve policy questions about a particular investment, the matter is kicked upstairs to the cabinet. But the cabinet also has never overtly taken steps to block a foreign investment.

The cabinet is where the Fujitsu-Fairchild deal was headed the morning that Baldrige had breakfast with reporters at the Sheraton Carlton. The emotional, sometimes heated debates within CFIUS and among top-level government officials had not resolved the conflicting viewpoints, and so the full cabinet was to take up the issue two weeks from that March morning.

Baldrige brought the debate into the public arena that morn-

ing when he attacked the sale as "bad policy." Baldrige told the
reporters he was drawing "a line in the sand" that Japan would
not cross without a fight.

In his view, the U.S. semiconductor industry was vital to the
nation's economic and military well-being, and it had been
damaged enough by Japan's predatory pricing tactics. Fujitsu's
acquisition of Fairchild would not go forth without a public
battle.

"I've come out against it," he said that morning. "That's [the
sale is] something that gives me great problems."

Baldrige's move insulted the Japanese, who have no stomach
for public controversy or embarrassment, and angered some in
the administration, who felt certain the opposition of Baldrige
and others had been doomed to quiet failure. They felt that
Baldrige had gone to the media to stir up support for his position
because he knew he was destined to lose when the matter came
before the cabinet.

But Baldrige's public opposition heartened the beleaguered
U.S. semiconductor industry and the techno hawks and supported their contention that the transaction could be the start of
a new phase in the Japanese attempt to conquer the U.S. high-
technology industry.

"If one of the flagship companies of our semiconductor industry could fall into the hands of the Japanese, we could end up
with no U.S. semiconductor industry. We could lose the technology race by default," warned Stephen Bryen, deputy undersecretary of defense, a specialist in international security affairs and a
card-carrying member of the techno hawks.

Part of the fuel used by the techno hawks to bolster their
opposition to the Fairchild sale was a secret report prepared for
an agency within the Defense Department called the Defense
Science Board. The report was done by a task force of government, military, academic, and industry experts. It took no position on the Fairchild sale, but it declared that the loss of semiconductor manufacturing capacity to foreign manufacturers might
someday be viewed regretfully as "a turning point in the history
of our nation."

While the report described Japan as a "strong and essential ally," it said the economic interests of the two nations diverge enough that "it would appear unwise for the U.S., a nation with worldwide interests and obligations, to accept . . . dependence upon foreign countries for critical military hardware or technology."

The report echoed a resolution passed by Congress more than thirty years before, which warned, "We must not depend on foreign factories for our industrial mobilization base."

This issue goes beyond allies and enemies. Advanced military weapons, from weapons systems on board jet fighters to the electronics systems of a tank, depend on the tiny semiconductors that are the real brains of every computer. If the United States relied on Japan for such key components, the supply would not have to be disrupted by an event as profound as a war between the two nations in order for U.S. national security to be damaged. More likely scenarios exist.

One involves a limited war between the United States and the Chinese or the Soviets. Japan, because of its proximity to both of those superpowers, would be vulnerable to intimidation to cut back production of components destined for the U.S. military machine. Sea lanes and air corridors between Japan and the United States could be blocked or endangered, persuading the Japanese not to take the economic risk of continuing shipments.

Further, in the event of a protracted war, could the Japanese be persuaded to gear up their production of semiconductors to supply the military needs of the United States at the expense of their own domestic markets? Or would they see this as another opportunity to penetrate world markets with consumer goods while the Americans devoted their resources to defense manufacturing?

The scenarios may seem implausible, but the danger of dependence on any foreign nation for goods vital to its national security puts the United States in jeopardy.

Fujitsu is not alone in raising the issues of Japanese ownership of U.S. defense and high-tech companies. In an episode that had striking similarities to the attempt to acquire Fairchild, another

Japanese company announced in the summer of 1988 that it had reached a deal to acquire Gould Inc., an ailing computer and electronics firm with headquarters outside Chicago.

The purchaser was Nippon Mining of Tokyo, an oil-refining and minerals company that had engaged in several joint ventures with Gould in recent years. The price was to be $1.1 billion, the fourth largest Japanese acquisition in U.S. history behind Firestone, CBS Records, and the Westin Hotel chain.

Gould maintained a substantial but dwindling defense electronics division in Southern California. The Navcom division in El Monte manufactured advanced communications equipment for the military and aircraft instruments.

Partly because Gould had been trimming its military operations, there were no immediate objections to the deal on national security grounds. Gould executives said the transaction had been approved in advance by the Department of Defense.

But the transaction did raise antitrust issues. Gould remained a major manufacturer of copper foil, a key ingredient in the manufacture of printed circuit boards. Nippon Mining also manufactures the foil, and the completed transaction would give the Japanese company control of 70 percent of the world's copper-foil resources.

Like Fairchild, Gould had fallen on tough times after once being a dominant player. After several mundane but prosperous decades producing batteries and industrial products, the firm's polo-playing chairman, William Ylvisaker, began an expansion in the 1970s toward the glamorous high-tech industries.

By 1980, Gould revenues had topped $2 billion a year, and it had several promising product lines. But there were mistakes, such as failing to reinvest profits in research and development, and shedding some of the old lines that had provided a base of sales and profits. They were the bad habits of American industry.

The big blow came in 1985, when Gould's semiconductor business was caught in an industry downturn created by an oversupply of underpriced chips dumped on the world's markets by the powerful Japanese manufacturers. Huge losses on contracts with the U.S. military crippled the company and set up the buyout by one of Japan's own, Nippon Mining.

Nippon already owned several smaller U.S. companies, including a titanium company in Michigan and some high-tech outfits in California.

A perfect example of what happens when a Japanese company acquires American technology occurred in August 1988, when Kubota Limited of Tokyo unveiled one of the world's most advanced mini-supercomputers.

Kubota is Japan's largest manufacturer of agricultural machinery, and the design, chips, and software in its new computer were all American as a result of shrewd investments in a series of small companies in Silicon Valley. All Kubota did was assemble the computer.

"It's perfectly legal, even admirable. But it is also a little scary," said John P. Stern, head of the Tokyo office of the United States Electronics Association.

Supercomputer technology is one of the few fields where the United States still maintains a lead over Japan. By investing $75 million in five small U.S. firms, Kubota bought the know-how to develop its own computer. And the company did so without raising complaints about national security by not seeking to control its American affiliates.

Instead of control, the Japanese firm filled a void left by the big American companies. It provided start-up capital and shared in the risks with its American partners. As a result, Kubota moved from tractors to supercomputers for a mere $75 million and in a very short time.

Unlike with Gould or the partners of Kubota, there was some irony to the debate over the Fujitsu-Fairchild deal because Fairchild was already foreign owned.

It had been acquired in 1979 by Schlumberger, the giant French-controlled oil-field services company. But there was a critical difference in the minds of U.S. officials between ownership by the French, a steadfast ally in two world wars, and the Japanese, enemies in a conflict still fresh in many American minds.

Indeed, while the British and French have acquired some defense-related companies in the United States, Japan and West Germany remain persona non grata in many corners of the government when it comes to buying shares in defense companies.

But memories of World War II only provided the background for opponents of the Fujitsu-Fairchild deal. Their main argument was the way the transaction fit so neatly into a Japanese strategy to dominate the semiconductor industry, and the implications that the potential dominance had for America's role as the world's technology leader.

The United States had already lost its world leadership to Japan in many important fields, such as consumer electronics, robotics, and microelectronics. While the nation remained the leader in other critical areas, such as artificial intelligence, the wholehearted commitment to developing cutting-edge technology and exploiting innovations for commercial and military products seemed to have disappeared from the U.S. manufacturing scene.

The same factors that had weakened other industrial sectors were at play in the high-tech arena. There was a fixation on quick research payoffs, an inattention to the value of research and development, and an inability to aim at creating new products for new markets.

"We were so much the world leader for a considerable number of years that people began to take for granted that most of the solutions lay in their own organizations," said Edwin Mansfield, director of the Center for Economics and Technology at the University of Pennsylvania. "After a while, there are new guys on the block, but the tendency is to not keep track of them as well as you might."

In the case of semiconductors, the new guys on the block are clearly the Japanese, and they were ignored for many years. But by the time Baldrige went public with the dispute over the Fairchild-Fujitsu deal, it was no longer a case of not keeping track of the Japanese. The question was, could they be stopped before they took over the critical industry?

The semiconductor, also known as a computer chip or integrated circuit, is the foundation for the modern computer. It is a miracle of technology that can store, channel, and manipulate millions of electrical signals on a sliver of silicon the size of a fingernail.

Its invention had allowed engineers to reduce the computer from the size of a room to the size of a typewriter. Calculators fit on watches, and televisions shrink to a matter of inches in dimension. Chips control pacemakers, video games, and the most sophisticated guided missiles. They are behind the voices in the dashboards of cars, and the intelligence in a range of goods from home appliances to spacecraft.

Literally scores of new products need chips of increasing power, which means more and more memory stored on tinier and tinier surfaces. Such new technologies as artificial intelligence, robotics, voice recognition systems, and digital television depend on production breakthroughs in chips. The Strategic Defense Initiative would be impossible even to conceive without an extraordinary faith in the potential for engineers and scientists to come up with dramatic increases in the memory and reliability of chips.

It was at Fairchild Semiconductor in the Silicon Valley of Northern California that a young engineer named Robert Noyce created the first practical integrated circuit, or chip. The invention turned Fairchild into the world's top computer-chip maker in 1966 and made it a nurturing ground for brilliant young electrical engineers and adventurous businessmen.

The astounding growth of Silicon Valley, and particularly the semiconductor industry on which it is built, is a tribute to the creative entrepreneurship of the United States. A few large firms, such as IBM, AT&T, and Hewlett Packard, developed substantial internal capabilities for producing semiconductors. But two-thirds of U.S. production, and virtually all of the chips sold on the open market, comes from the producers established in the last twenty years for the primary business of producing semiconductors.

Often these small, so-called merchant companies are financially unstable, with a transient employee base and a future pinned on developing the next hot product. While this type of industry growth played a vital role in the entrepreneurial spirit that made the United States the world's leader in semiconductor and computer advances, it is less conducive to long-term success as a mature and stable industry. But there was no denying the early successes, as American engineers reduced the size and expanded the memories of the tiny electronic brains.

At the height of its success in the middle 1970s, the U.S. industry held 95 percent of its domestic market, half of Europe's market, and 60 percent of the entire world market. But the U.S. firms were supplying less than one-third of the Japanese market.

The Japanese semiconductor industry had grown up on a far different path than its American rivals. The pattern was a classic of postwar Japan: a few diversified, integrated electronics companies, such as Nippon Electric Corporation (NEC) and Hitachi, were allowed to produce chips under protection from the government. U.S. technology and production equipment were imported and copied, but direct investment was prohibited and importation of actual chips was severely restricted.

The Japanese companies used about one-quarter of their chip production in their own electronics products, which constituted most of their business. They also developed lasting relationships with their suppliers and the national government. The only way a new chip manufacturer came into existence was when one of the established electronics firms, such as Sanyo or Sony, decided to produce its own chips.

Another advantage for the Japanese was their long relationships with banks, which meant that they could borrow money at low rates to finance expansion and research and absorb early losses as they built sales volume and quality.

During the late 1960s and 1970s, the Japanese were content to build up their domestic companies and refrain from exporting huge amounts of chips to the United States. But all that changed in the 1980s.

On February 26, 1987, a couple of weeks before the Baldrige breakfast at the Sheraton Carlton, Charles Ferguson of the Center for Technology, Policy and Industrial Development at Massachusetts Institute of Technology in Cambridge, Massachusetts, delivered a chilling diagnosis of the health of the U.S. semiconductor industry. He said the high-tech industry in general was in a crisis condition that was likely to worsen and send ripples through the economy in the coming years unless action was taken.

"In essence," he testified before a Senate subcommittee, "the deterioration of its high-technology industries confronts the United States with the prospect of a fundamentally weaker economic and geopolitical position, and a correspondingly greater dependence on Japan."

Between 1980 and 1986, the U.S. trade balance in high-tech goods had gone from a positive $27 billion to a minus $2 billion. A major component of that decline had been the severe erosion of the U.S. semiconductor industry in the face of what had become predatory competition from the Japanese.

Between 1978 and early 1987, Japan's share of the world semiconductor market had risen from 28 percent to 50 percent. The American industry's portion had dropped to less than 40 percent from 55 percent. In yet another industry, Japan had surpassed the United States.

In his testimony, Ferguson pointed out that the U.S. decline had started in the late 1970s as the worldwide semiconductor industry shifted from its earlier entrepreneurial flavor to one that required larger scale and more capital. Research and development costs soared as chip advances became harder and harder to develop. The cost of the average plant had soared to more than $100 million, labor costs had risen by as much as one-third, and many of the U.S. firms had been driven out of business.

At the same time, demand for chips was soaring. They were strategically critical to a growing range of major industries, including consumer electronics, weapons systems, and computers.

The environment was ideal for the Japanese giants, who could use multibillion-dollar corporate coffers to build advanced production facilities and finance research and development.

The Japanese had already been outspending their U.S. rivals on R&D. Between 1975 and 1982, the U.S. share of patents worldwide for chip technology had dropped to 27 percent from 43 percent. Japan's share more than doubled, going from 18 percent to 48 percent. By the mid-1980s, more than 40 percent of the research papers presented at international conferences on integrated circuits came from Japan.

As a result, the Japanese began producing higher-quality chips and making significant advances in technology. U.S. manufacturers of computers and electronic goods readily abandoned domestic suppliers in favor of cheaper and better Japanese chips.

Driven by the motivation of gaining market share, the Japanese companies began selling chips on the American market at below the cost of making them, the practice known as "dumping." Robert Noyce, by then the chief of Intel Corp., a leading U.S. chip producer, watched the price of a Japanese chip plummet from $17 to $4.50 in eight months, and he warned that the Japanese were "out to slit our throats."

The whole story of what happened can be told through the fate of the crucial market for semiconductors known as dynamic random access memory chips, or DRAMs. The latest DRAMs are known as 1-megabit chips, which means they store a million bits of data.

These immediate storage devices are found in every computer, as vital to computer production as steel is to automobiles. Without an adequate supply at a realistic price, advances in computer technology, one of the last areas of high technology where the United States held a commanding lead, would come to a standstill.

But by the mid-1980s, the Japanese share of the market had gone from 5 percent in 1981 to 90 percent. And the Japanese firms were pumping more and more cheap chips into the U.S. market, driving out American manufacturers and threatening the very existence of the industry in the United States.

One example of how the Japanese intended to capitalize on the weakness of the American companies was contained in an internal memo written on February 21, 1985, by an official at the American headquarters of Hitachi, one of Japan's biggest semiconductor and electronics manufacturers.

The memo instructed Hitachi's American distributors to undercut competitors' prices for semiconductors by 10 percent in order to raise the company's share of the market. The language was remarkably explicit:

"Quote 10 percent below competition. If they requote, bid 10 percent under again. The bidding stops when Hitachi wins."

The memo dealt primarily with chips called EPROMs, meaning erasable programmable read only memory. The prices for EPROMs already had declined nearly 75 percent in the previous year.

In a typical pattern, Hitachi executives denied any knowledge of the memo once it was made public by an official of the U.S. Commerce Department, claiming that it was unauthorized and unapproved. It was the type of hollow denial American competitors and trade negotiators had come to expect from the Japanese.

Denial notwithstanding, the predatory pricing outlined in the memo and carried out by the Japanese in many fields of chip sales took a toll on American firms. Many U.S. makers virtually had abandoned the market in DRAMs in 1985, despite the strategic importance of the chips. The U.S. semiconductor industry lost more than 40,000 jobs in 1985, and its five largest companies lost $343 million as their leads in chip markets eroded.

"We're at war with Japan—not with guns and ammunition, but an economic war with technology, productivity and quality," said Charles Sporck, president of National Semiconductor, a major U.S. producer.

Sporck's outcry was among many issued from the executives in the Silicon Valley. Many of them called on U.S. government intervention to stop Japanese dumping of chips, such as Fujitsu's sale of its DRAMs at 60 percent below their fair market value.

In 1987, the industry attempted to respond to the Japanese challenge by creating a consortium known as Sematech. With fourteen U.S. chipmakers contributing start-up capital and some staff members, the group set up operation in a tightly guarded building near the airport in Austin, Texas.

The group asked the federal government to provide $100 million a year out of Sematech's $250 million budget for the first five years, and the first installment was paid by the Defense Advanced Research Projects Agency, which oversees federal support for weapons research.

However, it was not until the summer of 1988 that Sematech could persuade one of its members to give up a senior executive to head the vital research operation. The executive who finally agreed to lead the charge against the Japanese was the legendary Bob Noyce, at the time a vice chairman of Intel Corp.

At the same time Sematech was being formed in 1987, the chip industry was complaining to Washington. One of those who heard the outcry was Malcolm Baldrige at Commerce, who moved to stop the destruction of the industry by filing an anti-dumping claim against the Japanese chipmakers. Clayton Yeutter, the U.S. trade representative, used the claim as the basis for what he later described as "hellishly difficult" negotiations with the Japanese to end the dumping and open Japan's markets to United States producers.

In September 1986, the negotiators signed a landmark agreement governing trade in semiconductors that both sides hailed as a breakthrough for the ailing U.S. industry. Japanese companies promised to quit dumping their chips in the United States. The Japanese government said informally that it would allow U.S. and other foreign manufacturers to increase chip sales in Japan.

For Fairchild, however, the accord appeared to come too late.

Schlumberger, the French-controlled multinational that owned Fairchild, had suffered setbacks in the oil industry and had run out of patience with the losses at its Silicon Valley subsidiary. Concerned about a possible shutdown of the entire operation, Fairchild executives opened talks with Fujitsu about a possible rescue.

After several weeks of secret negotiations, a deal was struck that would sell Fairchild to the Japanese electronics giant for $200 million. In the weeks before the agreement was unveiled, the Fairchild executives plotted a public relations campaign aimed at smoothing the way for what they knew would be a controversial acquisition.

Donald Brooks had been hired away from Texas Instruments by Schlumberger in 1983 to save the foundering Fairchild operation. Late in October 1986, Brooks was on his way to Washington to explain the details of his plan to save the company by selling it to the Japanese. Brooks expected to quiet any potential bureaucratic rumblings over the deal easily and head home.

But, as *Los Angeles Times* reporters William Rempel and Donna Walters wrote in an authoritative article on the controversy, "Brooks discovered that he and Fairchild had stepped from the financial frying pan into the political fire."

One of the first people he met in Washington was Stephen Bryen, the Defense Department techno hawk, who immediately voiced his skepticism about the effect on national security and the goals of the Japanese. At his next stop, the U.S. trade representative's office a block from the White House, Brooks encountered opposition from the officials who had just completed the accord they thought would spare the U.S. semiconductor industry.

"They gave me some indication that it was an unhappy situation with Japan and that this was another blow," Brooks later told Rempel and Walters.

While the proposed acquisition of Fairchild by Fujitsu was generating some headlines around the country by that time, sentiment about the deal was seething beneath the surface in Washington.

MIT's Charles Ferguson had picked up his telephone in Cambridge when he learned of the proposal and called contacts throughout the government, from Congress and the Defense Department to the intelligence community, to express his deep concerns. Bryen's initial skepticism hardened into a firm resolve to oppose the deal. Officials at the U.S. trade representative's office were angered at what some viewed as a Fairchild sellout, and opposition was heating up at the Commerce Department.

Adding to the woes of Brooks and the others backing the deal was the mushrooming of a routine Justice Department investigation into whether federal antitrust laws would be violated by the acquisition. One focus of the inquiry was what would happen to the market for a particular kind of chip essential to the operation of supercomputers, which play an important role in national security.

Cray Research, Inc., in Minneapolis, Minnesota, was the world's leading manufacturer of supercomputers, the giant machines that were pushing the frontiers of computer science to new levels. The supercomputers have numerous defense applications, most significantly their use for intercepting and decoding international communications by the supersecret National Security Agency.

Cray relied on two companies for essential chips called emitter-coupled logic chips. The companies were Fairchild and Fujitsu, and their merger would have eliminated a competing source for Cray. It also would have left Fujitsu with a unique ability to continue development of its competing supercomputer while obstructing Cray.

The Justice Department investigation was not expected to obstruct the deal, largely because the antitrust division at Justice had gone on a virtual vacation throughout the Reagan administration. But opponents of the transaction had persuaded the Justice Department lawyers on the case to demand massive documents from Fairchild and Fujitsu that would take months to assemble. Fujitsu was also extremely uneasy about supplying the material to U.S. authorities, particularly documentation dealing with its work in highly sensitive and competitive supercomputers.

Several members of Congress had also joined the camp of Baldrige and the techno hawks. Senator James Exon, a Democrat from Nebraska, wrote letters to several administration officials warning that the U.S. technological lead was being eroded and stressing the importance of the semiconductor industry to national defense. Senator Howard Metzenbaum, an Ohio Democrat and an influential member of the Judiciary Committee, cautioned the Justice Department in a letter that the Fairchild acquisition "could permit Fujitsu to dominate the American supercomputer market."

Fujitsu tried to eliminate those concerns with a secret agreement to provide Cray with the key chips for five years, and Brooks offered to license Fairchild's chipmaking process to other companies so there would be a diversity of suppliers for supercomputers.

But the efforts were too late and, more importantly, too little. They failed to address the substance of the fears expressed by the opponents: here was the mother of the U.S. semiconductor industry about to be bought up by the Japanese at a time when Japan's predatory pricing and superior quality had devastated that U.S. market.

The opposition concerned Fujitsu executives on several fronts. Delays in the deal were bothersome, particularly because of their public nature. If the transaction went through, Fujitsu could become a target for the widespread anti-Japanese feeling engendered by that nation's trade practices and its dominance over the United States in key sectors of the economy. Nonetheless, the Japanese hung tight in response to pleas from Fairchild executives to give the process a chance to work itself out.

But Baldrige's breakfast with reporters at the Sheraton Carlton changed all that. The public opposition of such an influential American government official was more than the Japanese could withstand. Five days after the comments from the breakfast were published in the nation's newspapers, Fujitsu withdrew from its agreement to buy Fairchild.

At a press conference on March 17, 1987, the morning after Fujitsu's announcement, Brooks tried to put the withdrawal in the best light. He said that the Japanese company remained interested in pursuing technological exchanges with Fairchild. He said that Fairchild's management was preparing a proposal to buy the company itself, with possible financial assistance from Fujitsu.

But he was also angry, accusing his Silicon Valley colleagues in the semiconductor business of "kindling the fires" that burned down his deal and complaining that the company and its employees had been victimized.

Brooks and his management team did eventually come up with a bid to buy Fairchild for $185 million, $24 million less than the Fujitsu offer. But the management bid was rejected because it required Schlumberger to come up with financing for much of the debt.

Six months after Fujitsu withdrew its bid, Schlumberger announced that Fairchild would be purchased by National Semiconductor, one of its Silicon Valley neighbors. The new company would be big enough to compete with the Japanese conglomerates, and some of Fairchild's advanced computer chips, such as those for the supercomputers, would fill a void in National's product lines. The price was $122 million.

Some of the people who had supported the sale to Fujitsu saw a bitter lesson in the price paid by National Semiconductor. They argued that the U.S. government had determined the price of Fairchild in a backhanded manner that had wound up helping another American company.

So what, said Charles Ferguson, the MIT expert who had opposed the Fujitsu deal early on. "I hope there's a lot more cases like that," he said. "I hope there's more $100 million price cuts. I hope it sends a signal to the entire U.S. semiconductor industry that they can't bail out of difficult competition by selling out to the Japanese."

15
STEALING THE CROWN JEWELS

THE LAVISH SUITE AT THE LANDMARK St. Francis Hotel over-looked Union Square in downtown San Francisco. The suite was filled with fresh-cut flowers and fine antiques, a perfect setting for the high-level international business deal under discussion by three men seated around a coffee table on April 23, 1982.

One of the men was Dr. Kisaburo Nakazawa, the general manager of Hitachi's plant in Kanagawa, fifty miles or so outside Tokyo and the facility where the giant electronics firm develops and manufactures its computers.

Hitachi, often called the General Electric of Japan, is the world's third largest electronics company and the third largest corporation of any type in Japan. In 1982, it had approximately 120,000 employees producing 20,000 kinds of products, which ranged from refrigerators and television sets to railroad cars and nuclear power plants.

Hitachi is also Japan's fourth largest computer manufacturer. The Tokyo-based company produced a line of computers and computer accessories compatible with IBM computers, though at a lower price. Hitachi was one of a number of companies that copied IBM products and sold them cheaper than the IBM originals.

These clones compete with IBM products in the United States and around the world for a share in the $100 billion computer industry. As long as they are produced within acceptable guidelines of what is called "reverse engineering," clones are legal.

In the reverse engineering process, new IBM products are dismantled by engineers to see how they were built, and then they are copied and produced as clones. In this way, a competitor can reap the benefits of IBM's technological advancements and also produce a system that can be hooked up to the IBM computers that dominate the business world.

Reverse engineering is expensive and time-consuming, but not nearly as expensive or lengthy as the research and development expended by IBM to develop the original computers.

Among Nakazawa's responsibilities was supervising the reverse engineering and doing whatever he could to get a jump on the other companies manufacturing IBM clones. Beating another manufacturer to market with a computer and peripherals compatible with the latest IBM was worth millions of dollars in sales and huge gains in market share.

If Hitachi could obtain actual IBM drawings and components or examine prototype machines, it could use the information to replicate the IBM hardware and get a jump on the other copycats in the huge market for clones. And without either the research costs or the price of reverse engineering, Hitachi could further undercut IBM prices.

The other two men in the suite at the St. Francis that day were Americans who had been introduced to Nakazawa as Alan Harrison and Richard Kerrigan.

Nakazawa had heard about both men extensively in recent weeks. He knew that Harrison, an engaging, round-faced man with a slight country accent, was president of a Silicon Valley computer consulting firm called Glenmar Associates. And it had been explained to the Japanese executive that Kerrigan, with a distinguished shock of white hair and an elegant manner, was a retired lawyer who had represented Harrison and once worked for IBM.

For nearly six months, Harrison had been selling confidential information to Nakazawa's associates from Hitachi about a top-secret new generation of IBM computers, the 3081 series, and other IBM equipment. Kerrigan had arranged early deals and remained involved in the scheme.

Using a sophisticated laundering operation set up by Hitachi through one of its subsidiaries and an American firm, Harrison's company had received about $55,000 for various IBM secrets from Hitachi. Up until that point, the material involved technical information and a clandestine opportunity to photograph one of the computers.

By late April, however, the stakes escalated. Harrison had offered to provide Hitachi with vital hardware from the powerful new IBM computer not yet on the market. And Kerrigan had held out the possibility that Hitachi could hire as consultants some high-level executives from IBM who were about to retire.

But Harrison was demanding more money this time, and he and Kerrigan both wanted assurances that the material and the identity of the retiring IBM executives would be closely guarded within Hitachi.

Their previous dealings had been primarily with Kenji Hayashi, a senior engineer from the Kanagawa works, and Takehiro Inoue, who was Hayashi's supervisor and a department manager at Kanagawa. The Americans' insistence on assurances from a higher level had brought Nakazawa, the highest-ranking Hitachi official yet involved in the operation, to the St. Francis that day.

As Harrison and Kerrigan listened attentively, Nakazawa told them that he was the person in charge of Hitachi's computer manufacturing and development plant. He said he could authorize expenditures on behalf of the plant of up to $1 million.

Nakazawa said he was aware of everything that Harrison's company had provided to Hitachi in recent months, and he acknowledged the risk that had been involved in obtaining the items, which he said had been very helpful to Hitachi.

The Japanese executive also said he was very interested in the recent suggestion from Kerrigan that some high-level IBM executives were interested in private consulting positions with Hitachi, if enough money were available.

Nakazawa assured the two Americans that arrangements were under way to guard carefully the information they were providing, plus any future information. He said only selected persons within the Hitachi organization would have access to the material, and he promised that it would be kept in a "secure" locked room at the Kanagawa works.

As an additional layer of security, he said the information would be rewritten or revised before it was provided to Hitachi engineers in order to disguise the fact that it was drawn directly from IBM documents and hardware.

The confidential plans and designs were being shared with experts at two other Hitachi plants in Japan, one of which developed software to instruct computers how to operate and the other of which manufactured disks to store information inside the computers.

Nakazawa said he could not give the same assurances about the way the material would be treated at the other plants. But he said he would contact his counterparts at both operations and insist that similar security steps be put in place.

As Kisaburo Nakazawa sat in the suite overlooking Union Square trying to reassure Harrison and Kerrigan of the secrecy of their joint operation, every word was being recorded by microphones hidden throughout the suite, including one in a flower arrangement on the coffee table, and every movement was being videotaped by cameras secreted at several locations in the suite. In an adjoining room, the audio and visual monitoring was being followed by a team of technical experts from the Federal Bureau of Investigation.

And a few blocks away, at a special command post established for the operation by the FBI and the United States attorney's office in San Francisco, supervisory agents and top prosecutors were receiving regular reports on what was taking place inside the bugged suite.

One of the men at the command post that day was John Gibbons, a Brooklyn-born veteran prosecutor who was chief of the criminal division in the U.S. attorney's office. After Nakazawa had introduced himself to Harrison and Kerrigan, Gibbons had leafed rapidly through an organization chart of the far-flung

Hitachi corporation. When he found Nakazawa at the head of the vital Kanagawa works, he looked up and said, to no one in particular, "This is a gong ringer."

The St. Francis Hotel meeting was one of about two dozen sessions recorded and videotaped by the FBI in an elaborate sting that demonstrated dramatically just how far the third largest corporation in Japan was willing to go in pursuit of a technological advantage. The sting revealed quite clearly why National Semiconductor's Charles Sporck could contend not long after, without being melodramatic, that the United States high-tech industry was at war with Japan.

It would be rash and unfair to accuse every Japanese corporation of engaging in industrial espionage. But the Hitachi sting, which also trapped the American computer-manufacturing arm of Mitsubishi, Japan's largest trading company, is almost a natural outgrowth of the zealous Japanese intelligence-gathering operations worldwide, which collect a steady stream of information on trade, commerce, technology, economic research, and anything else that might play a role in their drive for dominance.

Throughout history, spies have obtained vital nonmilitary secrets, but such secrets are normally picked up in the course of spying for military purposes. After World War II, however, a new breed of spies developed. They were experts in industrial espionage, primarily agents of the Soviet Union and its satellites whose mission was to steal U.S. technological secrets. The Rosenbergs and the secrets of the atom bomb are perhaps the best-known example.

For the Eastern bloc nations, however, this commercial spying existed as part of a thorough military espionage apparatus. For the Japanese in the postwar world, commercial spying became the primary focus of the nation's espionage network.

In a book about the Japanese intelligence service entitled *Kempe Tai*, British author Richard Deacon called the process "espionage for prosperity." It was, he said, the only intelligence service with the prime aim of making its nation more prosperous and improving the standard of living for its people.

After the war, Japan was limited to spending only enough on

its military to defend itself. Orthodox intelligence gathering for military purposes was also restricted substantially. Rather than dismantle the espionage apparatus, the Japanese government redirected its intelligence gathering to economic issues and broadened the roster of agents to include almost any Japanese businessman who went abroad. This activity was just as vital and patriotic as gathering military information in a time of war, for the Japanese viewed their economic survival as another type of war effort.

Spying for prosperity dovetailed well with Japan's historic trait of seeking useful information abroad and employing it at home. So the process played a natural role in Japan's economic rebuilding. It also had the added advantage of supplying another strong link between industry and government in what became essentially the government-planned capitalism of Japan.

The information gathered by Japanese businessmen around the world and fed into the government-industry alliance enabled the nation to foresee and capitalize on such events as the coming market for consumer electronic goods and the boom in worldwide camera sales. These were the types of shortcuts that played a significant role in helping the Japanese to catch up with their U.S. economic rivals in the 1960s and surpass them in many fields in the 1970s.

But no one in the world of computers had come close to catching up to the advances and market dominance of IBM, as the U.S.-based multinational International Business Machines Corp. was known.

It was not for lack of trying, however. Almost everything had been tried against IBM by its competitors, including attempts to steal its secrets. In the early 1970s, after suffering several losses of vital information to competitors, IBM had hired former United States Attorney General Nicholas Katzenbach to bolster its internal security operation and stop the hemorrhage of secrets. Katzenbach brought to IBM a team of security experts who had served with the government in various capacities at the FBI, the CIA, and other agencies.

Among the most outstanding men Katzenbach sent to work at IBM was Richard Callahan, a Marine captain during the Korean War who had joined the FBI in his early twenties on his way to a distinguished career in federal law enforcement. He had held several posts in counterintelligence and narcotics investigations before joining IBM as a full-time troubleshooter in 1973.

Callahan and the others established an aggressive security system at IBM that cost $50 million a year to run and became the envy of the corporate world. But it still was not enough to completely stop industrial espionage, not when the stakes were so enormous.

The Hitachi sting began in the summer of 1981 in the offices of a firm called Palyn Associates in San Jose, California, the capital of Silicon Valley.

The firm was run by Maxwell Paley, who spent two decades at IBM and rose to head its advanced computing laboratory before retiring in 1970 and opening his own consulting firm. As did many other small firms in the area, he kept track of developments at IBM through publicly available material on behalf of clients that produced IBM-compatible equipment. He and his associates compiled the material into frequent reports highlighting trends and technological advances and predicting what was coming next. One of Paley's major clients from the start had been Hitachi.

On August 19, 1981, Kenji Hayashi and another engineer from Hitachi Japan were in San Jose discussing IBM projects with two consultants who worked for Palyn at the firm's offices. George Rossman, a Palyn employee, offered to sell Hitachi a report the firm had prepared on future products at IBM based on the 3081 computer. Hayashi took a look at the report and said he would have to consult with associates back in Japan before making a decision on whether to buy the material.

A week later, Rossman received a telex from Hayashi in which the Japanese engineer said Hitachi already had ten volumes of IBM's "Adirondack workbook" outlining the operation of the 3081. While Hitachi was not interested in the written report, he said that Hitachi would be willing to buy any additional volumes of the Adirondack series that Palyn could provide.

Rossman brought the telex to Paley's attention, and the IBM veteran recognized immediately that "Adirondack" was IBM's code name for its new 3081 computers and that the workbooks undoubtedly contained highly confidential product-design information.

Paley telephoned Bob Evans, the vice president for engineering and technology at IBM in Poughkeepsie, New York, and told him, "Bob, I think one of my Japanese clients has gotten your crown jewels."

On September 14, 1981, Paley met with Richard Callahan, the IBM troubleshooter, and they put the final touches on a plan that had been laid out by IBM officials to discover the seriousness of the threat confronting the company.

At Callahan's instructions, Paley sent a telex to Hayashi in which Paley said he had "made a contact and was told information you requested is under strict security control but can be obtained." The telex also said that the sensitive nature of the subject matter necessitated a personal meeting in Tokyo, rather than further telex communications.

Paley and a colleague, Robert Domenico, met with Hayashi in a room at the Imperial Hotel in Tokyo on October 2 and showed Hayashi a copy of the index to the "Alpine" hardware design workbook. "Alpine" had taken the place of "Adirondack" as the code name for the 3081 computer development program, and the index was marked "Do Not Copy" and "IBM Confidential-Restricted." Hayashi was given a handwritten copy of the index.

Paley told the Japanese engineer that he was not in the business of acquiring confidential IBM information. However, he said that he might be able to locate someone who could help Hitachi. Hayashi said he would be grateful for any assistance, and he said that Hitachi would see that Paley received a commission and additional contracts if the search turned out well.

After the meeting, Paley described what had occurred to Callahan, who had accompanied him to Japan but remained out of sight.

Four days later, Hayashi returned to the Imperial Hotel for a second meeting. He brought back the handwritten index. On the index, he had indicated Hitachi's priorities for obtaining its contents by placing an A beside the items of the highest interest, a

B beside material of lesser priority, and a C beside items that Hitachi already possessed.

Hayashi also provided Paley with copies of several Adirondack-series workbooks, each of which was stamped "Do Not Copy" and "IBM Confidential." He volunteered that Hitachi already had a pipeline for obtaining IBM information, but that he was highly interested in opening a new avenue.

Hayashi suggested that the person Paley recruited to locate the IBM secrets should use code names and transfer the information through a Hitachi subsidiary, Nissei Electronics.

Following the meeting, Paley again reported on the substance of the conversation to Callahan and provided the IBM security official with the workbook copies that Hayashi had given to him. Callahan immediately recognized that the workbooks were authentic IBM material and knew he was on the trail of what appeared to be a major case of industrial espionage.

IBM had two options when Dick Callahan returned to the United States and reported the details of what had occurred at the Imperial Hotel. The company could file a civil lawsuit against Hitachi and hope for a court order stopping the plundering and voiding any benefits the Japanese firm may already have gotten. Or IBM could go to federal law-enforcement authorities.

Near the end of October, Callahan contacted Kenneth Thompson, a veteran FBI agent who worked on technology-transfer cases out of the bureau's San Jose field office. The decision had been made at IBM's executive level to try to persuade the government to pursue a criminal case against Hitachi.

Thompson is a handsome, middle-aged FBI agent who had spent many years pursuing organized-crime figures on the East Coast. After moving to the San Jose office, he was assigned in late 1980 to investigate possible violations of federal law in the theft and counterfeiting of electronic components in Silicon Valley. Within a month, Thompson concluded that the best way to discover the scope of the problem would be to create an undercover operation.

In March 1981, he submitted a proposal to FBI headquarters in Washington to set up an elaborate undercover operation. It would include creating employment histories and specialized training in the high-technology field for the undercover agents. For help, Thompson contacted IBM officials in San Jose, and in June of that year the company assigned Dick Callahan to help the bureau.

The FBI approved the undercover operation on July 30, 1981, and it was given the codename PENGEM, for "Penetrate Gray Electronics Market."

In August, Thompson met with Callahan and Joseph Rosetti, the head of worldwide security for IBM and a former Justice Department investigator who had played a central role in the political corruption case that sent Bobby Baker to jail during President Lyndon Johnson's administration.

The corporation approved an agreement under which IBM would establish cover for two FBI agents, providing them credentials and identification badges and agreeing to verify their employment if anyone tried to check them out. IBM also agreed to provide training to between two and seven FBI agents in the arcane world of computers, ranging from purchasing and testing to terminology. The training would cover both civilian and military uses.

The military aspect was important because PENGEM was conceived as an operation aimed at espionage by the Soviet Union and spies from other Eastern bloc countries who had become active in Silicon Valley in the 1970s.

In 1974, the CIA had thwarted an elaborate Soviet effort to buy several banks in Silicon Valley. U.S. intelligence and military officials said the scheme was designed to obtain critical credit information on companies and individual engineers in order to discover who was in financial trouble and vulnerable to the type of pressure that might persuade them to give up industrial secrets. A secondary goal, according to the officials, was to steal outright American technology based on information gleaned from the loan-approval process at the banks for high-tech companies.

As a front for the investigation, the FBI rented an office in a modern two-story building in Santa Clara, another Silicon

Valley town, and opened a consulting firm called Glenmar Associates.

When Callahan contacted Thompson in late October 1981, the FBI agent was surprised to find that PENGEM's first target would be Japanese, not Russian. But the bureau agreed to what the agents thought would be a temporary shift in focus.

Without telling him of the FBI involvement, Callahan persuaded Paley to telephone Hayashi at the New York Hilton and arrange a meeting in early November in Las Vegas, where Hayashi was traveling next. Paley told the Japanese engineer that he would be introducing him to someone who could help him.

At 3 P.M. on November 6, Hayashi came to room 1461 at the Las Vegas Hilton, where Paley introduced him to Callahan, identifying the IBM security official as Richard Kerrigan, a retired lawyer who had done work for Paley's firm and had worked at IBM. After the introduction was made, Paley left the room and his involvement in the sting was ended.

About 4 P.M. that day, another man came to room 1461 and was introduced to Hayashi as Alan Harrison, president of a San Jose consulting firm called Glenmar Associates and the person with access to confidential IBM information. Harrison was actually Alan Garretson, a veteran FBI agent.

After being briefed on the potential seriousness of the Hitachi investigation by Callahan, Thompson had asked FBI headquarters for an agent who had experience with computers and could do undercover work. When the FBI's own computers scanned through its thousands of agent profiles, one of the candidates was Alan Garretson, then assigned to the Washington field office.

Prior to joining the FBI, Garretson had been a salesman with IBM for a short time. He had the outgoing, engaging personality required of an undercover agent. His looks were also deceptive. Garretson was slightly overweight and round-faced and had a receding hairline, a description of a man more likely to be found at a consulting firm than within the nation's top law-enforcement agency.

Over that day and the next, Hayashi gave Garretson a detailed list of IBM material and equipment that Hitachi wanted. He explained that Hitachi was interested in "early information" on certain IBM products.

One of the company's top priorities was obtaining maintenance manuals for the IBM 3380, the most advanced disk storage device developed by IBM. The device would not be available for general sale for a few weeks, but early models had been shipped to some customers. Hayashi said Hitachi would pay $10,000 if Garretson could arrange a "viewing" of one of the 3380s by a senior engineer from Japan.

In addition, Hayashi asked for information about a new IBM program used to operate large computer systems that would not be on the market until sometime in 1983. He said Hitachi had already obtained some portions of the program from another source, but he said the company would pay $50,000 to $100,000 for the additional material.

In keeping with undercover guidelines, tapes show that Garretson made it clear to Hayashi that the IBM material would have to be stolen and that the people involved in its theft could go to jail if they were caught. The FBI agent said he wanted cash to cut down the risk. Hayashi said paying cash would be "indiscreet." Instead, he said, Hitachi usually used a "tunnel company" to channel the money and eliminate a link to Hitachi.

Callahan remained involved in the operation following the Hilton meeting. The presence of this distinguished older man was reassuring to the Japanese, and the continued involvement of IBM was reassuring to the FBI. In fact, it was Callahan who had the next contact with the Japanese.

A few days after the Las Vegas meeting, Jun Naruse telephoned Callahan and identified himself as a senior engineer from Hitachi's disk-storage facility in Odawara. The two men arranged for Naruse to view the 3380 in Hartford, Connecticut. Naruse said he had $10,000 in cash.

Naruse, however, said he was worried that, since he had traveled to the United States from Japan, if there was "any kind of trouble . . . it's real trouble for Hitachi." But Callahan reassured him that it was all set.

At 5 A.M. on November 15, 1981, Garretson met with Naruse in the lobby of the Sheraton Hotel in Hartford, Connecticut. They got in a car and drove through the predawn darkness to a parking lot near the Pratt & Whitney Aircraft jet engine plant in Hartford. There they met a Pratt & Whitney employee who had been recruited by the FBI, and he gave them company identification badges in exchange for an envelope from Garretson.

The three men drove to the plant, where Pratt & Whitney was operating a leased 3380, and were admitted after showing their ID badges to a security guard. As they made their way through the plant, they came to a door with a combination lock that the employee could not open. While Garretson and Naruse hid in a darkened office, the employee summoned a guard to come and open the door.

Once they reached the room where the storage device was located, Naruse was ecstatic. He began taking photographs, and Garretson had to caution him to avoid including any background in the pictures that might indicate the location of the machine. When he was finished, Naruse handed the camera to Garretson and had his own photograph taken, hugging the 3380.

After returning to the hotel, Garretson told Naruse that the maintenance manuals were on the West Coast. It was agreed that Naruse would pay $3,000 in cash immediately and the remaining $7,000 once he picked up the manuals in California.

Three days later, Naruse came to Glenmar's offices in Santa Clara and received maintenance volumes for the 3380. In exchange, he handed Garretson an envelope stuffed with $100 bills. The FBI agent withdrew the money and counted it aloud, placing it in stacks of $1,000. Then he counted the stacks, saying: "One, two, three, four, five, six, seven. Seven thousand dollars. With the $3,000 paid in Hartford, makes $10,000."

The transaction took place in a small conference room at Glenmar that the FBI had turned into a virtual production set, with microphones hidden at key points and a fish-eye lens tucked away in the ceiling.

The next day, November 19, Garretson took some additional manuals to Katsumi Takeda at the offices of Hitachi's chief American subsidiary in San Francisco. Takeda, an engineer with

Hitachi America, said that some engineers from Hitachi Japan would be visiting Garretson down at Glenmar in early December.

The engineers arrived and gave Garretson their shopping list for confidential IBM documents and equipment. One of them also said that Naruse had destroyed his copy of the receipt for the $10,000 he paid Garretson and that he wanted Garretson to do the same.

On the notable date of December 7, 1981, exactly forty years after the attack on Pearl Harbor, Garretson received a letter from Hayashi, who set forth Hitachi's requests for information, indicating the priority of each item and the amount Hitachi was willing to pay. The prices ranged from $3,000 to $100,000.

Over the next five months, Garretson filled many of those orders, with the help of Callahan and other IBM officials. It was necessary for IBM to provide legitimate material for two reasons.

First, in order for federal laws governing transportation of stolen material to apply, the goods had to have real value in excess of $5,000. Phony items would have been worthless and might have been grounds for dismissing the criminal case that the government expected to file eventually.

Second, the Japanese would have soon figured out that they were being scammed and would have dropped out of the operation. Each time when material was delivered, the Japanese engineers would perform preliminary checks on the equipment on the spot, and extensive tests were performed back in Japan. Only after the authenticity was established did the Japanese authorize full payment to Garretson in most instances.

To wash the payments, Garretson was introduced to a Japanese-American named Tom Yoshida, who operated a consulting firm in Santa Clara called NCL Data. Hitachi's Hayashi explained to Garretson that Hitachi would be sending money for him to Nissei Electronics, a Japanese subsidiary of Hitachi. Nissei in turn would transfer the funds to NCL Data, and Yoshida would make the payments to Garretson's company, Glenmar.

Lawyers for Hitachi would later raise the issue of whether the Japanese engineers really knew they were committing a crime in obtaining the confidential IBM material and establishing the means for washing the payments to Garretson. But the written material collected by the government shows clearly that the Japanese were aware of the risks and the illegality.

For instance, in a December 18, 1981, letter to Garretson, Hayashi wrote: "We had better to destroy our letter after reading and writing another memo of remembering the essence. So I have destroyed your letter yesterday. Please destroy every my letters after you recognize the essence."

The most damning evidence of how clearly the Japanese understood the illegality of what they were doing, however, is contained on the videotapes of their numerous meetings with Garretson and Callahan.

Meetings were recorded at Glenmar and at hotels in Las Vegas, San Francisco, and Hawaii. At each place, FBI technical experts arrived ahead of time and wired the hotel rooms for sound and video. Most of the videotapes have never been made public, but those who have viewed them have said the conversation was friendly and informal. But the most interesting aspect was the conversations in Japanese between the Hitachi employees.

They obviously felt comfortable that neither Garretson nor Callahan spoke Japanese, and they were blunt in their assessments of the great benefit they were receiving from the information that they were getting so cheaply from the Americans. It was also clear from the conversations that the Japanese were aware of the risks that they were taking.

"The tapes contain clear acknowledgements of the illegality of what they were doing," said one authoritative person who viewed the entire collection of sixty-five hours of videotaped meetings. "It was absolutely damning."

As the investigation proceeded, the Justice Department grew more interested in the case and it was elevated to Class 1 status, which meant that no resources were to be spared.

Gibbons, the criminal division chief in the U.S. attorney's office in San Francisco, and Gregory Ward, the assistant U.S. attorney who had developed the investigation with the FBI and was still handling the day-to-day legal matters, were sent to school at IBM so they could learn enough about computers to

understand what was going on and eventually draw up a techni-
cally accurate, understandable indictment.

Gibbons said later that his visit to IBM headquarters at
Poughkeepsie, New York, had made a lasting impression on him.

"I could see how well they protected their secrets, the great
lengths to which they went to keep everything in the shop," said
Gibbons, who left government in 1985 and became head of the
San Francisco office of Kroll Associates, a unique firm that
specializes in corporate intelligence and counterintelligence
work. "I began to realize the ripple effect across the American
economy caused by the loss of these corporate secrets. This was a
hemorrhage. It was that measurable. And if it could go out the
back door at IBM this way, what was going on at places that were
far less sophisticated in their own internal security?"

The agents involved in the case, Garretson and Thompson
and Mary Williams, a strikingly attractive blonde who was
working undercover at the Glenmar offices, were devoting enormous numbers of hours to the case. A supporting cast of agents
behind the scenes, including Japanese-speaking personnel, were
operating the electronic surveillance and helping transcribe the
conversations.

A key aim of the investigation was to draw high-level Hitachi
executives within range of the FBI's hidden cameras and microphones, and it was IBM's Callahan who came up with the idea
that baited the trap for the highest-ranking Japanese executive
caught in the net.

In March 1982, Callahan told Hayashi that he had been in
touch with some high-level executives at IBM who were retiring
soon and were interested in obtaining consulting contracts with
Hitachi. In a letter dated March 8, Hayashi said Hitachi would
be interested in using the IBM executives as private consultants
for twenty-five to thirty days a year at a rate of $30,000 to $40,000
a year each. Callahan said the amount was far too small and that
he wanted to discuss the arrangement with someone in authority
at Hitachi.

In response, the Hitachi officials decided to send Kisaburo
Nakazawa to San Francisco to meet with Garretson and Calla-

han to discuss the consultant arrangement and Garretson's efforts to obtain additional, more expensive IBM hardware.

The April 23, 1982, meeting at the St. Francis Hotel with Nakazawa was as high up within Hitachi as the undercover operation was able to get. While those involved were certain that Nakazawa could not operate in the rigid Japanese system without approval from the highest levels of the company, they were unable to obtain any proof.

At the same time, IBM executives who were aware of the sting operation were nervous about the extensive material that was being supplied to Hitachi, and some were anxious to wrap up the operation.

But the FBI kept trying to reach higher into Hitachi, with Garretson finally holding out the prospect of selling Hitachi a package that included almost everything it wanted, including the actual design documents for the 3081, at the time IBM's most sophisticated computer processing unit.

Garretson wanted $700,000 for the package, but after considerable haggling, he agreed to accept $525,000. On May 19, 1982, Yoshida gave Garretson a cashier's check for $30,000 as an advance on the $525,000, and Garretson agreed to collect the material for delivery in mid-June.

On June 21, Hayashi and another Hitachi official met with Garretson at the Glenmar offices and provided him with a letter to Callahan that set forth strict security arrangements. The letter said that a locked design room "controlled by top management" had been set aside to handle the information and that a limited number of people would have access at the Kanagawa computer plant.

The other Hitachi official, Isao Ohnishi, a section manager at the software plant in Odawara, diagrammed the offices at his plant and showed where the IBM software material would be kept secured. He said only four persons on his staff would have access to the material and that there was no security concern because all four were accustomed to seeing IBM material.

It was agreed that the Japanese would receive the 3081 design documents and the other material the following day, as soon as the remaining $495,000 was wired into Glenmar's bank account.

At 9 A.M. on June 22, Kenji Hayashi and Isao Ohnishi arrived at Glenmar in a brown Volkswagen van driven by Tom Yoshida. The van was necessary to carry away the IBM material they expected to receive. Yoshida waited in the van while the other two men went inside Glenmar's office and were escorted to the conference room, where Garretson and Callahan were waiting.

Glenmar had four offices in its second-floor suite. Throughout the investigation, one of them had been used as a monitoring site for the video and audio recording equipment trained on the conference room, where the business was conducted. Normally, the small room was occupied by two or three FBI agents. But on the day of the bust, it was filled with most of the agents and prosecutors who had played a role in the eight-month sting.

From their vantage point, the law-enforcement personnel could watch and hear what was taking place in the conference room. One of the most intent observers was Gregory Ward, the young prosecutor for whom this was the biggest and final case of his government career. Along with watching the screen, he was wearing a set of headphones so he could hear what was happening in the final moments.

As they entered the conference room, Garretson told the Japanese engineers that the $495,000 had been wire-transferred into his bank account. That brought the total paid by Hitachi to $612,000.

The IBM goods were stacked on a table in the room, and one of the Americans joked about going through customs with a piece of hardware bearing the words "Property of IBM" riveted to it. Hayashi laughed, opened a case he was carrying, and pulled out a pair of pliers. He said he wanted the label as a souvenir for Nakazawa.

As he headed toward the IBM hardware, Garretson said rather loudly, "Let's go ahead and do it."

Callahan responded with equal firmness, "Yeah, I think you're right."

No code word had been established to end the charade, but Ward recognized that the two men in the room were trying to wrap things up before Hayashi defaced the IBM equipment. Turning to two FBI agents, Ward said, "Go on. Get out there."

The agents entered the room and told Hayashi and Ohnishi that they were under arrest. Hayashi, so jubilant moments earlier, was visibly shocked as he put his head in his hands.

Later that day, two officials of Mitsubishi Electric Corp., a subsidiary of Japan's largest trading company, were arrested by FBI agents and also charged with transporting goods stolen from IBM. One of the Japanese was caught at San Francisco International Airport, where he was carrying a videocassette bearing an IBM sticker. What the agents thought was a great coup—catching him headed out of the country with actual secrets—turned out to be a great joke. The cassette contained a dirty movie.

Mitsubishi had entered the sting late in the game through the same route that brought Hitachi in.

Mitsubishi Electronics America is the U.S. sales and distribution arm for the giant trading company's line of IBM-compatible computers. The Mitsubishi computers were smaller, less sophisticated clones than Hitachi's, but like Hitachi their development depended on reverse engineering IBM products.

In January 1982, Takaya Ishida, assistant to the president of Mitsubishi Electronics, had sought confidential IBM material from Robert Domenico, a consultant at Maxwell Paley's firm. When Domenico and Paley reported the incident, they were instructed to see how far Mitsubishi was willing to go to obtain the material.

In a telephone conversation, Domenico told Ishida that Palyn Associates would not obtain confidential IBM material because it was illegal to do so. But he asked the executive if he wanted Palyn to arrange for someone who would get the information through an illegal channel.

After checking with his superiors, Ishida said that Mitsubishi wanted to go forward and obtain the information. Mitsubishi was then handed over to Garretson and the crew at Glenmar, and, over the next couple of months, the company that built the Zero fighter planes that attacked Pearl Harbor paid about

$26,000 for information about IBM computers and software.

The FBI agents and prosecutors suspected that the Mitsubishi sting could have gone on much longer, but they needed to close the net on Hitachi, and so both operations were brought down the same day.

The Japanese response to news of the sting was predictable. With Hitachi leading the way, various Japanese businessmen and government officials complained that IBM had simply used the FBI to thwart a competitor and that the U.S. law-enforcement officers were nothing more than Japan bashers.

The FBI and the prosecutors were accused, both in the Japanese press and in papers filed in court by Hitachi's lawyers, of entrapment of the engineers and of misconduct in the way the investigation was carried out. But the federal judge who heard the case, Spencer Williams, found that the U.S. government had behaved properly and within the law in carrying out the undercover operation, so he dismissed the motions and said he would allow the taped evidence to be used at trial.

Once that decision was handed down, even the big-name American defense lawyers hired by Hitachi and Mitsubishi, such as New York attorney Peter Fleming and Thomas Sullivan, the former U.S. attorney in Chicago, had no choice but to try to cut a deal for their clients. The information on the tapes was far too incriminating to get past a jury and far too embarrassing to become public.

Hitachi pleaded guilty to conspiracy to transport stolen property and was fined $10,000. Kenji Hayashi and Isao Ohnishi pleaded guilty to the same charge and were fined $10,000 and $4,000 respectively. Tom Yoshida, who had served as a conduit for the money to Garretson, pleaded no contest and was fined $7,500. The cases against eleven other Hitachi employees who had been involved in the illegal scheme were essentially dropped because those people were in Japan, outside the U.S. jurisdiction.

Mitsubishi Electronics America and two of its employees, including Takaya Ishido, also entered guilty pleas and paid fines.

No one went to jail.

There was an interesting and sad footnote to the biggest Japanese industrial-espionage case uncovered in the United States. Maxwell Paley, the former IBM executive who had set the whole chain of events in motion by alerting IBM to the theft of its "crown jewels," was criticized by some of his fellow consultants in Silicon Valley. They felt he had made a mistake in helping IBM at the expense of his Japanese clients.

16
INROADS ON
WALL STREET

WHEN GENERAL MOTORS DECIDED to reorganize its top management in 1984, the automotive giant turned the job over to the experts from McKinsey & Company, one of the most prestigious consulting firms in the United States.

When General Electric wanted to slash costs in the news division of NBC in 1987 after its acquisition of the network's parent, RCA, a team from McKinsey & Company was dispatched to do the job.

When First Interstate Bancorp decided to make a run at taking over its giant rival Bank of America in 1986, the calculations that the merger was a financially sound idea were done by partners from McKinsey & Company.

So when Sumitomo Bank of Japan, the world's third largest bank, allocated $500 million for an investment in the United States and wanted help deciding where to spend it, there is little wonder that the gnomes of Osaka turned to McKinsey & Company.

Although its roots are in New York and its headquarters remains there, McKinsey & Company is a truly international firm. It opened its first overseas office in 1959, when foreign companies were eager to learn the new American management techniques. Over the next two decades, McKinsey moved across Europe and opened branches in every major capital. Then it moved on to Japan and Australia. By the mid-1980s, a majority of the partners in the firm were non-Americans and the company was no longer selling American know-how. It was, as John Merwin of *Forbes* magazine put it in 1987, "selling the expertise of McKinsey itself."

Sometimes this transnational, consultant-without-a-country character caused dissension among the firm's partners.

In the early 1980s, McKinsey started a management training program to teach the ins and outs of American business to young executives from the twenty-five biggest corporations in Japan. The idea was for the rising stars from these corporations to spend four weeks in the United States and two weeks in Europe being exposed to the most advanced management techniques McKinsey could provide.

The program required that each corporation agree to participate for a minimum of ten years, which constituted an enormous commitment of time and money, because McKinsey does nothing cheaply.

The big Japanese corporations were persuaded to sign up partly through the influence of Kenichi Ohmae, the head of McKinsey's Tokyo office and a man often called Japan's only management guru. But the concept also fit neatly with the long-term outlook of the Japanese firms. These firms knew that they had little experience in international management and that they would need vast amounts of such knowledge to run their businesses in the coming era of a global economy.

The program was called the Multinational Business Institute, and its creation coincided with a time of great strain in relations between Japan and the United States. Largely because of these strains, there were complaints from American partners at McKinsey that the firm wasn't offering the same opportunity to American executives to learn about Japan. After all, their reasoning went, if the knowledge of the most powerful consulting firm in the United States was going to be sold to the Japanese, it ought to be sold to the Americans too, out of fairness.

But a funny thing happened on the way to consulting parity. When the offer went out to McKinsey's U.S. clients from the Fortune 500 list, there were no takers. The American firms were unwilling to make a ten-year commitment to the program. They could not see the need for diverting substantial amounts of money and executive talent to a training process that might not produce results by the end of the fiscal year.

"The Japanese were willing to make a ten-year commitment and spend a substantial amount of money," recalled a McKinsey partner who had lobbied hard for the creation of an American program. "We found it hard to get a commitment of one quarter [three months] from any American companies."

It was another example of the shortsighted nature of U.S. business leadership, and it quieted the critics of the Japanese program within McKinsey.

In mid-1985, a three-person team from McKinsey & Company, led by partner O. J. Hested, started a six-month study for Sumitomo Bank about possible investments in the United States. The amount of the investment was set in the range of $500 million, and the prospective field was the blue-chip investment banking houses in New York.

Sumitomo is viewed by most international banking experts as the toughest and smartest institution among the Japanese giants that have emerged as the world's dominant banks over the last decade. While only third largest among the Japanese banks in 1985, it was the most profitable. And by 1988, it would surpass Tokyo's Fuji Bank and climb into second place among the world's largest banks, behind Dai-Ichi Kangyo Bank in Tokyo.

Sumitomo's roots go back to the late sixteenth century, when the Sumitomo family formed a copper-refining business in Kyoto. In the next century the family began to finance commercial trade, and in 1895 the bank was incorporated. Sumitomo Bank became the center of a group of companies, including insurance, trading, and construction, and those companies remain informally associated today.

Sumitomo also has a history of reaching abroad for business. Within twenty-five years of its founding, the bank was operating small branches in London and Bombay. When the search began for a Wall Street connection, the bank already owned commercial

banks in Switzerland, Brazil, and California and a modest investment bank in London.

Sumitomo's executives recognized in 1985 that investment
banking was emerging as one of the most profitable banking
activities. This is the area in which financial institutions earn
huge fees by underwriting debt offerings by major corporations
and, more recently, serving as middlemen for takeovers and
acquisitions.

As was occurring in the United States, Japanese securities
firms had already made intrusions on banking customers, as big
corporations turned to debt offers to raise new money as an
alternative to the more expensive practice of borrowing from
banks. The year before, Nomura Securities had edged out Sumitomo as the Japanese financial institution turning the largest
profit. And several Japanese securities firms, including Nomura,
had already established operations in the United States. So the
pressure was heightened for a bold move into the heart of investment banking in the United States.

The executives in Osaka also recognized that Sumitomo, like
all the other Japanese banks, had limited experience in investment banking. Building its own staff from the small London
outpost would take years, and would mean missing out on
millions of dollars worth of deals and possibly being displaced
by another bank. The alternative was to purchase the expertise,
and the obvious hunting ground was the United States, particularly the five biggest houses on Wall Street that had dominated
the profession for decades.

In the end, Sumitomo probably could have chosen its quarry
on its own. But the patina of the six-month McKinsey study
satisfied the strong need for outside assurance that haunts every
Japanese executive. If things went wrong, the blame could always
be shifted to McKinsey & Company.

The target was Goldman, Sachs & Co., a New York investment
bank regarded as perhaps the best-managed house on Wall
Street. It was also the last of the five major houses to remain
independent, which meant that Goldman Sachs needed an outside source of capital to remain a major player in the deals that
were growing larger and larger. In fact, Sumitomo had already

loaned Goldman Sachs $100 million. The two institutions also had worked together to finance a new factory in Michigan for Matsushita, the giant Japanese electronics firm.

As Sumitomo zeroed in on Goldman Sachs, the bank hired another blue-chip Wall Street firm, Lazard Freres & Co., to be its investment banker on the deal. Lazard's senior partner, Felix Rohatyn, would be the lead negotiator.

In February 1986, Sumitomo president Koh Komatsu, accompanied by a delegation of investment bankers and lawyers, went to see John Weinberg, the chairman of Goldman Sachs, in his office on Wall Street. Komatsu and Weinberg hit it off personally, and secret negotiations were started that would last several months.

The central issue in the talks was whether Sumitomo wanted any control over Goldman Sachs, which was run by its seventy-nine partners and had a reputation as the most independent house on Wall Street. Attorneys involved on both sides said that the deal would have been dead if the Japanese, from Komatsu on down, had not promised that they intended to exert no control over the investment bank.

Once that was settled, the talks centered on the structure of the deal itself: how much would Sumitomo get for its $500 million?

The $500 million represented 34.9 percent of the capital of Goldman Sachs, but federal banking regulations prohibited a bank from owning more than 5 percent of a securities firm. So the two sides agreed that Sumitomo would have no voting stock. Instead, the Japanese bank was to receive 12.5 percent of Goldman Sachs's annual profits for the next ten years. After that, the terms would be open to renegotiation.

Both sides wanted the talks to remain confidential until a firm proposal was in hand for delivery to the Federal Reserve Board in Washington. Everyone involved recognized the potential for an enormous outcry—in Congress, on Wall Street, and from the public in general—along with the possibility of serious questions about the deal from the regulators.

After all, this was a landmark transaction. It marked the first time that a major foreign financial institution was purchasing a big share of a major Wall Street investment house. It was a venture that went to the very heart of American capitalism, and some negative reaction was anticipated.

"It was clear that we were in new ground," said John Carr, one of the key lawyers for Sumitomo on the deal. "We anticipated press interest and interest from the Hill. There was also a potential for an anti-foreign, anti-Japanese reaction."

Therefore, the proposal would present the controversial transaction in the best light, and the negotiators wanted to get the Fed on board before the deal became public. They also hoped to inform quietly several key congressmen in the hopes of heading off any negative reaction.

The Fed had jurisdiction because Sumitomo operated as a U.S.-chartered bank holding company, with a major consumer bank in California. In addition, Goldman Sachs was one of about forty elite firms with a lucrative position as a primary dealer in U.S. government securities issued by the Federal Reserve Bank of New York, and the firm did not want to jeopardize that.

Unfortunately for the participants, the aggressive Japanese press got wind of the deal before the way could be smoothed for the blessing of the Federal Reserve Board.

Rumors had swept Japan's financial community for weeks that Sumitomo was interested in acquiring a piece of an American financial company. Japanese reporters staked out Komatsu's office and home and followed him as often as possible. On August 6, 1986, news of the pending deal with Goldman Sachs was announced in the Japanese press.

The story quickly grabbed headlines in the United States, but the expected anti-Japanese reaction never really materialized. Most of the press accounts were relatively favorable. The limited criticism centered on the mistaken notion that the deal represented a joint venture between a bank and a securities firm that threatened to undermine the 1934 Glass-Steagall Act, which prohibited banks from owning securities firms.

The mistake was crystallized in an editorial that appeared in the *Washington Post* on November 20, 1986, the day after the Federal Reserve Board announced its approval of the $500 million investment. The *Post* lamented that the Fed had set a major precedent by allowing a Japanese bank to buy into an American securities firm when American banks were prohibited from doing so by Glass-Steagall. The *Post* feared an important safety line between commercial banking and the riskier investment banking had been jeopardized, despite some restrictions imposed on the transaction by the Federal Reserve.

Indeed, after several days of hearings and extensive written filings, the Fed had found that the deal offered Sumitomo "the power to exercise a controlling influence over the management or policies of Goldman." That would have violated a 1956 law governing permissible activities of bank holding companies, and possibly Glass-Steagall as well.

So the Fed demanded that the transaction be scaled back. Sumitomo was to limit its share in Goldman Sachs to no more than 24.9 percent of the investment bank's capital, not the 34 percent in the original agreement. That meant the $500 million would come into Goldman more slowly, as the firm raised enough additional capital to keep the Sumitomo investment below 25 percent.

Plans to create joint directorships between subsidiaries of the two firms in London and Tokyo would have to be abandoned, along with the proposal to share business contacts between the bank and the brokerage.

As a result of these changes, the Fed determined that the transaction did not conflict with securities and banking laws and was therefore permissible as a passive investment.

When Sumitomo agreed to the restructured deal, it appeared that the Japanese bank had gotten the short end of the stick. On the surface, Goldman would still get its $500 million with no dilution of its management control. One Wall Street analyst laughed about what he viewed as Goldman's success, joking, "It's like saying we won't invite you into the dining room but we will take your money."

This was naive.

Sumitomo never expected to exert any direct influence over Goldman Sachs. Its American lawyers, the respected Washington firm of Shaw, Pittman, Potts & Trowbridge, had advised the bankers from the start that a controlling interest was out of the

question, because of both legal and political considerations. And
that was fine with the Japanese bankers.

Furthermore, the opportunity to influence Goldman Sachs
would come later. The next time Goldman Sachs needed capital,
or when the date came around to renew the original agreement,
would be the chance for Sumitomo to exert its leverage.

The bank's view from the outset was long-term, and far
grander than partial control over a Wall Street investment bank a
fraction of its size. What Sumitomo sought was a foot in the
door, the opportunity to learn the business of investment banking from one of the most profitable and respected practitioners in
the world.

From the start, the key to the arrangement from the Japanese
side of the table had been the agreement for Goldman Sachs to
bring into its New York offices every year a specific number of
Sumitomo employees for training as investment bankers. They
would remain Sumitomo employees and would be rotated back to
Japan after their training period.

As they had done in many other types of joint ventures, the
Japanese had bought themselves an opportunity to learn skills
and processes from Americans so they could adapt them to their
own needs.

The proof of Sumitomo's success was soon evident. Within
months of the Fed's approval of Sumitomo's stake in Goldman
Sachs, Nippon Life Insurance Company of Tokyo would pay
$538 million for a 13 percent stake in Shearson Lehman Broth-
ers, the investment banking arm of American Express Company,
the largest financial organization in the United States. That in
turn was followed by Yasuda Mutual Life Insurance's investment
of $300 million in PaineWebber, another prominent Wall Street
firm.

The stakes in these blue-chip American investment firms
represent only one way in which the Japanese have moved into
the financial markets of New York. The four giant Japanese
securities houses—Nomura, Daiwa, Nikko, and Yamaichi—are
aiming to become major players on Wall Street in the coming
years. They have recruited American executives and traders from
virtually every major U.S. firm, and thrown the weight of their

enormous capital behind a strategic expansion in the United States.

In 1988, Yamaichi and Daiwa both took a step into the heart of another premier U.S. financial market, the Chicago Board of Trade, where the nation's futures market is concentrated. Each Japanese house was granted the right to settle trades directly with the board's financial arm, which eliminated the need to pay for the service through existing firms.

Japanese securities firms and the investors they serve have become so influential in the United States that the New York Stock Exchange decided in 1988 to establish an advisory committee to give them a voice in decision making on Wall Street and in Washington.

John Phelan, chairman of the New York Stock Exchange, unveiled the idea at a meeting in Tokyo in August of that year. He explained that the panel would be identical with one created three years earlier with Europeans. He said it would meet periodically with stock exchange members and federal officials.

The so-called Big Four already account for about one-fifth of all trading in U.S. government bonds through their New York subsidiaries, and they have moved into stocks and corporate finance with a competitiveness and pace that seem fierce even by Wall Street's superfast standards.

Their strategy is the same as that of the Japanese automakers and electronics giants of a decade ago: use high volumes and low markups to carve out a share of the market, and then consolidate your position for real profitability.

For the securities firms, that means selling large quantities of U.S. treasury bonds, corporate issues, and mortgage-backed securities to institutional investors at a thin profit. Then they advance to financing the more lucrative ventures, such as leveraged buyouts and mergers.

"No matter how long it takes—ten, twenty, fifty years—our ultimate goal is to be competitive," said Toshio Mori, the chairman of Nikko's New York subsidiary.

It probably won't take that long. But the Japanese securities firms and Japanese banks have had difficulty attracting and retaining topflight American executives. It is not a matter of money. The Japanese can study the salary charts for the industry as ably as the next person, and they have proven surprisingly willing to pay U.S. executives more than the Japanese nationals working in the U.S. offices.

The problem is that when an executive examines the responsibilities and chances for promotion available at one of the Japanese securities houses or banks, he finds that the real decisions are still being made in Tokyo, and the U.S. operation will almost always be run by a Japanese national. As for ever sitting on the board of the home company, forget it.

One consultant for McKinsey & Company who deals extensively with Japanese corporations described the closed-mindedness of the Japanese executives.

"The idea of a non-Japanese on the board," he said. "You mention that and they just stare at you. They cannot conceive of it. If you mention a Korean, they look at you as if you were from Mars."

As a result, the Japanese firms in the financial industry in the United States often must rely on second-class personnel.

One way around the problem is Sumitomo's relationship with Goldman Sachs, which will allow the Japanese bank to have its own top employees trained by the Americans. Another way to skirt the problem was found in the summer of 1988 by Nomura Securities.

The increasing pace of Japanese acquisitions of U.S. companies and real estate has not led to a corresponding increase in the lucrative advisory fees connected with the transactions for Japanese banks and securities houses. While the Japanese would clearly prefer to use their countrymen to keep the money in the family, they have been forced to rely on U.S. investment bankers because they have the expertise, even though the Japanese firms have the size.

Nomura, the biggest securities firm in the world, was founded in 1925 in Osaka by Tokushichi Nomura. He based his operation on the unusual idea that sound research into the financial history and prospects of a corporation could take the risk out of buying its stock. At the time, the Japanese stock market was highly speculative, and Nomura's ability to provide excellent analyses to his clients helped his firm grow into the largest securities company in Japan and, later, the world.

In 1969, Nomura formed an international branch in New York in an attempt to gain a share of the lucrative U.S. securities market. The company grew steadily, if not dramatically, gaining a seat on the New York Stock Exchange in 1981. Near the end of 1986, Nomura became a primary dealer in U.S. government securities through approval of the Federal Reserve Bank of New York. This status allowed it to be one of about forty firms that deal directly with the New York Fed when it buys and sells U.S. government securities on the open market. This is a highly prized status, because some large institutional investors do business only with institutions that are primary dealers.

The membership of Nomura and later three additional Japanese institutions in the group of primary dealers ruffled some feathers in Congress because Japanese financial markets refused to provide similar access to American investment firms. American firms complain that they are allocated a measly 0.8 percent share of the underwritings on the booming Tokyo markets, which are controlled by the Big Four.

Representative Charles Schumer, a New York Democrat, introduced legislation in 1987 to deny Japanese firms primary-dealer status until the Japanese opened their markets further to foreign firms. Schumer, who is viewed in Congress as the key representative of the interests of U.S. securities firms, was particularly concerned that U.S. institutions be permitted to underwrite Japanese corporate and government bonds on the Tokyo markets.

Schumer's legislation was approved as part of a massive trade bill in the summer of 1988. It banned foreign firms from status as primary dealers unless U.S. firms were granted equal access to the foreign country's market within a year's time.

There were indications that the U.S. pressure was working in the fall of 1988. With assistance from one of Nomura's Tokyo subsidiaries, some foreign securities firms began to share slightly in underwriting new public stock offerings of shares for domestic Japanese companies. Six foreign firms, including three American firms, were invited to participate in some small deals.

Unless Japan opens its financial markets to U.S. dealers or the

Japanese find some way around the new trade bill legislation, Nomura, Daiwa, and Nikko could be stripped of their status as dealers with the Fed.

However, Fuji Bank, the world's third largest, appears to have found its own way around the legislation. In 1988, it paid $14.5 million for a 24.9 percent share of a Chicago-based primary dealer owned by Britain's Kleinwort Benson Lonsdale. Insiders said Fuji was interested in buying a bigger chunk of the dealer but backed off after officials at the Fed in New York expressed reservations as a result of the legislation on the matter.

Ten of the forty-two primary dealers in 1988 were foreign, and applications were pending from two other Japanese banks at the time President Reagan signed the trade bill.

The Americans were not the only nation demanding reciprocity from the Japanese. Since London deregulated its financial markets in 1986, the Japanese had made significant inroads into financial services there without similar opportunities for British firms in Japan. As a result, the British also were pressuring the Japanese to open their financial markets.

Primary-dealer status, however, was only one avenue being pursued by Nomura in its expansion in the United States. The company was eagerly seeking a piece of the highly profitable mergers and acquisitions flourishing in the U.S. financial markets.

As the 1980s progressed, securities firms in New York had begun shifting their focus to the mergers and acquisitions that were sweeping the country and generating huge fees for the investment bankers who served as middlemen for the deals. Nomura and the other Japanese securities houses in New York were unsuccessful in gaining a sizable share of the M&A business, even though an increasing percentage of the deals involved acquisitions of U.S. companies by Japanese businesses.

Mergers and acquisitions, at least as the business was practiced in the 1980s on Wall Street, may be as opposite to the management outlook and strategies of the Japanese as anything that could be designed.

Any notion of long-term thinking had been abandoned in favor of the short-term transaction. No one seemed to look farther than the next deal. Corporations were taken over and dismantled without consideration for the jobs of workers or the fate of industries. A cadre of professionals on Wall Street, many still in their twenties, were driven by nothing more than greed and power. Individual initiative, always the backbone of Wall Street, had never enjoyed more glory. The stars who excelled at it, such as Bruce Wasserstein at First Boston and Martin Siegel at Kidder Peabody and at Drexel Burnham Lambert until he was caught in the great insider trading scandal, achieved cult status and were rewarded with salaries that topped $2 million a year.

Small wonder that the Japanese securities firms, wedded to a management structure that stressed consensus decision making and submerged individual initiative, were unable to make a go of it in the overheated world of mergers and acquisitions. Nomura and other Japanese houses recognized the need for American M&A executives, and sometimes they found willing executives. But the top ones rarely lasted, driven out by what they found to be a stifling atmosphere and a decision-making process in which the power always rested in Tokyo or Osaka. Between 1985 and 1988, the two American executives who headed Nomura's mergers and acquisitions department in New York quit.

During that time, Nomura had been buying up expertise in other areas to provide broader services to its huge Japanese investor base in the United States, acquiring half of a New York-based real estate company called Eastdil Realty in 1986 and forming a joint venture with Babcock & Brown, a San Francisco financing and leasing company, the same year. And the firm let it be known that it was in the market for an investment in a top-notch Wall Street firm to overcome its failure to break into the world of investment banking by hiring individual American executives.

As a result, almost any financial institution looking to sell a piece of itself to raise capital looked at Nomura because of its rich coffers and its access to some of Japan's wealthiest and most powerful corporations. At one point, Nomura discussed joint ventures with the brokerage house of Kidder Peabody and considered trying to buy the securities firm from its owner, General Electric. Before then, Nomura had studied a possible acquisition of another respected New York investment bank, Lazard Freres & Co.

So there was little surprise on July 27, 1988, when it was announced that Nomura was investing $100 million in capital in the aggressive new investment firm of Wasserstein, Perella & Company. In return, Nomura got control of a 20 percent stake in the New York company, which had formed just six months earlier to do high-stakes mergers and acquisitions.

The deal made big headlines because of the reputation of the American firm's leading partners, Bruce Wasserstein and Joseph Perella. They were regarded as two of the most brilliant mergers and acquisitions strategists in the United States when they headed the M&A department at the blue-chip investment house of First Boston Corp. They had quit to form their own firm, which catapulted to the front ranks of merger firms on the basis of their reputation alone.

For Wasserstein and Perella, the transaction brought a needed infusion of cash that would enable them to move to the next step of their plan and create a full-blown merchant bank that puts it own money into deals and stands to reap profits far exceeding the advisory fees paid to M&A firms.

The firm also gained access to Nomura's loyal Japanese clients, and a joint venture was planned to do merger and acquisition work for American, Japanese, and European companies.

For Nomura, the transaction was a long-term strategic investment that would enable the giant firm to get involved in merger work with a high-quality American partner and learn the ropes in the complex and lucrative business.

The deal actually was very similar to the investment made by Sumitomo in Goldman Sachs, although without many of the restrictions imposed on Sumitomo as a result of its status as a bank. And both deals promised to shorten the time it would take the Japanese to become tougher competitors in the financial services arena.

The operative philosophy at work in the financial services industry is actually very simple: If you can't beat them, buy them. And once they buy them, the Japanese have shown over the past two decades that they will study, study, study and learn to do it themselves so that they can compete effectively and efficiently in every sector of the financial services business in the United States and around the world.

Competition itself is no danger to the U.S. financial houses or the nation's markets. But if the Japanese cross the threshold from competition to concentration, if they begin to dominate financial markets in the fashion that they dominate, say, the consumer electronics arena, the threat to American independence becomes real and dangerous.

Ownership of financial institutions, far more than ownership of real estate and factories, implies power, and that power has the potential to jeopardize the sovereignty of the United States.

17
BUYING THE BANKS

ON THE NIGHT OF MAY 4, 1988, Harold Meyerman's telephone at his Pasadena, California, home rang shortly after 10:30 P.M. Meyerman is the chief of international banking at First Interstate Bank in nearby Los Angeles, the nation's eighth largest banking company.

On the other end of the telephone that night was Hisao Kobayashi, president of the California subsidiary of Dai-Ichi Kangyo Bank of Tokyo. He was calling from his office in a high rise in downtown Los Angeles.

Meyerman was surprised to receive a telephone call at that time of night from Kobayashi, but he was even more astonished by what the Japanese banker told him.

"Harold, your office is on fire," said Kobayashi.

Thus, Harold Meyerman became the first executive of First Interstate Bank to learn that the company's sixty-two-story headquarters, the tallest structure in Los Angeles, was burning. The blaze caused millions of dollars in damage to the building and kept bank offices there closed for months.

The most lasting image from that night for the financial

community in California, however, may be Hisao Kobayashi, chief executive of the American subsidiary of the world's largest bank, at work in his office well past 10 P.M.

This is one of those tired clichés that happens to be true, and it tells us a lot about how the Japanese are likely to overcome cultural barriers and other obstacles to become a force in U.S. banking just as they did in automaking and consumer electronics and computer components.

Los Angeles is the banking capital of the United States for the Japanese. There are more big branches of Japanese banks in New York, a sizable number in Chicago. But those offices deal almost exclusively with large corporate clients.

It is in Los Angeles and California that the Japanese banks have decided to get down in the pits and compete head-to-head with American banks for the hearts, minds, and bank accounts of American consumers.

There are several reasons why the Japanese have chosen California. First is its rich, diverse economy. If California were a sovereign nation, it would have the sixth largest gross national product in the world, right behind France and ahead of the United Kingdom, Italy, and Canada. The state boasts some of America's richest farmland and most productive manufacturing companies, from the high-tech corridor in Silicon Valley to the giant aerospace and defense firms surrounding Los Angeles.

Next on the list are proximity and familiarity. More than any other state, California is a natural port of entry for Japanese firms coming to the United States mainland to do business. It is the leading trading partner with the Japanese among U.S. states, a gateway to the Pacific Rim for the United States, and an open door to the United States for Japan and the rising economies of Asia. Indeed, by 1988, the Japan Business Association of Southern California estimated that 1,000 subsidiaries of Japanese companies were doing business in California, employing about 100,000 people.

The Japanese firms in the state ranged from the big ones, such as Fujitsu, Sony, Toyota, and Mitsubishi, to dozens of smaller operations that followed the large corporations abroad to maintain their relationship as suppliers. And of course, these firms brought with them a sizable population of Japanese nationals to run the operations. When combined with the large segment of Japanese-Americans who have been in California for generations, the pool of ready customers for Japanese banks is substantial.

The concentration of Japanese businesses in California also attracts the banks because they have the same type of long-term relationship with the major corporations as other suppliers. Japan adheres to the concept of "relationship banking" on a corporate level, a notion that passed from the American scene a couple of decades ago. Major Japanese corporations have long-standing ties to specific banks. In order to maintain the link, a bank is obligated to follow a company when it opens an operation abroad. If the banks do not, they run the risk of losing a share of the company's business not only overseas but at home, too.

For instance, when Toyota started construction of its auto plant near Georgetown, Kentucky, its two main banks from Japan, Tokai and Mitsui, quickly established offices there. For the manufacturer, this development ensures a reliable source of funds at reasonable rates. For the banks, it cements the relationship at home and means automatic business for the new U.S. office.

In addition, Japanese nationals transferred to the United States on three- or four-year rotations would not dare change something as sacred as a long-term banking relationship with its roots in the home country. Even if an American bank offered a superior rate, it would not be worth the possible damage to the company official's career hopes to accept the outsider.

This reliance on a family of suppliers, ranging from lawyers and accountants to janitorial firms, is consistent throughout the country with Japanese corporations. If a supplier cannot be Japanese, it must be "Japanese safe," which means it must have done business with other Japanese firms or have another entree.

The pattern has been followed across the country and, since California is home to more Japanese corporations than any other state, there are more Japanese banks operating there.

But the Japanese banks have had difficulty expanding beyond

Japanese companies. They have not cornered the consumer business in California, nor have they made significant inroads into commercial lending in the state. They are hobbled by cultural barriers, such as the Japanese aversion to making risky loans, and by a banking market that is one of the most fiercely competitive in the world. Plus, their refusal to grant real authority to their American executives is a strong disadvantage in a business as complex and peculiar as banking.

An American manager at Sumitomo's California subsidiary described his frustration in trying to get final approval on a big loan to a commercial customer. He telephoned the proper official in Osaka for approval and was asked whether the top Japanese executive at the Los Angeles bank had approved the loan. Even after the American said the executive had okayed the loan, the Osaka official said he would have to speak directly with the Japanese executive before okaying it.

Cumbersome approval procedures, aversion to risk, and other problems mean that the Japanese banks in California have turned in below-average profits year after year. Rather than pulling back, the Japanese continue to be driven by the same long-term strategy that has enabled them to overcome obstacles in other fields. They are expanding, driving for market share.

In 1988, a California affiliate of the Bank of Tokyo paid $750 million for Union Bank in Los Angeles, a $9 billion institution and the state's fifth largest bank. The transaction marked the largest investment by the Japanese in an American financial institution, surpassing Sumitomo's $500 million infusion into Goldman Sachs.

As in the Sumitomo-Goldman transaction, the acquisition of Union Bank was subject to approval by the Federal Reserve Board in Washington. The board okayed the application outlining the purchase by Bank of Tokyo's California First Bank on August 31, 1988. The vote was five to one.

The lone dissenter was Martha Seger, the conservative Michigan Republican, who had opposed earlier acquisitions of U.S. financial institutions by the Japanese because of what she felt was a lack of reciprocity.

"I am concerned that while this application would permit a large Japanese banking organization to acquire a bank in the U.S., U.S. banking organizations are not permitted to make comparable acquisitions in Japan," said Seger. "While some progress is being made in opening Japanese markets to U.S. banking organizations, U.S. banking organizations and other financial institutions, in my opinion, are still far from being afforded the full opportunity to compete in Japan."

But Japanese banks can compete freely in California, as acquisition of the powerful Union Bank demonstrated.

The deal was particularly astute for the Japanese because Union Bank's strength, lending to medium-sized businesses, was a lucrative field that the Japanese banks in the state had been completely unable to penetrate.

It gave the Japanese control of five of the ten largest banks in California. Those banks owned or controlled by Japanese banks are Union Bank, 77 percent owned by Bank of Tokyo; Sanwa Bank California, a subsidiary of the giant Japanese bank; Bank of California, a unit of Mitsubishi Bank; and Sumitomo Bank of California, a subsidiary of Sumitomo Bank, Ltd.; and Tokai Bank of California, a subsidiary of Tokai Bank Ltd.

In addition to those banks, five other Japanese banks operate full banking subsidiaries in California, including such giants as Dai-Ichi Kangyo, Mitsui, and Tokai.

The purchase of Union Bank marked the final step in the Japanese ascension over the British banks in California. The British were once the dominant foreign banking power in California, but their holdings fared no better than the Japanese ones. However, unlike the Japanese, the British lacked the capital and long-term outlook to remain in the face of losses or modest returns on their investments. Hence, there was little surprise in the financial community of Los Angeles when it was announced that Bank of Tokyo was purchasing Union from its British owners, Standard Chartered banking group.

Certainly Japanese banks are not short on capital. Throughout the 1980s, as the yen grew stronger and Japanese corporations spread around the globe, the Japanese banks spread out like financial Jesuits. By the end of 1987, the ten largest banks in the world were all Japanese. Seventeen of the twenty-five largest banks in the world were Japanese.

The biggest U.S. bank, New York's Citibank, ranked only twenty-eighth in terms of deposits on the list. San Francisco–based Bank of America, the biggest bank in California and once the world's largest, had fallen to forty-fifth place.

"It is shocking how fast Japanese banks have come up to dominate the banking industry," said William M. Isaac, the former chairman of the Federal Deposit Insurance Corp. and now the head of a Washington financial consulting firm. He said the dominance of the Japanese banks reflected a fundamental change in the competitiveness of the U.S. and Japanese banking systems.

Part of the reason for the size of the Japanese institutions was reflected in the appreciation of the yen and the concurrent decline of the dollar. And the Japanese banks benefit, too, from the ability to take deposits anywhere in Japan from their thrifty countrymen.

Japanese banks have benefited also from less stringent regulation at home than that for banks in most other industrialized nations. The Japanese banks have operated with much lower capital-to-asset ratios than their American counterparts. That means they are required to have less money invested in the bank in relation to its size, an additional leverage that translates into an ability to offer lower interest on loans both at home and abroad.

That competitive advantage is scheduled to disappear in 1992, when new international guidelines that are supposed to standardize capital ratios at the world's major banks will go into effect. Complying with those regulations may actually require the big Japanese banks to cut back on the dramatic growth of their lending around the world. But no astute analyst expects compliance to be anything more than a blip on the path to continued growth for the Japanese powerhouses.

In fact, raising new money or cutting back on lending may have a more dramatic effect on a dozen or so of the top American banks that are weakened by the load of their troubled loans to

Third World countries. Some analysts expect further declines among some American banks as they struggle to meet the new guidelines, which are slightly tougher than current U.S. standards. And one of the banks expected to have the hardest time is Bank of America.

No institution better illustrates the declining competitiveness of the U.S. banks against the Japanese referred to by Isaac than the San Francisco giant that once symbolized U.S. dominance of the world's financial industry. If you view the world as a teeter-totter, the Bank of America end has gone down dramatically in direct proportion to the rise of the Japanese end. The only problem with the comparison to a playground toy is the uncertainty over whether Bank of America will rise again to its former glory.

And no single incident better illustrates the downward course of Bank of America than a series of trips made to Tokyo in 1987 by its leading executives, climaxed by a hat-in-hand tour of the Japanese capital by Bank of America's chairman and chief executive, A. W. Clausen.

Clausen had retired from the bank in 1980 and spent five years as president of the World Bank in Washington. The World Bank finances development in poor countries, and Clausen's role as the benign lender of last resort to the developing nations echoed the stature of Bank of America when he left it. But in the fall of 1986, when he was called back to assume the helm once more, he was confronted by a far different institution.

Gone was the record of fifty-seven consecutive quarters of profits. Obliterated was its standing as the world's largest bank. In 1985 and again in 1986, the bank lost record amounts. It would be worse in 1987.

Within months of returning to the bank, Clausen was forced to go to Tokyo to ask for financial aid from the Japanese. He found himself in the position of supplicant, and Clausen is someone who would put himself in that position only as a last resort. Yet here was the chief executive of the bank that had been the chief lender for the reconstruction of Japan after World War II asking for a handout.

After a few weeks of haggling, a consortium of Japanese banks and insurance companies agreed to contribute $350 million in capital to prop up the sagging Bank of America. The Japanese drove a hard bargain, receiving premium interest rates and options which, if exercised, would give them about 7 percent of the stock in Bank of America, an enormous holding for a block of foreign investors.

"It was just a drop in the bucket for the twenty-three Japanese banks involved, but they strung out the negotiations with Bank of America just so everyone was reminded of where the power was," said the chief executive of a competing California bank.

Another bank executive familiar with the transaction said, "It was a deal that the Japanese pretty much dictated. It is so expensive that I cannot imagine we would ever do this again."

The Japanese investment was a passive one, but nonetheless it raised the question in financial circles of whether the San Francisco banking company would remain independent. Its capital base was weak and its stock price was low, making the $95 billion bank a potential takeover target for someone with a lust for its 900-branch network of consumer branches that still dominated California. Because of the enormous capital investment required to restore the bank to smooth operations, the speculation centered on the cash-rich Japanese banks.

"If someday the Japanese institutions decide to brush aside politics and go after banking, there are few banks in the United States that would give them pause, and Bank of America is not one of them," said Robert Albertson, a banking analyst at Goldman Sachs in New York.

Yet, as Albertson and others recognize, acquiring one of the giants of American banking, particularly one with "America" as part of its name, would set off a public and political backlash that would threaten to blow the lid off the basic strategy of "acquire and conquer" that the Japanese have pursued throughout the 1980s in the United States.

"The Japanese would never take over Bank of America," said Yukuo Takenaka, a Japanese-American Peat Marwick Main partner in Los Angeles, who is an adviser to the largest Japanese companies doing business in the United States and to their home offices. "People would be concerned about how it would look, about the political implications."

As he paused and reflected, Takenaka reassessed his position slightly and said: "They might come in, but only if they were asked to help, only if it was the only way that Bank of America could survive. But the Japanese know that if they are too aggressive, too excessive in any area, people will try to stop them."

While their troubled Third World debts and increased competition from investment banking firms have forced the major U.S. banks to reduce their international offices and slow the establishment of new offices for making loans abroad, Japanese institutions have expanded dramatically in the United States. From 1982 to 1986, Japanese banks opened forty-eight new U.S. offices, one-third of all foreign bank offices opened in the United States during that period. In 1987, the pace remained strong and the Japanese opened twelve more new offices.

At the end of 1987, the most numerous foreign banks in the United States were Japanese, with thirty institutions controlling ninety-nine full banking offices—a fifth of all foreign bank offices in the country. The British, who were reducing their U.S. presence after once playing the role of dominant foreign banking power in the United States, were a distant second, with twelve banks and forty-seven offices.

The Japanese banking presence in the United States can be divided into two categories: the consumer-oriented, U.S.-chartered banks, which are concentrated in California and are not performing up to U.S. standards, and the representative offices of the home banks, which concentrate on big loans and other services for Japanese businesses in the United States and, increasingly, for American corporations.

"You can't eke out a living by only dealing with Japanese businesses," said Michinori Nakajima, senior deputy general manager at the Chicago branch of Mitsui Bank of Japan.

The representative offices, which also scout for new investments in the United States on behalf of Japanese clients, are concentrated in major cities across the country—at last count in 1987, there were twenty-seven in Los Angeles, twelve in San

Francisco, six in Seattle, eighteen in Chicago, fifteen in Houston, eight in Atlanta, and forty-seven in New York.

By the middle of 1987, Japanese banks accounted for 9 percent of the banking assets in the United States, according to the Federal Reserve, which was more than double their share at the beginning of the decade. Their loans and assets in the United States totaled $270 billion at that time, more than the combined total of Citicorp, the nation's biggest domestic bank, and Bank of America, second largest at that time.

A survey published in 1988 by the *American Banker*, a respected financial industry newspaper, found that loans to U.S. businesses by foreign banks increased five times faster in 1987 than loans to U.S. businesses by American-owned banks. The Japanese accounted for most of the increase, grabbing more than three-quarters of all business lending by foreign banks in the United States.

The Japanese retail banks clustered in California have found it difficult adjusting to the sophisticated, sometimes eccentric demands of consumer banking. Indeed, even U.S. banks from outside California confront substantial problems making gains in the highly competitive state, which is home to four of the nation's ten largest banking companies and many of its largest and most profitable savings and loan associations.

But the representative offices do not face the same myriad of problems when they deal with business clients. While the names of the companies and the faces of the executives are different, corporate demands for financial services are very similar in both countries. As a result, the Japanese have done well by relying on their capital strength and the infrastructure in place back in Japan to make significant inroads into standard commercial banking services, such as corporate loans, letters of credit, and some lease financing.

These are areas, too, where the Japanese insistence on quality control and precise execution can surmount the cultural problems that plague U.S. consumer banking for them. An American businessman dealing with a Japanese bank was amazed when the bank telephoned him with corrections in the English version of some complicated loan documents prepared by his office.

In a 1988 article in the *Wall Street Journal*, reporter Michael R. Sesit recounted the story of the chief financial officer at a paper company in Tuscaloosa, Alabama, and his first encounter with Japanese commercial bankers. When a colleague suggested that the executive, James O'Brien, try a lender called Industrial Bank of Japan, O'Brien said his question was, "Do they lend in dollars?"

"They sent down two Japanese guys from the New York office and analyzed the numbers to death," said O'Brien, adding that in twenty-five years, the company's primary New York bank had never bothered to learn its business the way the Japanese did. "The joke around here was if we didn't understand something in our financial statements, we'd just ask the Japanese to explain it."

The paper company, Gulf States Paper, borrowed $15 million from Industrial Bank of Japan five months after its chief financial officer had asked whether the institution loaned in dollars. The answer, of course, was yes.

The Japanese bank offices have taken over a significant portion of the corporate letters-of-credit business in New York and other major cities by employing the time-honored tactic of reducing their profits to the lowest level possible. For instance, Mitsubishi Bank got a letter-of-credit deal for a $300 million bond issue by the City of Chicago with a bid of three-sixteenths of 1 percent. Sanwa Bank underwrote a thirty-year bond issue for Southern Methodist University in Dallas with a bid of one-twelfth of a percentage point. A short time later, the same bank provided a letter of credit for a $70 million revenue bond sale by the City of Boston with a fee of nine-tenths of a percentage point.

The aim of the Japanese banks is not so much to make money on these deals as to gain market share so that they can move into other bank services for the corporations and become the lead bank for top businesses.

"It is the way to get a start, the way any company often breaks into a new market where they are offering the same product as everyone else," said Steven Berman, a banking industry analyst with the New York investment firm of County Securities. "The

Japanese also are benefiting from the loss of anything resembling relationship banking in the United States. Banking in the last five or ten years has gone away from relationships and more toward transactions. That is what big corporations want. They want the cheapest price. They don't give a shit about loyalty. They can raise money other ways. They don't really need long-term relationships with banks anymore. So they go for the cheapest deal."

Japanese banks have been lending to U.S. corporate customers for the past decade in increasing amounts, and they have built up fairly substantial books of assets. They have stayed with standard banking services and with highly rated companies, making loans that Berman calls "no-brainers" because of their low risk.

A December 1987 study of Japanese bank activities in the United States by the Washington-based Council of Financial Competition, which is funded by American businesses, confirmed that the Japanese had had "stunning" success in penetrating commercial banking in the United States, but the study raised questions about whether they had been nearly as successful in becoming lead banks for America's largest corporations.

"In the council's interviews with both Japanese and American banks, one clear strategic theme emerged: The desire of Japanese banks to establish long-term relationships with American clients," said the study. "In pursuit of that goal, Japanese institutions have pursued (and in many cases, won) major deals; less clear is whether they have been successful in winning long-term relationships. Officers with American institutions generally said no."

American bankers comfort themselves with the notion that the Japanese are too cautious to engage in the most creative and often most lucrative lending practices. And they point out that the Japanese banks do not have the sophisticated cash-management services that major U.S. corporations demand of their lead banks.

This is precisely the kind of complacency exhibited two decades ago by American automakers and television manufacturers. Even in California, where the Japanese consumer banks have performed poorly, smart bankers do not expect them to remain second-class institutions forever. With purchases such as Union Bank and growing experience with American marketing and customer relations, gains are inevitable.

"So far we haven't run into any real competition from the Japanese banks," said Bram Goldsmith, chairman and chief executive of City National Bank in Beverly Hills, a highly profitable institution whose assets of $3 billion place it in the same league as most of the Japanese consumer banks in the state. "They have come in with some very aggressive, lowball pricing on letters of credit and auto loans. But they haven't learned the ropes yet. What bothers me, of course, is that we used to make those comments when they first started making automobiles, and look what they've done. At the moment, the culture is the problem. What will happen when they learn?"

Berman at County Securities said the major Japanese banks in New York also suffered a major setback when the stock market crashed on October 19, 1987. Wall Street securities firms and broker-dealer firms were scrambling for cash to cover their stock positions and mounting losses, and that meant they had to draw on their established lines of credit with the big banks.

"The Japanese banks had cut in on the low-end business, financing a lot of broker-dealers on Wall Street," said Berman. "It is a safe, no-risk business that provides these guys with money to support their inventories of stock. When the market crashed, the Japanese banks began to pull back on their lines of credit to Wall Street. They ran. This created a lot of problems for the brokers. Some big American banks ran, too. But the Federal Reserve stepped in and told the American banks they had to provide the liquidity that kept the market from a complete meltdown."

The Fed had no such control over the U.S. branches of Japanese banks, and many of them refused to provide the agreed-upon credit to brokers.

The episode raises again the issue of competition versus concentration. If the Japanese banks had a larger share of the Wall Street business, would their refusal to extend credit to brokers because the banks thought the brokers were headed toward bankruptcy in a plummeting market have actually turned the crash into a far more serious event? There is no answer to that, as there is no standard measure of when competition crosses the line to concentration. But the question remains, unanswered and troubling.

A similar issue was raised in the late 1970s, when the United States was awash with Arab petrodollars and some Middle Eastern nations were acquiring interests in U.S. financial institutions. The extraordinary influence that comes with owning a bank was described graphically by Representative Fernand St Germain, a Rhode Island Democrat and the chairman of the House Banking Committee, who said on a CBS network documentary:

"What you've got, once you own the bank or have control of the bank, is control of a good deal of economic power as far as where and how loans are to be made, and to whom. A manufacturing plant just manufactures whatever the product might be. That's an investment for profit. However, when we talk about the purchase of a bank, that's an investment for power."

18
THE TWENTY-FOURTH
WARD

IT WAS ONE OF THOSE RARE SPRING DAYS in Los Angeles. A steady wind had pushed away the brown layer of smog, baring the city's skyline against the backdrop of the San Gabriel Mountains. Standing at an upper-story window overlooking the most powerful financial center in the western United States, Yukuo Takenaka surveyed the skyscrapers that slashed the landscape and pointed to the many buildings owned by Japanese investors.

"The Japanese don't own all of downtown," said Takenaka, whose roster of 1,200 Japanese clients at the accounting firm of Peat Marwick Main includes several of those investors. "Not yet."

The list of what the Japanese owned in downtown Los Angeles that particular day in 1988 was already impressive: Arco Plaza, with a price tag of $620 million; Broadway Plaza, $210 million; Chase Bank Plaza, $137 million; Manulife Plaza, $62 million; World Trade Center, $75 million; Union Bank Building, $87.5 million; 1000 Wilshire Building, $145 million; 800 Wilshire Building, $47.5 million. And at least twelve other major downtown Los Angeles office buildings.

Japanese investors, ranging from wealthy individuals to major banks and insurance companies, control more than 25 percent of the office space in the center of Los Angeles, the nation's second largest city. The concentration of Japanese real estate ownership, Japanese-owned corporate offices, and businesses catering to the Japanese has resulted in a new nickname for downtown Los Angeles—"The Twenty-Fourth Ward." An ocean away, Tokyo is divided into twenty-three political wards.

"Japanese executives see downtown Los Angeles through the same eyes as they see downtown Tokyo," said Saturo Jo, a vice president with Cushman Realty Corporation, a major American firm. "They see it as a safe investment since it is in the center of activity. And, from a symbolic viewpoint, Japanese, like Europeans and Middle Easterners, believe that being in the center is the mark of a leader. In ancient cities, the ruler's palace was always in the center."

Thus, the Japanese have acquired "trophy" buildings, first in the centers of major cities where Japan Air Lines landed—Los Angeles, New York, and San Francisco—and more recently in cities throughout the country—Chicago, Boston, and Seattle.

More than any other aspect of Japanese investment in the United States, the acquisition of these important buildings, often at premium prices, demonstrates the apparently inexhaustible supply of dollars and the insatiable appetite for buying America on the part of the Japanese. The amount of U.S. real estate owned by the Japanese—a subject of considerable dispute in itself—is a mere fraction of the nation's total. But the Japanese have skimmed the cream off the top in city after city.

Since the beginning of 1986, most of the office buildings that have sold for $100 million or more were bought by Japanese. Of the sixteen largest real estate acquisitions by foreign investors from 1986 until the middle of 1987, all had Japanese buyers. The giant U.S. pension funds and insurance companies, even the British and the Canadian investors, that usually acquire these prime pieces of real estate for safe, long-term investments spent 1987 and 1988 on the sidelines, unable to compete with the cash-rich Japanese.

"There are several things going on here; it's important to separate the myth from the reality," said Sandy Goodkin, executive director of the Peat Marwick/Goodkin Real Estate Consulting Group in San Diego. "The Japanese were quite active in U.S. real estate—particularly in resort areas such as the Hawaiian Islands—in the '70s, just prior to the formation of OPEC. Those early acquisitions were what I would call 'frivolous.' The most important aspect of those projects was that they would have to have a golf course. Then the boycott hurt their liquidity and their government stopped money from leaving the country. That, of course, stopped the investment cold.

"Step two was the dawn of the '80s. The real momentum hit in '84. In the past ten years they have done a lot of research, which varied from company to company. A resort might become owned by a railroad. They formed symbiotic families. They began to form long-term strategies. The Japanese pay a lot of attention to strategy, as opposed to Americans whose main strategy is lunch for today.

"The evolution is such that they have gone from these frivolous investments to a period of buying nothing to a period of buying trophy properties."

Today, the Japanese have done their homework. The next steps will be land acquisition, development, and actual construction. "They will do this by acquiring or joint venturing, just as they have within the auto industry," said Goodkin. "Could they do the same thing in construction or housing that they already have within the electronics or auto industries? There's a fear they could."

Like other foreign investors, the Japanese have been drawn to the U.S. real estate for many reasons—relatively higher rates of return in the U.S. market because of its greater depth and size compared to other markets throughout the world, especially Tokyo; the decline of the value of the dollar, especially against the yen; an affinity for high-quality downtown office properties, a market that has been replenished throughout the 1980s by a commercial real estate boom; and, perhaps most importantly, because most Japanese investors view the U.S. real estate market as a safe haven from political and economic turmoil.

And then there are two additional reasons that the Japanese buying binge has expanded outside of the downtowns of major cities into all phases of commercial real estate, hotels and resorts, and more recently retail projects in the suburbs and secondary cities.

The first reason for the expansion of interest is a growing scarcity of prime buildings in the city centers; the Japanese and other foreigners, benefiting from the weak dollar in recent years, already have acquired many of the choice buildings in New York, Los Angeles, and San Francisco. The second reason is that the Japanese have done their homework and learned about commercial real estate, and they are now secure enough to begin applying what they have learned to new opportunities.

The question is what this expansion will mean for the American real estate industry. Will real estate go the route of the consumer electronics industry or the auto industry? Can the Japanese capture enough of the decentralized market to become a dominant force, setting rents and determining housing costs for a nation of tenants? By using the growing power of Japanese-owned banks and influencing policy through their cadre of lobbyists, can they affect zoning laws and wide-ranging government policies? And will the real estate market suffer dire consequences if the Japanese are forced to retreat suddenly because of economic difficulties at home, as the Mexicans did in the early 1980s?

These are real questions. The answers given by most industry leaders and government officials fall in a range between "certainly not" and "probably not." The "probably nots" have qualified their responses because they have a glimmering awareness about the same answers provided by the U.S. manufacturers of television sets and automobiles when they faced a similar invasion from Japan many years ago. The eventual defeat of the U.S. television industry at the hands of the Japanese wasn't even conceived by the proud giants of that industry. And Detroit's Big Three have been humbled, although not yet defeated, since they first denied that Americans would ever buy those little Japanese cars, forsaking the American automobile.

Proponents like to tout real estate investment by foreigners as a stabilizing factor in real estate markets. They view the growth in foreign investment as a positive and inevitable sign of the integration of the world's economies. If international relations or the economy sours, investors cannot take those buildings home with them, they like to point out.

"People get excited about Japanese investment. I remember when they were concerned ten or fifteen years ago about the Arab purchases. These things go in cycles," said Leonard Harlan, president of The Harlan Company, which has a joint venture agreement to build a Baltimore office building with Kajima Development Corporation. "I'm sure this will not be an endless stream of capital, but I can't tell you when it will stop.

"From a real estate point of view, the reason that people are upset is that the Japanese are buying these trophy buildings in high-profile areas. It's the media's dream for making headlines. There's a lot being made of this right now that belies the true facts about this Japanese investment," Harlan said. "The Japanese will, and already have, given this industry stability. They take a long-term view. Their emphasis is on quality. They will set a higher standard that all the folks in the industry will have to aim for."

But these proponents often ignore the perils posed by foreign ownership of real property in the United States and the dangers of allowing another vital segment of the domestic economy to become vulnerable to exchange-rate fluctuations and the other components of the global economy.

Already, rather than being a beneficial and stabilizing factor in the real estate market, the Japanese buying binge and overpayment for several prime properties has driven prices into excessive ranges in the cities where the Japanese have concentrated to date.

Examples of properties for which Japanese investors may have overpaid include the ABC Building in New York and Arco Plaza in Los Angeles.

Cecil E. Sears, director of economic research at Rountrey and Associates, said at a conference sponsored by the Japan Society in 1986 that Arco Plaza was sold to Shuwa for $620 million when the second highest bid was just $590 million, and that the ABC Building sold to Shuwa for roughly $165 million, when domestic bidders were offering $50 million to $90 million less. "Bids can be off by 5 or 10 percent, but seldom any more when everyone has done his homework," said one New York broker.

The prices paid per square foot by Japanese investors have reached record high levels. The Tiffany Building in New York sold for $94 million, or $940 per square foot, the highest amount ever paid for retail space. The U.S. News and World Report headquarters building in Washington sold for $80 million, or $480 per square foot, the highest price ever paid for office space in the nation's capital. The Westin Mauna Kea, a pricey hotel on the island of Hawaii, sold for $310 million, a record of $1 million per room.

More than ever in its history, the U.S. real estate market—a key component of the nation's economic health and a centerpiece of the American dream—is dependent on decisions made in a foreign country. And the Japanese influence in this sector of the economy is growing beyond the choice office buildings and high-class resorts and hotels to reach into every strong regional economy in the country.

"The future belongs to the Japanese," Coldwell Banker, the real estate arm of Sears, Roebuck and Co., declared in a July 1987 survey of international real estate investment in the United States. "The conclusion is inescapable that, considering the scope, scale, rapidity and methodical nature of their commitment, the Japanese will become at some point sooner than we might anticipate, the dominant force in the United States commercial real estate marketplace. In the words of one Japanese official, 'We are patient. We have studied. We have prepared. Now we are ready.' "

And more than any other major city on the American mainland, Los Angeles provides a look at the future of Japanese investment in U.S. real estate. Not only do the Japanese own one-quarter of the office space in the central business district. They are managing their own buildings. They are developing their own projects. They are using Japanese banks for the financing and Japanese construction firms for the building. They are buying up choice parcels of land to tie up future development sites.

To go along with the downtown trophy buildings, they are branching out into the regional and suburban business centers that ring the city, developing industrial parks and shopping centers and commercial office buildings in Century City, affluent Orange County, and the rapidly growing San Fernando Valley.

"This is more than just another wave," James O'Brien, a Coldwell Banker vice president, said in describing the Japanese buying across the country. "It's a sea change."

As with other forms of foreign investment, many Americans are eager to have the Japanese investors. For sellers in major urban markets, it has meant enormous price increases. In New York and Los Angeles, experts estimate that the extravagant bidding of the Japanese has pushed commercial real estate prices up 10 to 15 percent. For developers and owners in suburban areas, who have watched downtown prices skyrocket from the Japanese interest, the prospects are mouth-watering.

Others have qualms about what they see occurring, even including some of those who have profited from it.

Michael Zietsman is a native of South Africa who has sold real estate in Beverly Hills, California, for a major international company for several years. He sees his job as providing the best possible advice and negotiating services to his clients, regardless of their nationality. And when prime commercial property is involved, those customers more and more often have been Japanese.

"The Japanese are buying most of the prime real estate here," Zietsman said. "That is the sort of property that ought to be in the hands of the American pension funds and insurance companies. But those companies have been sitting on the sidelines for the last couple of years. These prime commercial properties are rare and highly sought after. They are irreplaceable."

But most real estate industry professionals never voice concern, because the Japanese investment boom has sent prices skyrocketing—and their commissions are pegged to prices. Goodkin was told by one seller of property that he actually was asked by a broker to raise his price to a Japanese buyer so the commission could be higher.

Less than a month after Takenaka surveyed the downtown skyline, the University of Southern California held its annual real estate development conference in the Westin Bonaventure Hotel, another downtown Los Angeles building owned by the Japanese. The best-attended session at the conference was an afternoon session entitled "Japanese Investments and the Pacific Rim Panel."

Approximately 2,000 real estate industry professionals jammed the California Ballroom at the Bonaventure—owned in part by the Japanese, to listen to representatives of some of Japan's biggest real estate companies outline their plans for the coming years and listen to U.S. experts talk about how to get a slice of the expanding Japanese pie.

Yoshio Yamashita, vice chairman of Shuwa Investments Corporation, the biggest Japanese landlord in the United States, described his company's arrival in Los Angeles a decade earlier without any real estate inventory. As Yamashita stood before the audience that day, Shuwa owned $2 billion worth of U.S. real estate and collected $210 million a year in rents alone.

In 1988, he said, Shuwa would spend between $500 million and $1 billion more on U.S. real estate, expanding out of downtowns to industrial parks and smaller commercial sites.

Okitami Komada, chief executive of Mitsui Fudosan, a subsidiary of one of Japan's biggest developers, provided a rare look at the philosophy and scope of Japanese investors.

"We have some very exacting development criteria," he said. "We look for prime locations in major cities throughout the world. We recognize that we are a foreign developer in many of these cities, with limited local experience, so we try to avoid speculative locations which might be desirable to those with a better knowledge about that particular market."

He described how Mitsui relies on its own corporate cash to finance developments. "Our financial commitments also allow us to keep our buildings," he said. "We do not have to give away equity to secure major tenants to get mortgage financing for the project. Giving away equity is one of the toughest United States marketing practices for us to accept because Japan has always been an owner's market."

Indeed, although Komada did not mention it that day, Japan's largest owner of real estate, Mitsubishi Estate Company, is said to have never sold a property in its fifty-year history—a clear definition of the owner's market. In Japan, the word for real estate is *fudosan*, and the literal translation of that term is "unmoving assets.".

While he said Mitsui recognizes the value of joint ventures in obtaining local expertise, Komada told his audience that the company will not enter a development unless it holds the controlling interest. As a result, he said, the firm has taken on American partners with a minority stake as it has expanded outside Los Angeles and New York to acquire industrial parks and other sites around the country.

But it was the trophy buildings that evoked the pride in Komada's voice as he flashed their photographs on a giant screen in the ballroom. A 250,000-square-foot office building under construction at 41st Street and Fifth Avenue in New York, 80 percent owned by Mitsui. A twenty-four-story office building in the heart of San Francisco's financial district, 95 percent owned by Mitsui but under development with an American firm. And a fifty-two-story tower under construction at Wilshire and Figueroa in downtown Los Angeles, a site that Mitsui acquired in 1979 and held until it believed the time was right for a major development. Again, Mitsui was using American companies as partners, but retained full ownership of the building.

Another speaker at the conference was Jack Rodman, managing partner of the Los Angeles office of Kenneth Leventhal & Company, an accounting and consulting firm. He was there to present the latest findings of the company's annual survey of Japanese real estate investments in the United States.

The extent of the investment described by Rodman and flashed on the screen that day was astonishing—twice as high as most other estimates. His prediction that the Japanese would surpass the British and become the biggest landlords in the United States by the end of 1988 was equally surprising.

According to Rodman, Japanese investors spent a record $12.7 billion on U.S. real estate in 1987, an increase of 70 percent over the previous year. In 1988, he said, the firm's calculations showed that the Japanese would invest another $16 billion to $19 billion in U.S. real estate holdings.

Other observers counted about half that amount of Japanese real estate investment in 1987. The Bank of America, for instance, said the Japanese acquired slightly more than $6 billion worth of U.S. properties. That was similar to the figure used by Salomon Brothers, the New York investment house generally recognized as the sharpest analyst of foreign buying trends. U.S. government figures were also in line with those estimates.

What the disparity points up is that in real estate, as with every other category of foreign investment, there are no accurate figures because there is no government-mandated mechanism for reporting purchases. "Foreign investment numbers are hard to come by," wrote Goodkin in a report. "Hidden deals are just as high in volume as those actually reported. These 'whisper' deals with foreigners occur in many big cities in the United States."

The only exception in real estate is agricultural purchases, which must be reported to the federal government. But these are often underreported, and the actual identity of the purchaser can be concealed easily. And in many other real estate purchases, foreign investors can easily conceal their identities through a maze of offshore corporations.

The Leventhal survey, which is based on data compiled from the firm's own transactions, those of various investment banks and other real estate firms, and publicly available information, concluded that the Japanese own $26.34 billion worth of U.S. real estate.

That figure is slightly more than 1 percent of the value of all developed real estate in the United States. So, even using Leventhal's high-end figure, the total impact of Japanese investment is still relatively small. But the investment has been concentrated on such narrow, choice parts of the market that its impact is magnified.

Salomon Brothers estimates that total foreign investment in U.S. real estate is about $24 billion. But the investment bank also pointed out that the concentration in big-city downtowns, hotels, and resorts creates an impact greater than the total amount of the purchases would indicate.

Where the Bank of America and Salomon Brothers and Leventhal & Company do agree is on the trend in Japanese investment.

"While Japanese investors will continue to focus on the West Coast and the East Coast, they also will be much more interested in other strong economic growth regions across the United States," said Jack Cooper, managing director of Bank of America's investment real estate group.

At the conference at the Bonaventure, Rodman described the Japanese investment boom diversifying beyond office buildings and hotels into industrial property and big residential developments and expanding into secondary markets.

Traditionally, he said, the Japanese have invested in real estate in Honolulu, Los Angeles, San Francisco, and New York. In 1985 and 1986, those four markets accounted for more than two-thirds of all Japanese real estate purchases. But in 1987, the Leventhal survey found that the Japanese had diversified into areas surrounding those cities and into other major cities. In 1987, Japanese investors spent 56 percent of their real estate dollars outside the four cities.

New magnets for Japanese money were Orange County, San Diego, Boston, Chicago, Miami, Phoenix, and Seattle.

Office buildings and resorts still accounted for the bulk of Japanese investments in 1987. But the report found that the Japanese were now investing heavily in retail, industrial, and residential property.

"Clearly the Japanese strategy of coming into the major markets is expanding into the secondary markets as they gain familiarity with the United States," said Rodman.

In addition to buying real estate, the Japanese have shown that they intend to manage their own properties in the future, too, rather than depending on American companies. This trend was highlighted when Japan's Orient Leasing Company acquired a 23.3 percent stake in Rubloff Incorporated, a nationwide real estate management company based in Chicago.

This step is similar to Nomura's earlier 20 percent investment in the San Francisco–based Babcock & Brown, which was later renamed Nomura Babcock & Brown, and similar also to Nomura Babcock & Brown's purchase of a 50 percent interest of Eastdil Realty in New York. These acquisitions represent a recognizable pattern in the Japanese striving to keep everything in one family. They are examples of the historical *keiretsu*, or business group relationship, which bonds the Japanese trading corporations, real estate companies, and financial institutions.

While the Japanese have been acquiring more real estate and are set to expand into the management of their projects, Japanese construction companies have stepped up their U.S. development activity.

According to a 1988 analysis by David Shulman and Susan Jordan of Salomon Brothers in New York, the financial strength of the huge Japanese construction companies and their ties with Japanese banks provide them with a strong competitive advantage over their U.S. rivals. Joint ventures with U.S. developers have provided them with experience in local markets, so that they can now play the major roles in building new projects for Japanese industrial firms as they increase their penetration of the United States.

Construction and management contracts won by Japanese companies in the United States have gone from less than $50 million in 1981 to about $2 billion in 1986 and roughly $3 billion in 1987, according to *International Construction Week*, an authoritative industry newsletter.

The newsletter's editor, Charles Pinyan, said that the Japanese construction companies probably moved into first place among foreign firms in the United States in 1987, ahead of Great Britain, France, and West Germany, which do business through American companies.

The Japanese construction firms combined their ability to borrow money more cheaply from Japanese banks with their thin profit margins to underbid American firms on hotels in Hawaii, skyscrapers in Manhattan, and Japanese auto plants in the Midwest.

In Long Beach, California, Kajima, one of the giant Japanese construction firms, is building a behemoth $550 million complex, called the Greater Los Angeles World Trade Center, with a local firm. Kajima is supplying inexpensive financing and the local firm, IDM Corp., will supervise construction development.

Ohbayashi-Gumi, another big Japanese firm, beat out such American companies as Bechtel and Morrison-Knudsen to build a $63 million dam in Oregon.

Kumagai Gumi, another leading Japanese firm, is in various stages of seven projects valued at more than $1 billion as a joint venture with a prominent New York developer, the Zeckendorf Organization. Among the projects is a $500 million office complex at the former site of Madison Square Garden on the west side of Manhattan.

"Is the construction industry where Detroit was twenty years ago?" asked Barbara Alexander, an industry analyst at the investment firm of Salomon Brothers, in a 1987 report.

William Triplett, a staff member of the Senate Foreign Relations Committee, had an answer: "These guys (the construction industry) are next. It's the same game. No question about it. It all fits the same pattern."

Indeed, another important element of the pattern is the closed construction industry in Japan. While Japanese construction firms have been expanding in the United States, including such government-funded projects as work on the subway system in Washington, D.C., U.S. construction firms have fought a losing battle to gain a toehold in Japan.

In the fall of 1987, *International Construction Week* said that U.S. construction contracts in Japan were so small that it listed their value as zero. The Japanese government disputed the zero, claiming that five American companies won $34 million worth of Japanese public works projects in 1986. But the Japanese have steadfastly refused to open their public works bidding to foreign companies.

So far, Japanese real estate activity has been concentrated on commercial projects. Although there have been many individual purchases of residential property for personal use, the Japanese involvement in residential real estate has been relatively minor to date. The exception is Honolulu, where entire condominium buildings have been sold to Japanese investors, occasionally one floor at a time.

Because of Japan's small size, Japanese home builders have been able to form large, national companies in their own country. The U.S. market is different, however—much larger and much more diverse. Building codes vary from state to state. More than 80 percent of the houses built in the United States are built by builders who construct ten or fewer houses a year. However, the U.S. housing market is moving toward nationalization. The industrialized housing segment of the market is growing. At some point in the not-too-distant future, it is possible that the housing industry will become vulnerable to competition from Japan and its extremely advanced industrialized housing industry.

Like Rodman at Leventhal, Shulman and Jordan also expect increased Japanese investments in U.S. property, reaching $7 billion to $10 billion in 1988, depending on various economic factors.

The most common explanation for the surge in Japanese real estate buying in the United States is the rapid depreciation of the dollar against the yen. As late as 1970, the official exchange rate was 360 yen per dollar. From 285 yen to the dollar in early 1977, the dollar had declined to about 151 yen in October 1986 and 124 yen in early 1988.

This change is significant because it gives the Japanese a strong competitive advantage in purchasing real estate. A Japanese investor who needed 500 million yen to buy a U.S. building in early 1985 needed only 300 million yen at the end of 1986 to buy a building of the same value on the U.S. market, and about 275 million yen in early 1988. Essentially, the United States has been having a real estate sale for Japanese investors, with all properties marked down 30 percent to 60 percent or more.

The huge dollar holdings accumulated by the Japanese in their trade surplus with the United States have to be invested somewhere. By 1986, the Japanese surplus in dollars had reached $86 billion, surpassing the OPEC surpluses of the previous decade. Real estate has been a traditional investment for the Japanese and, given the relative illiquidity of real estate in

Japan, the United States was a natural outlet for some of the wealth accumulated by selling Sony televisions and Toyota cars and thousands of other products.

Prices for Japanese real estate, particularly office buildings in Tokyo, doubled in 1986, driving yields for investors down to 1 percent. The result was that the U.S. market looked even more attractive because yields, even if the Japanese overpay initially, routinely exceed 5 percent per year.

At the same time that these factors have been making U.S. properties more attractive, the Japanese government has eased its restrictions on how much money corporations can invest abroad. Before 1980, foreign investments were prohibited unless approved specifically by Japan's Ministry of Finance. After that date, the ministry began a slow period of relaxation on overseas investments.

For instance, in March 1986, the ministry increased the amount of foreign investment allowed from 10 percent of an insurance company's assets to 25 percent. In August of the same year, the limit was pushed up to 30 percent. That meant that an insurance company with assets of $100 billion could invest $10 billion abroad at the beginning of 1986 and up to $30 billion before the end of the year. This tripling came at a time when the insurance companies themselves were growing richer than ever, largely through appreciation of the yen.

Coupled with these attractions, the Japanese also see the same attributes of political and economic stability that bring other foreign investors into the U.S. real estate market. But no other nation's investors have been able to match the sums paid out by the Japanese in recent years for the choicest office buildings and resorts as they were en route to becoming the most active purchasers of U.S. real estate.

In some cities, the Japanese have already pushed up rents on office buildings as a result of their willingness and ability to pay above-market prices for prime locations.

"A number of buildings have been sold to the Japanese," said Alair Townsend, deputy mayor in charge of business development for New York City. "They can easily outbid a local or domestic investor and, given the exchange rate, they are not paying more. As a result, prices have gone up sharply and unpredictably in many cases, and there has been hell to pay."

The reason is the way commercial real estate leases are structured in New York City. Most of the leases allow the landlord to pass through increases in taxes by raising rents. Since the sale price of a building is used by the city assessor to determine the taxes, tenants never like to see a building sold because it means their rents will soon be going up. When a Japanese investor pays an above-market price, it means the rent will go up that much more.

Townsend said that the problem has not reached the stage of hostilities, but she said many tenants have attempted to negate the impact by trying to get binding rents. The landlords object because that makes a building harder to sell, since it would limit the new owner's ability to raise rents.

The high-priced sales to Japanese investors of even a relatively small number of office buildings in New York and other major cities can also have a ripple effect on many nearby properties uninvolved in the deals. Tax assessors will use those high-priced sales to raise assessed values on neighboring buildings.

For example, Japanese investors have acquired only about 10 percent of the office space in downtown Chicago in recent years. But the prices they have paid for such landmarks as the forty-one-story Prudential Plaza ($140 million by Nissei Realty) and Xerox Center ($50 million by Sumitomo Trust Bank) evoked concern among other building owners that their taxes would be raised as a result. A private consultant was hired to compile a report for the Cook County assessor which concluded that tax assessments should not be based on sale prices of buildings because of the inflation stemming from the Japanese purchases. The argument was rejected.

There is another effect here: the prices paid by Japanese investors are contributing to the tendency of office-building prices to remain high, even though recent overbuilding in many cities dictates that they should be falling or at least remaining stable. The net result is that the supply-demand aspect of the market is bypassed, at least as long as the Japanese are paying premium prices.

There are other justifiable fears of what would happen if the Japanese buyers decide to abandon the U.S. real estate market because of economic reversals here or at home, or because of some other factor that makes it less advantageous for them to be in the United States.

Proponents of foreign investment argue that real estate investments are safe because the buildings cannot be moved if the foreigners decide to leave. But real estate is one of the most volatile, market-sensitive industries in the United States, and a massive retreat by the Japanese would rob the industry of huge amounts of value, even if the buildings themselves remained.

In the early 1980s, the bottom fell out of the market in several major U.S. cities when the Latin American recession forced Latin investors to sell out at low prices. Similarly, the value of property dropped dramatically in Southern California and Texas when the Mexican currency crisis forced Mexican owners to walk away from commercial property or sell their residential investments at huge losses.

These events were precipitated by withdrawals on a far smaller scale than what would happen if the Japanese suddenly began to move out of the U.S. property market. And the potential impact is heightened because the Japanese have so far focused their purchases upon relatively narrow parts of the U.S. real estate market. This would be true even if the Japanese expand to buy property in suburban and secondary cities in the coming years, because they will still be relatively concentrated within the vast U.S. market.

There may be some irony in the ultimate impact of Japanese acquisitions on the real estate sales industry itself. As explained by Komada and evidenced by Mitsubishi's refusal to sell property, the Japanese will buy and hold the choicest U.S. real estate for long periods of time. The lack of turnover may mean that big U.S. institutional investors will be robbed of the opportunity to diversify their portfolios.

Along with ownership of the United States itself, real estate provides a route for the further expansion of Japanese influence on American economic and political policies.

In January 1988, a new organization to promote the interests of foreign investors in the U.S. real estate market was formed in Washington by a coalition of big international investment concerns. Among the founders were Japan's Mitsubishi Trust & Banking Corp., a French bank, and a group of Dutch pension funds.

Called the Association of Foreign Investors in U.S. Real Estate, or AFIRE, the organization said it would engage in both educational and lobbying activities. Its founding statement also said AFIRE "will seek to establish a dialogue between foreign investors and government officials on interests of mutual importance."

Its new chief, a former U.S. ambassador named William Middendorf, sounded a familiar if thinly veiled threat from the start. He said the organizers believe that any concerns about foreign ownership of U.S. land and industry "are unfounded and, if even marginally successful in limiting foreign investment, raise the specter of slower economic growth, fewer jobs and lower real income."

That is an argument that panders to American fears and clouds the dangers of the nation's rising dependence on foreign investment, including real estate.

The folly of that dependence is seen in the relationship between the increasing U.S. real estate purchases by rich Japanese individuals, and major corporations who are using the inflated values of their Tokyo real estate holdings as leverage to expand into the United States. The result is that the American real estate market becomes vulnerable to the house of cards constructed on hyperinflated Tokyo real estate. This is the downside of globalization.

To understand Tokyo real estate, consider a story told by Kenichi Ohmae, director of McKinsey & Company's Tokyo office. A well-known noodle shop in Tokyo's downtown financial district closed in January 1987. According to rumor, the owner had been paid $14 million by a person whose business it is to assemble small bits of real estate into a package large enough to sell. The noodle shop was on a 450-square-foot parcel of land.

Such tales are not restricted to the rumor mills. In a 1988 report, the Japanese government reported that the choicest piece of commercial real estate in central Tokyo was worth $6.7 billion an acre. Residential real estate prices in the capital city rose 68.9 percent in 1987.

These escalating prices are fueling the export of capital to the United States by investors who are leveraging against their real estate holdings in Tokyo.

Property owners, including major corporations and financial institutions as well as rich individuals, borrow money for investments from banks, using real estate as collateral. Because of yields and availability and a host of other reasons cited already, U.S. real estate is an attractive home for the borrowed money.

As real estate prices in Tokyo increase, the property owners borrow more money and invest it again in the United States. Many of those individual and institutional investors also buy U.S. stocks and bonds. In addition, they have pumped huge sums of borrowed money into the Tokyo stock market, accounting for a large part of its stunning rise in recent years.

This works great, as long as property values in Tokyo keep rising. But in an effort to solve its own problems of overcrowding and hyperinflated land prices that are contributing to the most expensive housing situation in the industrialized world, the Japanese government is considering a combination of measures—liberalization of land policy to allow more agricultural land to be used for residential purposes, a ten-year moratorium on the famous "right to sunlight" rule that allows residents to block new development in Tokyo, and dispersement of the government bureaucracy from Tokyo to nearby cities—that could increase the Tokyo land supply threefold. Such an increase, although beneficial to the average worker searching for reasonably priced housing, could be devastating to the wealthy landowner.

When the property values drop, as real estate cycles throughout the world indicate is inevitable, banks might begin calling in loans. To pay the loans, borrowers will be forced to sell property. Given the Japanese attachment to land, it is a sure bet that their foreign holdings—from real estate to stocks—will be sold off first.

19

"I AM HERE TO HELP YOU"

SHIGERU KOBAYASHI WAS ENTERTAINING two Japanese-American businessmen in a nightclub in Tokyo's lively Ginza district, where he is one of the largest landowners. As sometimes happens in the racy bars of the district, Kobayashi was pawing a waitress, who giggled as she tried to serve the men drinks without spilling them.

Suddenly Kobayashi snaked a hand up under the waitress's skirt and, as she tried to back away with a slight scream, he quickly withdrew his hand and held up a trophy to his two companions. Between two fingers he grasped a pubic hair.

Kobayashi, one of the richest men in the world, made a short, impassioned speech about the mystical powers of pubic hair. Then he ceremoniously dropped the hair into the scotch sitting in front of one of the Japanese-Americans, a young lawyer, and stirred the drink with a finger. He then held the glass aloft and demanded of his guest: "Drink that. You will be powerful."

The flustered young lawyer looked at his companion, who provided no clue about how to handle the bizarre experience. The lawyer grabbed the glass, gamely put it to his mouth, and drained it.

The episode, which was related by one of the participants, was pure Kobayashi: arrogant and disdainful of others, particularly Americans. Now in his early sixties, he is still feared by his employees and has a record of driving away top personnel with his petulant outbursts.

Yet, through the real estate firm he founded in 1956, he is also one of the wealthiest landowners in Japan, where his holdings are worth an estimated $8 billion. And the U.S. arm of his company, Shuwa Investments, has acquired more than $2 billion worth of U.S. property and sends home to Tokyo in excess of $200 million each year in rental income.

Increasingly in recent years, the Kobayashi empire has focused its acquisitions on the United States, benefiting from the yen-dollar relationship that has helped all Japanese investors. Exercising the bold, aggressive strokes that marked its origins in Japan, it has been able to establish itself as the Japanese landlord with the most extensive holdings in the United States.

At the same time, Kobayashi has taken steps to secure influence in the United States in order to help protect his expanding realm.

Shortly after the U.S. subsidiary of Shuwa paid $620 million for the twin-towered Arco Plaza in downtown Los Angeles in 1986, Kobayashi came calling on Los Angeles Mayor Tom Bradley. In a demonstration of neighborliness, Kobayashi presented Bradley with a check for $100,000 as the first donation toward a monument to immigrants Bradley is still trying to build.

"When we come over from Tokyo, after a nineteen-hour flight, if when we reach the city we could see a monument like the Statue of Liberty, people would be very happy," Kobayashi said through an interpreter at the ceremony marking the check's presentation.

A few months later—and a few acquisitions later—Kobayashi made a major donation to the Museum of Contemporary Art in Los Angeles. Museum officials refused to specify the size of the donation, except to say that it was "a six-figure amount."

As his power and prominence grow in the United States, it is worthwhile to examine how Shigeru Kobayashi went from being the son of a middle-class furniture manufacturer to one of the richest men in the world, with a personal net worth estimated by *Forbes* magazine at $6 billion.

Kobayashi went to work instead of to college after graduating from high school. After World War II, he persuaded his father to provide him with a financial stake and set up a small ferry operation on Tokyo Bay. The company prospered during the time of the Korean War but collapsed a short time later.

In selling his ferry site in 1956, Kobayashi discovered that the price of the land beneath the structure had shot up during Japan's economic recovery following World War II. He had discovered the means to great wealth, but the problem was how a virtually penniless businessman could acquire more land.

"He recognized the potential of Tokyo real estate and said, 'I can get rich by owning these buildings. How am I going to own these buildings? I want to own Tokyo. If I own it, I am going to be rich,' " a Japanese-American businessman recalled being told by Kobayashi during a long night of drinking in Tokyo.

What confronted the would-be rich man was an important question: "How do I get the money to buy the land? I cannot steal it. The only way I can get the money is to borrow it. Who has it? Japanese banks. I have got to develop relationships with the banks."

Kobayashi then set about systematically identifying the key loan officers, executives, and presidents of Tokyo's banks, which had indeed emerged in postwar Japan as the most powerful private institutions in the country. He developed friendships with these bankers. He found out their birthdays and wedding anniversaries and the birthdays of their wives.

On the morning of a bank executive's birthday, Kobayashi would show up at the banker's house with a big cake and a present. He also employed an intelligence network that told him when a banker was moving. On the day of the move, he would show up at the house with ten or fifteen former workers from his old ferry operation and shout, "I am Kobayashi. I am here to help you."

The earnest building of relationships paid off, because Kobayashi soon found himself with an ample supply of loans from those same banks. He poured the money into real estate, starting with the construction of what are known as "social buildings" in the Ginza district. His first project involved five of these rental buildings, and it was an enormous success.

These structures are narrow, tall buildings that may house an art gallery or a coffee shop on the street level and a collection of colorful bars, restaurants, and nightclubs crammed onto the upper levels. In demonstrating his determination to make a go of it, Kobayashi himself often opened the first bar in the building and hired B-girls to keep the customers happy and help attract tenants.

During this period, he also developed a strategy that he still employs today. He borrowed substantial amounts of money from many banks. Along with minimizing the risk to his own capital, a tactic often employed by opportunistic investors, the practice meant that the banks found themselves with a substantial interest in seeing his projects succeed.

"If I have borrowed a little, they can close me," he explained to the Japanese-American. "If I have borrowed a lot, they can never close me. So I have borrowed from many banks."

Alongside his financial cunning, Kobayashi proved himself to be a visionary in developing real estate in Tokyo. He capitalized on the post–World War II housing shortage in the early 1960s by building the first condominiums in Japan—apartment towers in affluent neighborhoods designed to look like European buildings and topped with blue tiling. The usually cramped, apartment-style quarters were called *manshon* in Japanese, ironically after the English "mansion."

When the demand for these condos slumped after the Tokyo Olympic Games in 1964, Kobayashi smoothly switched to building middle-class condos and taking the unprecedented step of financing the buyers himself. By 1971, he was the biggest landlord in Tokyo.

When the Arabs pushed the price of oil through the roof in 1973 and killed the condo market, Kobayashi again landed on his feet. He sold much of his land, but shifted to building office buildings on his remaining property.

By 1988 the Tokyo-based parent company, Shuwa Corporation, had a staggering portfolio of Tokyo real estate: 56 major office buildings, including the fifteen-story Shuwa Shiba Park Building, which was nicknamed the Warship Building because of its bulky profile, and 139 apartment buildings. "Shuwa" is the first word in each of the buildings.

Kobayashi runs his empire with an iron hand. One Japanese-American who is familiar with how he rose to wealth and has dealt with him extensively described Kobayashi this way: "He spent a lot of time kissing peoples' behinds. Now he wants everybody to kiss his."

Most Japanese office buildings have austere lobbies, even by American standards. But when the name Shuwa appears on the building, there is likely to be an opulent lobby behind the entry doors. None is more elegant than the pale creamy marble floors and exquisite antiques and sculptures that mark the entry to Shuwa Kioicho TBR Building, the sleek structure where the company has its Tokyo headquarters.

The hallway to Kobayashi's office is nearly forty feet long, with a white marble floor and porcelain dogs lining the walls. The dogs get progressively larger as a visitor approaches the inner sanctum. Tucked in a corner of the enormous office is a sound booth for interpreters for the non-Japanese-speaking visitors, who are given headsets to wear. Translations are provided through the headsets.

The same instincts that made him wealthy in Japan took Kobayashi to the United States in 1978. He had seen real estate prices soaring in Japan and wanted to find a new outlet for his construction projects. So Shuwa Investments Corporation was established in Los Angeles to buy and build office buildings and residential projects. The boss installed his young son Takaji Kobayashi as president of the U.S. operation, but insiders have steadfastly maintained that the father makes every decision, regardless of its significance.

"Every day there is a telephone call," his son once said rue-fully. "Sometimes, there are three."

Between 1978 and 1985, Shuwa Investments spent about $25 million building apartments, homes, and office parks throughout California. The ventures were largely unsuccessful because the Japanese lacked the skills to sell them properly in the United

States market. "The Japanese have studied our housing market for years. They are interested in it because of its massive size, but they don't really understand it for the same reason," said Sandy Goodkin, the San Diego consultant. "Unlike the Japanese market, which is really just one national market, the U.S. market is too regionalized, too diversified for the Japanese to compete. They're pragmatic. They will continue to study it until the U.S. market is nationalized."

"We could build this kind of property, but we cannot sell it very well," conceded the younger Kobayashi in a rare interview with Tom Furlong and Nancy Yoshihara of the *Los Angeles Times* in 1987.

The company's fortunes changed dramatically, however, in 1986 when it plunged into the commercial real estate market in a fashion reminiscent of the 1970s buying binge in New York by the Canadian super-developers Olympia & York.

The list of major acquisitions that year by Shuwa would constitute a nice real estate portfolio for a good-sized insurance company. In California, there were 1900 and 1901 Avenue of the Stars, the two most prominent buildings in the affluent Century City area of west Los Angeles; the Hughes Aircraft Building in El Segundo; the former Crocker Bank Center in Irvine; the architecturally distinctive 500 Washington Building in downtown San Francisco; the Xidex Building in Fremont; the Guardian Bank Building in downtown Los Angeles; a few blocks away, the twenty-five-story, $101 million Chase Plaza; and Downey Savings Building in Costa Mesa.

In Boston, Shuwa bought the PaineWebber Building, a granite tower in the heart of the city's financial district. In New York, the company paid $165 million for the ABC Building at 1330 Avenue of the Americas.

The New York acquisition caught the attention of the real estate industry there, because Shuwa clearly overpaid significantly for the building.

When one Manhattan broker was asked how much below Shuwa's $165 million his client had bid, the broker responded, "Why don't you ask me how much below $100 million our bid was?" Another broker said the second highest bid for the building

had been $150 million, and his client had offered $105 million.
"It is not unusual for bids to be off by 5 or 10 percent, but never
any more when all the parties have done their homework," he
said.

But the transaction that put Shuwa on the map in the United
States that year was its $620 million purchase of Arco Plaza, a
downtown Los Angeles building with two fifty-two-story towers
that housed the headquarters for Atlantic Richfield, one of the
nation's largest oil companies, and the Southern California
headquarters of Bank of America, the nation's third largest
banking company.

At the time it was announced, the deal was reported as a record
price for a U.S. office building, and real estate industry insiders
speculated that Shuwa had overpaid by at least $30 million. But
the Japanese company was undaunted by any criticism, and
happily moved its headquarters into its most prominent U.S.
acquisition.

"Shuwa paid a lot more than any domestic investor would
have," Rob McGuire, a prominent Los Angeles developer, told a
reporter at the time. "We've all just been watching their purchases and going, 'Wowie.' "

But the value of the yen in relation to the dollar still made the
purchase a good buy from the Japanese perspective. And the deal
was structured in the style that has become the hallmark of the
elder Kobayashi. Shuwa borrowed $62 million from each of ten
U.S. branches of Japanese banks. The interest rate on the loans
was less than 7 percent, well below what any American borrower
was paying at the time for a big commercial loan.

By the end of 1986, Shuwa had spent $1.6 billion in acquiring
eighteen office buildings from Boston and New York to Los
Angeles and San Francisco. In the visionary fashion of its
founder, the company had also expanded into the secondary
markets surrounding Los Angeles and San Francisco, blazing
the trail for other Japanese investors who are just now beginning
to follow.

The elder Kobayashi was so proud of his accomplishments in
the United States that early in 1987 he ordered the kind of
corporate coming-out advertisement that American companies

sometimes use to trumpet milestones. Full-page ads in major newspapers across the country showed photographs of Arco Plaza and the ABC Building and proclaimed:

"A landmark year. If you followed the Shuwa Group's 1986 acquisitions, stay tuned for future developments."

By the end of 1987, along with spending another $500 million on acquisitions, Shuwa had established another landmark for its countrymen to heed. On the drawing board was the company's first venture in the development of a major U.S. office building— a $650 million development on a full city block in downtown Los Angeles where Shuwa plans to build a hotel, office building, and retail space.

But in late 1987 and 1988 Shuwa encountered some new problems which could foreshadow serious difficulties for its huge real estate portfolio and possibly hint at widespread difficulties for other Japanese investors.

After the stock market crash in October 1987, Shuwa backed away from two agreements to purchase U.S. office buildings in a single week. One of the deals involved two buildings in Chicago, and the other was for a single building in Boston. The total price for the three structures was around $300 million.

"In this environment they didn't want to have empty buildings," said Paul Alanis, a broker involved in the Chicago deal. "They are going to be more cautious."

A few months later, however, long after the stock market had settled down, Shuwa backed out of agreements to buy a $90 million office building in downtown Los Angeles and a $50 million office building in nearby Santa Monica.

"They telephoned up and said they had reworked the numbers and couldn't make the deal work for them," said a broker involved in the downtown Los Angeles transaction. "The documentation had already been ordered and hands had been shaken. And they were just gone."

Shuwa had also underbid significantly on several other office buildings in Los Angeles in recent weeks, causing speculation among real estate industry insiders that the firm was simply making a pretense of being involved when actually it had all but stopped its acquisitions.

A spokesman for Shuwa refused to comment on the dead deals, but he did say that Shuwa faced heavy expenses in providing sprinkler systems and other updating for their Los Angeles buildings.

As 1988 came to a close, however, Shuwa was showing signs of a resurrection. Several American architects were asked to submit proposals to build a new office building on a prime site in downtown Los Angeles acquired by Shuwa. The mandate handed down from the senior Kobayashi was a simple one: design a building eighty-five stories high, the tallest structure in the Western United States.

20
COLONIZING HAWAII

ON THE EVENING OF MARCH 28, 1988, about 150 people gathered in a grade-school gymnasium in a middle-class neighborhood on the outskirts of Honolulu. They were just ordinary people, not great statesmen or brilliant economists.

They had come together that night to debate the problem of foreign investment in its most personal and elementary form. They were scared that they and their children would no longer be able to afford to own homes. They were worried about the quality of life in the face of an unprecedented onslaught of foreign money.

Japanese investment was changing the economic balance in Hawaii, particularly on the island of Oahu, where most of the state's people live and where the state's only large city, Honolulu, is located. After buying up more than half of the hotels on famous Waikiki Beach, dozens of choice office buildings, and numerous oceanfront condominiums, the Japanese had begun moving into the residential neighborhoods of Honolulu and the surrounding area, snapping up home after home.

They started in the affluent neighborhoods overlooking the Pacific Ocean and Diamond Head. The owner of a $1 million house would come home one day and find a formal offer, escrow receipt attached, slipped under the front door for $3 million cash. A 2,000-square-foot, beachfront house with a view of Diamond Head sold for $1 million in 1985, $3.2 million in July 1987. Two months later, a Japanese investor paid $5.9 million for the property.

These were not isolated incidents. In the twelve months before the grade-school meeting, thirty-one waterfront homes had been sold for an average price of $6.3 million to Japanese investors or to speculators hoping to resell them to the Japanese. Homeowners in the nicest neighborhoods had seen the value of their property triple or quadruple almost overnight.

As available homes in the rich neighborhoods grew scarce, the Japanese and their real estate agents had moved inland to the middle-class neighborhoods. And that was what had brought the small businessmen, teachers, and housewives to the auditorium that night.

The speculative nature of the buying binge had driven the average price of a home in Honolulu, already the nation's most expensive residential market, up by one-third in the past year to $227,100. In the ritzy Kahala section, the average price of a single-family home soared 60 percent, rising to $475,800 from $297,000. Great for home sellers, but death for home buyers or people who do not want to sell.

The lightning rod for much of the anger of Hawaii's residents was an ostentatious Japanese billionaire who drove through middle-class neighborhoods in a long, white limousine, buying up houses as he went. Sometimes he did not even bother to get out of the car, simply peering through the smoked-glass window and pointing at properties he liked. His representatives would then add them to the shopping list and go negotiate a price with the owners.

The man's name is Genshiro Kawamoto, and by the spring of 1988 his name was synonymous with the dollar-flush Japanese investment wave that had swept over the islands in the Pacific. His wealth had soared with the prices of land in Tokyo, where he owns a string of hostess bars and nightclubs in high-priced locations.

Using that wealth, between late 1987 and early 1988 Kawamoto bought 160 houses for more than $80 million on the island of Oahu. He boasted to a *Boston Globe* reporter, Tom Ashbrook, that he planned to buy 500 or 1,000 homes in all. He then had the gall to complain about the lack of quality in the housing, telling Ashbrook the homes were poorly built. He called them "lousy candy houses."

All except one. In March 1988, Kawamoto bought the entire estate of the late pioneer industrialist Henry Kaiser for $40 million, the most ever paid for a residential property anywhere in the United States. Actually, Kawamoto had already acquired one of three homes on the estate for $4.5 million. But the extra $40 million brought him two more homes on the 5.5-acre, ocean-front property, complete with pools and tennis courts.

"He has replaced the Ugly American," said Wallace Fujiyama, a respected Japanese-American lawyer in Honolulu who was as disturbed by the behavior of Kawamoto and some other Japanese investors as he was by what he perceived to be an unfair overreaction to Japanese investment overall by the state's residents.

For the 150 or so middle-class residents gathered at the grade school that evening in March 1988, however, Kawamoto symbolized a threat to their way of life with his acquisitions in their neighborhood. Even those who had no intention of selling out knew they were going to feel the impact of the Japanese residential buying spree.

As in most places in the United States, the value of a house for tax purposes in Honolulu is based in part on the value of other property in the same neighborhood. This meant that the hyper-inflated prices paid by the Japanese would send the values of neighboring homes skyrocketing once they worked their way through the tax assessment process.

The 1987 prices would be reflected in tax bills in 1989, and the people at the grade school were well aware of the bombshells awaiting them and of the potential impact on the quality of life for years to come of the virtual colonization of their island paradise.

"Will my children be able to live here in the year 2000 and will I be able to live here in the year 2000?" Annetta Kinnicutt, a local homeowner and one of the meeting organizers, asked the crowd. "Will I want to live here in the year 2000?"

Kinnicut said she had lived in Japan for five years, and she cautioned against Japan bashing. But she added forcefully, "This is my land and I intend to stay here."

Ray Sweeney, sales manager for a local radio station, was more direct: "Don't be so timid about Japan bashing. Let's get their attention."

Getting their attention is precisely what had been done a week before by a man who arrived at the meeting forty-five minutes late but to great applause. Honolulu Mayor Frank Fasi created an international stir when he asked the state legislature in March 1988 to stop foreign investors from buying residential and agricultural land in Hawaii.

"It's your children and grandchildren who won't be able to buy a home here," Fasi warned the audience. "This is the tip of the iceberg."

Fasi's proposal to restrict foreign investments in Hawaii had evoked strong reactions on both sides of the emotion-charged issue. The state's lieutenant governor had accused the mayor of Japan bashing, and others were alarmed that Fasi and the homeowners would anger the Japanese and create a backlash that would result in Japanese tourists staying home or going to Australia.

Tourism is the major industry in Hawaii, and by the 1980s the islands had become so dependent on Japan that a significant reduction in visitors from there would send the islands' economy into a tailspin.

"There is a danger," David Ramsour, chief economist for the Bank of Hawaii, cautioned a visitor over lunch a few weeks after Fasi's legislation was proposed. "We may not see the investors leave, but the visitors will leave if they feel unwelcome. And we are vulnerable to a downturn in tourism, just as Texas was vulnerable to energy prices. We have a lot of eggs in one basket."

The concern was echoed by Jim Ohlman as he drove through the upscale residential subdivision called Hawaii Loa Ridge that he was developing on a hill overlooking the ocean.

With lots priced from $350,000 to $1.85 million, there had

been many months in the past seven years when he sold only one lot. An earlier developer had gone bankrupt trying to finish the project. But since Japanese investors had discovered the project the year before, business had picked up dramatically. In just three weeks during February 1988, Ohlman had sold 112 lots— an entire phase of the project and some leftovers from three earlier phases. Ohlman's total sales for the month were $22 million.

One Japanese investor had watched patiently during those three weeks as the properties were being gobbled up. One day he approached Ohlman and said he would take the remainder of the lots. Hawaiian law requires a real estate purchaser to actually see the land, so they climbed into Ohlman's BMW and toured the lots in less than fifteen minutes before signing contracts for the remaining eight lots. The investor wrote out a check for $2 million as earnest money on the properties.

Japanese buyers had stopped surprising Ohlman on the day a few weeks earlier when he got a telephone call from a U.S. Customs Service agent at the Honolulu airport.

"There's a guy here with $400,000 in greenbacks," the customs agent told Ohlman on the phone. "He says it's money he owes you for some land."

The "guy" was a Japanese investor who had bought the four most expensive lots in the development, and he was to provide $400,000 in earnest money on the lots within thirty days. Ohlman raced to the airport, vouched for his investor, and drove him straight to a bank. At the bank, employees took the investor down to the vault and counted the money.

"When I said that it was a 'cash deal,' " Ohlman said, "he thought I literally meant greenbacks."

Yet Ohlman said his worries over Japanese reaction to the mayor's proposal extended beyond the threat of eliminating the investors who were finally making his project successful.

"Fasi's freeze is being disguised as anti-speculator when it is really anti-Japanese," said Ohlman. "That's dangerous because the Japanese are very sensitive. If they perceive that the *aloha* is gone, it won't be just real estate that suffers, but tourism, too. The hotels, the shops, everything."

Yet critics and supporters alike recognized that Fasi, a seasoned political pro, had tapped a provocative issue in a year when he was running hard for reelection. And there was precedent for the dapper mayor's proposal, although not in any place that had nearly the level of foreign investment as Hawaii.

At least three states, Mississippi, Nebraska, and Oklahoma, already prohibit land ownership by nonresident foreigners. Wisconsin limits foreign ownership to 640 acres, and Minnesota bars ownership of farmland by foreigners.

Whether or not Fasi's proposal represented the best course of action, he had gotten the attention of the Japanese and helped provide a forum for airing genuine concerns over the long-term desirability of the incredible concentration of Japanese investment in Hawaii.

It is a debate that is important to all Americans because it is destined to be repeated countless times on the mainland as the level of Japanese investment increases in cities such as Los Angeles, Atlanta, San Diego, Chicago, Boston, and even New York City.

"The rest of the United States must look closely at what is happening here," said Honolulu attorney Anthony Locricchio. "Because it is eventually going to spread."

Bruce Stark, a developer in Hawaii working with the Japanese on major projects in the islands and on the mainland, said: "My prediction is that the present investment in Hawaii will continue elsewhere. They have just chosen Hawaii as a launchpad."

Already, there are signs that the impact has reached the mainland. Recent studies by the Bank of America in San Francisco and by Salomon Brothers, the New York investment house, say that Japanese investment has spread from the city centers to suburban areas. And the Los Angeles metropolitan area has experienced a strong surge in residential buying by Japanese investors as well as by people from other Asian nations.

"The closest play to Japan was Hawaii," said Jon Douglas, a Beverly Hills, California, real estate agent, in the summer of 1988. "Los Angeles is the next closest."

Backers of foreign investment in real estate—who often tend to be those who are profiting from it—love to defend the purchases by pointing out that it is impossible to remove the assets from the country and that no sensitive technology changes hands. These supporters are correct when they argue that most tenants do not care who owns the building, although even that argument is weakened by the increased rents being passed through as a result of the premium prices paid by the Japanese.

But what Hawaii demonstrates is that investment in real estate, when it is as concentrated as Japanese investment has been in the islands, does pose a threat to stability. Right now, Hawaii is a petri dish where the dangers of Japanese investment in real estate are festering. The rest of the nation should watch as the culture grows, to see what protective measures may become necessary.

Hawaii has had a long, profitable, and sometimes rocky history of involvement with foreign investors. In the 1820s and 1830s, when the islands were on their way to becoming a truck stop for trans-Pacific trade, the first foreigner to establish a business there was an American named James Hunnewell, who opened a trading store in Honolulu in 1826. Over the years, other Americans as well as British, German, and Dutch businessmen set up shop in Hawaii.

The capital provided by the foreign investors was essential to developing the agricultural resources of Hawaii, and it financed the first sugar plantations in the 1830s. By the end of the century, sugar was Hawaii's main industry, and foreigners owned the plantations and most of the commercial trading houses set up to ship the sugar and other exports abroad.

The United States annexed Hawaii as a territory in 1898, and Americans were thereby removed from the category of foreign investors, although mainland money is still considered foreign by many island residents.

The first recorded major Japanese investment in Hawaii came in 1892 when a Yokohama bank was started in Honolulu to serve the growing number of Japanese workers employed in the agriculture industry. Sumitomo Bank followed with an office in 1916. Some Japanese merchants followed the banks and workers, but their presence was small before World War II.

After the attack on Honolulu's Pearl Harbor on December 7, 1941, the Japanese businesses in the islands were seized by the government. Foreign investment in Hawaii dropped off in the decade after World War II, as the nations that had once invested there—Britain, Japan, and Germany particularly—devoted their resources to rebuilding their own countries.

The Japanese were the first to return. In October 1959, Shirokiya, the department store subsidiary of Tokyo Corp., opened a $1 million store in Honolulu. That was the same year Hawaii was granted statehood.

At the time, Hawaii was actively seeking new capital, and the Japanese investment was welcomed. In 1961 the state legislature passed a foreign-lenders law that said, in part: "The capital needs of the economy of the State have grown to such an extent that available local capital is insufficient to meet those needs. Among the consequences of the inability of Hawaii to meet its capital requirements out of its own local funds has been a shortage of mortgage funds for home and commercial financing."

Two years later, a Japanese developer named Kenji Osana bought two hotels on Waikiki Beach. Over the next few years Osano bought several additional hotels in Honolulu, and for many years he was the largest foreign investor in Hawaii. His countrymen were slow to follow, partly because the Japanese government kept a tight rein on investments abroad by the Japanese in order to insure sufficient capital for rebuilding the country's domestic industries and housing.

The Japanese binge started in 1971, when the country's rebuilt economy was growing at a rate of 10 percent a year and Japan had $20 billion in reserves from its foreign trade surplus. At the same time, the government in Tokyo eased restrictions on foreign investment.

Within two years, the Japanese spent $280 million on Hawaiian hotels, restaurants, golf courses, land, and shops. The investments coincided with a dramatic growth in Japanese tourism to the islands. The Japanese government and businesses wanted to make sure that the money stayed in the family. So the Japanese tourists would fly to Honolulu aboard a Japanese airline, stay at a Japanese-owned hotel, eat at a Japanese-owned restaurant, and shop at a Japanese-owned store. It was a pattern that would be repeated in the next decade by Japan's industrial investors.

The Japanese acquisitions created a wave of criticism among local residents in Hawaii. In complaints that would be echoed in Hawaii and elsewhere throughout the United States more than a decade later, the residents criticized the Japanese for buying too many hotels, driving up real estate prices, hiring too many Japanese nationals, and threatening to take control of the state's economy.

Rather than stimulating new jobs and a more diverse economy, the Japanese were threatening the economic stability of the islands and pushing the limits of one of the most tolerant, easygoing cultures in the United States.

On December 27, 1973, a U.S. Senate subcommittee on foreign commerce and tourism held a hearing in Honolulu on the controversy surrounding foreign investment. The chief concern of the American public in those days was the escalating investment of Arab petrodollars in the United States. But the chairman of the subcommittee was also worried about the extensive Japanese investment in Hawaii. The chairman was Senator Daniel Inouye, a Democrat who had served with distinction earlier that year on the Senate committee investigating the Watergate scandal.

Inouye had expressed his own concern over the practice of the Japanese to keep their tourist dollars within Japanese-owned businesses. And Inouye was concerned about the limited knowledge Americans had of the full effects and extent of foreign investment.

At the hearing, Hawaii Governor George Ariyoshi acknowledged the fears and suspicions in the islands. However, he praised foreign investment as a vital ingredient in the state's economy. What Hawaii wanted, he said, was long-term foreign investment that would help create jobs and diversify the economy. What the state did not want or need, he said, was short-term speculative investments, adding, "This applies to businessmen from our own U.S. mainland as well as those from elsewhere."

The public reaction chastened the Japanese, and the skyrocketing price of oil as a result of the Arab embargo trimmed Japan's financial sails, too. So they cut back on their purchases in Hawaii for several years.

When they resumed in the 1980s, the Japanese were more dollar-rich than ever. The character of their investments had changed little from the type of speculative purchases that had angered Hawaiians a decade before. They were buying hotels, golf courses, and blocks of the best office space. And they had added single-family housing to their shopping list, turning entire condominium projects and residential neighborhoods into Japanese ghettoes. It was the money that was different—the Japanese had more of it than ever before.

Instead of providing fresh capital for such economy boosters as home mortgages, the role the state legislature had foreseen for foreign investment in 1961, the Japanese were buying the houses themselves. Rather than investing in projects to contribute to the diversification of the economy and stimulate new jobs, the Japanese were concentrating on existing projects and sending the profits back home.

By 1986, the Japanese owned one out of every four hotel rooms in Hawaii. The following year, the ratio increased to one out of two, and plans were on the drawing board for enormous new projects that combined resorts with residential and retail areas.

In 1987 Japanese investors bought four out of every ten condominiums sold on Waikiki Beach and three out of every ten homes sold in the posh Kahala neighborhood, according to a survey by a local real estate company called Locations.

Tracking down the extent of Japanese investment in Hawaii is as difficult as it is anywhere else in the United States. In addition to the lack of reliable figures from the federal government, the state monitoring process is basically nonexistent because of fears of angering foreign investors.

Even the definition of "foreign" is muddied. For instance, a corporation is considered foreign in Hawaii if it was organized outside the state border. Yet a corporation created by foreigners or mainlanders is considered domestic if formed in Hawaii.

As a result, estimates of the extent of Japanese investment in Hawaiian real estate in recent years are all over the ballpark. The state's Department of Business and Economic Development said the Japanese invested $1.7 billion during 1985, 1986, and half of 1987. Yet *Forbes* magazine estimated that the Japanese had invested $6.5 billion in Hawaii in 1986 and 1987 alone. A study by Kenneth Leventhal & Company, the Los Angeles accounting and consulting firm, put the Japanese real estate investments in Hawaii at $7.2 billion from 1985 through 1987.

It was the greatest concentration of Japanese money in the United States, according to the Leventhal study. And the potential impact on the Hawaiian economy dwarfed the leverage of Japan's investments of $7 billion in California and $5.8 billion in New York—both far larger and more diverse economies.

In testimony before the Honolulu City Council on April 15, 1988, Gregory Pai, the chief economist for First Hawaiian Bank, noted the discrepancy between the state figures and the Leventhal numbers. He said the government agencies faced "an appalling lack of credibility as to the actual extent and penetration of Japanese investment in Hawaii" which created enormous problems in formulating an effective strategy for dealing with Japanese investment.

"And," he added, "if any credence is to be given to the Leventhal estimate, then the problem may be far larger than we had thought."

The state's numbers simply are not to be believed, and even if *Forbes* and Leventhal have overshot the mark by a billion or so, the trend is clear: Hawaii is on the verge of becoming a colony of Japan, with its major industry—tourism—dependent on the Japanese and with the value of its real estate linked to the price of land or the well-being of the stock market in Tokyo.

Here in Hawaii, East has met West, and the result has been the shackling of the local economy to events a six-hour plane ride away.

As an example of the new dependency on Japan, consider the case of a privately held Tokyo company called Azabu Group. The company spent $565 million in Hawaii to buy six hotels, a shopping center, and land for a golf course between mid-1986 and the end of 1987. The company earns its money from real estate development and imported-car sales in Japan. The $565 million spent acquiring property in Hawaii came from loans collateralized by the inflated value of its Tokyo real estate holdings.

Thus, if the price of land in Tokyo plummets, as real estate cycles indicate it someday must, the Azabu Group may be forced to dump its highly leveraged Hawaiian holdings to pay off the loans. And if this scenario were repeated among many other major Japanese investors, the bottom would fall out of the real estate market and land values would be in the dumper.

But it is within the tourist industry that the greatest peril to the Hawaiian economy exists. The extensive Japanese purchases of hotel and resort properties, coupled with the rising number of Japanese tourists, makes the leading industry in Hawaii a hostage to economic events in Tokyo.

Along Waikiki Beach in Honolulu, the most popular tourist location in Hawaii, the Japanese own more than half the hotels. Throughout the islands, they control more than one-third of the hotel rooms. Most of those hotels were bought between 1986 and 1988 at premium prices, and the results demonstrate quite clearly the dynamics of such acquisitions.

"The recent spate of purchases of existing hotels at above-market prices creates no new net economic activity and has contributed to cost cutting, higher prices, and greater potential volatility in the visitor industry," First Hawaiian Bank's Gregory Pai said in the spring of 1988.

At the same time, the number of Japanese tourists has shot up nearly fourfold in the past fifteen years. The more than 1 million Japanese who visited the islands in 1988 accounted for nearly 20 percent of the total tourists. And the Japanese stayed longer and spent more than tourists from elsewhere did.

Travel and leisure activities have become increasingly important in Japan, and that is one reason behind the drive by Japanese companies to acquire resort and hotel properties in Hawaii at almost any cost.

In April 1987, Kokusai Motorcars Company, a taxi operator in Tokyo, bought the Hyatt Regency Maui for $319 million. The price was the highest total ever paid for a U.S. hotel at the time. Less than a year later, Japan's Seibu Railway paid $310 million for one of the state's most prestigious resorts, the Westin Mauna

Kea on the big island of Hawaii. The price of $1 million per room for the 310-room hotel topped the previous per-room price by 40 percent. The previous record was $710,000 per room, paid by the Sultan of Brunei for the Beverly Hills Hotel in late 1987.

Forbes magazine quoted industry sources as saying the only way Seibu can make money on its "million-dollar rooms" is by charging a minimum of $500 a night. The price range in 1989 was from $220 to $481 per room, depending on the season.

By mid-1988, the Japanese also owned eighteen of the forty-seven golf courses in Hawaii. Given the staggering cost of a golf club membership in Japan, which can run as high as $3 million, these acquisitions stirred concern among Hawaiians that the cost of golfing would go the same route as housing prices—up, up, up. Along with freezing out middle-class Hawaiians, that trend would damage the tourist appeal of the islands. Those concerns have been fueled by the fact that some of the Japanese-owned courses are closed to Americans.

Another cause of worry is the use of agricultural land for new resort and golf course developments by the Japanese, a trend that adds to the reliance on tourism by undercutting the agriculture industry.

The two concerns—exclusion of Americans and misuse of land—came together in 1988 when it was disclosed that a Japanese company, Minami Group (USA), was developing a $60 million golf course on conservation land on Oahu and would not allow the public to play on the course for at least the first year it was open.

Through the assistance of Wallace Fujiyama, the Japanese-American attorney, the company had received state approval to build what the lawyer described as "the finest golf course in the state of Hawaii and maybe the country" on land that had been set aside for conservation.

The permit for the course, issued by the state Board of Land and Natural Resources, said: "Within one year after the opening of the club facility, the applicant shall complete a study to assess both the need for public play and the economic feasibility for some form of limited public play at that facility."

In other words, it was left up to the Japanese developer to

decide, at the end of one year, whether it would be sound economics to allow the public to play on a course being built on land that was previously set aside as open space.

Just as they find golf a bargain in Hawaii, the cash-rich Japanese can afford to pay the higher room prices that the Japanese hotel owners are charging to pay off the premium prices they paid for the properties. But the prices for hotels and restrictions on golf threaten to drive away tourists from the U.S. mainland, who still account for better than 60 percent of Hawaii's visitors. If that happens, the result will be an increasing dependence on tourism from Japan.

The Japanese have countered that their projects create new jobs, and to a degree they are correct. However, once construction is completed, even the new projects are concentrated in the tourist industry.

One example most often cited by the defenders of Japanese investment is a $3 billion project under way on 642 acres of vacant land fronting on two miles of ocean beach. Once completed in the mid-1990s, the development, called Ko Olina, will have eight hotels with a total of 4,000 rooms, 5,200 condominiums and townhouses, a 450-slip marina, an eighteen-acre shopping center, four man-made lagoons, and a championship golf course.

It is the most ambitious project ever undertaken in the islands. Its developers envision Ko Olina as an upscale version of Waikiki, with room rates already projected at $300 a night. Not a bad price for the Japanese visitors, but a bit stiff for most American visitors.

The $3 billion venture is being developed jointly by Herbert Horita, one of Hawaii's most successful home builders, and two Japanese companies—the giant Japanese construction firm Kumagai Gumi and TSA International, a small development firm owned by Japanese entrepreneur Takeshi Sekiguchi. Horita will provide most of the management for the project and hold a 40 percent interest. The two Japanese companies will provide the financing and share the remaining 60 percent.

Kumagai Gumi and TSA already have spent $700 million developing the Westin Maui and Westin Kauai hotels and the Hyatt Regency Waikoloa Hotel under construction in 1988 on the big island of Hawaii. But it is through the Ko Olina project that the two partners appear destined to have their greatest impact on Hawaii.

As described by Bill Blaisdell, one of the planners, Ko Olina will provide a mini-job boom all of its own for the Hawaiian construction industry. The development agreement calls for all subcontracting to be done by local companies, and the construction work will be spread out over several years, which should mean steady jobs for local workers.

And once the construction is completed, Ko Olina projections foresee 5,000 new jobs in the complex and another 10,000 or so jobs generated indirectly. In addition, the resort is providing a major boost to the prospects of a long-dormant plan to build a totally new city on several hundred acres of land once part of the island's largest sugar plantations.

More than any other Japanese investment in the islands, Ko Olina holds out the promise of performing one of the tasks sought from foreign capital by the state's leaders for more than a century—creating new jobs.

But some local developers complain that the Japanese, with their access to seemingly limitless funds, are monopolizing the choice development projects and relegating domestic companies to subcontracting roles.

"Every piece of prime real estate has gone," said Jerry Kremkow, a Honolulu developer. "The Japanese own it. You can't even bid because they get there first and they have the capital to do it out of pocket. They don't have to go to the bank like the rest of us."

There are also concerns that the project will increase dramatically the level of Japanese ownership within the tourism industry, and with that will come an increasing dependence on Japan. Further, rather than using capital to diversify the Hawaiian economy, the Japanese purchases have emphasized tourism and increased the state's economic reliance on that single industry.

"You don't know how reliable these people are as owners," said Bill Wood, the editor of *Hawaii Investor* magazine, the state's most authoritative business publication. "What will happen if there is a serious drop in the Japanese economy? It's all a little like whistling in the graveyard. You simply don't know."

21
ASSAULT ON
HOLLYWOOD

FOR EIGHT DAYS IN FEBRUARY 1988, the elegant Beverly Hilton Hotel in Beverly Hills, California, was transformed into an international film bazaar. More than 200 of the hotel's rooms were converted into mini-screening rooms, with the beds moved out and chairs and projection equipment moved in. Nearby movie houses were pressed into service to show the most prominent of the new releases.

In all, about 500 films were shown for prospective buyers from around the world at the annual American Film Market, Hollywood's yearly exposition of its products and the largest international marketplace for independent, English-language films.

In addition to buyers from many American distribution companies, representatives from fifty-five foreign countries were also present. Japan sent ninety-seven buyers, the most by far of any foreign country, and 1988 was the second year in a row that Japanese buyers have outnumbered all others when it comes to foreign purchases of American films. Among the Japanese who circulated among the viewing rooms at the Beverly Hilton were representatives of such giant trading companies as Mitsubishi and Mitsui, along with the nation's entertainment-related companies, such as Tokyo Broadcasting Systems and NHK, which already airs the most popular U.S. television show in Japan, "Little House on the Prairie."

"Japan is the largest market for American movies outside of America," said Timothy Kittleson, executive director of the American Film Marketing Association, the collection of independent film producers that sponsored the event. "That has been true for the last five or six years. Japan has an insatiable appetite, certainly for blockbuster films, but also for films that died on the vine in the United States. It is what you see happening in the whole Pacific Rim."

In this era of American trade deficits, the U.S. entertainment industry was the second most successful export in 1987, topped only by the aerospace industry. Films, television shows, videocassettes, and musical records and tapes produced a trade surplus of almost $5 billion. Videocassettes led the way with an export surplus of $1.8 billion, followed by movies at $1.2 billion, recordings and tapes at $1.4 billion, and television programs at $500 million.

"One thing we still do really well in the United States is make movies," said Kittleson.

Indeed, despite the objections from intellectuals and cultural figures in some foreign countries, people around the world simply cannot seem to get enough of American entertainment. "Little House on the Prairie" is broadcast in 110 countries, "Dallas" in 97 countries, and "Love Boat" in 86 countries. Revenue from television exports was expected to top $600 million in 1988.

Japan is Hollywood's biggest customer for movies, followed by France, West Germany, Canada, and Britain. In most foreign countries, U.S. films have at least half of the local market.

These products—movies, TV shows, videos, and recordings— are referred to within the industry as the "software," in contrast to the "hardware," which is composed of VCRs and televisions and such. In the hardware category, the U.S. ran a $2.6 billion deficit, mostly with Japan, in 1987.

But the software more than made up the difference, and ana-

lysts project that the entertainment industry is on the verge of
great growth as a result of the growth of television in developing
countries and expansions in established nations, creating bigger
and bigger markets for American programs. The most optimistic
analysts and industry executives predict that foreign revenues
soon will top domestic revenues for the television industry.

The proliferation of direct-broadcast cable and satellite-based
channels has multiplied demand for television programming in
Europe and Japan. France has gone from three television networks to five, and the government turned one of its channels
private. France also has created Europe's first pay-cable service,
and the three-year-old system, Canal Plus, had 2.5 million homes
signed up by late 1988.

Britain plans to have two direct-broadcast satellites in service
sometime in 1989. One of them will be launched by media
magnate Rupert Murdoch, whose satellite will double the number of commercial TV channels in England to eight from four.
The other satellite, from British Satellite Broadcasting, has a
first-year budget of $30 million for buying movie rights, and at
least half of the money is earmarked for American films.

In Japan, two new satellite-based channels are scheduled to
begin broadcasting in 1989. They will be added to the nation's
five private television stations, which are attracting record audi-
ences.

There is no way that Japanese producers—or those in Europe
either—can provide enough programming to fill all the time
slots. The problem is particularly pressing in Japan, where
viewers, accustomed only to original programs, will not tolerate
reruns.

So these new broadcasters must turn to the most popular
entertainment medium in the world, American movies and
television shows. And the Japanese businessmen eyeing Hollywood are keenly aware of the profit potential down the road if
they can buy a piece of the place that will be supplying that new
programming.

For instance, Lorimar Telepictures was unable to sell its
nighttime soap series "Knots Landing" in France in 1986. In
1988, the company sold the complete series of more than 200

episodes to TF 1, the recently privatized French channel, for $11 million—about $55,000 per episode.

Prices like that were behind the acquisition of Mary Tyler Moore's MTM Entertainment for $320 million in 1988 by Television South, a British commercial station, and Canal Plus, the new French pay channel.

Perhaps the surprise is that the Japanese have been slow to react. But that reflects their natural caution and the sharp cultural differences between the Japanese and the American entertainment industry.

But it is no surprise that Japanese buyers have been turning up in droves in Hollywood at the American Film Market and smaller gatherings. And while the talk among the movie moguls at the February 1988 film fair in Beverly Hills was dominated by sales of foreign rights, the background discussion in the bars and restaurants centered on rumors that the Japanese were interested in buying a major studio.

"All the big trading companies, as well as the networks, are interested in creating, producing and holding film properties," explained Yasuhiro Kuno, the president of Viacom Japan, a subsidiary of the New York–based entertainment company Viacom International. "It's being driven by the rising yen and a lack of good-quality movies for TV."

Yasuyoshi Tokuma, chairman of a Japanese investment group in Los Angeles, told a gathering of film industry executives in Las Vegas in September 1988 that the Japanese are interested in backing any type of films. He said the Japanese know "that to be international, they have to come to Hollywood."

Toward that end, Fujisankei Communications, Japan's largest mass communications company, agreed in late 1988 to provide a chunk of the financing for a joint venture agreement between British producer David Puttnam and Warner Brothers. In exchange for contributing an undisclosed amount to a $50 million fund to finance films, Fujisankei gets video and television distribution rights in Japan. A British satellite broadcasting company also contributed to the fund in exchange for British satellite television rights.

Rather than purchasing the foreign rights for films and television programs that have already been produced in the United States, the Japanese are eyeing the possibility of acquiring the production facilities themselves. More than a dozen Japanese companies have established entertainment offices in Los Angeles and New York, and their investment bankers have been exploring possible acquisitions of such major American studios as MGM and the troubled MCA's Universal Pictures unit.

"It's about to take off," predicted Lisbeth Barron, an entertainment industry specialist at a New York securities firm. "No serious bids have been made yet, but names like Sony keep coming up whenever a studio comes up for sale."

John Olds, an analyst at the Carmel, California, investment firm of Paul Kagan Associates, Inc., agrees, saying: "There will be some acquisitions by the Japanese. Do I want to put a dollar amount on it? No. How soon will it happen? I don't know."

While the British and French are also casting about for a major purchase in Hollywood, a big studio such as Columbia or Universal will cost $3 billion or more. That kind of money makes the Japanese the most likely buyers.

Kenji Kitatani, a professor of telecommunications at Indiana University and a consultant to many Japanese telecommunications and entertainment companies, foresees Japanese investors acquiring Hollywood studios in much the same fashion that they have bought premier office buildings and resorts in the United States.

"The next wave," Kitatani called it. "The entertainment area is the last area in which Japanese companies could start pouring money. They have done, of course, a very careful study and survey of contemporary Hollywood. The study concluded that it is not as risky as before."

According to Kitatani, one reason the Japanese have decided the film industry is less risky is the burgeoning revenue from foreign sales and videocassette rights. Hefty proceeds in these areas can easily make a winner out of a film that loses money in the American market.

In addition, Kitatani said, the need for more programming to supply the growing Japanese television system means that the Japanese will be competing among themselves to buy American movies and television shows. The competition would force the prices higher and leave the Japanese open to manipulation by the American distributors.

"So instead of simply spending money to buy programs, they thought it would be better to feed the money for investments in software so they not only have software produced for them but an equity position in whatever is produced," he explained. "There is a very natural evolution of thinking here."

So natural that it fits the pattern the Japanese have followed in gaining a foothold in other industries, whether it is tourism in Hawaii, investment banking in New York, or auto parts suppliers in the Midwest. If they are going to have to spend money on American programming to fill up new television channels at home, they want to get in on the profits that will be generated at the production end and share in the anticipated revenues from burgeoning sales around the world. Equally importantly, they do not want to leave themselves vulnerable to suppliers from outside the family.

Kitatani said the prospective Japanese investors also were encouraged to find that most executives in the major studios are lawyers or MBAs who speak the same language they do when it comes to the bottom line. "They found out it was not producer types or artist types running things, but rather people with legal and financial knowledge," he said.

Still, Hollywood is far different from Detroit. The film and television industries are peculiarly American institutions, and tampering with the creative process through the introduction of Japanese management methods would be doomed to failure. So the Japanese have proceeded cautiously in their forays into the entertainment industry.

The biggest acquisition so far has been Sony's $2 billion purchase of the CBS Records division in 1988. One reason that deal came first was the recognition at Sony that records are the sort of hard goods that do not require enormous risks and allow the Japanese to leave the existing management in place for handling the artists. The transaction also was done at a time when the yen was strongest, making the price easier for Sony to swallow.

The acquisition also fits into Sony's long-range plans for developing new lines of consumer stereos and dovetailing CBS production with its advances to assure a steady supply of software. One area under development is laser-disc compact disc players that combine music and videos. Owning CBS would ensure a source of software and make certain Sony does not repeat the disaster that resulted from its development of VCRs that played Beta movies when the industry was turning out VHS movies.

Sony also has seen its profit margins getting thinner from televisions, VCRs, and other entertainment hardware as a result of competition from Korea and Taiwan. Moving into the software side of the entertainment business represents a means for developing a new profit center. And the acquisition of CBS Records provided Sony with an invaluable international distribution system that can be readily expanded to additional entertainment software.

A fascinating examination of the motivations behind CBS and Sony was provided by Peter J. Boyer in an article in the *New York Times Sunday Magazine*. Boyer, one of the newspaper's television reporters, explained that Laurence A. Tisch, the investor who had become president and chief executive of CBS, wanted to amass a stockpile of cash while Sony's founder and chairman, Akio Morita, was looking for a deal that would merge hardware and software in a fashion destined to pay off for decades to come.

"Stock management on one side, company management on the other," wrote Boyer.

"Twenty years from now, history will prove us right," said Morita of the deal that made his company the new home of such recording stars as Michael Jackson, Billy Joel, Bruce Springsteen, Cyndi Lauper, and Barbra Streisand as well as a repository of invaluable old recordings.

Sony's appetite goes beyond CBS Records. The electronics giant was part of a consortium of Japanese companies that conducted a formal study of MGM/UA in the spring of 1988 to determine whether or not to purchase the studio created from two legendary Hollywood names.

"We are interested," says Michael Schulhof, an executive of

Sony of America. "Worldwide, we have a 25 percent market share in audio hardware, a 20 percent share in video hardware. Thanks to CBS we now have 24 percent of audio software. We need the fourth leg of the chair, a video software producer."

Investing in movie production, either in individual pictures or by acquiring an entire studio, is a much riskier venture than buying a major recording label. The stakes are higher because a film costs far more to develop—an average of $30 million at a major studio, $17 million at an independent studio. And conflicts between commercial interests and creative ones occur more frequently, creating more potential pitfalls for the Japanese owners or investors.

So far, the most active investing in the movie industry has come from a consortium of three big Japanese companies—C. Itoh, the giant trading company; Suntory, the nation's largest brewer; and Tokyo Broadcasting Systems. They formed a joint venture called CST Communications in July 1987 after spending a year and a half studying the feasibility of a major investment in Hollywood. CST opened a small office in Hollywood and signed a deal with MGM/UA Communications, the successor company to Metro-Goldwyn-Mayer and United Artists, to invest $5 million in each of three pictures produced by the studio.

The first two pictures, Whoopi Goldberg's *Fatal Beauty* and Michael J. Fox's *Bright Lights, Big City*, were commercial failures. The third film is *Last Rites* starring Tom Berenger, released in late 1988. Unless *Last Rites* is a blockbuster, the Japanese will not get their investments back on any of the three films. But they knew that going in.

The amounts were piddling compared with the vast resources of the companies. The investments amounted to little more than tuition to get a lesson in how Hollywood works. It is part of the long-term view that marks the strategies of every Japanese company.

What CST learned was that, since very few movies turn into hits and far fewer are blockbusters, the current structure offers the investor little hope of recouping his money at the box office or even through the complicated system of allocating revenue from other rights constructed by the studios.

"The manner in which Hollywood structures deals has gone on a long time and studios can't afford to change it," said Barron, the analyst. "The one way they have to recoup their losses [on a picture] is manipulating the accounting so that by the time it trickles down to the investors, there is little money there. Many investors don't understand the accounting. But they invest to be able to go to a cocktail party and talk about it. That alone is worth it to them. If it's a hit, they'll be rich, like playing the lottery."

Some wealthy Japanese individuals will invest in the movies for those reasons, just as rich Americans do. But the three big Japanese businesses behind CST are interested in far more than bragging rights over a sip of sake.

"We are not willing to gamble," said Toshihiro Nagayama as he sat in CST's nondescript office with a view of the famous "Hollywood" sign in the hills above Los Angeles. "Responsible companies can't use company money for Las Vegas–style investments. We are waiting to renegotiate with MGM. We were not happy with the first deal. At the moment, we feel the deal we made was very favorable for the studio side. But I am not sure we can recoup our investment, much less get a profit."

Nagayama declined to say how much money CST has at its disposal, but he said the joint venture wants to continue investing in Hollywood. However, he said the company will not participate in deals structured to provide all the advantages to the studios.

"We'd like to change the structures," he said. "Deals must be more favorable to the investor because without his money no one can produce pictures. Money goes where it can expect profit."

That last sentence reveals the clout that the new wave of Japanese investment will be bringing to Hollywood. With the exception of the immensely successful film efforts at Walt Disney Productions, Hollywood's major studios often have to scrape for cash to make movies. And the Japanese have the cash. In order to get it, however, Hollywood will have to bend its terms to suit the new breed of investors from across the Pacific.

Nagayama was purposely vague in discussing the changes that CST wants in its future deals. He mentioned investing in multiple-film packages in order to improve the odds of owning a piece of a blockbuster. And he talked about percentages of gross profits, and revenue from world distribution rights and video-cassettes.

Such lucrative terms can only be commanded by a handful of major stars in Hollywood these days in return for their participation in a movie, not by outside investors. Nagayama is savvy enough to know that the only way to structure deals that ensure the investor a share in the revenue is to coproduce the movies or buy a studio. But on this subject, too, he declined to reveal details of what CST plans.

Acquisition of a major studio would also provide the Japanese with another enormous profit center—the studio's archives of old movies. At virtually no additional cost, these movies can be distributed to the hungry television channels around the world and generate a steady flow of profits.

Ted Turner of Turner Broadcasting recognized the value of old films when he paid $1.5 billion for MGM/UA in 1986. After stripping out the invaluable collection of 3,700 feature films, including such classics as *Gone with the Wind*, *Casablanca*, and *Citizen Kane*, Turner resold parts of the company back to its primary previous owner, Kirk Kerkorian, for about $700 million. What he was left with was a vault of movies that can be run and rerun forever on his Turner Broadcasting System, insulating him from the studios and television production companies.

"The long-term value of a studio library is immeasurable," said Kitatani, the Japanese consultant. "By just looking at the future market for the upcoming twenty years, the market is expanding so that even if they were to acquire a library with deficit financing now, at least they know the cash flow would be positive."

Kitatani and others who have analyzed Hollywood are certain that the Japanese corporations are on the verge of a major acquisition drive. But this will not be like moving in on the American auto industry, where superior Japanese quality control and modern management allowed them to make inroads in an industry where U.S. consumers were dissatisfied with the products.

In the case of Hollywood, the Japanese will acquire the company but leave the operation basically in the hands of the local managers. No analysts expect that the Japanese would impose their rigid structures on the industry's work habits and risk stifling the creativity that makes American films and television programs the most popular in the world.

But there will be changes. The Japanese are tremendously afraid of taking risks, and they will most certainly try to find a way to cut down on the gamble associated with producing a major motion picture or undertaking a new television series. The result is likely to be fewer movies and television programs that take risks.

Marketing movies to different cultures is dicey, and as the stakes increase, so do the efforts to reduce the risks. Already the potential money from foreign sales has caused Hollywood to require that major movies contain some elements to enhance their value on the international resale market. These pressures would increase, subtly but inevitably, under Japanese ownership.

Many experts, including Kitatani, anticipate a gradual shifting of movie production away from Hollywood and New York to the less expensive, right-to-work states of the Midwest and South, where the Japanese will not have to contend with union labor. This pattern has been well established in Japanese-owned manufacturing companies, particularly the automakers and their suppliers.

And gradually more and more of the profits from the entertainment industry will be sent back to Tokyo and Osaka, eroding the benefits of the trade surplus in the second most successful exporting industry in the United States.

The lesson is simple: Japan's domestic industry cannot approach the quality and international appeal of the American entertainment business, so they will buy what they cannot match and pocket the profits in that way.

Those who say no foreigner can dominate such a uniquely American industry need look no farther than the publishing industry to see how it can be done, if one has the money.

Australian-born Rupert Murdoch has used sheer economic power and an aggressive acquisition strategy to become a major force in publishing in the United States and the world. Indeed, when he purchased *TV Guide, Seventeen* magazine, and the *Daily Racing Form* for $3 billion in mid-1988, Murdoch became the biggest publisher of consumer magazines in the country.

When the new properties are added to his existing empire, the breadth is staggering. By the end of 1988, Murdoch owned 150 newspapers and magazines, book publishers, television stations, and the satellite channel under development in England. His U.S. holdings included television stations in Boston, Chicago, Dallas, Houston, Los Angeles, New York, and Washington; the fourth major network, Fox Television, as well as Fox Films; newspapers in Boston and San Antonio, Texas; the magazines *Star, New Woman, New York, Automobile, Premiere, In Fashion,* and *European Travel and Life*; and the book publisher Harper & Row.

In Britain, he owned the *Times of London*, the *Sunday Times*, the *Sun*, and *Today*. In Australia, he owned six daily newspapers with an average daily circulation of 2 million. In Hong Kong, he owned the *South China Morning Post*.

"He's acquiring a larger and larger ability to shape and influence public policy," said David Wagenhauser, staff attorney for the Telecommunications Research Action Center, a consumer watchdog organization. "One of the best ways to influence public opinion without holding a political office is to control the media—from past experience it does seem that Mr. Murdoch wants to influence public opinion."

In much the same fashion that Murdoch has created a media empire, the world's book publishing industry is undergoing a massive consolidation which has left a handful of multinationals controlling half of the world's market. The new giants are companies such as West Germany's Bertelsmann AG, England's Pearson Group (in which Murdoch holds a 14 percent interest), and America's Gulf + Western, Hearst, and MCA.

In 1988, Bertelsmann paid $475 million to add Doubleday to an American stable that already included Bantam, and the French media giant Hachette SA acquired Grolier for $448 million. As a result, American publishers have been scrambling to merge and avoid being taken over by foreigners or swallowed up by one of the U.S. giants.

Thus, in the summer of 1988, Random House, a unit of the S. I. Newhouse media empire, bought Crown Publishers Group, one of the most successful U.S. houses, in a deal that cost Random House in the neighborhood of $100 million.

Publishing industry executives are divided over the effects of the consolidation of their business. Michael Korda, editor in chief of Gulf + Western's Simon & Schuster unit, says it does not matter who owns the companies and puts up the money for the books so long as the editorial staffs remain the same.

"This is a quirky business," Korda told the *New York Times* in August 1988. "If Simon & Schuster were to buy Farrar Straus & Giroux, we'd be crazy to change it. If you bought it and the authors left and the corporate identity and quality went down the drain, why buy it?"

Yet others within the industry worry that the corporate mentality of the dominant owners will stifle risky new ventures and rely on proven bestsellers, just as some fear will occur in the movie industry if the Japanese make significant purchases.

"My concern is with the editorial integrity of the various book lines," warned Steven Mason, president of Ingram Book Company, in the *New York Times*. "In the past, each company tried to maintain its integrity. With the concentration, you could have less bidding competition among publishers for authors."

As with the backlog of old movies, one of the appeals of American publishers for foreign purchasers is their libraries of old titles. Most American publishers are unaware of the value of these old titles in the face of growing world demand for literature in England. But foreign publishers recognize the potential and consider it when they make a bid for an American house.

This is one acquisitions arena that the Japanese have avoided so far. The cultural gulf is enormous, far more than confronts a naturalized American citizen such as Australia's Murdoch or even Germany's huge publisher Bertelsmann.

Yet few lucrative industries have avoided their scrutiny, and the attractions of a globalized publishing empire are bound to be strong for the Japanese. In addition, there is the nearly irresistible opportunity to influence public opinion in the United States that would come with the creation of a major media empire.

Certainly the Japanese have demonstrated that they are willing and able to influence U.S. opinion when necessary to protect their interests. One wonders how long they will be able to remain on the sidelines of this burgeoning field of play.

22
BILINGUAL SPIES

NISSAN, THE BIG JAPANESE AUTOMAKER, has its U.S. sales and distribution headquarters in a campuslike complex at the intersection of two freeways southwest of Los Angeles. Shortly after 5 P.M. each work day, several dozen Japanese men race up and down the halls of those buildings.

This is not some weird variation of the Japanese penchant for workplace calisthenics. Five o'clock Pacific Time is the start of the business day in Japan, and these mid-level Japanese executives are scurrying back and forth between their offices and the facsimile machines, sending messages to Tokyo and receiving replies.

American workers at Nissan refer to these fast-moving men as "bilingual spies." They are viewed by the Americans as the eyes and ears of Nissan's Japan-based management.

"Spies" is a term to which the Japanese managers in the United States object strenuously. After the *Los Angeles Times* wrote about the practice and used the phrase as part of a series about working for the Japanese in the middle of 1988, a contingent of Japanese businessmen descended on the newspaper with a laundry list of complaints. At the top of the list was the use of the phrase "bilingual spies."

The Japanese businessmen justifiably pointed out that constant communication is really no more than one would expect in a foreign-owned company. American multinationals, despite their longer experience abroad, still consult their home offices daily for advice. But the executives also lamented the fact that they had to keep so many Japanese nationals in the United States to do the same work assigned to American executives. In objecting to the terminology, they confirmed the practice.

At Nissan and dozens of other Japanese-owned operations across America, the practice of reporting back to Japan daily and shadowing each American manager with a Japanese counterpart has assumed an ominous quality. The practice has arisen partly because Americans have so little experience working under foreign bosses. And partly because many U.S. workers possess a streak that leads them to distrust any authority, particularly one 5,000 miles and an ocean away.

But some of the blame belongs to the Japanese. They have fostered an atmosphere of mystery and secrecy in the workplace, which feeds the distrust. And the Japanese often make no secret of their disdain for American managers and workers.

Americans are almost unanimously unable to penetrate the inner circle of management at Japanese-owned firms in the United States. They are shut out of the top jobs, and they know it. Foreigners working for U.S. firms often head the foreign division and sometimes return to the U.S. headquarters in highly responsible positions. However, it is rare that an American holds the top spot in any Japanese-owned firm in the United States, and impossible to imagine a scenario that would place an American in a position of ultimate responsibility in Tokyo.

For example, at Mitsubishi International Corp., the U.S. arm of Japan's biggest trading company, a succession of executives from Tokyo have promised since the 1970s to open up the ranks of upper management to their American employees, who make up 80 percent of the work force. Yet by 1988, Americans headed just two of the firm's forty-one divisions, and one of the two was in a position that required an American, general counsel. Americans on the board of the subsidiary are not allowed to vote.

"It has been extremely frustrating for a lot of people," said Ray Lippincott, second in command behind a Japanese national at Mitsubishi's Atlanta office.

These factors create the atmosphere in which routine reporting assumes a clandestine flavor, and it all contributes to the increasing sense that Americans are not involved in making the key decisions.

"Each important American is shadowed by a Japanese," explained a top American manager at Nissan. "On the organization chart, there is a dotted line from each American executive to a bilingual Japanese. The Japanese are assistant vice presidents. But they are not really assistants. They are bilingual spies."

In other places, the Americans call them watchdogs or shadows.

"If you were the manager of a department, you would have a shadow," said Robert Wilkinson, who was corporate controller at the U.S. subsidiary of Kubota Tractor Corporation in Compton, California, until he resigned in 1987. "You would have a man who was assigned to learn what you were doing, and assigned to 'help' what you were doing. They were actually grading you, whether you realized it or not."

Wilkinson said he quit working for the Osaka-based manufacturing firm because the problem of the shadows—the anxieties they created, the subtle signal about where the real power would always lie—left him feeling that he had no future with a Japanese-owned company.

However, increasing numbers of American workers do have a Japanese employer in their future, whether they like the idea or not. And many already have a Japanese boss.

The problem of shadows and bilingual spies is just one symptom of the conflicts between U.S. employees and their Japanese bosses that are likely to emerge as a major social and economic issue over the next decade as more Japanese companies set up shop in the United States. The cultural gap between Japan and the United States is wide, and the workplace is an important and far-reaching example of the difficulty presented in bridging that gap.

Frequently, however, any notion of problems is swept aside as droves of Americans rush to sign up when, as *Newsweek* magazine phrased it in 1987, "Japan Inc. holds out the 'Help Wanted' sign."

The promise of lifetime employment, a Japanese idea that has been greatly exaggerated by hopeful Americans, is an enormous lure for workers left behind when U.S. manufacturers shut their doors. The new plants and new jobs and new technologies represented by the Japanese investment have indeed had a positive effect on numerous communities around the United States, most notably Marysville, Ohio, as noted earlier.

But the effects of fast-growing employment of Americans by Japan-based companies go far beyond small towns in the Midwest. The concept of lifetime employment is merely one of the myths that have died as more and more Americans find that working for the Japanese can present all the difficulties of working for Americans, along with a host of new challenges.

As with everything connected with foreign investment in the United States, accurate figures on the number of Americans working for Japanese bosses are impossible to find. Estimates have ranged from a ridiculously low 160,000 to more than 500,000, which is probably too high.

The latest official figures on foreign employment from the U.S. Commerce Department cover only up to 1986, and estimate that 216,392 Americans were working then for the Japanese. Since then, the pace of Japanese acquisitions in the United States and Japanese construction of new factories has increased substantially. In one fell swoop, for example, Bridgestone added 55,000 to its payroll with the 1988 purchase of Firestone Tire & Rubber.

Tokyo's Ministry of International Trade and Industry predicts that Japanese investment will create an additional 850,000 American jobs in the coming decade. Many experts consider that a conservative estimate.

Despite the lack of precise figures, the trend is clearly toward growing employment of Americans by Japanese-owned companies.

There is a rising disillusionment among American workers

after less than a decade of experience under Japanese bosses, particularly among the low-skilled workers who constitute most of the employees. As James Risen pointed out in the *Los Angeles Times* series on the subject, "The honeymoon between the Japanese and some of their American blue-collar workers seems to be coming to an end."

Americans are finding that the Japanese do lay off workers when economics turn sour. Invariably the first workers to go are Americans and the last are Japanese, because the Japanese work for the home office.

Americans also are discovering that the routine sacrifices expected of workers in Japan prove too demanding for many Americans, who are unaccustomed to the paternalism of Japanese corporations. Executives find that there is a glass ceiling above which they cannot rise because the top positions are filled by Japanese nationals, usually on three- or four-year tours from Tokyo or Osaka. And women and minorities confront the sharp contrasts in the attitudes of the Japanese toward them and their role in the workplace.

Some of these problems have spawned lawsuits. Executives and assembly line workers alike have claimed they were fired after being promised lifetime employment. Women have accused the Japanese of sexual discrimination by refusing to promote them or provide them with equal pay. The federal Equal Employment Opportunity Commission has found that Japanese automakers, particularly and surprisingly Honda, have discriminated against women and minorities.

"As there are more Japanese firms here, there will be more attention paid to their operating practices because they will be affecting more and more people and there will be more instances where you have that cultural gap," explained Harley Shaiken, a specialist on the workplace and a professor at the University of California in San Diego.

Perhaps some Americans are so bitter because their hopes were so high. They were attracted by a philosophy that they understood blended a degree of moral commitment to business practices. It was different from the start.

When Mazda announced that it was accepting applications at

its Flat Rock, Michigan, plant, the company expected 40,000 applications for the 3,100 jobs. As it turned out, the company got 130,000 written requests for application forms, and 96,500 completed forms were turned in.

American hiring is basically divided into two types—stressing basic skills at lower job levels and an emphasis on psychological testing at the upper-management ranks. But at Mazda, the evaluation of every employee was divided into five steps—two hours of written tests covering mechanical and oral comprehension and numerical skills; an interview examining previous work experience aimed at determining whether the person will fit into the Mazda environment; a social assessment in which the individual is placed in a real-life situation to see how he or she reacts to interpersonal problems; a medical examination, including screening for alcohol and drug abuse; and a physical test that simulates the actual job the person would perform.

The battery of tests takes a lot of time to complete, particularly by U.S. standards. The social assessment required about four hours, and part of it involved splitting applicants into groups that were given problems to solve through teamwork. The emphasis was on arriving at a consensus, on cooperating with fellow workers. In one of the physical tests, workers had to bolt down a floor mat with six bolts and then attach an electric light and a fan within a set period of time.

"After you are done they say good luck. We will call you," recalled one person who took the test.

The overall testing took as long as six months, and three weeks might pass before an applicant was told if he or she had passed one phase of the examination process. Even the successful applicant faces an additional three months of training before actually starting to work.

During training, workers are lectured on various aspects of their specific jobs and Mazda's philosophy, and they get plenty of hands-on experience. By the time they are ready for the assembly line itself, they are expected to be able to do their assigned task blindfolded.

There is much to admire in this thoughtful process, which stresses teamwork and sacrificing individual recognition in favor of the success of the group. But it is fraught with dangers, particularly among a work force with a tradition of self-reliance and independent behavior, and the Japanese have had difficulty adapting their methods to American workers.

The blame for these problems has been shifted to the American workers and managers, a recurring theme in Japanese relations with the United States. Just as they have deftly tried to shift the blame for the trade imbalance to U.S. consumers and manufacturers, the Japanese refuse to take any responsibility for failures in the workplace. This permits them to avoid admitting that they may have made a mistake, an embarrassing and rare admission among the Japanese.

The most serious problems between American workers and Japanese bosses have occurred when the Japanese have taken over plants with existing work forces. The Japanese have a strong preference for what is called "green fields"—building new plants and hiring new, nonunion workers who are indebted to them for the jobs.

"They don't want to acquire an existing company and take on an existing work force," explained William Davidson, a professor of international management at the University of Southern California in Los Angeles and author of *The Amazing Race,* a book on the technology race between the United States and Japan. "The Japanese have a fanatical preference for starting from scratch. In doing that, they are able to build in the kind of system and worker attitudes they want to see."

But Davidson does not think the policy will keep problems at bay for long. For one thing, the growth and expansion that comes with starting a new factory will not last forever, and when the growth rate slows or layoffs begin, problems will surface. Also, he said, the work forces at the Japanese-owned plants will get older and wiser and possibly unionized. And he, like many others, expects the Japanese to undertake more direct acquisitions.

Indeed, by 1987 the sinking dollar had made American factories so inexpensive that the Japanese could not resist the bargains, and they acquired a growing number of existing operations.

23
"THEY'RE THE BOSS"

ONE EXAMPLE OF WHAT HAPPENS when the Japanese take over
a U.S. manufacturing plant with an existing work force comes
from the little town of Forrest City, Arkansas.

An American firm, Warwick Electronics, manufactured televisions at a Forrest City plant for Sears, Roebuck and Co. But in
the 1970s, the televisions began to suffer from the impact of
Japanese imports and their own quality problems. Employment
at the plant began to decrease, and there were fears that it might
be closed when Japan's Sanyo took over the operation in late
1976.

From a low of 500 workers, Sanyo increased the work force to
2,400, and production rose from 500 sets a day to 3,000. The
company then added an assembly line for microwave ovens, and
things were booming in the little town. Sanyo sponsored com-
panywide picnics and sports celebrations, and the rejuvenation
of the plant was hailed as a major step in labor relations and
industrial rebirth.

Union officials said Sanyo management even promised not to
repeat the pattern of layoffs and recalls that had destabilized

the work force under its American owners, an assertion that Sanyo has denied.

But there were problems from the start, right below the surface. One was that the early success of the plant was not based on its own economics, but on the use of high-quality component parts manufactured in Japan and shipped to Arkansas for assembly. Once the yen started to rise against the dollar, the economic sense of that tactic would evaporate. Also, the little town was beset with its own black-white problems, and the addition of Japanese managers to the mix only stirred up discontent in some quarters.

In addition, there was sometimes open hostility toward the new management by members of the union that represented the workers, the International Union of Electronic, Electrical, Salaried, Machine and Furniture Workers. Some of the hostility had been left over from the previous management, but the Japanese created some of their own problems, too.

There was a brief strike in 1979, but labor relations at the plant soured completely and turned violent in 1985. Workers were already angry over the death of a worker in a fall and the firing of the union president. The strike turned into a violent, stone-throwing melee in which local police arrested pickets as well as truck drivers who tried to force their vehicles through picket lines to deliver supplies.

Faced with growing pressure from imports from Taiwan and South Korea and the rising cost of bringing in its own components, Sanyo took a tough stance, demanding cuts in medical insurance, changes in the seniority system, and the right to shift workers from job to job. Even when the strike was settled, Sanyo began cutting back on television and microwave production at the plant and laying off workers. Early in 1988, the microwave assembly line was dropped completely, and the production of large television sets was moved to Mexico, where Sanyo could take advantage of cheaper labor right across the border from the United States.

A Japanese-owned plant that once employed 2,400 was down to 300 hourly workers by mid-1988, and hundreds of disillusioned, bitter Americans were left behind in a community where the unemployment rate was suddenly back up to 25 percent.

"I don't know if it was bad management or bad parts, but I know one thing was they could get cheaper labor in Mexico," said Annette Bradley, a former Sanyo worker. "They are taking jobs from the U.S. to Mexico because of cheaper labor, and it hurts the states and it hurts the people. I know they are human, they are out to make a dollar just like the rest of us are, but it's just that it would have been better if they would have just tried to work a little bit more with us, instead of just ship everything out."

There was an irony in the Japanese moving to Mexico. A decade earlier, competition from the Japanese had provided American companies with a convenient excuse for moving their factories to underdeveloped countries, outside the reach of American labor unions.

Abandoning the American worker had been taboo in the past. But the threat of cheaper goods flowing in from Japan muted the outcry, as American manufacturing moved to Taiwan and Singapore and Mexico to take advantage of the cheaper labor in what was described as the only way to compete with the Japanese.

And Sanyo was not the only Japanese firm to imitate American manufacturers by transferring labor-intensive production to Mexico. An entire industry has sprung up along the 2,000-mile border with the United States. Mexican workers assemble U.S. parts and supplies for reexport to the United States at wages of 60 cents to $1 an hour—about one-eighth the rate in Japan and the United States and half that of Hong Kong and Taiwan.

The result is a great boon to U.S. companies and to Japanese companies operating in the United States. For Mexico, its vast unskilled and low-skilled work force has a growing source of jobs. The plants account for about half of the country's manufactured exports and helped that sector surpass tourism to become the second leading industry in the country behind oil.

By 1988, more than 300,000 Mexicans were employed by 1,000 U.S. and foreign firms along the United States–Mexico border turning out everything from television sets and refrigerators to water beds and garage-door openers. They are called *maquilado-*

ras, from the Mexican word for "handwork." By the end of the century, most experts on both sides of the border predict there will be more than 1 million *maquiladoras*. A large percentage of them will be working for the Japanese companies that are flocking to the areas just south of the U.S. border.

The attractions for U.S. and Japanese industry alike are the rock-bottom labor cost and the duty-free provisions of the arrangement. A provision of the U.S. tariff code allows duty-free movement of U.S. goods across the border, as long as the items are assembled into finished products and reimported into the United States. The only tariff is applied to the value added by the assembly process, which is minimal given the cheap labor involved.

But the Japanese firms have flocked south of the border for an equally important bonus reason. The *maquiladoras* provide yet another avenue for the Japanese to escape any protectionist measures imposed by the United States, a threat that plays a central role in all of Japan's direct investments in the United States and Mexico, too.

For example, in April 1987, when the United States announced retaliatory tariffs on Japanese semiconductors as a result of dumping, the measure stated that Japanese firms in Mexico would be exempt from the penalties.

So in addition to Sanyo, some of Japan's other household names have established plants in Mexico, including Sony, Hitachi, Matsushita, and Mitsubishi. In Tijuana, about one-third of the 28,000 *maquiladoras* work for Japanese companies in the sprawling, drab, one-story buildings that line the dusty streets.

The Japanese make no apologies for their presence in Mexico. Indeed, while many of the American plants in Mexico are not designated by signs, the Japanese proudly display their names on the plants where they are assembling goods for U.S. consumers.

"These are the rules they gave us," said Alan Foster, an executive in San Diego for Sanyo Industries of America. "If we can use the rules to make something and label it 'Made in Mexico,' that's what we will do."

Teri Ritter Cardot, vice president of marketing for a San Diego company that sets up and manages *maquiladoras* in Tijuana,

Mexico, thirty miles away, puts it another way: "They [the Japanese] are probably saying, 'If they are going to slam the door on us bringing in products from the Far East, we won't bring them from the Far East.' "

This is a trend that worries some Americans. U.S. labor unions claim that the migration to Mexico by American and Japanese firms is costing their members jobs. They argue that there is a direct link between layoffs in the United States and the expansion of the *maquiladoras.*

American companies are sensitive to the argument, which is one of the reasons they decline to provide specific numbers of their size in Mexico and often do not label their factories there. But they respond to the unions and other critics that these are jobs that would be in Taiwan or Singapore if they were not in Mexico. And in Mexico, they are at least helping an important neighbor.

The Japanese can make no such argument. The jobs that they are switching to Mexico are ones that would normally have been moved to the United States. Yet they have found a way around U.S. tariff regulations, and potential future protectionism, while reducing their reliance on the higher-paid U.S. work force.

The industrial explosion on the Mexican border threatens U.S. jobs in another long-term manner, too. Japanese auto-parts makers are beginning to set up shops in Mexico, from which they expect to become a major supply source for the Japanese automakers in the United States.

For instance, Yazaki Corporation, a Japanese manufacturer of auto parts and air conditioners for cars, has operated two plants in Ciudad Juarez, just across the Rio Grande from El Paso, Texas, since 1982. The company's work force at the plants is slightly less than 2,000, but Yazaki expects to more than triple that figure by 1990 when four additional plants are completed.

Alexander Good, director general of the U.S. Commerce Department division that promotes U.S. exports, warned a meeting of border states in late 1987 that the notion that Japan has found a back door into the United States could increase the possibility of legislation threatening the existence of the entire *maquiladoras* industry.

If Congress becomes convinced that Japan is using its Mexican border plants "as a vehicle to enter the U.S. market inappropriately, it could have a very strong effect that could erode the support that we have for the *maquiladoras*," Good told the governors.

Despite the threat, the number of Japanese firms in Mexico is increasing. One Mexican official said in early 1988 that he had hosted more than 150 representatives of Japanese firms in the last three months. At a one-day seminar in Santa Clara, California, on June 28, 1988, dozens of Japanese businessmen and their American managers listened as participants extolled the virtues of manufacturing goods duty-free in Mexico. The keynote address was delivered by Carlos de Orduna, general manager of Sanyo's subsidiary in Mexico. Its title was "How the Japanese Miracle Works in Mexico."

The unemployed ex-Sanyo workers in Forrest City see no miracle in the Japanese move to Mexico. They are bitter and angered because the Japanese promise did not work in Arkansas.

There is a similar disillusionment among dozens more Americans just north of the Mexican border in San Diego, California.

Kyocera International, the Japanese company that is one of the world's leading manufacturers of ceramic chips for the computer industry, had bought a San Diego plant from its American owners in 1980. The ex-workers claim that they were given the impression by Kyocera executives that they would have lifetime jobs in exchange for devoting themselves to the company and performing even the most menial tasks.

Eighteen months later, Kyocera closed the plant without notice. When the nonunion employees went to work one day in August 1981, they were gathered together in a parking lot and told that they were terminated. According to some of the workers, the plant reopened the following day with a staff of lower-paid workers.

Some of the workers filed a lawsuit, charging that Kyocera had broken its promise of lifetime work. "These people were taken in," said Robert Rothman, an attorney for the ex-workers. "They did what they were asked to, some washed floors, because they thought they had lifetime jobs. Kyocera very deliberately used that policy to get workers to do what they wanted, and to keep unions out."

For its part, the plant's management denied that it ever promised lifetime employment. One of its lawyers called the concept ridiculous. Kyocera said the plant was closed because it was a financial failure, and the only workers brought in the day after it was shuttered were there to perform cleanup chores.

Executives claim broken promises, too.

James Ristow spent thirteen years as vice president of sales in New Jersey and Southern California for the American subsidiary of Toshiba, the giant Japanese electronics firm. It all came to an abrupt end when he was fired in 1984 as the plant was cutting back his division. He said that during his years at the company there had never been a Japanese employee fired, and the layoffs associated with the cutbacks were no different. No Japanese lost his job.

"I thought of American companies as being very cold, calculating and ruthless," said Ristow, who sued Toshiba on charges of racial discrimination after his firing. "But the Japanese have arrived, haven't they? They're cold. They're ruthless."

Michael K. Young is a professor of Japanese law and director of the Center for Japanese Legal Studies at Columbia University in New York City. While he said that only about one-third of the workers in Japan are actually covered by the promise of lifetime employment, there should be no surprise that Americans are fired first at Japanese-owned plants in the United States.

"One thing is crystal clear," he said. "In layoffs that occur, the Americans get axed and the Japanese don't. The Japanese work for the home company. Japanese don't get fired. They are just sent back to Japan. That doesn't look to Americans as equal sharing of benefits and burdens. When you ask the Japanese about it, they draw the comparison with the family. When you ask what is the family all about, they say it is that they rise and fall together."

The entrenched social attitudes of the Japanese also spark tensions and conflicts when it comes to dealing with employees who are women or members of minorities. The Japanese have little experience at home dealing with assertive women who expect to be treated as equals, and less background in handling relations with minority employees who have the same demands.

In Japan, women earn about half of what men do, and they are expected to leave their jobs to raise a family after marrying by the age of twenty-five. The small percentage of women who do not leave work or who return after having children find themselves relegated to part-time clerical positions.

Young recalled a lawsuit in Japan against a broadcasting company by two women fired from their jobs at the age of thirty. "One of the male executives said something to the effect that 'I fired my female employees because they are not so beautiful after thirty,' " Young said.

The women's movement is new in Japan, and women managers in business are rare. Young cited a survey of 310,000 junior managers in Japan that found less than one-half of 1 percent were women.

Alair Townsend, deputy mayor of New York City, learned about the status of women in Japan during a trip there in 1985 in search of Japanese investment for the city. She was asked to speak by representatives of a charitable foundation funded by Panasonic.

The speech she delivered was reasoned and cool, intended to ruffle no feathers. She talked about women having two role models, one for the home and one in the workplace. Problems exist with both arrangements, she told her audience, but Japan will have to face the inevitable changes in women's roles and plan for them sensibly.

After the speech, Townsend was mobbed by women from the audience. Her sensible, moderate speech was perceived as a barnburner in staid Japan. A few months later, the impact became even clearer. Two Japanese men visited her office in New York's historic City Hall. Townsend was not there, so the men presented their gift to her staff—a videotape of her speech.

"She very famous in Japan," the Japanese men told the staff.

Townsend later learned that 1 million copies of the videotape had been sold in a nation hungry for candid talk about women's issues, even though the substance of her speech had been low-key. It was a clear measure of how far women in Japan have to go.

But minorities fare even worse in Japan. About 700,000 Koreans make up the largest minority in a nation of 120 million, and few white-collar jobs are available to them. Even though they are born in Japan of Korean parents who were brought there as cheap labor after World War II, the Korean-Japanese usually are unable to become Japanese citizens.

The Japanese are proud of their homogeneity and see it as a primary factor in their economic success.

The issue of Japanese racism attracted international attention in 1986 when Yasuhiro Nakasone, then the prime minister, suggested that blacks, Latinos, and other minorities were pulling down educational levels in the United States. Nakasone later apologized for his remarks, but not until a fire storm of controversy had been ignited that highlighted the racist attitudes that pervade Japanese culture.

These attitudes are part of the baggage carried to the United States by Japanese managers when they arrive for their three- or four-year stints running the U.S. subsidiaries of Japan-based corporations. Their adjustment to U.S. laws and customs has been confusing, difficult, and discouraging.

Indeed, in the spring of 1988, Honda's American manufacturing arm agreed to pay $6 million to 377 blacks and women who were denied jobs at the company's Ohio plants between 1983 and 1986. The agreement settled discrimination charges raised as a result of a sweeping investigation into hiring and promotion practices at Honda by the federal Equal Employment Opportunity Commission, the agency responsible for enforcing civil rights laws in the workplace.

At the same time, it was disclosed that the EEOC had recently settled a similar but much smaller case involving hiring practices at Toyota's sales and distribution center in California and was wrapping up an investigation into apparent sexual and racial discrimination at Nissan's California headquarters.

"Homogeneity is antagonistic to what we believe in this country," said Clarence Thomas, chairman of the EEOC in Washington.

Judith Keeler, district director of the EEOC's office in Los Angeles, said in mid-1988 that the office had received numerous complaints about Japanese companies failing to promote minorities, women, and older people to upper management slots.

"There are also complaints that banks, real estate companies and other Japanese firms catering mainly to Japanese clientele here fail to hire non-Japanese," said Keeler, whose office was conducting a broad inquiry into the practices at the time.

In August 1988, leaders of the American black community confronted the issue head-on after another leading Japanese politician, Michio Watanabe, told a political meeting that American blacks have no qualms about declaring bankruptcy. A short time later, there were news reports that Japanese stores were using black mannequins with exaggerated racial features and selling toys and beachware featuring a "Sambo" figure, also with distorted features.

Although Watanabe apologized for his remarks and the products were withdrawn, the episodes caused black leaders to say they believe racism is deeply imbedded in the Japanese culture. The leaders said racial discrimination also appeared to be behind the fact that Japanese-owned companies in the United States have given few business opportunities to blacks and members of other minorities. As an example, they said there are almost no black-owned dealerships for Japanese automobiles.

In addition, blacks were angered by Japan's emergence as the number one trading partner with South Africa, with Japanese corporations eagerly fulfilling the role vacated upon the departure of European and American companies.

As a result, in August the black leaders said they were going to begin planning for a possible boycott of Japanese goods and other forms of public protests to demonstrate to the Japanese that they must develop a racial sensitivity.

"The black leadership is angry," said Representative Mervyn Dymally, a California Democrat who is chairman of the Congressional Black Caucus and who headed up a visit of black leaders to Japan after Nakasone's remarks. "We've tried to have a conciliatory approach and gotten nothing. Now civil rights groups are going to get involved, and they are not going to have quiet meetings, and nice teas and visits to Japan."

The worsening relations with blacks concerned officials in the

Japanese embassy in Washington, who feared an escalation of the racial backlash could contribute to tensions already heightened over trade problems with the United States.

"I'm recommending to Tokyo that they not take cosmetic measures, but real actions to deal with this," Taizo Watanabe, charge d'affaires at the Japanese embassy in Washington, told the *Los Angeles Times*. "It's a serious situation."

A study by Robert Cole and Donald Deskins, Jr. of the University of Michigan demonstrated how serious the problem has become, at least from the point of view of black American workers.

The 1988 study published in the fall 1988 *California Management Review*, a publication of the University of California, Berkeley Business School, found that the Japanese auto firms have systematically avoided locating manufacturing plants in areas with sizable black populations. Without voicing a conclusion about the motives of the Japanese, the authors warned that "their plant site locations contribute to a drying up of opportunities for black workers in an industry that has traditionally supplied large opportunities to minority workers."

The study raised the issue of whether states should be using the taxes of all of their citizens to subsidize the location of Japanese firms that contribute to the already overwhelming unemployment problem confronting blacks.

There has also been an increasing number of lawsuits filed by women and minorities who claim they were victims of discrimination while working for Japanese-owned companies in the United States. In a landmark case, Sumitomo Corporation of America agreed to pay $2.6 million in back pay and institute broad employment reforms to settle a federal lawsuit that accused the company of favoring Japanese and American males over females. The case took twelve years to resolve and generated a decision by the U.S. Supreme Court which declared that civil rights laws apply to U.S. subsidiaries of foreign companies.

"We have spoken to women from many other subsidiaries of Japanese corporations, and they have given us the same story," said Lewis Steel, a New York lawyer who represented the women in the Sumitomo lawsuit. "Women are treated as inferiors. They are expected to serve coffee or tea, but they are not expected to deal with outside clients. To get even minimal promotions, they have got to be superwomen."

A study by Columbia University's Graduate School of Business found that 2 percent of the management positions at Japanese-owned firms in the United States were held by women in 1985, a figure that was unchanged from 1982. In contrast, roughly 37 percent of the managers in American-owned companies were women.

Thousands of Americans have avoided the problems that have plagued some of their countrymen in working for the Japanese. Their upbeat experiences reflect both the diversity of the Japanese-owned companies in the United States and progress by some Japanese managers in adapting to the demands of the American workplace.

Susan Insley, vice president of corporate planning at Honda's American manufacturing arm in Marysville, Ohio, is one of the highest-ranking women in the auto industry in the United States. She is a lawyer who first worked with Honda in helping the firm negotiate with the small Ohio communities surrounding its auto plant. Ultimately, she went to work for the Japanese company.

"There is a basic philosophy here of respecting the individual," she said. "It doesn't seem to make any difference whether you are a woman or a man."

Yet another woman lawyer who went to work for Toyota in its Southern California sales and distribution headquarters found that there was a difference, although she echoed Insley in saying that she was treated fairly and her opinions were respected.

"The Japanese were more respectful of my opinions and position than I expected," said Margaret Henry, who spent several years as a senior counsel at Toyota, a management position. "It would be hard to get past the Americans and accuse the Japanese of discrimination. There were a number of American men in management positions and they came from Detroit, where Henry Ford once said the auto industry is no place for women. These men were old chauvinists."

Yet Henry was worried before she took the job with Toyota, so she asked a former judge whose law firm represented many Japanese clients what she would encounter as a woman working for the Japanese.

"He said that the Japanese tend to look upon American women as a third sex and they are actually very good at working with them," recalled Henry, who is now in private law practice in Los Angeles. "After I went to work at Toyota, I found that that was true. They don't treat you like a man, and underneath it all they may suspect you aren't as good as a man, but that doesn't mean they don't take your advice."

Henry said she thought the Japanese managers made progress during the years she worked for Toyota in dealing with their American employees, though she acknowledged some rough spots remained. Nonetheless, her comments and those of Insley were not as harsh as those of other women and many men who have worked for the Japanese.

But whether the experience is generally good or roundly awful, there is one hard fact that can never be changed, no matter how well the Japanese eventually adjust to the American work force or the American work force adjusts to the Japanese bosses. That hard fact was expressed succinctly by Douglas Mazza, a vice president and the highest-ranking American at the U.S. automotive division of Suzuki, who said:

"An important thing to remember is that when you come to work in the morning, you work for the Japanese. It's their company. They're the boss."

24
NICs ARE NEXT

WHEN THE OLYMPIC FLAME WAS CARRIED into Seoul in September 1988 to signal the start of the Summer Olympic Games, the hoopla centered on a sports extravaganza. But the real symbolism of the event was the emergence of South Korea as a world economic power.

The Olympics, broadcast direct to millions of viewers in the United States, provided the name recognition and modern image that the Koreans have been seeking in their all-out drive to build exports. The Koreans want nothing so much as to make their products, from cars and computers to steel and televisions, as prominent and sought after in the United States as those of their rival and model, Japan.

The Japanese used their sponsorship of the 1964 Olympics as an effective springboard for consumer exports. Whether the effects of 1988 are as dramatic or not, the Koreans are already challenging the Japanese in many fields, both in the United States and Japan.

In the past twenty-five years, South Korea had led the way in the transformation of four previously backward countries into industrial powers—Hong Kong, Singapore, and Taiwan in addition to South Korea. The export-driven rise of these four Asian nations, known collectively as the newly industrialized countries, or NICs, is an economic success story nearly as dramatic as the ascension of Japan.

More important is the potential impact of this success story on the attempts of the United States to reassert its place as a leader in innovation and trade. The emergence of the NICs also is a driving force in the efforts of the Japanese to expand their share of the U.S. market and solidify their position as leaders in high technology before the NICs reach full strength.

The pattern in relations between the United States and the NICs already is startlingly similar to the conflicts that began nearly two decades ago with the Japanese.

All four of the NICs have recorded rapid economic growth in recent years. In 1987 alone, Korea, Hong Kong, and Taiwan grew at double-digit rates, while Singapore's economy expanded by almost 9 percent. This economic vigor stems from the growth of exports to the United States, which is the biggest market for all four nations. As a result, all four have registered huge surpluses in their trade with America.

In 1987, the Asian NICs registered a total surplus of $37.2 billion in trade with the United States, approximately 22 percent of the total U.S. trade deficit. The largest surplus was $16 billion with Taiwan, followed by Korea at $9.6 billion, Hong Kong at $9.4 billion, and Singapore at $2.2 billion. All four countries combined have a smaller surplus with the United States than Japan's $55 billion for 1987, but the direction—up—is the same, and the NICs appear in many ways to be simply a couple of decades behind the Japanese.

The NICs have built their surpluses in the same way the Japanese did—on the backs of cheap labor and imported technology, undercutting the prices of competitors around the world and striving desperately to improve the quality of their goods.

The demand for improved quality is another lesson learned from the Japanese. As Japan did in the 1960s, the NICs are using their trade surplus to develop and improve domestic industries aimed at exporting more goods abroad. In return, they expect a greater share of the world's business and a higher standard of living down the road.

The NICs have not yet reached the stage where their governments are comfortable in easing tight restrictions on foreign investments. As a result, the NICs have not become substantial investors in the United States, although there have been some exceptions, particularly in the field of high-tech joint ventures.

But if the growth and trading patterns continue, there is every reason to believe the NICs will turn their growing dollar surpluses into direct U.S. investments in the coming decade, leaving the United States to cope with a new wave of foreign acquisitions and inroads into its domestic markets.

Lumping these four countries into a single category is a bit simplistic. They have different strengths and weaknesses. Nonetheless, they have progressed along a similar path from being marginal producers of cheap clothing and toys to being industrial powers.

Hong Kong has what is probably the world's most purely capitalist economy, allowing goods to flow in and out of its ports with virtually no restrictions. The former British colony, which still exports enormous quantities of stylish clothing, has become one of the world's leading financial centers. Almost every major bank in the world has an office there.

Hong Kong also produces electronics goods that compete with the Japanese for American business. One of the best examples is Johnson Electric Industrial Manufactory, the world's second-largest independent producer of micromotors behind Japan's Mabuchi Motor Company. American companies have virtually abandoned the field.

Johnson micromotors are used in a disparate range of products, including Kodak cameras, Conair hair dryers, and Black & Decker cordless tools. They also have a growing number of uses in the automotive industry, driving electric aerials, headlight wipers, adjustable mirrors, and fuel injection systems.

Alongside competing with the Japanese, Johnson demonstrates how good businessmen can work with the communist leaders of China. This is a particularly important lesson, as Britain's lease on Hong Kong expires in 1997 and the Chinese will regain control over the colony.

Johnson subcontracts much of the most labor-intensive work to factories just across the border in China close to the city of Zhongshan. The labor and factory space come from the Chinese, while the equipment and technical know-how are provided by Johnson. This is particularly important in keeping operating costs down because the cost of labor in Hong Kong has been driven up by the booming service industry.

Although the approaching sovereignty of China over Hong Kong caused some initial fears and an exodus of some capital and capitalists, experiences such as Johnson's have helped restore confidence and enhance Hong Kong's role as the gateway to China. That is a position that could be of enormous economic benefit to the burgeoning financial power as China's reform government seeks outside capital to stimulate its moribund industrial base.

While Hong Kong may be freewheeling, Taiwan has kept its markets and economy closed to outsiders while benefiting from its one-way trade relations with the United States. The $16 billion surplus rolled up by Taiwan's corporations in 1987 angered U.S. officials and led to threats of retaliation unless Taiwan opened its domestic markets and allowed its currency to rise.

The Taiwanese have specialized in creating numerous small companies that produce a diverse line of products for export, ranging from consumer electronics to medical supplies.

Singapore is also strong in electronics production and is trying to create a biotechnology industry in an attempt to reduce its dependence on the oil industry. Like Hong Kong, the tiny island nation also hopes to become a financial and communications center to serve the rising economies of Asia.

None of the other NICs has matched the success of South Korea. A nation of 42 million people with a land area about the size of Indiana, South Korea's economy is growing at twice the rate of Japan's, and it is emerging, in the words of *Forbes* magazine, as "another major challenge to the U.S. industrial recovery."

Far more impressive than its staging of the Olympics, the government in Seoul has orchestrated the growth of giant industrial conglomerates along the lines of the Japanese corporations and aimed them at the same economy—the United States'. The triumphs have begun to pile up, led by Hyundai's subcompact Excel, which became the bestselling imported car in U.S. history within months of its arrival in 1986, and the emergence of Pohang Iron & Steel as a rival to the world's leading steel producer, Japan's Nippon Steel Corporation.

Posco, as the Korean steelmaker is known, has risen from obscurity in the last twenty years to become one of the world's most efficient steelmakers. Its prices are from 15 to 50 percent lower than those of its chief competitors in the United States, Japan, and Taiwan. By 1990, Posco expects to be on a production par with Nippon.

One sign of its stature is a fifty-fifty joint venture with America's USX Corporation to run a steel mill in California. The mill, in operation only since 1986, is already turning a profit. One reason is that its workers are trained at Posco's most technologically advanced plant in Pohang.

Another star in Korea's economic lineup is the Samsung Group, a conglomerate whose 150,000 employees generated revenues of $24 billion in 1987 from products as diverse as televisions, textiles, sugar, and insurance. The sales rank the company alongside such American biggies as K mart, Philip Morris, and Chrysler.

Samsung is Korea's largest and most profitable *chaebol*, or family-operated corporation. It is the country's leading producer of consumer electronics, semiconductors, sugar, and paper.

The company was founded to export fruit and dried fish in 1938 by B. C. Lee, the son of a wealthy farming family who obtained his college education at Tokyo's Waseda University. He retained his ties to Japan, frequently returning to learn from its industrialists and keeping a mistress and two children in Tokyo.

In the 1950s, Samsung provided consumer necessities, such as sugar, wool, and flour, to earn cash in a poor nation. In the following decade the company expanded into paper, electronics, retailing, and life insurance before moving into petrochemicals, hotels, semiconductors, computers, and aerospace in the 1970s and 1980s.

Now, Samsung is spearheading Korea's push into new fields of high technology, such as robotics and genetic engineering, by investing record amounts in research and development and, in some cases, pooling its efforts with other Korean companies.

For example, Samsung's Cheil Sugar & Company, Korea's largest food processor, is spending heavily on genetic engineering and has opened a laboratory in New Jersey in an attempt to tap U.S. scientists. Another Samsung division operates a semiconductor pilot plant in the heart of California's Silicon Valley, and its aerospace arm received a contract from the Korean government in 1988 to produce a new fighter plane under technology licensed by McDonnell Douglas of the United States.

The parallel between the emergence of South Korea and the other NICs may be best illustrated by the success of Masayuki Ohyama, a small businessman in Tokyo who set up two shops selling only imports from the NICs in early 1988. The goods on the shelves of his Inbix shops—clothes, food, televisions, and VCRs—cost 20 to 30 percent less than equivalent products made by the Japanese. And the quality is high enough to have sent sales above the $1 million-a-month mark and engender plans for a chain of Inbix shops.

It is a far cry from the days when the Japanese shunned products from the NICs as poor-quality and cheap—just the way the world once characterized the goods of Japan. And it is a lesson that American industry must not ignore as it calculates how to cope with the rising threat from abroad.

25
SECRETARY OF TRADE

NONE OF THE MANY ILLUSIONS manufactured during the Reagan era is more dangerous than the shortsighted, politically expedient myth that the sharp increase in foreign investment over the last few years reflects the nation's economic revitalization and stability.

The reality is that this dramatic escalation is the direct result of the economic decline of the United States, from the deficit spending that turned the nation into the world's biggest borrower to the failures of American industry to keep pace with technological advances.

The reality is that the influx of foreign capital, particularly from Japan, threatens to hobble efforts to create an American industrial renaissance. The reality is that the sellout of the United States raises the distinct possibility that the nation will lack the political and economic sovereignty to solve the long-term economic problems that have lowered its standard of living in the past decade.

The United States is too vast, too rich in resources, and too vital to the world's political balance to become a colony of Japan or any other foreign power. But that does not insulate the nation from further deterioration in its economic health and global power unless substantial reforms are instituted.

Indeed, the effects of colonization have been felt already in the stock market crash of 1987, the discrimination experienced in the workplace by growing numbers of American employees of Japanese-owned companies, the widening influence of the Japanese on the political process, and their domination of industry after industry.

The simple fact is that decisions that should be made in Washington or New York or Los Angeles or Marysville, Ohio, are being made in Tokyo and Osaka. While this does not mean the United States is likely to become a colony, it does convey the warning that the nation is at risk. Unless a way is found to control foreign investment, particularly that of the Japanese because of their staggering concentration of investments, the future of the United States' sovereignty looks bleak.

Mapping these reforms is tricky business. Japanese investment in the United States has had many positive effects. Further, the nation has grown so dependent on the Japanese that it cannot risk driving them away with onerous new restrictions, although that risk has been greatly exaggerated by opponents of reform abroad and in the United States.

The task confronting policymakers in the new administration is four-pronged: design a means of controlling and monitoring foreign investment; curb the excessive government spending that opened the door to the foreign investors; create incentives for American industries to invest in the research and development to regain the ability to make things better; and demand that foreign governments open their doors to U.S. companies as widely as America has opened its.

Only through that combination of steps can the United States hope to reverse the trade deficit and restore the standard of living. But, as Robert Hormats, an investment banker and former senior trade official in the Carter administration, says, none of the nations with trade surpluses will volunteer to give up their advantages. It will be up to the new administration in Washington to adopt policies that start reducing the nation's growing foreign debt while minimizing rancor and retaliation among its trading partners.

The first step in this delicate task should be the creation of a secretary of trade. The establishment of a cabinet-level post would elevate the problems of trade to a national priority. Equally important, the new department would provide a mechanism for coordinating the nation's response to the dilemma of foreign investment and the revitalization of American industry.

For instance, the 1988 trade bill increased the likelihood that the United States will retaliate against unfair trade practices, particularly in countries with huge surpluses, such as Japan, Taiwan, and South Korea. If the administration is unable to resolve what it considers inequities through negotiations, it now has broad authority to challenge entrenched practices in the foreign country, such as Japan's distribution system which restricts marketing of American goods.

This systemic approach offers an increased possibility for broad reforms in Japan and elsewhere that are not provided by the previous means of approaching problems sector by sector.

But this new authority ups the stakes in any potential trade war, making it all the more essential to create a new department to coordinate policies and responses.

A secretary of trade also could play a pivotal role in redefining the concept of national security so that it reflects the importance of global economic matters. As surveys of the public have found, Americans are more concerned about economic competition from the Japanese than confrontation with the Soviets. And in this instance, the people are well ahead of their leaders.

"Containment of the Soviet Union has succeeded," former Defense Secretary Harold Brown told the *Wall Street Journal* in August 1988. "But the containment model doesn't manage all these new issues: Third World debt, sub-Saharan Africa. Clearly the world's more complicated now. In many areas of competition, it's not the Soviet Union we have to watch, but Japan, to some extent Europe, and increasingly the newly industrializing countries."

One consideration in developing a new national security policy should be forging a new pact with U.S. allies to share some of the costs of their common defense.

The concept, called "burden sharing," is seen as a way of plugging economic considerations into defense issues and relieving the enormous costs to the U.S. economy. Japan spends less than 1 percent of its gross national product on defense, gaining a tremendous advantage over the United States, which devotes 7 percent of its GNP to the military.

The fact is that the United States pays a disproportionate share for the defense of the western alliance, a luxury that it can no longer afford.

Another central theme in the debate should be the role of foreign investment in the United States, for the level of investment from abroad clearly has jeopardized the nation's economic security and, in some cases, its military security.

One of the first things the new secretary would have to understand is that foreign money is not a passive or even a neutral force. That was the description that the Reagan administration tried to foist onto the public for eight years. One need look only as far as ITT's role in the overthrow of the Allende government in Chile or the manner in which United Fruit ran Guatemala to see the lengths to which foreign investors will go to protect their interests.

It is inevitable that the interests of the foreign powers investing heavily in the United States will conflict with those of the United States. This divergence of interests will take place with all foreign investors, but it is destined to be most pronounced with the Japanese. This is especially true when it comes to the creation of new businesses.

Walter Russell Mead, the author of *Mortal Splendor: The American Empire in Transition*, explained the potential conflict in the Summer 1988 issue of *New Perspectives Quarterly*.

In order to pay off its huge debt and avoid new troubles, the U.S. economy needs rapid growth, even at the expense of rising inflation. But the Japanese, as the world's largest creditors, can be expected to back slow growth and low inflation. In addition, Japan is an importer of raw material, and a rapid expansion of the global economy would mean an increase in raw material prices.

There is also the very elementary argument that the Japanese, more than the people of any other nation, are obsessed with gaining market share and would not support the creation of new competition in any field.

As seen already in the experiences of Americans working for the Japanese, discrimination against women and minorities is inbred in the Japanese culture and has followed Japanese managers to the United States. In addition, the ponderous, consensus-style of the management structure does not lend itself to the spirit of individualism and creativity that fueled America's ascendance to the top of the world economy.

"An American economy funded by Japanese capital would not be [an] open and dynamic paradise," wrote Mead. "It is far more likely to be a highly structured, financially centralized and slow growth behemoth."

By grasping the inevitable conflict between these divergent interests, the new secretary of trade would be able to fashion an honest debate over the measures that should be taken to control foreign investment in the United States.

Controls already exist for some foreign investments. Foreigners are not allowed to own airlines or television stations, and there are restrictions on their ability to control defense contractors. Further, the 1988 trade bill gave the president the right to block foreign investments for reasons of national security.

Additional steps, however, are needed as foreign investment mounts. Chief among them is requiring the registration of all foreign investments over a certain size. This was the basic concept behind the hotly controversial legislation proposed by Congressman John Bryant of Texas, and it is a worthwhile idea that should be resurrected and approved by Congress.

Up to sixteen federal agencies currently monitor various aspects of foreign investment. But none provides a complete monitoring, and some of them keep their data secret, even from Congress. As a result of this incomplete hodgepodge, the federal government does not have sufficient information to gauge the extent of foreign investment or the identity of the investors.

Therefore, efforts to formulate a policy for dealing with the issue are hobbled.

The idea here is not to restrict foreign investment, but simply to determine its extent and the identity of the buyers. However, there are instances where restrictions are justified.

One such area involves hostile takeovers by foreign corporations. The merger mania that swept the United States in the 1980s did enormous damage to the nation's industrial base. Allowing foreign companies to play this game merely increases the chances of danger. There are enough willing domestic sellers to justify a prohibition against hostile acquisitions by foreigners.

The British have been particularly aggressive in initiating hostile takeovers of U.S. companies. The most notable example of a hostile foreign acquisition was the 1988 takeover of the Farmers Group, a Los Angeles–based insurance holding company, by British-owned Batus, which already owned the third largest U.S. cigarette maker, Brown & Williamson Tobacco. The $5.2 billion takeover was the largest in California history and occurred after a bitter six-month fight by the Farmers Group.

So far, the Japanese have shied away from hostile takeovers. But going from friendly to hostile deals is an evolutionary process, and there is evidence that the Japanese are climbing that ladder.

For instance, when they believe the stakes are high enough, the Japanese have demonstrated enormous resolve and financial power in making an acquisition. Bridgestone waged an expensive battle against Pirelli for the right to buy Firestone Tire & Rubber in 1988. The step from that type of battle to an unfriendly acquisition is a short one.

And there are indications that the Japanese are preparing to play a harder brand of ball. In 1988, several major Japanese corporations used Kroll Associates, the best-known corporate intelligence firm in the United States, to dig into the personal and corporate backgrounds of potential acquisition targets. Kroll's expensive services, which include investigations for former federal prosecutors and ex-FBI and CIA personnel, are frequently used by corporate raiders.

Further, thanks to their joint ventures with U.S. investment houses, Japan's financial institutions will soon have a cadre of experts trained in the methods and strategies of American take-over experts.

There should also be a prohibition on political contributions by foreign-owned subsidiaries in the United States. The American political process should be as free as possible from foreign influence. That is why resident noncitizens are not allowed to vote. Yet current federal election laws permit foreign corporations to contribute money to elections by failing to differentiate between contributions from the political action committee of an American-owned corporation and a foreign-owned one.

Similarly, consideration should be given to placing restrictions on former federal employees going to work for foreign governments or entities. The abuses have been well chronicled, and there is no sense in allowing U.S. government agencies to continue serving as training grounds and information pools for influence peddlers destined for the payrolls of foreign interests.

A Department of Trade could also establish and implement a national policy on directing foreign investments to areas where the money will provide jobs and opportunities for Americans. Mechanisms could vary, but would presumably rely on a system of tax credits. This overall policy would also eliminate the fratricide in which various states and local governments engage in their competition to lure foreign money.

The mistakes of American industry over the last two decades have been plentiful, and so have its excuses. But U.S. executives are justified when they complain that their ability to devote resources to long-term developments and improvements has been damaged severely by the demands of the marketplace for short-term profits. The obvious solution is finding ways to encourage farsighted management and relieve the pressures of the marketplace.

One means of relieving the pressure for short-term profits would be the elimination of the tax-free status of pension funds on short-term stock market transactions. Allow them to maintain their tax-exempt status for profits made on investments held over several years.

This radical approach has been pushed by several prominent

economists and consultants, including investment banker Felix
Rohatyn, investor Warren Buffett, and the Greenwich Associates,
an international management consulting firm in Greenwich,
Connecticut.

Pension funds control $2 trillion in capital and own roughly
half of the stock of major U.S. companies. At the first signs of an
earnings decline or an enticing offer from a corporate raider, the
pension funds managers sell out.

Changing the tax law could force the institutional investors to
pay a premium for getting out quick, and the result would be a
more stable market and an increase in the ability of corporate
managers to do long-range planning and development.

In order for this to work, of course, American industry must be
willing to make the investments in research and development
necessary to regain the edge in manufacturing and marketing.
The federal government should enhance this opportunity by
offering incentives to industries that are carrying out complex
production work in the United States.

Robert B. Reich, an author and political economy professor at
Harvard's Kennedy School of Government, and a colleague, Eric
D. Mankin, have proposed that the government subsidize investments in production expertise with a human investment tax
credit.

"The object would be for government to accept part of the
economic cost of creating an important national economic good:
more highly skilled, trained, and experienced workers and engineers," the pair said in an influential article published in the
Harvard Business Review.

In addition, Reich and Mankin suggested that the government
establish "technology extension services" to share information
on the latest manufacturing techniques with the small businesses that are the underpinnings of the U.S. industrial base.
The service, modeled after the successful agriculture extension
service, would conduct classes and seminars.

The federal government needs to recognize that certain strategic industries are essential to the continued prosperity and
security of the country and the reallocation of resources to those
industries. What is called for here is an adaptation of the Japa-

nese concept of communitarian good over individualist good.

This is a legitimate function of government in the new era of global economic relations, and it could take several forms. One could be a modification of antitrust laws to spread the costs of research and development among several corporations. Another could be the government assuming the role of facilitator in forming partnerships between business and labor aimed at the long-term well-being of the nation's economy.

Business executives and government leaders alike must be concerned that the national wealth is at stake. The inroads made by foreign investors, particularly the strategic acquisitions made by the Japanese, are symptoms of a larger malaise within the U.S. economy. There is an opportunity to deal with this malaise through a revitalization of the industrial base, and the means to harness the positive impact of foreign capital.

The Japanese have demonstrated enormous skill in adapting American concepts to benefit their country. The United States has the opportunity to adapt the Japanese concept of strategic planning for the overall good of the nation, to rescue its own economy.

Doing so will require casting aside the illusions of the Reagan era in favor of a reality that will demand some tough choices from government and business. The alternative is further deterioration in the nation's standard of living and its security as more and more sway over the United States is sold to owners in Tokyo and London and Bonn.

APPENDIX A:
THE FIVE MOST ACTIVE FOREIGN REAL ESTATE
INVESTORS, 1980 AND 1986

1980
Total Investment $3.5 billion

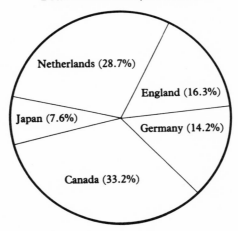

1986 (Preliminary Estimate)
Total Investment $16.2 billion

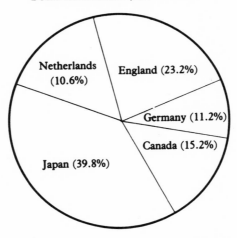

Source: "Japanese Real Estate Investment in the United States" by Cecil E. Sears of Rountrey & Associates, summary of conference October 2, 1986, cosponsored by the Japan Society and Urban Land Institute. Used by permission.

341

APPENDIX B:
THE TOTAL VALUE OF
FOREIGN DIRECT INVESTMENT

1980: $83.046

Netherlands	$19.140	23.0%
United Kingdom	$14.105	17.0%
Canada	$12.162	14.6%
West Germany	$ 7.596	9.1%
Netherland Antilles	$ 6.651	8.0%
Switzerland	$ 5.070	6.1%
Japan	$ 4.723	5.7%
Other		16.5%

1987: $261.927

United Kingdom	$74.941	28.6%
Netherlands	$47.048	18.0%
Japan	$33.361	12.7%
Canada	$21.732	8.3%
West Germany	$19.637	7.5%
Other		24.9%

NOTE: Dollar figures in billions
Source: the U.S. Department of Commerce

APPENDIX C:
THE WORLD'S BIGGEST BANKS

	Bank	Nation	1987 Deposits	1986 Deposits	1986 Rank
1	Dai-Ichi Kangyo Bank	Japan	$275.3	$186.0	1
2	Sumitomo Bank	Japan	257.6	164.5	3
3	Fuji Bank	Japan	249.4	166.5	2
4	Mitsubishi Bank	Japan	242.2	158.7	4
5	Sanwa Bank	Japan	238.2	151.9	5
6	Norinchukin Bank	Japan	210.5	144.2	6
7	Indus. Bank of Japan	Japan	206.1	137.4	7
8	Mitsubishi Trust	Japan	174.9	110.5	13
9	Tokai Bank	Japan	167.2	113.3	12
10	Sumitomo Trust	Japan	159.3	110.1	14
11	Deutsche Bank	W. Germany	155.4	121.6	10
12	Credit Agricole Mutuel	France	151.1	113.7	12
13	Banque Nationale	France	150.2	121.8	9
14	Mitsui Bank	Japan	149.4	104.4	16
15	Mitsui Trust	Japan	148.7	98.9	19
16	National Westminster	Britain	144.0	107.8	15
17	Credit Lyonnais	France	142.1	115.2	11
18	Long-Term Credit Bank	Japan	142.0	98.6	20
19	Barclays Bank	Britain	139.3	96.8	21
20	Taiyo Kobe Bank	Japan	129.4	91.2	23
21	Societe Generale	France	128.3	99.1	18
22	Yasuda Trust	Japan	124.6	85.9	26
23	Daiwa Bank	Japan	124.1	88.3	24
24	Dresdner Bank	W. Germany	123.3	95.7	22
25	Bank of Tokyo	Japan	113.5	86.7	25

NOTE: Dollar figures in billions
Source: American Banker

APPENDIX D:
THE EIGHTEEN LARGEST ACQUISITIONS BY INTERNATIONAL INVESTORS OF EXISTING U.S. OFFICE TOWERS, 1986–1987

	Property/City	Size/Sq.Ft.	Price	Year Acquired	Country	Price/Sq.Ft.
1	Arco Plaza, Los Angeles	2,200,000	$640,000,000	1986	Japan	$291
2	Exxon, New York	2,285,000	610,000,000	1986	Japan	270
3	666-5th Avenue, New York	1,370,000	500,000,000	1987	Japan	365[1]
4	Tower 49, New York	600,000	301,000,000	1987	Japan	500
5-6	1900-01 Ave. of Stars, Los Angeles	1,200,000	235,000,000	1986	Japan	200[2]
7	ABC Tower, 1330 Avenue of Americas, New York	48,000	175,000,000	1986	Japan	365
8	One Montgomery Street, San Francisco	600,000	150,000,000	1986	Japan	250
9	One Prudential Plaza, Chicago	1,130,000	141,000,000	1986	Japan	—
10	265 Franklin Street, Boston	316,000	107,000,000	1986	Japan	339
11	One Sansome Street, Chicago	545,000	100,000,000 (50%)	1986	Japan	367
12	555 4th Street, Washington, D.C.	330,000	87,000,000	1987	Japan	264
13	Union Bank, Los Angeles	605,000	87,000,000 (50%)	1987	Japan	287
14	101 North Wacker, Chicago	567,000	85,000,000	1987	Japan	150
15	111 Sutter Street, San Francisco	260,000	75,000,000	1986	Japan	288
16	Manulife Plaza, Los Angeles	400,000	65,000,000 (50%)	1986	Japan	325
17	100 Spean Street, San Francisco	200,000	65,000,000	1980	Japan	325
18	AT&T, Los Angeles	651,000	60,000,000 (50%)	1986	Japan	180

[1]Under contract, due to close Summer 1987, *Wall St. Journal*, June 5, 1987.
[2]Century City not in downtown Los Angeles market and acquisition not included in downtown totals.
NOTE: Survey does not include purchase or joint venture of new projects under construction.
Source: Coldwell Banker Survey of 19 major United States downtown office markets, May 1987.

APPENDIX E:
MAJOR JAPANESE INVESTMENTS IN THE UNITED STATES 1987–1988

Acquirer	Target	Price (in millions)
Bridgestone	Firestone	$2,600
Seibu Saison Group	Inter-Continental Hotels	2,270
Sony	CBS Records	2,000
Aoki, Bass Group	Westin Hotels	1,530
Nippon Mining	Gould Inc.	1,100
Paloma Industries	Pace Industries, Inc.	820
Bank of Tokyo	Union Bank	750
Dai Nippon Ink & Chemicals	Reichhold Chemicals	540
Nippon	Shearson Lehman*	538
Sumitomo Bank	Goldman Sachs*	500
23 Japanese banks	BankAmerica*	350
Shiseido Co.	Zotes International	345
Poyobi Ltd.	Motor Products division of Singer Co.	325
Jusco Co.	Talbot's	325
Onoda Cement Co.	California Portland Cement	310
Yasuda Mutual Life	PaineWebber*	300
Komori Printing Machinery	Harris Graphics division of AM International	250
Mitsubishi Mining & Cement Co.	Lucerne Valley plant of Kaiser Cement Corp.	195
Sunstar Inc.	John O. Butler Co.	161
Mitsui & Co.	Joseph Horne Co.	150
Long-Term Credit Bank	Greenwich Capital Markets	144
Showa Denko K.K.	Airco division of BOC Group	100

*Minority stake

Source: Compiled from newspaper reports and excludes real estate purchases.

APPENDIX F:
U.S. PASSENGER CAR SALES

Year	Total U.S. Sales	Domestic Sales[1] U.S. Controlled(D)	Foreign[2] Controlled(T)	Total Domestic(D+T)	Import[3] Sales(I)	% Import(I)	% Foreign Linked(T+I)
1991F	11,100,000	6,140,000	1,760,000	7,900,000	3,200,000	28.8	44.7
1990F	11,000,000	6,090,000	1,760,000	7,850,000	3,150,000	28.6	44.6
1989F	10,700,000	5,980,000	1,670,000	7,650,000	3,050,000	28.5	44.1
1988F	10,700,000	6,260,000	1,340,000	7,600,000	3,100,000	29.0	41.5
1987	10,277,949	6,402,422	678,436	7,080,858	3,197,091	31.1	37.7
1986	11,452,566	7,609,496	605,392	8,214,888	3,237,678	28.3	33.6
1985	11,043,768	7,794,968	409,753	8,204,542	2,839,226	25.7	29.4
1984	10,393,230	7,574,477	377,040	7,951,517	2,441,713	23.5	27.1
1983	9,181,036	6,513,665	281,637	6,795,302	2,385,734	26.0	29.0
1982	7,978,177	5,635,321	121,339	5,756,660	2,221,517	27.8	29.4
1981	8,532,672	6,043,851	162,445	6,206,296	2,326,376	27.3	29.2

[1]Includes passenger cars built in the U.S. and Canada.

[2]Includes output from Volkswagen (PA), Honda (OH and Ont.), Nissan (TN), NUMMI (CA), Mazda (MI), Toyota (KY and Ont.), DSM (IL), Hyundai (Que.), Renault-AMC (WI and Ont.), GM-Suzuki (Ont.), and Fuji Heavy Industries-Isuzu venture (IN).

[3]Includes captive imports of U.S. auto companies.
Statistics compiled and forecasts prepared by Motor & Equipment Manufacturers Association January 1987.

NOTES

CHAPTER 1: LOSING SOVEREIGNTY

Page 7. **"People ask me . . .":** Thomas E. Ricks, "Task Force's Brady Says Japanese Sale of U.S. Bonds Touched Off Oct. 19 Crash," *Wall Street Journal*, April 22, 1988.

Page 8. **Richard Koo, a senior economist:** Edwin A. Finn, Jr., "In Japan We (Must) Trust," *Forbes*, Sept. 21, 1987.

Page 8. **zooming upward in 1983:** "Japanese Investment in Foreign Securities: A New Era Dawns," Tokyo Financial Review, Bank of Tokyo, July 1988.

Page 10. **productivity of U.S. workers:** The Cuomo Commission on Trade and Competitiveness, *The Cuomo Commission Report* (New York: Simon and Schuster, 1988), 53.

Page 10. **"Is this the beginning . . .":** Robert Johnson, "More U.S. Companies Are Selling Operations to Foreign Concerns," *Wall Street Journal*, Feb. 24, 1988.

Page 10. **"Sooner or later . . .":** Johnson, "More U.S. Companies."

Page 11. **More than 300,000 Americans:** Douglas Frantz, "Roles of Working Women, Minorities Pose Challenge," *Los Angeles Times*, July 13, 1988.

Page 12. **"I don't think we should . . ."**: Frantz, "Roles of Working Women."

Page 12. **"We're *gaijin* (foreigners)"**: James Risen, "Japanese Plants in U.S. — Is the Honeymoon Over?," *Los Angeles Times*, July 12, 1988.

Page 13. **the successful muting:** Robert A. Rosenblatt, "Intense Lobbying Cools U.S. Anger at Toshiba," *Los Angeles Times*, May 1, 1988.

Page 14. **"Despite allegations . . ."**: David E. Sanger, "U.S. Reverses Position on Damage by Toshiba," *New York Times*, March 13, 1988.

Page 14. **"They came in waves . . ."**: Rosenblatt, "Intense Lobbying."

Page 15. **"In all the 21 years . . ."**: Stuart Auerbach, "Toshiba Corp. Costly Lobbying," *Washington Post*, Oct. 13, 1988.

Page 15. **"It marks a new dimension . . ."**: Auerbach, "Toshiba Corp."

Page 15. **As for the Japanese:** Karl Schoenberger, "Toshiba Unit, 2 Executives Guilty in Export Case," *Los Angeles Times*, March 22, 1988.

Page 16. **"single worst case . . ."**: Sanger, "U.S. Reverses Position."

Page 16. **an unnamed Reagan administration representative:** Hobart Rowen, "Is Japan's Investment Really a Threat?," *Washington Post*, Feb. 4, 1988.

Page 16. **Budget experts said:** Walter S. Mossberg, "Cost of Paying the Foreign Piper," *Wall Street Journal*, Jan. 18, 1988.

CHAPTER 2: A NATION FOR SALE

Page 20. **The most recent figures:** Office of Trade & Investment Analysis, International Trade Administration, U.S. Commerce Department, 1988.

Page 21. **"there is no escape":** Thomas K. McCraw, *America v. Japan* (Boston: Harvard Business School Press, revised 1988), 5.

Page 23. **"If they perceive . . ."**: Tom Furlong, "Japanese Will Buy Landmark Country Club," *Los Angeles Times*, May 4, 1988.

Page 23. **In Chicago alone:** John Hillkirk, "Japanese Hike USA Holdings," *USA Today*, Aug. 22, 1988.

Page 24. **"real estate is cheap":** Jerry C. Davis, "Foreign Buyers Snapping Up Chicago Realty," *Chicago Sun-Times*, April 28, 1988.

Page 24. **Japanese interests have acquired:** Lawrence S. Bacow, "Understanding Foreign Investment in U.S. Real Estate," Massachusetts Institute of Technology Center for Real Estate Development, 1987.

Page 24. **the list is almost as long:** Bacow, "Understanding Foreign Investment."

Page 25. **While the hotels:** Jonathan Peterson, "Tokyo Group to Buy Hotel Chain for $2.27 Billion," *Los Angeles Times*, Oct. 1, 1988.

Page 26. **Los Angeles–based accounting firm:** Jack Rodman, "Japanese Investment in U.S. Real Estate," Kenneth Leventhal & Co., 1988.

Page 27. **dozens of little-noticed:** Keith Bradsher, "A Reluctant Brierly Will Sell Holdings in CalMat to Japanese," *Los Angeles Times*, July 21, 1988.

Page 29. **foreign bargain hunters:** Stephen Koepp and others, "The Selling of America," *Time*, Sept. 14, 1987.

Page 30. **growing much faster:** Office of Trade & Investment Analysis, reports for 1984, 1985, and 1986.

Page 31. **the expansionist drive:** Hitoshi Sugimoto, "Japan Merger Fever Grows," United Press International, April 25, 1988.

CHAPTER 3: A FAILING POWER

Page 35. **early nineteenth century:** Harry N. Schreiber, Harold G. Vatter, and Harold Underwood, *American Economic History* (New York: Harper & Row, 1976), 277–97.

Page 36. **American firms in France:** Jean-Jacque Servan-Schreiber, *The American Challenge* (New York: Atheneum, 1969), multiple pages.

Page 38. **decline was inevitable:** McCraw, *America v. Japan*, 51.

Page 38. **But others see a peril:** Felix G. Rohatyn, speech to the Economic Club of Washington, Jan. 26, 1988.

Page 39. **"a failing economic power"**: Rohatyn, speech.

Page 39. **"a wealthy family"**: Carol J. Loomis, "The Inside Story of Warren Buffett," *Fortune*, April 11, 1988.

Page 39. **"family jewels"**: Rep. John Bryant in talk to Brookings Institution, April 1, 1987.

Page 40. **"Toyotas are coming back"**: Matthew L. Wald, "Foreign Investors Step Into More Active Roles," *New York Times* special real estate section, May 15, 1988.

CHAPTER 4: WHO OWNS AMERICA?

Page 46. **the lack of data:** Edward Ray, testimony before House Energy and Commerce Subcommittee on Telecommunications, Consumer Protection, and Finance, May 8, 1986.

Page 52. **watered-down amendment:** Rep. Norman Lent, testimony before House of Representatives, April 29, 1987.

Page 53. **dragooning letter:** From a copy of letter by Gary J. Campkin to C. J. Webster, Metrocrest Chamber of Commerce, dated Sept. 25, 1987.

Page 54. **hotly contested issues:** Mike Robinson, "Fight Still Raging Over Putting Spotlight on Foreign Investors," Associated Press, April 14, 1988.

Page 56. **"It seems the measures . . .":** Oswald Johnston, "Japanese See Racial Bias in U.S. Trade Bill," *Los Angeles Times*, April 23, 1988.

CHAPTER 5: CAPITOL CLOUT

Page 57. **152 Japanese companies:** Pat Choate, "Money Talks: How Foreign Firms Buy U.S. Clout," *Washington Post*, June 19, 1988.

Page 57. **Overall, Japan's government:** William J. Holstein and Amy Borrus, "Japan's Clout in the U.S.," *Business Week*, July 11, 1988.

Page 57. **"They are interested . . .":** Holstein and Borrus, "Japan's Clout."

Page 58. **Senior statesman Elliot Richardson:** Filing under Foreign Agents Registration Act (FARA), U.S. Department of Justice.

Page 58. **key adviser:** FARA filing (many of the examples in this chapter are drawn from the authors' examination of the Justice Department files).

Page 58. **resigned as national security adviser:** Documents prepared by office of Rep. Marcy Kaptur, 1988.

Page 59. **Eric Garfinkel:** Rep. Kaptur, testifying before House Committee on the Judiciary, Aug. 6, 1987.

Page 59. **Walter Lenahan:** Kaptur testimony, Aug. 6, 1987.

Page 60. **One Washington reporter:** From authors' interview with reporter, who asked that his name be withheld.

Page 60. **unable to muster support:** Eduardo Lachica, "Capital Campaign: Japanese Are Lobbying Hard in U.S. to Offset Big Protectionist Push," *Wall Street Journal*, Aug. 23, 1985.

Page 61. **The GAO identified:** "Foreign Representation: Former High-Level Federal Officials Representing Foreign Interests," General Accounting Office, July 1986.

Page 62. **"A few years ago . . .":** Kaptur testimony, Aug. 6, 1987.

Page 63. **"an American original":** Deborah M. Levy, "Foreign Agents' Registration Act of 1938—Interpretation and Construction," Foreign Policy, Summer 1987.

Page 63. **point that was made forcefully:** Choate, "Money Talks."

Page 63. **sign up with the Japanese:** Mary Thornton, "Trade Official Solicited Job with Japanese," *Washington Post*, Oct. 28, 1987. Also, Hilary Stout, "The Questions Posed by an Exodus," *New York Times*, Nov. 12, 1987, and "Conflict is Disclosed; Trade Negotiator Quits," Associated Press, Oct. 6, 1987.

Page 65. **"the king of clout":** Robert A. Rosenblatt and Ronald J. Ostrow, "Robert Gray—Capitol's King of Clout," *Los Angeles Times*, May 13, 1984.

Page 66. **outlined the campaign:** FARA files.

Page 67. **For the last six months:** FARA files.

Page 68. **$121,000 to political candidates:** FARA files.

Page 68. **"no pretense of constituency":** Lachica, "Capital Campaign."

Page 68. **"philosophically akin":** John J. Fialka, "Making Friends: Legal Profession Tops All Others in Financing Candidates for Congress," *Wall Street Journal*, Aug. 18, 1983.

Page 69. **"assisting foreign correspondents":** FARA files.

Page 69. **cited a 1981 study:** Choate, "Money Talks."

CHAPTER 6: THE SHADOW LOBBY

Page 71. **three former high-ranking:** Retreat for House Ways and Means Committee official document, "Faculty Assignments, Not to Be Released to Public," 1986. This section relies on this and other documents and interviews obtained by the authors. In addition, research assistance was provided by the International Economic Policy Association in Washington, which is financed by American manufacturers.

Page 74. **foreign interests on trade policy:** Ronald L. Danielian, "U.S. Foreign Policy in the 80s," International Economic Policy Association, 1986.

Page 76. **a whopping eighty-three times:** From an examination of all *Washington Post* articles on foreign trade issues, January 1984 through June 1988.

Page 76. **a $100,000 grant:** Annual report, United States Japan Foundation, 1984.

Page 77. **"there are no trade barriers":** Clyde Prestowitz in interview with the authors.

Page 78. **"a whitewash for the Japanese":** Hobart Towen, "Japan's Trade Barriers Called Exaggerated," *Washington Post*, July 12, 1985.

Page 79. **"influence the agenda":** Frederick Bergsten letter published in *Business Week*, Aug. 15, 1988.

Page 80. **not become a lobbying organization:** Kathleen Teltsch, "Foundation Hopes to Strengthen U.S.-Japan Ties," *New York Times*, March 29, 1981.

Page 80. **"influence public opinion":** U.S.-Japan Foundation annual report, 1982.

Page 80. **son of a poor sake brewer:** Biographical material about Sasakawa comes primarily from an article by Leslie Helm, "Would You Give This Man the Nobel Peace Prize?," *Business Week*, July 28, 1986, and a segment of the NBC network television program "1986," aired Nov. 11, 1986.

CHAPTER 7: OPEN DOORS, CLOSED DOORS

Page 85. **congressional study:** Congressional staff study, "Protectionist Investment Policies of Selected Foreign Nations," May 22, 1987.

Page 85. **confidential report prepared:** A copy of this document was provided to the authors.

Page 87. **how Japan has benefited:** Confidential report by U.S. Trade Representative's office.

Page 87. **"Japanese are always complaining":** Sam Jameson, "Most U.S. Exporters Eat Up Japanese Trade Agreement," *Los Angeles Times*, June 21, 1988.

Page 88. **removing the restrictions:** Damon Darlin, "U.S. and Tokyo Are Near Pact on Beef Quotas," *Wall Street Journal*, June 20, 1988.

Page 89. **intestines thirty feet longer:** Sam Jameson, "In Japan, Unique Is a State of Mind," *Los Angeles Times*, Aug. 2, 1988.

Page 90. **the television wars:** Varied sources were used for the section on television wars, including Clyde V. Prestowitz, Jr., *Trading Places: How We Allowed Japan to Take the Lead* (New York: Basic Books, 1988); McCraw, *America v. Japan*; and Marvin J. Wolf, *The Japanese Conspiracy* (New York: Empire Books, 1983).

Page 94. **"broad latitude":** Ronald L. Danielian, testimony before House Ways and Means Subcommittee on Trade, Sept. 24, 1986.

Page 95. **"Systemic Japanese governmental measures":** Confidential report, U.S. Trade Representative's Office.

Page 95. **disadvantages for U.S. investors:** Congressional staff study, May 22, 1985. Information updated by authors.

Page 98. **It is a mistake:** Martin and Susan Tolchin, *Buying into America* (New York: Times Books, 1988), 225–26.

CHAPTER 8: UNDERSTANDING THE COMPETITION

Page 103. **"manufacturing is not un-American":** Prestowitz, *Trading Places*, 187.

Page 109. **middle class was earning large salaries:** James Flanigan, "Middle Class in Japan Finally Gaining Weight," *Los Angeles Times*, June 12, 1988.

Page 109. **a *soba* (noodle) shop:** "Tokyo: $6.7 billion an Acre," Associated Press, March 31, 1988.

Page 110. **world's richest man:** Andrew Tanzer, "Land of the Rising Billionaires," *Forbes*, July 27, 1987.

Page 110. **the 1953 Nissan strike:** David Halberstam, *The Reckoning* (New York: William Morrow, 1986).

Page 111. **rice farmers make up:** Michael A. Hiltzik, "Japan Rice System Faces a Challenge," *Los Angeles Times*, Feb. 15, 1988.

Page 111. **trying to explain the Japanese:** James Fallows, "The Rice Plot: How Rice Farmers Control Japan's Politics and Distort Its Economic System," *Atlantic*, January 1987.

Page 111. **One of Japan's acknowledged masters:** Stephen Kreider Yoder, "If Japan Poses Threat in Superconductors, Shoji Tanaka Is Why," *Wall Street Journal*, April 29, 1988.

Page 112. **A consortium of Japan's shipbuilders:** Stephen Kreider Yoder, "Japan Plans Speedy Superconductor Ships," *Wall Street Journal*, Aug. 17, 1988.

Page 113. **A study by the U.S. Naval Research Laboratory:** Yoder, "Japan Plans."

CHAPTER 9: SELLOUT AT FIRESTONE

Page 119. **the third largest U.S. tire company:** Zachary Schiller, "Japan vs. Europe: Firestone May Be Just the Appetizer," *Business Week*, March 21, 1988.

Page 120. **"It isn't that Firestone . . .":** Jonathan Peterson, "Firestone Wasn't Pushed Out of Tires—It Jumped," *Los Angeles Times*, March 19, 1988.

Page 120. **General Motors said it would end:** Reuters, April 24, 1988.

Page 120. **Nevin was the president:** Cindy Skrzycki, "Japanese Deal Is Ironic for Firestone's Nevin," *Washington Post*, March 21, 1988.

Page 121. **"it was the perception":** Skrzycki, "Japanese Deal."

Page 122. **the fifty-five-acre site:** Tolchin, *Buying into America*, 68–80.

Page 123. **"Fixated on quick research payoffs . . .":** Jim Schachter, "As a Giant Dozes, Ideas Tiptoe Away," *Los Angeles Times*, Feb. 21, 1988.

CHAPTER 10: TROJAN HORSE

Page 127. **another 540,000:** "Assembly Is Not Enough: The Transplant Strategy in the U.S. Motor Vehicle Market," United Autoworkers Research Department, 1987.

Page 128. **almost no concession is too great:** Bill Powell, "War Between the States," *Newsweek*, May 30, 1988.

Page 128. **"Their expectations . . .":** Powell, "War Between."

Page 130. **paper was prepared:** Richard C. Hill, Michael Indergaard, and Kuniko Fujita, "Flat Rock, Home of Mazda: The Social Impact of a Japanese Company on an American Community," Michigan State University, March 22, 1988.

Page 131. **Mazda got about $120 million:** Hill et al., "Flat Rock."

Page 132. **offset an increase in city services:** Hill et al., "Flat Rock."

Page 132. **"As long as there are people . . .":** Powell, "War Between."

Page 133. **"Industrial rationalization":** Prestowitz, *Trading Places*, 108.

Page 133. **The law attempted:** Prestowitz, *Trading Places*, 108.

Page 133. **could have delivered:** James A. Mateyka, "Perspectives on Transplants," Booz, Allen, and Hamilton, May 3, 1988.

Page 134. **decline of the domestic:** James Risen, "Detroit Still Singing the Blues," *Los Angeles Times*, May 25, 1988.

Page 135. **producing 1.77 million cars:** Risen, "Detroit Still Singing."

Page 135. **For example, Toyota:** Gregory A. Patterson, "Ford-Nissan Minivan Project to Pioneer Managerial Role for a Big Three Concern," *Wall Street Journal*, Sept. 13, 1988.

CHAPTER 11: THE HONDA STORY

Page 138. **"Americanization of Honda":** Stewart Toy, Neil Gross, and James B. Treece, "The Americanization of Honda," *Business Week*, April 25, 1988.

Page 143. **"genius with a legendary ego":** Richard T. Pascale, "Honda," case study for Harvard Business School, 1983.

Page 143. **Honda's first breakthrough:** Pascale, "Honda."

Page 146. **its philosophic cornerstone:** "Elements of Honda's Strategy," Honda of America Manufacturing, undated.

Page 149. **Honda's share:** Data from Honda of America and *Ward's Automotive Reports*, various issues.

Page 150. **random sample:** Toy et al., "The Americanization."

Page 150. **On a chilly Monday:** Brian S. Akre, "Honda Ships First Exports of U.S.-Made Cars to Japan," Associated Press, March 7, 1988.

Page 150. **"we can do anything"**: Akre, "Honda Ships."

Page 151. **The case that Honda settled**: Douglas Frantz, "Honda to Pay 377 Women and Blacks for Hiring Bias," *Los Angeles Times*, March 24, 1988.

CHAPTER 12: CATTAILS & SUN VISORS

Page 154. **told a House committee**: William F. Busker testimony before House Committee on Small Business, July 21, 1987.

Page 154. **far blunter that same year:** Julian C. Morris testimony before U.S. International Trade Commission, Feb. 24, 1987.

Page 155. **new plant in Shelbyville**: "Japan Auto Parts Firm to Indiana," Associated Press, July 19, 1988.

Page 155. **despite years of trade talks**: "U.S. Global Competitiveness: The U.S. Automotive Parts Industry," United States International Trade Commission, December 1987.

Page 157. **"unnatural growth in productivity"**: Morris testimony before Trade Commission.

Page 162. **"transplants grab more"**: Mateyka, "Perspectives on Transplants."

Page 162. **"other major American industries"**: Busker testimony before House.

CHAPTER 13: GIVING AWAY THE FUTURE

Page 163. **U.S., firms would receive:** "U.S., Japan Resolve Issues on Codevelopment of FS-X Fighter," *Aviation Week and Space Technology*, June 13, 1988.

Page 164. **civilian air transportation industry:** Virginia C. Lopez and Loren Yager, "The U.S. Aerospace Industry and the Trend Toward Internationalization," The Aerospace Research Center, March 1988.

Page 165. **"frontiers of technology"**: A high-ranking Defense Department official who spoke only on the condition that he remain anonymous.

Page 168. **perils of these business partnerships:** Robert B. Reich and Eric D. Mankin, "Joint Ventures with Japan Give Away Our Future," *Harvard Business Review*, March-April 1986.

Page 171. **drawings and technical data:** Prestowitz, *Trading Places*, 300–301, plus interviews with authors.

Page 172. **Carlucci promised:** "U.S., Japan Resolve," *Aviation Week*.

CHAPTER 14: TECHNO HAWKS

Page 174. **"Cowboys don't talk . . .":** Donna K. H. Walters and William C. Rempel, "A One-Time Winner Is Out of Chips," *Los Angeles Times*, Dec. 1, 1987. This excellent article was part of a two-part series by Walters and Rempel that explored the Fujitsu-Fairchild transaction in unprecedented depth.

Page 176. **"a line in the sand":** William C. Rempel and Donna K. H. Walters, "Trade War: When Chips Were Down," *Los Angeles Times*, Nov. 30, 1987.

Page 176. **"We could lose . . .":** Rempel and Walters, "Trade War."

Page 176. **"turning point in the history":** Walters and Rempel, "One-Time Winner."

Page 178. **Nippon Mining of Tokyo:** Victor F. Zonana, "Nippon Mining to Buy Gould for $1.1 Billion," *Los Angeles Times*, Aug. 31, 1988.

Page 179. **"It's perfectly legal . . .":** David E. Sanger, "Kubota's Strategy Sparks Fears About Technology Losses," *New York Times*, Sept. 7, 1988.

Page 182. **a chilling diagnosis:** Charles H. Ferguson, "The Competitive Decline of the U.S. Semiconductor Industry," testimony before U.S. Senate Subcommittee on Technology and the Law, Feb. 26, 1987.

Page 183. **U.S. share of patents:** Ferguson, "The Competitive Decline."

Page 184. **"slit our throats":** Rempel and Walters, "Trade War."

Page 184. **5 percent in 1981:** George Gilder, "How the Computer Companies Lost Their Memories," *Forbes*, June 13, 1988.

Page 185. **semiconductor industry lost:** Ferguson, "The Competitive Decline."

Page 185. **"at war with Japan":** Rempel and Walters, "Trade War."

Page 185. **executive who finally agreed:** Otis Port, "Bob Noyce Created Silicon Valley. Can He Save It?" *Business Week*, Aug. 15, 1988.

Page 187. **picked up his telephone:** Walters and Rempel, "One-Time Winner."

CHAPTER 15: STEALING THE CROWN JEWELS

Page 193. **Harrison had been selling:** Virtually all of the information in this chapter comes from public records in the federal criminal prosecution of Hitachi and its employees for stealing IBM secrets. Among the court records are transcripts of conversations recorded by hidden listening devices. In addition to the previously available information, the authors obtained the full record of FBI transcripts, which had not been available previously. The records were augmented by extensive interviews with present and former government agents who participated in the operation. Most of them did not want their names used.

Page 195. **Japanese intelligence service:** Richard Deacon, *A History of the Japanese Secret Service* (London: Frederick Muller, 1976), 251–76.

Page 198. **"gotten your crown jewels":** Conversation was related to the authors by a third party connected with the investigation.

Page 200. **elaborate Soviet effort:** Tolchin, *Buying Into America*, 142–48; also James Bartholomew, "Moscow Nardony's Hidden Loss," *Far Eastern Economic Review*, Sept. 29, 1978.

Page 209. **Mitsubishi had entered:** Robert A. Rosenblatt, "U.S. Charges 6 in Japanese Plot to Steal IBM Secrets," *Los Angeles Times*, June 23, 1982. In addition, information about Mitsubishi's role was provided by persons involved in the investigation and court records.

CHAPTER 16: INROADS ON WALL STREET

Page 213. **a truly international firm:** John Merwin, " 'We Don't Learn from Our Clients, We Learn from Each Other,' " *Forbes*, Oct. 19, 1987.

Page 214. **Multinational Business Institute:** The background and controversy on this little-known operation with McKinsey was described to the authors by two McKinsey employees who did not want their names used.

Page 215. **a three-person team:** Background information about the origins and details of the Sumitomo-Goldman transaction were provided by a lawyer involved in every stage of the discussions who did not want his name used.

Page 215. **among the world's largest banks:** *American Banker*, a daily newspaper for the industry, compiles its rankings annually; 1988 rankings were published on July 18, 1988.

Page 215. **Sumitomo's roots:** Nicholas D. Kristof, "Japanese Maverick Expands," *New York Times*, Aug. 7, 1986.

Page 217. **delegation of investment bankers:** This meeting was described to the authors by a participant who requested anonymity.

Page 218. **mistake was crystallized:** "Banking in the New Style," *Washington Post*, Nov. 20, 1986.

Page 219. **the Fed demanded:** John E. Yang, "Fed Approves Goldman Stake For Sumitomo," *Wall Street Journal*, Nov. 20, 1986.

Page 220. **Nippon Life Insurance:** William Glasgall and Toshio Aritake, "It Won't Stop with the Shearson Deal," *Business Week*, April 6, 1987.

Page 220. **Yasuda Mutual Life:** Michael R. Sesit, "Japanese Acquisitions in U.S. Jumped to $5.9 Billion in '87; Strong Yen Cited," *Wall Street Journal*, Jan. 21, 1988.

Page 221. **John Phelan:** Sam Jameson, "NYSE Sets up Panel to Give Japanese a Voice on Wall Street," *Los Angeles Times*, Aug. 25, 1988.

Page 222. **founded in 1925 in Osaka:** Milton Moskowitz, *The Global Marketplace* (New York: MacMillan Publishing, 1988), 413–17.

Page 223. **ruffled some feathers:** Michael R. Sesit and Tom Herman, "New York Fed to Admit Nikko Unit as Primary U.S. Dealer, Sources Say," *Wall Street Journal*, Dec. 22, 1987.

Page 223. **With assistance:** Marcus W. Brauchli, "Foreign Securities Firms in Japan, Aided by Nomura's Jafco, Crack Initial Issues," *Wall Street Journal*, Sept. 2, 1988.

Page 224. **Fuji Bank:** Michael R. Sesit, "Fuji Bank Buys Stake in Kleinwort Unit, Gaining Toehold as Primary U.S. Dealer," *Wall Street Journal*, May 22, 1988.

Page 225. **Nomura had been buying:** Michael R. Sesit and Bryan Burrough, "Nomura Securities Is Negotiating to Buy Stake in Wasserstein Perella, Sources Say," *Wall Street Journal*, July 27, 1988.

Page 226. **there was little surprise:** Mariann Caprino, "Nomura

Securities to Buy Stake in Investment Boutique," Associated Press, July 27, 1988.

CHAPTER 17: BUYING THE BANKS

Page 229. **first executive of First Interstate:** Conversation related to the authors by Harold Meyerman.

Page 230. **1,000 subsidiaries of Japanese companies:** "Employment/Economic Impact of Japanese Firms in California," Japan Business Association of California, 1988.

Page 232. **Bank of Tokyo paid $750 million:** Douglas Frantz, "Japanese to Pay $750 Million for Union Bank," *Los Angeles Times*, Feb. 16, 1988.

Page 234. **Seventeen of the twenty-five largest:** *American Banker* survey, July 18, 1988.

Page 235. **no single incident better illustrates:** Richard B. Schmitt, "BankAmerica to Sell Stock and Notes To Japanese Investors for $350 Million," *Wall Street Journal*, Oct. 8, 1987.

Page 236. **"It was a deal . . .":** Schmitt, "BankAmerica to Sell Stock."

Page 237. **most numerous foreign banks:** Kenneth J. Hicks, "Japan Increases Presence in US; UK Banks Decline," *American Banker*, Feb. 23, 1988.

Page 237. **"can't eke out a living":** Hisanobu Ohse, "Japanese Banks Set up Shop in U.S. Heartland," Reuters, Nov. 11, 1987.

Page 237. **at last count in 1987:** Hicks, "Japan Increases."

Page 239. **recounted the story:** Michael R. Sesit, "Japan's Banks Become Ever-Bigger Lenders to American Business," *Wall Street Journal*, Jan. 1, 1988.

Page 240. **study of Japanese bank activities:** Barbara A. Coffin, "Competitive Challenge: Japanese Bank Activities in the U.S.," Council on Financial Competition, December 1987.

Page 242. **extraordinary influence:** CBS News Special, "Foreign Investment in America: Sales or Sellout?," March 31, 1979.

CHAPTER 18: THE 24TH WARD

Page 243. **list of what the Japanese owned:** Dick Turpin, "Foreigners See L.A. Center as 'Mark of Leader,' " *Los Angeles Times*, March 13, 1988.

Page 244. **"executives see downtown":** Turpin, "Foreigners See."

Page 244. **Of the sixteen largest:** James B. O'Brien, "Survey of International Investment," Coldwell Banker Commercial Real Estate Services, July 1987.

Page 248. **prices paid per square foot:** David Shulman and Julia D. Fernald, "Japanese Investment in U.S. Real Estate," Salomon Brothers, March 1987.

Page 248. **"future belongs to the Japanese":** O'Brien, "Survey of International Investment."

Page 251. **a record $12.7 billion:** Douglas Frantz, "Japanese Buy Record $12.7 Billion of U.S. Property," *Los Angeles Times,* April 5, 1988.

Page 252. **slightly more than $6 billion:** "Japanese Investment in U.S. Real Estate to Remain High in 1988," Bank of America, April 7, 1988.

Page 252. **"Hidden deals are . . .":** Sandy Goodkin, "Foreign Capital Investment in U.S. Real Estate," Peat Marwick Goodkin Report, 1988.

Page 253. **"continue to focus on the West Coast":** "Japanese Investment," Bank of America.

Page 254. **Japanese construction companies:** David Shulman and Susan Jordan, "Japanese Construction Firms Increase Role in U.S.," Salomon Brothers, April 1988.

Page 254. **Construction and management contracts:** Peter Coy, "Japanese Builders Garnering Big Share of U.S. Market," Associated Press, Nov. 11, 1987.

Page 255. **behemoth $550 million complex:** Tom Furlong, "Foreigners Building New Base in U.S.," *Los Angeles Times,* Oct. 28, 1986.

Page 255. **"where Detroit was twenty years ago":** Coy, "Japanese Builders."

Page 256. **Japanese investor who needed:** Anthony Downs, "Foreign Capital in U.S. Real Estate Markets," Salomon Brothers, April 1987.

Page 260. **well-known noodle shop:** Kenichi Ohmae, "Tokyo's Soaring Property Prices; If They Fall, So Will Our Stock Markets," *New York Times,* Oct. 11, 1987.

CHAPTER 19: "I AM HERE TO HELP YOU"

Page 263. **a short, impassioned speech:** This incident was described to the authors by one of the participants, who requested anonymity.

Page 264. **one of the wealthiest landowners:** Hiroko Asami, "Shigeru Kobayashi: Yield Gap," *Forbes*, July 25, 1988.

Page 264. **a check for $100,000:** Cathleen Decker, "Firm Presents Bradley Check for Monument," *Los Angeles Times*, Sept. 16, 1986.

Page 265. **"the potential of Tokyo real estate":** This material came from a businessman who had listened to Kobayashi describe his rise to power over a long friendship. The businessman requested anonymity.

Page 266. **a staggering portfolio:** *Faces of Shuwa*, Shuwa Corporation, 1988.

Page 267. **hallway to Kobayashi's office:** This was described by several visitors.

Page 267. **"Every day there is . . .":** Tom Furlong and Nancy Yoshihara, "The Japanese Land Rush in America," *Los Angeles Times*, Feb. 1, 1987.

Page 268. **list of major acquisitions:** *Faces of Shuwa*.

Page 268. **"Why don't you ask me . . .":** Robert Guenther and Masayoshi Kanabayashi, "Japanese Firms Boost Purchases of Real Estate in U.S.," *Wall Street Journal*, Oct. 20, 1986.

Page 269. **"Shuwa paid a lot more . . .":** Guenther and Kanabayashi, "Japanese Firms."

Page 270. **Shuwa backed away:** Roger Lowenstein, "Shuwa Calls Off 2 Deals in U.S., Brokers Assert," *Wall Street Journal*, Dec. 11, 1987.

Page 270. **"didn't want to have":** Lowenstein, "Shuwa Calls Off."

Page 270. **A few months later:** These incidents were described to the authors by a broker involved in one of the deals and privy to details of the second. He requested anonymity.

CHAPTER 20: COLONIZING HAWAII

Page 275. **He boasted:** Tom Ashbrook of *Boston Globe*, "Biggest Japan Buyer Calls Isle Homes 'Lousy,' " *Honolulu Advertiser*, April 21, 1988.

Page 275. **"replaced the Ugly American":** Ashbrook, "Biggest Japan Buyer."

Page 275. **"Will my children be able . . .":** Tom Furlong, *Los Angeles Times* reporter who attended the meeting, was interviewed by the authors.

Page 278. **At least three states:** Kit Smith, "Many States Restricting Foreign Investment," *Honolulu Advertiser*, April 3, 1988, and material from authors.

Page 278. **"The closest play to Japan . . .":** Tom Furlong, "Growing Influence of Asians on California Real Estate," *Los Angeles Times*, Aug. 14, 1988.

Page 279. **a long, profitable, and sometimes rocky history:** The history of foreign investment in Hawaii is drawn from several sources, primarily "Foreign Investment in Hawaii," a study done in December 1979 by the Hawaii International Services Agency of the State Department of Planning and Economic Development and the U.S. Department of Commerce.

Page 281. **hearing in Honolulu:** Transcript of testimony before U.S. Senate Subcommittee on Foreign Commerce and Tourism, Dec. 27, 1973.

Page 283. **$6.5 billion in Hawaii:** John Heins, "A Mixed Blessing," *Forbes*, Feb. 22, 1988.

Page 283. **chief economist for First Hawaiian Bank:** Gregory Pai, testimony before Honolulu City Council, April 15, 1988.

Page 283. **Azabu Group:** Heins, "A Mixed Blessing."

Page 285. **quoted industry sources:** "Land of the Rising Prices," *Forbes*, March 12, 1988.

Page 285. **eighteen of the forty-seven golf courses:** Robert Green, "Japanese Investors Move on U.S. Golf Properties," *Golf Digest*, September 1988.

Page 285. **"the finest golf course":** James Dooley, "Golf Course Gets to Bar Public Play a Year," *Honolulu Advertiser*, March 31, 1988.

Page 286. **most ambitious project ever undertaken:** Bill Wood, "All That Money Can Buy," *Hawaii Investor*, February 1987.

CHAPTER 21: ASSAULT ON HOLLYWOOD

Page 290. **second most successful export:** Al Delugach, "Hollywood Finds a Gold Mine in Foreign Markets," *Los Angeles Times*, Aug. 8, 1988.

Page 290. **broadcast in 110 countries:** Delugach, "Hollywood Finds."

Page 291. **"Knots Landing" in France:** Lisa Gubernick, "Why Rent When You Can Own?," Forbes, Sept. 5, 1988.

Page 292. **"All the big trading companies . . .":** Ron Grover and Neil Gross, "On Location in Hollywood: The Japanese," *Business Week*, March 21, 1988.

Page 292. **Toward that end:** Geraldine Fabrikant, "Putnam Group Forms Venture with Warner's," *New York Times*, Sept. 15, 1988.

Page 295. **A fascinating examination:** Peter J. Boyer, "Sony and CBS Records: What a Romance!," *New York Times Sunday Magazine*, Sept. 18, 1988.

Page 295. **a formal study of MGM/UA:** James Flanigan, "Why Sony Is Checking out the Box Office," *Los Angeles Times*, May 4, 1988.

Page 300. **Murdoch owned 150 newspapers:** Johnnie L. Roberts, "Murdoch's News Corp. Will Buy Triangle Publications for $3 Billion," *Wall Street Journal*, Aug. 3, 1988.

Page 300. **"ability to shape and influence public policy":** Mark Clayton, "What Murdoch Wants," *Christian Science Monitor*, Aug. 10, 1988.

Page 301. **"a quirky business":** Joel Kurtzman, "Book Houses Consolidate," *New York Times*, Aug. 21, 1988.

Page 301. **"concern is with the editorial integrity":** Kurtzman, "Book Houses."

CHAPTER 22: BILINGUAL SPIES

Page 305. **"extremely frustrating":** Jim Schachter, "When Hope Turns to Frustration," *Los Angeles Times*, July 10, 1988. This was one of a series of twelve in-depth articles, "Working for the Japanese," compiled by a team of *Times* business writers and run in July 1988.

Page 305. **"you would have a shadow":** Jonathan Peterson, "Americans as 'Watched' Executives," *Los Angeles Times*, July 11, 1988.

Page 306. **Americans rush to sign up:** Bill Powell, "Where the Jobs Are," *Newsweek*, Feb. 2, 1987.

Page 307. **"The honeymoon between . . .":** James Risen, "Japanese Plants in U.S.—Is the Honeymoon Over?," *Los Angeles Times*, July 12, 1988.

Page 307. **"As there are more Japanese . . .":** Douglas Frantz, "Roles of Working Women, Minorities Pose Challenge," *Los Angeles Times*, July 13, 1988.

Page 308. **130,000 written requests:** Hill, "Flat Rock: Home of Mazda."

Page 308. **"they say good luck":** Hill, "Fiat Rock: Home of Mazda."

CHAPTER 23: "THEY'RE THE BOSS"

Page 313. **"bad management or bad parts":** Risen, "Japanese Plants in U.S."

Page 314. **"the rules they gave us":** Leon Teeboom, "Japanese Using Maquiladora Program to Protect Markets," *Orange County Business Journal*, Feb. 15, 1988.

Page 315. **'slam the door on us':** Teeboom, "Japanese Using."

Page 316. **Good told the governors:** Eugene Carlson, "Japanese Companies Increase Presence Near Mexican Border," *Wall Street Journal*, Dec. 12, 1987.

Page 317. **"very cold, calculating and ruthless":** Jim Schachter and Nancy Yoshihara, "Bosses from Japan Bring Alien Habits," *Los Angeles Times*, July 10, 1988.

Page 319. **"Homogeneity is antagonistic . . .":** Frantz, "Roles of Working Women."

Page 320. **"black leadership is angry":** James Risen, "Accusations of Racism," *Los Angeles Times*, Aug. 9, 1988.

Page 321. **"It's a serious situation":** Risen, "Accusations of Racism."

CHAPTER 24: NICs ARE NEXT

Page 326. **registered a total surplus:** Toshio Yamasaki, "The Asian NICs: Trends in Exchange Rates and Trade Patterns," *Tokyo Financial Review*, August 1988.

Page 328. **"another major challenge":** Andrew Tanzer, "Samsung: South Korea Marches to Its Own Drummer," *Forbes*, May 16, 1988.

Page 329. **Posco, as the Korean steelmaker:** Joseph P. Manguno, "Korean Steel Firm Takes on the Japanese," *Wall Street Journal*, April 29, 1988.

Page 329. **The company was founded:** Tanzer, "Samsung."

Page 330. **shops selling only imports:** "It's So Cheap," *The Economist*, May 14, 1988.

CHAPTER 25: SECRETARY OF TRADE

Page 333. **"Containment of the Soviet Union . . .":** Walter S. Mossberg and John Walcott, "U.S. Redefines Policy on Security to Place Less Stress on Soviets," *Wall Street Journal*, Aug. 11, 1988.

Page 334. **the potential conflict:** Walter Russell Mead, "Capitalism Bound," *New Perspectives Quarterly*, Summer 1988.

Page 335. **"American economy funded by Japanese":** Mead, "Capitalism Bound."

Page 338. **"The object would be . . .":** Robert B. Reich and Eric D. Mankin, "Joint Ventures with Japan Give Away Our Future," *Harvard Business Review*, March-April 1986.

INDEX